Pastoral and Ideology

The publisher gratefully acknowledges the generous contribution provided by the Director's Circle of the Associates of the University of California Press, whose members are

VIRGINIA AND RICHARD ADLOFF
EDMUND CORVELLI, JR.
DIANE AND CHUCK FRANKEL
FLORENCE AND LEO HELZEL
SANDRA AND CHARLES HOBSON
VALERIE AND JOEL KATZ
PENNY AND ROBERT MARSHALL
LUCIA AND PAUL MATZGER

RUTH AND DAVID MELLINKOFF
ELVIRA AND BYRON NISHKIAN
HELENE H. OPPENHEIMER
AVA JEAN PISCHEL
LYDIA AND MARTIN TITCOMB
ADELLE AND ERWIN TOMASH
MRS. PAUL WATTIS
MARCIA WEISMAN

The publisher also gratefully acknowledges the assistance of the J. Paul Getty Trust in the publication of this book.

Pastoral and Ideology

Virgil to Valéry

ANNABEL PATTERSON

University of California Press

BERKELEY   LOS ANGELES

Published with the assistance of
the J. Paul Getty Trust

University of California Press
Berkeley and Los Angeles, California

© 1987 by
The Regents of the University of California

Library of Congress Cataloging-in-Publication Data
Patterson, Annabel M.
Pastoral and ideology.
Includes index.
1. Virgil. Bucolica.   2. Virgil—Criticism and
interpretation—History.   3. Pastoral literature—History and criticism.   I. Title.
PA6804.B7P38   1987   809'.93321734   86–24970
ISBN 0–520–05862–3 (alk. paper)

Printed in the United States of America

1 2 3 4 5 6 7 8 9

This one is for Charles, and his future

It's a free country, they say.

Daniel Berrigan

Contents

Illustrations

Acknowledgments

This project has been so generously supported by so many, in so many ways, that my claim to authorship is, if not a fiction, certainly a convention. First and foremost, the uninterrupted time to grapple it all together was provided by a Guggenheim Fellowship, a Senior Fellowship at the Society for the Humanities, Cornell University, and a General Research Board Leave Fellowship from the University of Maryland. Second, I am particularly indebted to the curators of rare books and special collections at Cornell, at Princeton, at the British Library, at the Library of Congress where the Rosenwald Collection of illustrated *Virgils* is housed, at the Bibliothèque Nationale, and above all at the Folger Shakespeare Library, whose staff have been unfailingly and extraordinarily supportive. And third, the quality of the illustrations (for which separate acknowledgments will be made hereafter) is due in part to generous subsidies by the J. Paul Getty Trust and Duke University, and in part to the University of California Press, which committed itself to making a beautiful book.

But beyond these institutional benevolences, whose value no formal acknowledgment can intimate, this book has been especially blessed by individuals—colleagues and friends who have given me their time, their interest, a reference, a warning, a leg up. Whole long chapters were read by Paul Alpers, Jonathan Arac, Sacvan Berkovitch, Stuart Curran, Leopold Damrosch, Charles Dempsey, William Frost, Robert Gleckner, Anthony Grafton, Wallace Jackson, Stanley Stewart, and Joseph Wittreich, and were accordingly enriched or chastened. Virginia Brown went considerably out of her way to proffer her vast knowledge of early editions of Virgil, and David Wright gave me, in effect, a private tutorial on the manuscript tradition in antiquity. Alan Cameron taught me about Servius, Vincent Carretta about the illustrations to Pope's *Pastorals,* Peter Van Egmond about Frost's "political pastoral." Marjorie Levinson shared her work on Wordsworth with me, George Pigman his personal Virgil archive; Frederick Ahl, David Erdman, John Fyler, Frederick Garber, and William Klein all, though they may not all remember it, own a piece of the stock. Perhaps the ultimate selflessness came from three wonderful research assistants, Linda Meriens, Elizabeth Carmichael, and Rebecca Spracklen, who claimed they enjoyed what they were doing. It has been, in truth, a collaborative enterprise.

Finally, I am grateful to the editors of *English Literary Renaissance, Harvard English Studies,* the *Huntington Library Quarterly,* and *Criticism* for permission to reprint the sections of this work that have already appeared in their journals.

Introduction

More than two thousand years ago, certain privileged Roman readers unrolled a "book" of poems and encountered the following greeting:

> Tityre, tu patulae recubans sub tegmine fagi
> silvestrem tenui musam meditaris avena;
> nos patriae finis et dulcia linquimus arva.
> nos patriam fugimus; tu, Tityre, lentus in umbra
> formosam resonare doces Amaryllida silvas.[1]

> You, Tityrus, reclining under the spreading shelter of the beech,
> meditate pastoral poetics on your slender pipe; we are leaving the
> borders of our country and its sweet fields. We are in flight from our
> fatherland; you, Tityrus, relaxed in the shade, teach the woods to
> echo the name of fair Amaryllis.[2]

These lines have been echoing ever since; not, I would argue, because of their graceful memorability, but because those Roman readers faced, even in these first five lines, a challenge that has remained intensely audible. Almost every word in this apparently translucent opening is overdetermined, making demands on interpretation that translators in every genera-

---

[1]The Latin text cited throughout is that of R. A. B. Mynors (Oxford, 1969), as modified by Paul Alpers, *The Singer of the Eclogues: A Study of Virgilian Pastoral* (Berkeley, Los Angeles, London, 1979). Readers unfamiliar with Virgil may find the subject easiest of approach through Alpers's attractive and useful volume, with its text facing a "new" verse translation, and a commentary highly sensitive to differences of opinion.

[2]Unless otherwise specified, all translations from the *Eclogues* and other non-English texts are my own.

1

tion have wrestled with, only to the dissatisfaction of the new translators who follow with wrestlings of their own. Among the most pressing textual exigencies are the relationships between the pronouns, so insistent in their chiastic structure, "tu . . . nos . . . nos . . . tu"; the presence of those Greek names, Tityrus and Amaryllis, which invite speculation into Virgil's recall of Theocritus, and hence the full meaning of *resonare,* echo; and the question of how to translate *silvestrem . . . musam meditaris,* which permits a more cerebral response than its equally permissible alternative, "practice woodland music." Neither option, however, is innocent. Each carries with it a rival theory of pastoral.

All these issues will be explored, directly or indirectly, in the chapters that follow, but it is the first, the relationship between "tu" and "nos," that most economically represents this book's concerns. Modern thought has done much for the status of the pronoun, and particularly for the Latinate "ego," with its privileged status in the various disciplines that seek to define (or to erase) subjectivity. "Est 'ego' qui *dit* 'ego,'" writes, for example, Emile Benveniste, developing an argument for the linguistic expression both of subjectivity and of its essentially dialogic nature.[3] But Virgil, who also begins with dialogue, indicates in his opening statement the limitations of a discourse centered on the first person singular. The relational structure of the first eclogue is not between the ego and its audience but between "tu" and "nos," a plural that immediately confronts the reader with a choice of identifications. If *I* is normally the index of subjectivity, and *you* the audience who permits its expression, *we* is the sign of community, of some common communicative ground. But here, as Virgil insists by his *contrastive* positioning of the pronouns, the *we* represented by Meliboeus must exclude the *you* represented by Tityrus. And every other aspect of those first five lines explains and passionately justifies that exclusion. While the selfhood of Tityrus is associated with reflection (*meditaris*), with echoes, with song, with literary allusion, and especially with leisure and protection, the community to which Meliboeus belongs is connected to (at the moment of its severance from) the most value-laden word in Roman culture, the *patria,* subsuming the concepts of origin, national identity, and home. To which of these sets of values should Virgil's readers (by definition here, readers of poetry) be expected to affiliate themselves?

As the dialogue continues, the ethical indeterminacy posited in its opening lines steadily increases. We learn that the community at risk, for whom Meliboeus claims to speak, does not "flee" the land of their fathers voluntarily, but rather that they have been expelled by an apparently unjust military force:

---

[3] Emile Benveniste, *Problèmes de linguistique générale* (Paris, 1966), p. 260.

impius haec tam culta novalia miles habebit,
barbarus has segetes. en quo discordia cives
produxit miseros: his nos consevimus agros!

(lines 70–72)

Shall the impious soldier possess these well-tilled grounds? A
barbarian possess these crops? See where fighting has brought our
miserable countrymen. See for whom we have sown our fields!

In these lines, especially as their implications were developed in the ninth
eclogue, the ground was laid for early recognition that Virgilian pastoral
referred to something other than itself, and specifically to the historical circumstances in which it was produced—the last phases of the civil war between Brutus and Cassius, representing the old republic, and Antony and
Octavian, agents and heirs of Caesarian centrism. Here, too, words that
Roman culture had already saturated with value competed with each other,
impius and *barbarus* in apparently oxymoronic proximity to *miles* (member
of a disciplined armed force), *discordia* undoing the *corporate* semantics of
cives. Thousands of years of scholarly quarreling as to how much of recent
Roman history was here embedded, and why it matters, have not resolved
the tensions here established—between words whose social function, we
may suppose, was normally to go unexamined.

The status of Tityrus also becomes increasingly problematic. However
we read the dialogue, it speaks dramatically of the barriers that inhibit the
exchange of values or even of information. Questions go unanswered. Lis-
teners do not listen. Especially, many commentators have felt, Tityrus fails
to attend to the obvious, if indirect, appeals for his sympathy and concern.
So oblivious is he of the responsibilities of the fortunate toward the unfortunate that he misses the ethical force of Meliboeus's pronouns, declaring,
in defiance of all evidence to the contrary, that "deus *nobis* haec otia fecit"
("a god gives *us* this leisure"). The ambiguity of *deus* as the source of protected leisure and the continued enjoyment of one's patrimony is intensified
at the opening of the sixth eclogue, where, in eight lines full of allusions to
the opening of the first, Virgil attaches the speaking ego to himself; elliptically suggests his reasons for writing pastoral at such a time; names a god,
Apollo, as his somewhat playful superego; and identifies himself as Tityrus:

Prima Syracosia dignata est ludere versu
nostra neque erubuit silvas habitare Thalea.
cum canerem reges et proelia, Cynthius aurem
vellit et admonuit: "pastorem, Tityre, pinguis
pascere oportet ovis, deductum dicere carmen."
nunc ego (namque super tibi erunt qui dicere laudes,

Vare, tuas cupiant et tristia condere bella)
agrestem tenui meditabor harundine Musam.
non iniussa cano.

From the beginning our Thalea deigned to amuse herself with
Sicilian verse, nor did she blush to inhabit the woods. When I would
sing of kings and battles, Apollo tweaked my ear and warned me: "A
shepherd, Tityrus, ought to feed fat sheep, to sing a slender song."
Now I (for there will be plenty who wish to sing your praises, Varus,
and to celebrate melancholy wars) will meditate the country Muse on
my narrow reed. I do not sing unbidden.

So, astonishingly, Virgil lays claim to the character of the protégé whose
limitations the opening dialogue had exposed; the Tityrus of the first
poem must be recognized retrospectively as one aspect of the *authorial*
ego, and his pastoral project, however externally or transcendentally authorized, as supported precisely by his exclusiveness, his difference from the
civic "we" who are dispossessed.

We may recognize these maneuvers, pronominal and nominal play, as
one of the earliest analyses we have of the problematic author-function defined by Michel Foucault, but operating here, manifestly, to thicken rather
than to erase the historical presence of a writer. The very deviousness of
the ploys by which "persons" are represented in the *Eclogues* invites our
forming the most basic questions about authorship—questions about how
an artist survives in society and what are his obligations: to his fellow-
citizens, to his patrons, to himself. Especially in Eclogue 6, we can see the
relevance to Virgil of Foucault's notion of a link between authorship as a
convention or strategy, and a controlling state authority.[4] The naming of
one actual Roman patron, Varus, supports the inference that the god who
controls the media, here and in Eclogue 1, is Octavian. And by throwing
into structural and linguistic question the location of his own voice throughout the ten poems, Virgil effectively demonstrated how a writer can *protect*
himself by dismemberment, how he can best assert his ownership of the
text by a wickedly shifting authorial presence. Servius was the first to observe that Tityrus sometimes functions as an authorial persona and sometimes merely as the name of a Greek shepherd. The sign "Menalcas" behaves
in the same unsettling way, being attached to singers of very different character in Eclogues 3 and 5, and in Eclogue 9 denoting the master singer
(again, perhaps, Virgil) whose significance in this poem is marked by his
physical absence from it, his songs recorded only in fragments, those frag-

---

[4] Michel Foucault, "What Is an Author?" in *Language, Counter-Memory, Practice,* trans.
Donald Bouchard and Sherry Simon (Ithaca, N.Y., 1977), pp. 124–25.

ments carefully balanced between echoes of Theocritus and allusions to recent Roman history. Menalcas, then, is a name for Virgil to invest *momentarily* with his own cultural ambitions: his desire to reinvent the Greek pastoral in the Roman historical context, and his doubts (expressed also in the lament of Moeris for his loss of voice and memory) that the fusion can be managed, or that Rome and its current leaders deserve it. But Menalcas's absence from the ninth eclogue is not the disabling absence of a deconstructive theory of language. The poem speaks of doubt and vocational anxiety, but it ends on a note of pragmatism:

> Desine plura, puer, et quod nunc instat agamus;
> carmina tum melius, cum venerit ipse, canemus.

> No more singing, boy; let us do what needs to be done now; when he himself comes, then we will sing better songs.

The contrast between doing and singing at the end of the ninth eclogue retains, therefore, the possibility that singing is doing. It alerts us to the argument woven through the *Eclogues* as to whether poetry has a social function, and if so, where it rates on the scale of social usefulness. At one end of the argument stand the lovelorn, idle Corydon of Eclogue 2 and his counterpart Gallus in Eclogue 10, the former defined by his opening quality, *formosus,* the lovely one, as belonging to a pastoral in which formal and aesthetic properties count for almost everything, provided the mirror of art does not lie, "si numquam fallit imago." Yet even this poem, with its reduction of *otium* to solipsism, ends with the self-injunction to "at least do something useful," and so points against itself to the limited instrumentality of Eclogue 9, whose saddest moment is Moeris's complaint that poetry has not *worked* to protect its singers from a hostile environment:

> carmina tantum
> nostra valent, Lycida, tela inter Martia quantum
> Chaonias dicunt aquila veniente columbas.

> (lines 11–13)

> Our songs, Lycidas, are worth about as much in wartime as, so the saying goes, the Chaonian doves when the eagle comes.

These lines would later become a trope of humanist discourse. In their own context they point to the other most obviously provocative aspect of the *Eclogues;* that the tight network of cross-references between them only serves to accentuate their generic disparities, the doubts at the heart of Virgil's pastoral theory.

Critics from Servius onward have tried to account for the striking variations in tone and range, dealing in oppositions such as serious/light, high/ low, idyllic/ironic, Theocritean/Roman, or "forward-looking, peaceful, conciliatory, and patriotic" versus "neoteric, ambiguous, or polemic."[5] Virgil himself invited such activity by his cryptic suggestion, at the opening of Eclogue 4, that the pastoral could have both gradations of seriousness and political relevance: he there proposed to sing a *little* more grandly ("paulo maiora canamus"), producing a silvan song worthy of a consul's attention ("silvae sint consule dignae"). But, as the history of his reception shows, he absolutely prevented any neat decisions as to how the eclogues might be rearranged in preferential order. To recognize Eclogues 2, 3, 7, and 8 as directly modeled on Theocritus, while Eclogues 1, 4, 5, 9, and 10 require a Roman perspective, is not to determine their relative value, a question that would not only be hotly debated ever after but that would bring to the surface, for all later readers, their own ideological requirements. For some early Christian readers, the series was only worthy of preservation for the sake of the messianic fourth eclogue; for others, Virgil's higher mood extended also to Silenus's account of creation in the sixth eclogue and to the lament for Daphnis in the fifth; while for others, all complexity, whether political or philosophical, was hopelessly out of place in pastoral, and only the Theocritean songs of love or lovely grief deserved imitation. All such revealing decisions—revealing of *their* authors' cultural premises—were set in motion by the dialectical structure that Virgil bequeathed to us, an ancient poetics no less elliptical than those of Plato and Aristotle, and one that has been, I would argue, at least as influential.

In the chapters that follow, more will be said about the metapoetic or self-theorizing aspect of the *Eclogues,* insofar as that was addressed by Virgil's later readers. But this will not be another book describing or debating the meaning, structure, or origins, whether literary or historical, of Virgil's text, a kind of criticism that has been remarkably fertile in the second half of the twentieth century. I do not wish to augment or challenge the work of scholars such as Paul Alpers, Friedrich Klingner, Eleanor Winsor Leach, Brooks Otis, Michael Putnam, Charles Segal, and Bruno Snell, to name those who have developed perhaps the most distinctive positions on the *Eclogues.*[6] Rather, I wish to shift the focus of inquiry to Virgil's readers,

---

[5] Brooks Otis, *Virgil: A Study in Civilized Poetry* (Oxford, 1964), p. 130.

[6] See Alpers, *Singer of the Eclogues;* Friedrich Klingner, "Die Einheit des Vergilischen Lebenswerkes" and "Virgil und die geschichtliche Welt," in his *Römische Geisteswelt* (2nd ed. Munich, 1961), pp. 274–311; Klingner, *Virgil: Bucolica, Georgica, Aeneis* (Zurich, 1967); Eleanor Winsor Leach, *Vergil's Eclogues: Landscapes of Experience* (Ithaca, N.Y., 1974); Otis, *Virgil;* Michael Putnam, *Virgil's Pastoral Art* (Princeton, 1970); Charles Segal, *Poetry and Myth in Ancient Pastoral* (Princeton, 1981); Bruno Snell, *The Discovery of the Mind: The Greek Origins of European Thought,* trans. Thomas Rosenmeyer (New York, 1960), pp. 281–310. While Leach, Putnam, and Otis all emphasize the Roman context of the *Eclogues,* Leach

from Varus and Octavian to my own contemporaries, whose views are only the most recent phase in the long history of Virgilian reception and interpretation. What interests me, and will I hope interest others, is the nature of the investment that has been made in this remarkable text over time, and what we can learn from the curves in its reception history about the larger history of which it is the shadow.

Nor will this book launch another attempt to define the nature of pastoral—a cause lost as early as the sixteenth century, when the genre began to manifest the tendency of most strong literary forms to propagate by miscegenation, and a cause reduced to total confusion by modern criticism's search for "versions of pastoral" in the most unlikely places. If William Empson's *Some Versions of Pastoral* has been, in the second half of our century, "the most important and the least helpful" approach to the problem of definition,[7] perhaps now is the time for the central question to be restated. It is not what pastoral *is* that should matter to us. On that, agreement is impossible, and its discussion inevitably leads to the narrowing strictures of normative criticism, statements of what constitutes the "genuine" or the "true" to the exclusion of exemplars that the critic regards as "perverse." What can be described and, at least in terms of coverage, with some neutrality, is what pastoral since Virgil can do and has always done; or rather, to put the agency back where it belongs—how writers, artists, and intellectuals of all persuasions have *used* pastoral for a range of functions and intentions that the *Eclogues* first articulated.

This will, therefore, be a book about the history of Virgil's *Eclogues* in Western culture; about the fact that, despite statements to the contrary, Europeans have never lost interest in this remarkable collection of short poems; and about the drive (the Freudian term is not misplaced) that has kept them coming back to it again and again. I shall here argue that what people think of Virgil's *Eclogues* is a key to their own cultural assumptions, because the text was so structured as to provoke, consciously or unconsciously, an ideological response.

By *ideology* I mean both a more capacious and a less totalizing concept than is sometimes invoked by that term: not only the dominant structure

---

stresses the poetry's absorption of actual Roman landscape and customs, of the literary milieu and the decorative arts; Otis puts most emphasis on the Julio-Augustan themes in the *Eclogues,* but sees them as essentially benign; and Putnam offers a considerably darker view of Virgil's attitude toward Octavian and the death of the republic. In contrast, both Klingner and Snell define Arcadia, which they equate with Virgil's pastoral world, as an ideal interior landscape to which the poet can retreat from the brutal realities of history. To anticipate one of the central arguments of my Chapter 5, it is no coincidence that both Klingner's and Snell's positions were originally formulated in Germany in the period marked by the rise of the National Socialist party and its consequences in the Second World War: Klingner's two essays were first published in 1930 and 1943, respectively, Snell's in 1944.

[7] Andrew Ettin, *Literature and the Pastoral* (New Haven, 1984), p. 189.

of beliefs in a society, but also the singular view (heterodox, subversive, maverick); not only the biases inherent in class differentiation and structured by large-scale, long-term economics, but also the lonely strictures of personal ambition or its restraint; and, especially, sets of aesthetic or metaphysical premises, whether held at large or idiosyncratically. For aesthetic beliefs are seldom fully insulated from the first two categories and frequently serve as acceptable metaphors for them.

Among the competing ideologies proleptically displayed in the *Eclogues* are Roman republicanism, the classic statement of the claims of the many to equal consideration; the counter-claim of the privileged few to special treatment on the grounds of special talent; the hegemonic needs of the holders of power for cultural authentication; the responsibility of the intellectual for providing that authentication, in the interests of stability; the value of political or social stability in nurturing the arts; the responsibility of the intellectual for telling the whole truth, in the interests of social justice; the intellectual's claim to personal autonomy. At various stages in European cultural history one or more of these positions has become dominant in a society or at least among those most able to establish themselves as its spokesmen, and among the most powerful ideologies in our own century has been the position that literature, and pastoral in particular, is or should be nonideological. This book charts the growth of that view from the eighteenth century onward, while at the same time attempting to show both that it has consistently been challenged by thinkers and artists of stature, and that it is no less "political" in intention and effect than opinions whose exile it has sought.

This project began in an attempt to explain why it was that modern theorists of pastoral were often hostile to or contemptuous of the one era in which the genre could fairly be said to be ubiquitous, namely, the Renaissance. Trying to answer that question took me back to Virgil, and thence to the Virgilian interpretation that most influenced the Renaissance, the system of commentary associated with the name of Servius. My first chapter records the products of that inquiry and is partly structured defensively, as a revisionist account of the Servian hermeneutics as they were developed in the later Roman Empire. But the inquiry itself opened my eyes to some remarkable facts about Virgil's *Eclogues*. The size of the Virgil collections of the British Library, Princeton University Library, and the Library of Congress suggested that few texts can have been so frequently edited, annotated, translated, imitated, and illustrated in visual form. Moreover, the fame of the names involved indicated that here was a ready-made instrument for doing cultural history with a certain rigor, while at the same time raising the suspicion that there was more here than met the eye, that more had been invested in this text over time than our own cultural system anywhere admitted. Among early editors and commentators were Landino, Politian, and Vives; among translators, Clément Marot, John Dryden, and Paul Valéry; among imitators, Petrarch, Spenser, Milton, Pope, Wordsworth, Frost; among illustrators, Sebastian Brant, Franz Cleyn, William Blake, Jacques-Louis David, Samuel Palmer, Aristide Maillol, Jacques Villon. It was true, of course, that not all of this interpretive energy was limited to the *Eclogues*—some of it was directed to the Virgilian canon as a whole; but it also appeared to be true that the *Eclogues* had acquired a special role as a cultural catalyst and emblem. On the one hand, they came first in editions of Virgil; their brevity made them, until the classics ceased to be part of our curriculum, a natural exercise for elementary education, so that they entered the European consciousness at a formative stage. On the other, there was an interesting pattern of *return* to the *Eclogues* at a late stage in the intellectual life, as though this were the one text that would make all things clear. This was the case for Vives in the sixteenth century, for Blake at the turn of the eighteenth, for Samuel Palmer in Victorian England, and for Paul Valéry at the end of his career in Vichy France.

Beginning, therefore, as an exploration of Renaissance poetics, the project became impossible to complete without retracing the whole story of Virgilian interpretation, from its first major formulations in the early Middle Ages to developments that at least as I write can be spoken of as recent. The book is therefore divided into five large blocks, whose contents roughly correspond to our most common divisions of literary and art history into "periods"; the first, focused on Servius and Petrarch, represents the Middle Ages, both early and late; the second, the Renaissance, from the mid-Quattrocento to the end of the sixteenth century; the third, the seventeenth century; the fourth, Neoclassicism; and the fifth, in one fell swoop, both Romanticism and modernism. The logic of this arrangement, so apparently conventional, produced some controversial results. The material created its own narrative structures, which sometimes, as with Neoclassicism and Romanticism, called into further question the already fragile demarcations that periodization suggests, and sometimes, as with medievalism and again Romanticism, subjected to skepticism even the semantic content of those terms.

Gradually I perceived that the topic I had stumbled upon was infinitely richer than I could have imagined. Not only could I, by focusing on Virgil's text and its reception, acquire some structural purchase on the slippery topic of pastoral theory; not only might this focus, because of the significance of the figures involved, provide an integrated account of European cultural history that might interrogate or demonstrate anew our most cherished assumptions about how and when significant *change* occurred;

but, most important, here was a perspective from which it might be possible to speak with some precision about at least one of the many relationships between art and society. For as distinct from Marxist discussions of art's means of production, of the economics of the imagination, the issue here, statistically insignificant, was therefore analytically manageable: the question, pressing to no one but themselves, of how the intellectuals in any society define themselves, their sanctions and functions. Whether they called themselves writers, artists, poets, *grammatici, ingeniosi, docti, philosophes, Dichter,* men of letters, or professors, the arbiters of European culture since Virgil turned to Virgil's *Eclogues,* apparently, as a paradigm of the intellectual's dilemma. The models for self- and societal analysis they found there were often, but not always, those I have already suggested. Often they repressed or suppressed half of what they found there or what others had found, in the interests of projects that could not afford a fully dialectical inspection. Sometimes they turned to the *Eclogues* as both outlet and authorization for the expression of vocational anxiety.

This book, then, is candid in its admission that the culture spoken of throughout is high culture; although there are moments at which pastoral theory, as we shall see, attempts to manage—to represent, to speak on behalf of or to silence—other, less privileged social groups. The *we* in my rhetoric, however, are imagined to be all or any who make a living by practicing one of the liberal arts, who must occasionally wonder to what end they do so. Three examples may suggest the applicability to ourselves of what will follow, a relation not necessarily contravened when the case before us seems obscure or even eccentric. Such was certainly the career profile of Nicodemus Frischlin, German humanist scholar and philologist in the second half of the sixteenth century, and author of a commentary on the *Eclogues.* Having been a professor at the university of Tübingen for several years, and even crowned as a Count Palatine by the emperor, in 1582, in the urbane words of the *Encyclopedia Britannica,* "his unguarded language and reckless life made it necessary that he should leave Tübingen." Returning to the university after a judicious visiting appointment elsewhere, "he was threatened with a criminal prosecution on a charge of immoral conduct, and the threat led to his withdrawal to Frankfurt-am-Main." It was there that the commentary on the *Eclogues* was written and, later, published under the title *Introductiones oeconomicae simul & politicae.*[8]

Considering his somewhat precarious existence as a scholar, it is not surprising that Frischlin responded to the *Eclogues* as an extended allegory of worth unappreciated. In particular, he provided an original reading of

---

[8] Nicodemus Frischlin, *Introductiones oeconomicae simul & politicae; Historiis, fabulis, allegoriis, virtumque adeo ac vitiorum imaginibus admirandis* (Frankfurt-am-Main, 1614).

the second eclogue, the lament of Corydon for his unreciprocated love for Alexis. Whereas Byron would note the homoerotic content of the poem with derisive glee,[9] as one of the "naughty bits" of the European cultural anatomy,[10] and Erasmus had already reacted with dismay, converting it into an allegory of friendship between like rather than unlike natures,[11] Frischlin saw in the poem a metaphoric account of intelligence despised. For him, the "formosum pastor" is Cornelius Gallus, who is "urbanus" and despises Virgil/Corydon as a country hick. Everywhere, he complains, the Roman world is enjoying peace; he alone is solitary, living an unquiet life, morose and irritable because it is so difficult to make friends in Rome:

> Poeta rusticus & plebeius: ut qui nullam adhuc ingenii documentum in lucem emiserit. At tu quaerito ab iis, qui hac de re judicium ferre possunt: quo animi cultu, quibus disciplinis ornatus sim: & quas res versuum monumentis comprehenderim. Neque enim solum humanitatis artes, & haec liberaliora studia memoria teneo: sed carmina etiam pango, quae . . . cum erudita antiquitate, non immerito comparari queant.
>
> (p. 36)

> The poet is a peasant and lower-class: so he has not yet published any proof of his intelligence. But I seek you out from among those who can judge of these matters: by what mental exercise and disciplines should I improve myself, and what subjects should I celebrate in verse? For I have mastered not only the humanities and those liberal studies, but I also write songs, which can, not undeservedly, be compared with the accomplishments of antiquity.

The self-reflexive function of this translation, by a disgraced humanist and classical scholar, seems simultaneously comic and sad (as, by most accounts, was Virgil's Corydon), and the narcissistic aspect of both the original and Frischlin's translation is in fact strikingly foregrounded in what follows. For Frischlin glosses the extraordinary passage in which Virgil's shepherd consoles himself that he is not bad-looking:

> nec sum adeo informis: nuper me in litore vidi,
> cum placidum ventis staret mare. non ego Daphnin
> iudice te metuam, si numquam fallit imago.
>
> (2.25–28)

---

[9] George Gordon, Lord Byron, *Don Juan,* Canto 1: 48: "But Virgil's songs are pure, except that horrid one / Beginning with 'Formosum Pastor Corydon.'"
[10] The phrase is, of course, Monty Python's.
[11] Desiderius Erasmus, *De ratione studii,* ed. J.-C Margolin, *ASD* 1, 2 (1971): 139–40.

> Nor am I so ugly: recently I saw myself, by the shore, when the sea
> was becalmed. If you were judge, I should not fear Daphnis,
> provided that reflection is not deceptive.

Instead of finding it, as a modern reader might be tempted to do, a statement of phenomenological doubt, he produces a two-stage historical allegory of personal ambition. The becalmed sea is postwar Italy; Corydon's
image in the water stands for Virgil's favorable reception in peace and leisure ("in ocio & pace") into the company of Maecenas, Pollio, Tucca, Varus,
and Caesar Octavian himself, who have all approved his life and his customs ("vitam ac mores meos"); and the only remaining doubt is whether
Gallus, with his exceptional refinement, can be brought to concur. There
could scarcely be a more egregious example of damaged self-esteem consoling itself in the mirror of the text. The 1614 edition of Frischlin's commentary reminded its audience that its author was "Orator & Poeta coro-
natus." It is somehow dramatically fitting that Frischlin's career concluded
as it did: in 1590 he was arrested for writing libelous letters and imprisoned in the fortress of Hohenurach; he broke his neck while trying to
escape.

The second example comes from England in the eighteenth century,
when Robert Andrews, a North Country Nonconformist minister, produced a translation of Virgil's *Works* and dedicated it to the Hon. Booth
Grey. The dedication, which is of much more interest than Andrews's eccentric, line-by-line, completely unreadable translation, consists of a personalized account of Virgil's career as seen through the lens of English
politics in 1766. This was a year marked by the English parliament's repeal
of the Stamp Act in a vain effort to head off the American revolution, a
year that ended with constitutional crisis and corn riots at home. The word
of the day was *liberty,* a key word particularly associated with the propaganda of John Wilkes, the spectacular radical organizer and polemicist
who, though dismissed from the House of Commons and sent into political exile, quietly returned in the summer of 1766. Again, then, it is not
exactly surprising that this eighteenth-century Virgil was introduced to his
public in the language of the times:

> He never inspires in his intelligent and unaffected Admirers any other
> than the Spirit of Liberty, and of universal Justice, which tho' founded
> originally in the natural Equality between Man and Man, cannot be
> executed without the civil subordination of Ranks and Offices under
> the inviolable Authority of a British King and Parliament: That our
> happy Constitution![12]

[12] Robert Andrews, *The Works of Virgil, Englished* (Birmingham, 1766), n.p.

Andrews here registered as a conformist in state if not in church polity. But his defense of Virgil against the charge of supporting tyranny (a charge that Blake would make, unmake, and make again) was subsequently developed into a far more sophisticated defense against the other possibility, namely, that Virgil was apolitical:

> Yet he was not a trifling Virtuoso, or mere idle Spectator of the world. . . . And Liberty which like the nightingale ever sings the sweetest in its dying agonies, had with the murder'd and immortal Cicero breathed her last, and left the world to Augustus now settled on a Tyrant's throne. In such a situation what did Virgil do? What could he do, more than the virtuous Messala? Those high Ideas of national Independency and civil liberty, which he had suck'd with his Mother's milk, and which to me seem clearly in his writings to have been heighten'd in him by the philosophy of Plato, these were really become visionary. In this, the severest trial to a generous soul, he yet proved himself superior: did not, like Cato, to shew his courage, prove his madness: nor yet chose to sleep life away, dissolved to annihilation in the dreams and pleasures of the gay philosophy in vogue. Neither was he like those who because they cannot do all the good they wish, will therefore do none: nor again like those who because they cannot be absolute, will therefore have no influence, except that of a sly and virulent opposition to the public wisdom, in order to multiply the public calamities, and thereby prove the bad consequences of any measures but their own. He had other views of patriotism: saw that now the world had arrived to its full measure of iniquity, nothing more remained for man to do, than if possible to soften the rigours of divine justice to be apprehended in a line of despotic Princes: at least himself certainly could do nothing but by the inspiration of the gentle Muses.
>
> (pp. 10–11)

Although Andrews did not himself make the point, this passage functions as an extended gloss on one of the most tendentious sections of Virgil's first eclogue, when, in response to Meliboeus's question as to the motives of his journey to Rome, Tityrus replies, "Libertas"—a mysterious answer that, as we shall see in Chapters 1 and 2, had from Servius onward suggested a republican subtext. By the time Andrews wrote his own commentary, the arguments for and against such a reading had multiplied to the point that no Virgilian scholar could possibly have invoked the word without recalling its ideological history. Andrews's defense of Virgil from the charge of escapism had, therefore, the same self-reflexive potential as Frischlin's more labored efforts at self-defense, for to "English" Virgil at a time like this was a way of reenacting the strategy he attributed to Virgil, of working to ameliorate the system from within. If Andrews hoped, like his original, to soften the consequences for his nation of "a line of despotic Princes" by using the "gentle Muses" as the vehicle of his own principles, it was only prudent to begin with an act of egregious submission, by formally saluting the third in a line of Georges.

The third and considerably more distinguished example comes from our own century: Hermann Broch's *Death of Virgil*, a lyric novel conceived in the 1930s as an essay on the death of culture. An Austrian intellectual who in 1938 fled from the Nazis and whose work was banned in Germany until 1945, when *Der Tod des Vergil* appeared both there and in America, Broch is a powerful instance of the writer in exile, a Meliboeus, as it were, of a later and greater expropriation.[13] But the connection with the *Eclogues* goes deeper than analogy. It is true that the *Death of Virgil* focuses whatever narrative it contains on the *Aeneid*, on the question of whether Virgil will persist in his dying determination to destroy the unfinished poem or whether he will, as actually happens, bequeath it to his friends, along with its carefully unwritten dedication to Augustus. But Broch's characterization of Virgil as author and, indeed, his novel's central debate depend on a profoundly inventive (yet not unprecedented) reading of the *Eclogues*.

For Broch, Virgil as author was explicable primarily as a peasant, but one who had come to conceptualize his own origins, or, as the second georgic has it, to know his own happiness. Early in the novel, as the invalid poet is carried from the port at Brundisium up to the imperial palace, he is torn between pastoral and political impulses. A scent of lumber makes him think

> of forests, of olive groves, the bucolic peace from which he himself a peasant's son had emerged, the peace of his constant nostalgia and of his earth-bound, earth-bent, always earthly longing, the peace to which his song had been dedicated since days of yore, oh the peace of his longing, unattainable; and as if this lack of attainment reflected itself here, as if everywhere it must come to be the image of his selfhood, this peace was constrained here between stones, subserviated and misused for ambition, for gain, for bribery, for headlong greed, for worldliness, for servitude, for discord.[14]

---

[13] For Broch's circumstances, including his abandonment of "a well-established career as industrialist, engineer and director of a Viennese textile concern for philosophy and letters," see R. Hinton Thomas, "The Novels of Hermann Broch," *Cambridge Journal* 6 (1953): 591–604; for Broch's own account of his novel's evolution, see H. J. Weigand, "Broch's *Death of Vergil:* Program Notes," *PMLA* 62 (1947): 551–54; and for an essay on its contributions to poetics and cultural history, see Lawrence Lipking, *The Life of the Poet: Beginning and Ending Poetic Careers* (Chicago and London, 1981), pp. 130–37.

[14] *The Death of Virgil*, trans. Jean Starr Untermeyer (New York, 1965), p. 36.

The novel's lyric movement will be to resolve this conflict through a series of visonary memories, on the one hand, and on the other, by debating with the emperor the meaning of his own work.

Like Frischlin and Andrews, though with infinitely greater provocation, Broch interprets the *Eclogues* in the light of his own situation. Watching the war in Europe from the safety of the United States, writing his novel with the support of a Guggenheim Fellowship, he found the meaning of Virgil's career in the *Eclogues,* and the meaning of the *Eclogues* in Eclogue 4, with its prophecies of peace in one's own time and the desuetude of nostalgia.[15] It was this vision that empowered Broch's Virgil in his last confrontation with Augustus and permitted him to challenge the emperor's view that the *Aeneid* was his greatest, because most Roman, work. The fourth eclogue, in that argument, is reinterpreted *not* as Augustus would have it, as a statement that "the glory of the ages had been fulfilled by our time" (p. 336), but as a new provisional statement poised between epochs and already receding before the "stronger metaphor" of a new perception. "In the kingdom of that perception the sword will come to be superfluous" (p. 360), Broch's dying Virgil is capable of asserting, and his Augustus, grasping its radical (transgressive) spiritualism, remarks: "These are extremely dangerous and novel ideas, Virgil: they are derogatory to the state" (p. 377).

Yet to focus on the confrontation between poet and emperor, between transcendence and historical pragmatism, art and politics, pastoral and epic, is to oversimplify. This spoken debate comes late in the novel, as if narrative and dramatic modes can only reappear in a last moment of "normal" lucidity prior to death; and it is preceded by wave after wave of lyric self-analysis, during which Virgil takes, if one can put it so sharply, the other side of the argument. Watching the slaves rowing, he muses on the probable fate of the *Aeneid:* "Nothing availed the poet, he could right no wrongs; he is heeded only if he extols the world, never if he portrays it as it is . . . only the agreeable things would be extracted from it, and . . . there was neither danger nor hope that the exhortations would be heeded" (p. 15). Meditating on his own dependency as an intellectual, a man "who had never fought for anything," he knows himself as a man "endowed, fed,

---

[15] On the role of the fourth eclogue in Broch's thought, see Timm Collmann, *Zeit und Geschichte in Hermann Brochs Roman "Der Tod des Vergil"* (Bonn, 1967), pp. 159–64. The novel is also saturated with allusions to, quotations from, and interpretations of other eclogues: see *Death of Virgil,* pp. 65, 251, 273, 281, 301, 305, 412. Significantly, Broch assumes a political context for the *Eclogues,* referring (p. 305) to their connection with the Treaty of Brundisium; and his Virgil confesses that, despite his own homoerotic experiences, the second eclogue "had not come to be love-song, but an Eclogue of thanks for Asinius Pollio, dealing but in a most negligible way with love in a longed-for landscape" (p. 251).

and kept by Asinius Pollio and by Augustus—they who had fought for Rome" (p. 244). And, most importantly, forcing himself in interior monologue to scrutinize his aesthetics, Broch's Virgil (and, surely, Broch himself), contemplated one of the most obvious dangers facing the pastoral lyric (and even the lyric novel):

> he knew also that the beauty of the symbol, were it ever so precise in its reality, was never its own excuse for being, that whenever such was the case, whenever beauty existed for its own sake, there art was attacked at its very roots . . . there was only intoxication with empty forms and empty words, whereby art through this lack of discrimination and even of fidelity, was reduced to un-art, and poetry to mere literarity.
>
> (pp. 141–42)

The pleasure of the text and the allure of constant revision (a terrible insight, this one) are temptations in the same family as the final temptation for the artist: to destroy the *Aeneid* because it is less than perfect.[16] Passing beyond it, Virgil allows himself to become the *Aeneid's* author, an act of submission to history marked by the dictation of his "will" and its formal dating, "at Brundisium, the ninth day before the calends of October in the seven hundredth and thirtieth year after the founding of the city of Rome" (p. 432).

This book, also written from a protected position, with the help of a Guggenheim Fellowship and other institutional supports, but without any of the shocks and hazards that must have stimulated Broch's return to Virgil, is my own imperfect contribution to the topic he embraced with such self-analytical rigor: the long debate on the author-function, the role of the intellectual in society, and the cultural work that pastoral, as a metaphoric poetics, has apparently being doing. It should already be clear that the structural neutrality I aim for is undermined by a commitment to a socially conscious, or rather self-consciously social, aesthetic. Such self-contradictions are endemic to our profession, and I make no apology for mine. But I must make one appeal to my readers. As this book's scope is broad, so the argument is essentially incremental. It depends less on the depth or intricacy of individual "readings" than on a network of connections and cross-references that stretch from the first chapter to the last, as writers and artists themselves looked back to earlier stages of interpreta-

---

[16] Lipking, *Life of the Poet,* p. 135, cites Broch on the analogy between Virgil's vocational *angst* and his own: "I have renounced the thought of completing the book in a genuinely artistic way, because in this time of horrors I could not dare to put still more years into a work that, with each additional page, would have become increasingly esoteric."

tion in order to take their own personal stance, to locate themselves and *their* version of the *Eclogues* in their own historical moment. If the book is read selectively, it will disappoint; and it certainly cannot be used as a work of reference, having neither the completeness of coverage nor the density of bibliographical reference necessary to that genre.

As usual, Virgil (and one of his readers) said it for me. In Fielding's *Tom Jones* (book 8, chapter 4) Partridge the ex-schoolmaster has a habit of classical allusion, which leads the hero to remark, "I find, Friend, you are a scholar." "A poor one," was the reply, "non omnia possumus omnes." His source was Virgil's eighth eclogue; his citation, a phrase that had become a commonplace of humanist scholarship;[17] its sensible if self-forgiving meaning: we cannot all do everything.

---

[17] Eclogue 8.63; it is also cited by Broch, *Death of Virgil*, p. 281.

1
MEDIEVALISM:
Petrarch and the Servian Hermeneutic

Allegories are, in the realm of thoughts, what
ruins are in the realm of things.

Walter Benjamin, *The Origin of German Tragic Drama*

In the front of Francis Petrarch's own manuscript of Virgil is an extraordinary painting (Plate 1) by Simone Martini—extraordinary not only for its
beauty and preservation, but for the story it tells about certain principles
of interpretation.[1] On the upper right sits Virgil himself, pen in hand,
under a tree. Below him, sheep (or perhaps goats) are being milked, and
trees pruned. Beside him stand two figures, the one in armor completing
the triple allusion to the *Eclogues, Georgics,* and *Aeneid.* Yet the ambience of

The chapter epigraph is from Walter Benjamin, *The Origin of German Tragic Drama,*
trans. John Osborne (London, 1977), p. 178; first published as *Ursprung des deutschen Trauerspiels* (Berlin, 1928).
[1] Biblioteca Ambrosiana, Milan, codex A.49. inf.; reproduced in facsimile (Milan, 1930).

19

the painting is predominantly pastoral, Virgil's own pose reflecting the rural leisure that makes writing possible, the pose and role that he, in the first eclogue, had permanently assigned to Tityrus. Even more telling is the presence of the other standing figure, not onlooker but interpreter, who draws away the veil (actually a neat muslin curtain, rings and all), behind which, without his mediation, Virgil would have remained partially obscured. Within the frame of the painting are two Latin epigrams which, according to Pierre de Nolhac, were added in Petrarch's own hand.[2] They explain, first, the significance of the manuscript, and second, the identity and function of the interpreter:

> Ytala perclaros tellus alis alma poetas:
> Sed tibi grecorum dedit hic attingere metas.
>
> Servius altiloqui retegens archana maronis
> ut pateant ducibus pastoribus atque colonis.

> Italy, kind country, you feed famous poets. So this one [Virgil] allowed you to attain the Grecian goals. [Here is] Servius, recovering the enigmas of high-spoken Virgil, so that they are revealed in generals, shepherds, and farmers.

Below the frame of the painting is a third epigram which adds, as it were, a third stage to the story of interpretation. Here Petrarch pays tribute to the importance of the *visual* commentary, in a statement simultaneously of the doctrine of *ut pictura poesis,* of the collaboration of the sister arts in a humanist adventure, and of the historical time and place of that collaboration:

> Mantua Virgilium qui talia carmine finxit,
> Sena tulit Symonem digito qui talia pinxit.

> Mantua bore Virgil, who fashioned such things in poetry; Sienna bore Simone, who painted such things with his own hand.

This frontispiece represents, then, an iconic hermeneutic—a graceful and lucid pictorial account of a system of interpretation that relates specifically to Virgil, and especially to his *Eclogues*—as well as certain propositions about the originator of that system, Maurus Servius Honoratus, grammarian and teacher of rhetoric in Rome at the end of the fourth century A.D. His career can be dated only conjecturally, by virtue of his ap-

---

[2] Pierre de Nolhac, *Pétrarque et l'humanisme,* 2 vols. (Paris, 1907), 1: 141.

pearance in the *Saturnalia* of Macrobius, as one of the interlocutors in a dialogue supposed to have taken place in Rome in 384;[3] but it belongs to what seems to have been a crucial phase in the history of Virgilian interpretation. The fourth and early fifth centuries produced, in what may have been a series of conservationist efforts, a *Life* of Virgil by Aelius Donatus, teacher of St. Jerome from 359 to 367 and also the author of a commentary on Virgil that now survives only in the interstices of the Servian one; the chapters in Macrobius's *Saturnalia* that deal in Virgilian criticism; and the two most ancient manuscripts of Virgil, with illustrations derived from classical iconography.[4] The commentary of Servius himself, which also collates older sources, especially Donatus, in the format of a variorum, was the first major reading of Virgil's work to survive in its entirety and was, in terms of subsequent influence, the greatest. Yet since at least the middle of the nineteenth century both Servius and his interpretive methods have been subjected to various kinds of criticism, suppression, and even abuse; and, by a coincidence that serves our purpose, something of the same fate has attended Simone Martini's painting.

The reasons for this are far from simple. They combine misunderstanding of what truly distinguished Servian commentary on Virgil, a vague but historically recurrent prejudice against "medieval" habits of thought, a revaluation downward of any metaphorical structures that could be designated *allegory,* a loss of confidence in the actual text of Servius, and a modernist bias (which actually has its roots in Neoclassicism) against any contamination of literature, and especially of pastoral, by an explicit political ideology or purpose. The reception of Servian commentary is, therefore, an inextricable part of the reception history of Virgil's *Eclogues,* and

[3] On the internal and external evidence for dating the *Saturnalia* see H. Georgii, "Zur Bestimmung der Zeit des Servius," *Philologus* 71 (1912): 518–26; Alan Cameron, "The Date and Identity of Macrobius," *Journal of Roman Studies* 56 (1966): 25–38, and Jacques Flamant, *Macrobe et le Néo-Platonisme latin, à la Fin du IVe siècle* (Leiden, 1977), pp. 15–141. The imaginary dialogue took place in the house of the prefect Vettius Praetextatus, who died in 384; but its date of composition remains conjectural. Cameron and Flamant disagree absolutely on the relationship of Macrobius to the pagan revival, Cameron arguing that "the non-militant and sentimentally pagan atmosphere of the *Saturnalia*" required a late date in the 1430s (p. 36), Flamant that the work was precisely suited to evade the proscriptions against the Roman religion, both by concealing its militant paganism "sous le couvert de l'erudition" and by its limited circulation among a few aristocratic Roman families (pp. 137–38).
[4] Both are in the Vatican Library: Codex Vaticanus Latinus 3225, the Vatican Virgil, and Codex Vaticanus 3867, better known as the Vergilius Romanus. For the dating of the Vatican Virgil, see the convenient summary of scholarship in T. B. Stevenson, *Miniature Decoration in the Vatican Vergil* (Tübingen, 1983), pp. 1–23. Stevenson concludes tentatively that the manuscript derives from the height of the pagan reaction in Rome during the late fourth century (p. 223). See also David Wright, *Vergilius Vaticanus: Commentarium,* in *Codices Selecti* (Graz, 1985), vol. 71, and in *Codices e Vaticanis selecti,* vol. 40. For the Romanus, Erwin Rosenthal, *The Illuminations of the Vergilius Romanus* (Zurich, 1972), pp. 102–5, proposed an early sixth-century date but had to posit a late-fourth-century intermediary.

no exercise could more sharply illustrate my contention that all interpretation of the *Eclogues* is subject to cultural shift than the attempt in this chapter to restore to Servius the credit he once possessed. By first examining
the unspoken premises of some of those past negative judgments, both
of the painting and of the hermeneutics it represents, and then by re-
investigating the Servian approach to the *Eclogues,* I hope to establish the
direction of this project, that is, to demonstrate the ideological substratum
of all cultural history and the evaluative decisions of which it is the cumulative record. Without making Servius the hero of the story, we can certainly
make an informed attempt to recover the meaning of Simone Martini's
painting and of Petrarch's three verses, the content of their joint enthusiasm. What later chapters will, among other things, attempt to confirm is
that the "medieval" understanding of the *Eclogues* could not be erased from
the cultural system. What Servius had seen in Virgil, and Petrarch in Servius,
became part of the genetic structure of pastoral and could never be completely unwritten.

First, then, the painting. There is a highly instructive comparison to
be made of attitudes and assumptions it has generated even in the twentieth century. In 1902 there appeared a volume entitled *Pétrarque, ses études
d'art,* the joint product of Prince Essling and Eugène Müntz. Here Simone
Martini was blamed for his anachronistic costuming of the figures—having
never had the opportunity, it is supposed, to see a Greek or Roman statue—
and for his ignorance of "the laws of perspective and the rules of order," an
ignorance resulting in the arrangement of figures on a flat plane, before a
row of stage trees, with no illusion of distance or landscape. But into the
faces of the central protagonists Müntz read a mixture of that which in-
trigued and repelled him, a statement of cultural and aesthetic ambivalence:

> Under some trees, in a quite primitive structure before which a curtain
> is clumsily hung, Virgil reposes, represented with the features of a man
> in his sixties . . . he appears to be searching for inspiration which is
> slow in coming. It is a less than happy face, with a morose expression,
> a vast distance from our own image of the divine poet. . . . Finally, in
> this skinny arm, in this seemingly atrophied hand, one feels too much
> of the preoccupation with asceticism that we associate with the Sien-
> nese school. Near Virgil, and in absolute contrast with him, appears
> Servius the commentator, shining with youth and beauty, his hair
> blond, his gaze eager, his mustache and beard youthfully crisp, his
> color heightened; one of the noblest creations of the Middle Ages.[5]

[5] Victor Masséna, Prince Essling, and Eugène Müntz, *Pétrarque, ses études d'art* (Paris,
1902), pp. 12–13. Compare, however, the account of P. Rossi, *Simone Martini e Petrarca*
(Sienna, 1904), pp. 16–200, which, while repeating much of Müntz's description, qualifies
his attack on the supposed anachronism of the painting.

In this remarkable passage are displayed with unusual candor an appreciative, rather than a formalist, approach to art history; a focus on human personality and genius as the value-bearing ingredients of art; and a conflict between the standards of Enlightenment rationalism (the source of the concept of anachronism) and the nineteenth-century recuperation of medievalism as a positive cultural construct.

This turn-of-the-century ambivalence is strikingly absent from an account of Petrarch published in 1982 by Thomas Greene. Or, rather, such ambivalence as the subject of Virgil and Servius might hold was transferred by Greene to Petrarch himself, who in Greene's view alternated between a genuinely Renaissance sense of the classics and a residual medievalism, expressed in visual terms on the frontispiece to the Virgil manuscript. "In this miniature," wrote Greene,

> Virgil appears crowned with ivy behind a thin curtain in a pose often assigned to biblical prophets or evangelists. The pointed finger of a grammarian, possibly Servius, directs the attention of a knight, Aeneas, to his creator. . . . The miniature breathes the spirit of late medieval allegory, represented in a heavily stylized Gothic manner. Facing the manuscript and the civilization behind it, how could we expect Petrarch to erase the hermeneutic sedimentation of fourteen centuries? We know in fact that he did not. On the folios containing the first eclogue, he inserted an interlineated gloss based on a mechanical and reductive interpretation inspired by Donatus but spelled out now with a relentlessly heavy hand.[6]

While at first sight startling in its lack of sympathy, this passage is rich in "hermeneutic sedimentation" of its own and is therefore of much analytic value. Compared to Müntz's critique of what is maladroit in the visual composition, Greene's animus is clearly directed against what, again in his view, it represents: the "spirit of late medieval allegory," which for Greene is associated both with the medieval church (hence the references to biblical illumination) and with a style of textual exegesis (the line-by-line commentary) that can dyslogistically be designated "the grammarian's approach."

Now Servius was indeed a grammarian, that is to say, a teacher whose primary responsibility to his students was in making intelligible to them in detail the linguistic structure of Virgil's works. The use of the term as opprobrium is found even in Macrobius[7] and was prevalent in the early

---

[6]Thomas M. Greene, *The Light in Troy: Imitation and Discovery in Renaissance Poetry* (New Haven, 1982), p. 35. This view of the Virgil manuscript as "puerile" and "bizarre" was established at the beginning of the century by de Nolhac, *Pétrarque et l'humanisme*, 1: 147.

[7]See *Macrobius: The Saturnalia*, trans. Percival Vaughan Davies (New York, 1969), p. 156 (1.24): "What Virgil says here . . . is consistent with that wealth of material which al-

Italian Renaissance among those who wished to make claims for their own version of classical commentary. One of the first to do so was Cristoforo Landino, with the object of promoting, in place of grammatical or rhetorical exegesis of Virgil, his own uncompromisingly allegorical reading of the *Aeneid,* yet, ironically, Landino's own edition of Virgil was, as we shall see, deeply dependent on Servius.[8] As a result of such necessary gestures of self-placement in a tradition, conveniently directed by Servius' nickname, Grammaticus, the dictum became accepted that Servius cared for nothing but petty linguistic detail. Thus at the end of the nineteenth century the scholar James Henry remarked that Servian commentary bore the same relation to recent work on the *Aeneid* "as we may suppose critiques of the dramas of Shakespeare, written some two hundred years ago by the master of a village grammar school in Yorkshire, would bear to those of Schlegel."[9]

On the other hand, it is distinctly misleading to allude so broadly to the "spirit of late medieval allegory," since the commentary of Servius is utterly distinct in content and method from any subsequent allegorizing connected with Christianity, whether it be, to speak only of Virgilian interpretation, the prophetic readings of the "messianic" eclogue by the Church Fathers, the moral subtext discovered throughout Virgil's canon by Fulgentius in the fifth century, or the Christian eclogues of the Carolingian renaissance.[10] The allegory for which Servius was chiefly responsible was of quite another kind, namely, political or historical allegory, or topical allusion. Both Servius and Donatus had read the *Eclogues,* the first and ninth in particular, as a figurative comment on Virgil's experience of the civil war and its aftermath, his relationships with some of the political figures of that unsettled period, and the loss and subsequent recovery of his patrimonial estate. And not only had Servius expanded on the presence and significance of the various historical persons whom Virgil had inserted into the *Eclogues*—Maecenas, Pollio, Varus, Gallus—but he had also recorded the

---

most all the literary critics carelessly pass by with (as the proverb says) 'dusty feet,'—as though a grammarian were permitted to understand nothing beyond the meaning of words. . . . But we who claim to have a finer taste shall not suffer the secret places of this sacred poem to remain concealed, but we shall examine the approaches to its hidden meanings and throw open its inmost shrine to the worship of the learned." Despite this language, the preoccupations of the *Saturnalia* remain Roman ritual and rhetorical figures and strategies.

[8] For Landino's anti-grammarian stance, see Chapter 2, p. 63.

[9] James Henry, *Aeneida, or Critical, Exegetical and Aesthetical Remarks on the Aeneis,* 3 vols. (London, 1873–89), 3: 77.

[10] Fabius Planciades Fulgentius, *De expositione Virgilianae continentia,* written in the fifth century and published in 1589. See Fulgentius, *Opera,* ed. Rudolf Helm (Leipzig, 1898), pp. 83–107; trans. L. G. Whitbread, in *Fulgentius the Mythographer* (Columbus, 1971), pp. 105–53, esp. p. 119. For the Carolingian eclogues and their successors, see Helen Cooper, *Pastoral: Mediaeval into Renaissance* (Ipswich, 1977), pp. 8–33.

hypothesis that the wondrous child of the fourth eclogue was Saloninus, the otherwise unknown infant son of Pollio, and that the Daphnis of the fifth eclogue was a figurative representation of, among other candidates, the murdered Julius Caesar. All later commentary had to take some cognizance of these proposals, if only to refute them, but undoubtedly the most powerful of them was the Servian assumption that Virgil himself was present in the *Eclogues* in figurative form, under the persona of Tityrus in the first eclogue, and that the pastoral *umbra,* the shade under which Tityrus reposes, represented the protection of Augustus.

The impact of Servian commentary on Virgilian interpretation in general, then, was to bring the entire canon under, as it were, the shade of the *Eclogues* by making that early work a figure of the relationship between poet and political patronage. It was precisely because this argument carried a timeless force, providing an endlessly reusable paradigm for the relation between writers and the holders of power, that it was repeatedly denied—from the eighteenth century onward, increasingly successfully. And it was an early strategy, deriving from the Enlightenment, to blur the line between the Roman-historical readings of Virgil and the habit of allegorizing associated with the medieval church; thus the Victorian Thomas Keightley protested against the Julian reading of the fifth eclogue in the following remarkable terms:

> We are here required to believe that Virgil, who was perhaps the least original poet of antiquity, was the inventor of a new species of poetry [i.e., allegory]. . . . We think, on the contrary, that it was the progress of Christianity and the doctrine of the typical character of the personages and narratives of the Old Testament that led the heathens [i.e., Servius] to look for something similar in their own literature.[11]

It would be unjust not to point out, however, that Greene arrived at his reading of Petrarch's Virgil frontispiece in the course of a brilliant analysis of Petrarch's cultural liminality, the birth of his historical self-consciousness, stimulated equally by the ruins of Rome and the ancient texts for whose fragments he also used the term *ruinae,* and his archeological excavation of both the physical and the intellectual traces of Virgil's Rome. But by designating this cultural archeology "sub-reading," Greene found himself opposing such historicist investigation to another, in his view faulty, hermeneutic, the "Alexandrian method that presumed a poetic truth concealed by an allegorical veil."[12] It is that veil, of course, that is

[11] Thomas Keightley, *Notes on the Bucolics and Georgics of Virgil* (London, 1846), p. 75.
[12] Greene, *The Light in Troy,* p. 94.

represented on the frontispiece of Petrarch's precious Virgil manuscript; and in reaction against it, the entire painting fell under Greene's critical disesteem.

As it happened, another response to the painting already existed, offered in 1977 by Joel Brink specifically to medievalists in the current professional sense of the term. Arguing that the painting cannot be construed correctly without due attention to the verses built into its structure, and beyond them to Petrarch's other writings and known concerns, Brink produced an account of Petrarch that was both sympathetic to his investment in allegory and alert to his historical self-consciousness.[13] Thus in the third of the three pairs of verses, recognized as classical hexameters, "by emphasizing the Italian origins" of Virgil and Simone Martini Petrarch was linking his own fourteenth-century culture "historically with that of Augustan Rome," while the three figures of general, farmer, and shepherd represent not only the three major works of Virgil but also the three *genera dicendi* and hence the whole tradition of classical rhetoric with which Petrarch wished to identify. To Brink there was nothing "maladroit" in the composition, no "heavily stylized Gothic manner," but a symbolic account of Petrarch's interests and personal icons, including the laurel (not ivy) wreathing Virgil's brow. He even discovered in the placing of the figures an example of the symbolic geometry widely practiced in early Renaissance art: the root-two of a rectangle from a square, in which "the top of the square cuts the rectangle at precisely the point where Simone Martini places the telling gesture of Servius."[14]

We might take this argument further, beginning with the Latin epigrams, which are literally "winged words," shown in the painting with their own motor principle attached. What the epigrams tell us is more than the identity of the figures represented, and the historical argument they make is more precise and more complete than even Brink suggests. The epigrams articulate, with absolute economy, a three-stage *translatio studii*. In the first, Virgil receives and passes on to Italy the Greek cultural heritage; in the second, Servius (with a younger perspective?) mediates the transfer of the text from antiquity through the Middle Ages, revealing its *arcana;* and in the third, as Mantua and Siena meet under a single verb, *tulit,* so poet and painter collaborate in exploring for the earliest Renaissance what was perhaps to be its central text—or so at least Petrarch thought. We can narrow the historical time and place of the third stage still further by noting that Petrarch and Simone Martini met as exiles in the papal court at Avignon and that the painting was probably commissioned

[13] Joel Brink, "Simone Martini, Francesco Petrarca and the Humanistic Program of the Virgil Frontispiece," *Mediaevalia* 3 (1977): 83–109.

[14] Ibid., pp. 107–8.

there sometime between 1338 (when the precious manuscript was re-covered after its theft) and 1344, when Simone Martini died at Avignon.[15] Given that ironic glimpse of mid-fourteenth-century problems, of the re-moval of the papal seat from Rome and of the nonexistence of a single *patria* to which a humanist program might adhere, the assurance of the frontispiece is all the more remarkable; but we might well read the meeting of Mantua and Siena under a single verb as a grammarian's wish for Italian unity.

To read the epigrams in this way is to dispose once and for all of the charge of anachronism, for a *translatio studii* must always implicitly argue that textual transfers are culturally mediated and that interpretation is inevitably an ongoing historical process. In that spirit we can reenter Simone Martini's composition, looking for what more it might tell us about Petrarch's hermeneutics and the place of Servius within them. For as the physical presence of the veil and the interpreter indicates that interpreta-tion itself is the primary subject of the painting, all its viewers (though none of the three quoted above had mentioned it) must surely be con-scious to some degree of an upward movement, of a curve from the lower level of the painting, where resides the overt content of Virgil's works, to the upper level, where their enigmatic subtexts are revealed. Yet we can make no firm appropriation of verticality to altiloquence, or between levels of meaning. The line between the sign and the signified, the literal and the allegorical, has been crossed by Aeneas, who is both the representative of the "highest" work in the Virgilian canon and also a representation of Augustus.

The other point that the painting makes, of course, and more force-fully even than the epigrams, is the centrality of the interpreter as a person. As Servius stands between Virgil and his greatest character, Aeneas, so the interpreter himself becomes a new character in the story of understanding, we might even say an author in his own right of one phase of that story. So for Petrarch and for many of his Renaissance successors, Servius had in-deed become a personal presence to be reckoned with. It was this person-alization that came undone at the end of the nineteenth century, as a result of the-then-modern procedures of textual scholarship. Skepticism and con-fusion now hang over the text of the commentary that Petrarch was able to take for granted as the work of a single mind. It is now generally known that there are two major versions, a shorter or Vulgate text, and a longer version printed for the first time by Peter Daniel and now known as Servius Danielis. The longer version was at first assumed to be more authentic, but

---

[15] Fredrik Wulff, *Deux Discours sur Pétrarque en résumé* (Uppsala, 1902), p. 4, suggests that the painting was added to the manuscript in 1341, when Petrarch met Simone Martini in Avignon.

at the end of the nineteenth century it was discovered to be an amalgamation of the Vulgate with another commentary, subsequently attributed to Donatus. The main part of his commentary, presumed lost, was thus theoretically restored to Donatus, but his gain was Servius's loss.[16] His text had been deconstructed. By 1880 the possibility of a still more radical de-authorization was glimpsed by Emile Thomas, who remarked that "all the world agrees that the commentary that gives us the editions under the name of Servius are the work neither of one man nor of one epoch."[17] Despite the fact that subsequent scholarly editions of Servius replaced this state of potential anarchy with something admissible as "the text," his credibility as an author, and hence as an authority, had been damaged.[18] Yet such distrust exaggerates, ignoring the complex intentions and implications of a variorum commentary and even, as we shall see, the evidence in Servius of an independent critical mind.

Whether or not it was connected to this textual uncertainty, there developed in classical studies at about the same time another kind of skepticism, a tendency to discredit the reliability of Servius, and with him Donatus, with respect to matters of fact. Classical scholars were aware, as others were sometimes not, of precisely what kind of allegory Servian commentary had permitted or promoted, and the textual problematic had refocused the historical one. To what extent were Servius and Donatus authorities for the genesis of the *Eclogues* in a Roman historical occasion, the expropriations of land in favor of Octavian's veterans that took place after the battle of Philippi? Could they be trusted as the repositories of an earlier historical tradition, or had they merely worked backward from the apparent allusions to the expropriations in the first and ninth eclogues and constructed a *vita* for the poet to fit the poems?

Editors in earlier centuries had often quarrelled with specific aspects of Servian interpretation, noting (with an astonishing literalism) that Tityrus, for instance, as an elderly and only recently manumitted slave, was an unfit image of Virgil, but in the modern period there was a decided tendency in classical studies altogether to discredit the Servian approach to the *Eclogues*. A not atypical approach, though more rhetorically flamboyant than most, was Tenney Frank's 1922 biography of Virgil, which declared in its preface that a substantial part of the Servian tradition was

---

[16] See E. K. Rand, "Is Donatus' Commentary on Virgil Lost?" *Classical Quarterly* 1 (1916): 158–64.

[17] Emile Thomas, *Scoliastes de Virgile: Essai sur Servius et son commentaire sur Virgile* (Paris, 1880), pp. ii–vi.

[18] The standard edition for the *Eclogues* remains G. Thilo and H. Hagen, *Servii Grammatici qui feruntur in Vergilii Carmina commentarii*, 3 vols. (Leipzig, 1881–87), vol. 3, part 1; pending, that is, the appearance of the long-awaited first volume of the Harvard edition. All subsequent citations from Servius are from Thilo and Hagen.

nothing but "a conglomeration of a few chance facts set into a mass of later conjecture derived from a literal-minded interpretation of the *Eclogues,* to which there gathered during the credulous and neurotic decades of the second and third centuries an accretion of irresponsible gossip." For Frank the chief villain in that story of misprision was Donatus, but his mode of argument was to lump together, as equally unreliable, all "the obsequious scholiasts of the Empire," who were never to be trusted unless their accounts could be squared with those of "reliable historians" such as Appian and Dio.[19]

Most revealing was Frank's recommendation to the twentieth-century reader as to how the *Eclogues* were to be understood:

> The visitor to Arcadia should perhaps be urged to leave his microscope at home. Happiest, at any rate, is the reader of Vergil's pastorals who can take an unannotated pocket edition to his vacation retreat, forgetting what every inquisitive Donatus has conjectured about the possible hidden meanings that lie in them. . . . The safest way is to . . . interpret the *Eclogues* primarily as imaginative pastoral poetry, and not, except when they demand it, as a personal record.[20]

With unconscious irony Frank echoed Virgil's "happy man" passage from the second georgic (lines 490ff.), as he stated his version of the modernist creed. The ideological basis of this passage is unmistakable, and companion statements about the *Eclogues,* and indeed about pastoral in general, have characterized the literary criticism of much of the twentieth century. All such critical statements manifest, in addition to their own inevitable biases, the profound investment that Western culture has made in the concept of pastoral, and the fact that that investment has constantly to be protected against what appear to be damaging alterations in the currency. Frank's recommendation of the "safest way" to proceed in interpretation is indeed telling, suggesting that there were dangerous hermeneutical procedures afoot, procedures that would impugn the disinterested nature of intellectual activity by contaminating them with politics; and his distrust of the "obsequious scholiasts" was particularly focused on the theory that Virgil needed to express his gratitude to Augustus for the return of the patrimonial estate. Only those who kowtowed to Domitian and the later emperors, thought Frank, could possibly have so reduced the *Eclogues* to the status of a "bread-and-butter letter."

Frank's reclusive aesthetics leave unresolved the problem that every editor and commentator on Virgil is required to face. How are we to respond

[19] Tenney Frank, *Vergil: A Biography* (New York, 1922), pp. v, 122, 111.
[20] Ibid., pp. 110–11.

to the injunction to ignore the possible historical context of the *Eclogues* "except when they demand it"? How do we recognize such a demand from the text when we see it? What is to be done with the Pollio of Eclogue 4, the Gallus of Eclogue 10, and the fact that Virgil refers to himself as Tityrus at the beginning of Eclogue 6:[21]

> cum canerem reges et proelia, Cynthius aurem
> vellit et admonuit: "pastorem, Tityre, pinguis
> pascere oportet ovis, deductum dicere carmen."

> When I would sing of kings and battles, Apollo plucked my ear and warned: "It behooves a shepherd, Tityrus, to feed fat sheep, but to sing a slender song."

I shall make no attempt to answer such questions—especially since the governing premise of this study is that there are no right answers, only interpretations—but shall argue, rather, that Servius himself appears to have been alert to precisely this problematic. It was of course Servius who introduced into European critical discourse the crucial word *polysemous,* as a comment on Virgil's *cano* in the opening lines of the *Aeneid.*[22] But in his commentary on the *Eclogues* he shows, in addition to a respect for poly-semantics, a theoretical grasp of the problem of referentiality in a "literary" text, as well as of the critical methodology such a problem requires.

In order to follow the exegetical methods of Servius we need to recall that in late antiquity the commentary had a well-defined formal structure. That structure we now call an *accessus,* or formal introduction, access, to a work, by means of a series of accepted categories of analysis. On the basis of the only early theoretical discussion of the *accessus* that has survived, the *Dialogus super auctores* by Conrad of Hirschau, a Benedictine monk of the twelfth century, it was at one time assumed that the system originated with Servius.[23] E. A. Quain, however, decisively demonstrated that the origins of the system went at least as far back as the Alexandrian philosophers of the second century B.C.[24] Now the obvious advantage of a well-established system of analysis is that its very conventionality, its structure of options and limitations, allows the analyst to display his personal system of choices,

---

[21] Both Calpurnius *Bucolica* 5.160–64 and Martial 8.56.8–13 made use of the Virgil-Tityrus identification, though not without a sense of its complexities.

[22] See D. C. Allen, *Mysteriously Meant: The Rediscovery of Pagan Symbolism and Allegorical Interpretation in the Renaissance* (Baltimore, 1970), p. 96.

[23] *Conradi Hirsaugiensis: Dialogus super actores sive Didascalon,* ed. G. Schepss (Wurzburg, 1889).

[24] E. A. Quain, "The Medieval Accessus ad Auctores," *Traditio* 3 (1945): 215–64.

his own sensibility and concerns. The basic structure that Servius used to explain the *Aeneid*, which was the text he placed first in his commentary, had six categories of analysis: "Poeta vita; titulus operis; qualitas carminis; scribentis intentio; numerus librorum; explanatio"; that is, a biography of the poet, the title of the work, the type of poetry or its genre, the poet's intentions in writing, the numerical organization of the work (which can encompass questions of internal structure), and the explanation or detailed commentary on the text. The last category of analysis, therefore, was far the most extensive. But when Servius approached the *Eclogues,* he inserted into his *accessus* to them another term, *causa,* that relates complexly to *intentio* and becomes the heart of his distinctive interpretation. In doing so he was partly following Donatus; both of them discuss the problem of cause and intention in ways that are utterly different from the prevailing practice of the later Middle Ages.

By the time that Conrad of Hirschau defined the *accessus, causa* and *intentio* were almost invariably used to justify the existence of a text according to neo-Aristotelian or Christian premises, to assimilate into religion or ethics something secular or pagan or playful or imaginative (to use terms from several discursive systems). Nowhere is this more evident than in the commentary tradition on Ovid, where quite subtle distinctions can be made between original, authorial intention and those other, "better" intentions that the text, in the light of later revelation, can be made to show. The terms are interchangeable, and their meanings and value can vary. Thus Conrad distinguished between *intentio* as that "quid auctor intendat" and *causa finalis* or the pious "fructus legentis," a hermeneutics penetrable, of course, by God's intentions.[25] Another twelfth-century grammarian would make *intentio* the higher term, ethically speaking, while relegating *causa* to a form of socioeconomic motive; in translating the legends of the *Heroides* from Greek into Latin, Ovid sought the favor of the Roman ladies.[26]

What we find in Donatus is equally fluid, but it leads in a different direction. Donatus professed uncertainty as to whether the *causa* of the *Eclogues,* which he merges with *intentio,* was a desire to imitate Theocritus or to make a statement about the progress of civilization or, rather, to gain the indulgence of Caesar and the recovery of Virgil's lands, which he had lost for the following reason ("quem amiserat ob hanc causam"). He then proceeded to the famous story of the expropriations that followed Philippi, of Virgil's belief that he had won the right to reclaim his estate, and of how he was violently rebuffed by the centurion Arius and nearly lost his life in

---

[25] Ibid., pp. 219–20.
[26] See Judson Boyce Allen, *The Ethical Poetic of the Later Middle Ages* (Toronto, 1982), p. 28.

the scuffle. This part of the story, according to Donatus, was reflected in Virgil's ninth eclogue, but "sed postea et per Maecenatem et per triumviros agris dividendis Varum, Pollionem et Cornelium Gallum fama carminum commendatus Augusto et agros recepit et deinceps imperatoris familiari amore perfruitus est"[27] ("afterward, both through Maecenas and through the triumvirate for the division of the land, Varus, Pollio, and Cornelius Gallus, he was commended to Augustus for the fame of his poetry and received back his lands and was thereafter on the best of terms with the emperor"). Donatus left it ambiguous, because of his rather offhand use of conjunctions, as to whether there were two separate stages in the recovery of Virgil's property and what role the *Eclogues* played in the story. Were they, as "fama carminum commendatus Augusto" implies, the cause of the recovery of the lost lands or, rather, as Donatus subsequently suggests, were they written as an expression of gratitude to those who had intervened on his behalf?

Such questions are not, as I have already suggested, capable of resolution, not even by the commonsense recogition that the composition of the *Eclogues* spanned a period of several years, from before Philippi through the more stable and hopeful days of the peace of Brundisium. What the Donatan *accessus* imports are, rather, its inventive and powerful moves in interpretation: first, the invasion of the categories of *causa* and *intentio* by material that really belongs to the *vita,* the penetration of the work by the life; second, a clear attempt to link the category of *causa,* essentially an empty compartment of thought, with the concept of historical causation—Virgil lost his lands "ob hanc causam," a phrase that introduces a carefully linked chain of historical causes, starting from an original cause, the assassination of Julius Caesar on the Ides of March, 44 B.C.; third, the statement that *because* of this structure of causality, the *Eclogues* require a different hermeneutics than that presupposed by a reader of Theocritus:

> In bucolicis Vergilii neque nusquam neque ubique aliquid figurate dici, hoc est per allegoriam. vix enim propter laudem Caesaris et amissos agros haec Vergilio conceduntur, cum Theocritus simpliciter conscripserit.

> (pp. 16–17)

> In the *Bucolics* of Virgil there is a certain amount of figurative discourse, neither nowhere nor everywhere, that is, allegory. For these things were allowed to Virgil, on account of the praise of Ceasar and the lost lands, although Theocritus had written simply.

[27] For Donatus, see Jacob Brummer, ed., *Vitae Vergilianae* (Leipzig, 1912), pp. 15–16. For some of the historical implications of Donatus's account, see J. Bayet, "Virgile et les triumvirs 'agris dividundis,'" *Revue des Etudes Latines* 5–6 (1927–28): 271–99.

The presence of figurative discourse or allegory—not found in Theocritus, who wrote literally about shepherds and their songs—is permitted to Virgil (note the shadow of an apology) because of the historical context in which his pastorals were written. And along with the note of apology goes a note of methodological caution: figuration is to be found in the *Eclogues* "neque nusquam neque ubique," a remarkably opaque and provocative locution.

None of this escaped Servius. In his own *accessus* to the *Eclogues* he stated firmly that the *intentio* of Virgil was the imitation of Theocritus, a purely literary ambition. But he then introduced the other category of *causa,* under which he retold, though with significant differences of phrasing, the Donatan account. He attempted to straighten out the chronology by suggesting two stages of territorial recovery, one in which Virgil was exempted "solus," the only lucky man, and another in which, after a second appeal, he was also successful in obtaining relief for his Mantuan neighbors. He explicitly used the text of the *Eclogues* as documentary support, showing how the story of Arius was necessary to explain otherwise mysterious statements in the ninth eclogue, such as the complaint by Moeris of the inefficacy of poetry in violent times ("all our songs, Lycidas, no more prevail among weapons than Chaonian doves, as they say, when eagles come," 9.11–13). And, most significantly, he expanded and meditated on the contrast between two different types of pastoral, the simple and the complex, the literal and the figurative:

> Et aliquibus locis per allegoriam agit gratias Augusto, vel aliis no-
> bilibus, quorum favore amissum agrum recepit; in qua re tantum dis-
> sentit a Theocrito. Ille enim ubique simplex est: hic necessitate com-
> pulsus aliquibus locis miscet figuras, quas perite plerumque etiam ex
> Theocrito versibus facit: quos ab illo dictos constat esse simpliciter.
> Hoc autem fit poetica urbanitate.
>
> (p. 2)

> And in certain places by means of allegory Virgil gives thanks to
> Augustus or to other leading men, by whose favor he received back
> his lost estate; in which he greatly departed from Theocritus. For
> Theocritus is always simple. Compelled by this necessity, Virgil
> mingles figures in certain places, which for the most part he skillfully
> constructs out of Theocritus's verses; things well known to be spoken
> literally by Theocritus. But this makes for poetic sophistication.

While it would be going too far to claim for this passage the paternity of all subsequent distinctions between Virgil and Theocritus, it probably *was* the origin of the recurrent habit, among those who have tried to define the

nature of pastoral, of framing their definitions (and their ideological prefer-
ences) in terms of a competition between the founding fathers. And it is
important to see how Servius promoted that side of the perpetual argument in which Virgil is valued above Theocritus, precisely by having
moved the genre away from semantic transparency and innocence. It is ir-
relevant for these purposes whether Theocritean pastoral can in fact be accurately described as written simply, without any figurative intention.
What matters for the cultural history of pastoral is that Servius said it was
so and attributed to Virgil a sophistication that Theocritus lacked: namely,
a grasp of the uses of the pastoral as a metaphor for something other than
itself.

Two other aspects of this statement of intention were to be of incalculable influence. The first was the recognition of the principle of discon-
tinuous allegory or of inconsistent historical reference. What Servius
meant by the phrase "aliquibus locis" is further explained in his gloss to the
opening of the first eclogue: "Et hoc loco sub persona Tityri Virgilium
debemus intelligere; non tam ubique, sed tantum ubi exigit ratio" ("And
in this place, under the persona of Tityrus, we ought to understand Virgil;
yet not everywhere, but only where reason demands"). This is the Donatan
"neque nusquam neque ubique," rendered considerably less opaque by
adding the notion that reason exerts interpretive controls. And it makes an
interesting comparison with the Tenney Frank position that one should
not read the *Eclogues*, "except where they demand it, as a personal record."
Servius was not interested in finding the safest way to read, though occasionally, in rejecting the allegories of his predecessors, he declared that a
simple or literal reading was "melius," better. Rather, he seems to have
grasped the infinitely complex manner in which different kinds of meaning
and intentionality are entangled in any text, especially one that is attempting to adapt an earlier text, a pre-text, to a new cultural context. Thus he
notes that the song-fragment quoted by Lycidas in Eclogue 9—"Tityre,
dum redeo (brevis est via) pasce capellas" ("Tityrus, until I return, for the
way is short, feed my flocks," line 23)—is an actual quotation from the
third Idyll of Theocritus. The fact that it is a quotation brings to the surface of the text the literariness of Virgil's intention, Theocritean recall; yet
for Servius the song-fragment is genuinely polysemous. It is both a word-
for-word translation ("verbum ad verbum translati") and an allusion to
Virgil's own Roman historical affairs: "for allegorically he thereby left instructions to his men to take care of his estate, and for the present to obey
Arius the centurion."

When Servius rejected, in his commentary on the third eclogue, the
suggestion that the Tityrus mentioned there is also Virgil and that his
sneaking up to steal someone else's goat alluded to an adulterous affair he
was supposed to have had, his response was not moral prudishness but a

grasp of how a historicist theory of intention and allusion must work. "It is better," he says, "that we should take this simply ("sed melius simpliciter accipimus"). For allegories in pastoral ought to be rejected, unless, as I said above, they derive from that necessity of the lost lands" (p. 33). This statement was later appropriated by those who, like the Victorian Keightley, would banish all allegory from pastoral,[28] and on the other hand repudiated by those who, like the sixteenth-century Spanish scholar Ludovico Vives, would have liked to extend the allegorical potential of the text beyond the territory delimited by Servius. What Servius meant by the "necessity" of the lost lands, however, was the historical circumstance that had originally directed Virgil to figurative expression. The range of meanings that could plausibly be extracted from the text was, therefore, to be governed by the reader's sense of authorial motive and the historical facts that had helped to shape it.

Even on the identification of Virgil with the Tityrus of the first eclogue, it appears that it has been the critics of Servius, rather than Servius himself, who have been too literal in their response to the interpretive problem that Virgil himself set up. Whenever the identification has been subsequently disputed, it has always been on the grounds that Virgil was neither *senex* nor manumitted slave, but "free-born and . . . about the age of thirty" when the *Eclogues* were written.[29] Such responses overlook the evidence that Servius was not making a naive identification, but was, rather, discussing the urbane strategy of using a persona, a much more delicate and shifty notion. On the lines (27–28) in which Tityrus appears to refer to his white beard, Servius remarks that "either we have a change in the function of the persona, so that we must receive him speaking as an elderly rustic, not as Virgil, allegorically . . . or certainly there must be a change in punctuation, so that it is not his beard which is whiter, but liberty."

And on the word *libertas* itself the grammarian and the Roman historian met in Servius, to create a gloss that would not only resonate through the subsequent history of pastoral, but by its placement in the commentary would generate ironies throughout the *Eclogues*, if not the whole Virgilian canon. *Libertas* is explained as meaning "the love of liberty," which, Servius indicates, is an inappropriate locution for Tityrus as erstwhile slave:

Et aliter dicit servus, libertatem cupio, aliter ingenuus: ille enim carere vult servitute, hic habere liberam vitam, pro suo scilicet arbitrio agere: sicut nunc Vergilius sub persona Tityri dicit se amore libertatis Ro-

---

[28] Keightley, *Notes on the Bucolics*, was delighted to find in the text of Servius certain restrictions on the use of allegory which, taken out of context, could be used as a support for his own position: "Servius . . . elsewhere seems to give us the opinions of the more judicious critics, when he says, 'Melius simpliciter accipimus.'" (p. 76).

[29] H. J. Rose, *The Eclogues of Vergil* (Berkeley and Los Angeles, 1942), p. 49.

mam venire compulsum, et item latenter carpit tempora, quibus libertas non nisi in urbe Roma erat.

And a slave speaks one way ("I want liberty"), a freeborn man quite another; for the first desires to be quit of his servitude, the second to have a free life, to act, of course, by his own free will: so now Virgil in the persona of Tityrus tells how he was compelled by his love of liberty to come to Rome, and covertly blames the times, in which there is no liberty except in the city of Rome.

Here the grammarian's sense of linguistic nuance alerts Servius to what he sees as a sign of intentionality, and by that word *latenter* he allows into his commentary another level of meaning or source of ambiguity, permitting the inference that Virgil did not always say, even through metaphor, exactly what he meant. As the term *libertas* itself was powerful but elusive ideological currency in the affairs of Rome preceding the civil wars, having been used as a slogan by both Pompey and Julius Caesar (and it would later be incorporated into the imperial coinage), its presence in the context could scarcely be innocent.[30] Servius's gloss, especially when compared with the "compulsion" ("hic necessitate compulsus") behind the *Eclogues* and their figural structure, considerably qualifies the premise that the entire text is a work of gratitude for favors received. Rather, he suggests the peculiarly difficult and equivocal stance that a poet like Virgil would have had, *by necessity*, to adopt toward the political leadership at the end of the civil war, when the need for a national settlement and personal security were both no less apparent than their costs; on the one hand, the irretrievable loss of the republican system; on the other, the inevitable loss of intellectual autonomy.

There are other important glosses that perform the same function. Most complex, perhaps, is what looks at first sight merely like an act of textual criticism. On the phrase "turbatur agris" (1.12), the words in which Virgil expresses, through Meliboeus, the sufferings that have been caused by the expropriations and from which Tityrus is so fortunate to have been exempted, Servius wrote that the reading *turbamur* found in some manuscripts is without "any distinction of blame or merit; and enviously he covertly blames the times of Augustus" ("et invidiose tempora Augusti carpit latenter"). "Doubtless," he continues, "the right reading is *turbatur*, since it is impersonal, pertaining to all in general: for the expulsion of the Mantuans was communal. For if you read *turbamur*, it seems to

---

[30] See Ronald Syme, *The Roman Revolution* (Oxford, 1939; reprinted 1952), pp. 154–55, 320–21, 515–17; and C. Wirszubski, *Libertas as a Political Idea at Rome during the Late Republic and Early Empire* (Cambridge, 1950).

refer to a few." The effect of this gloss is to introduce the problem of the reader's inevitable sympathy with Meliboeus—the sympathy that Tityrus so noticeably fails to feel—and therefore to recognize the dialectical force of the poem, the tension between the aesthetic value represented by *otium* and the ethical claims of justice and equity. Striking, too, is the Servian term *invidiose,* in its allusion to Meliboeus's own statement ("Non equidem invideo," line 11) that he does *not* envy the protected leisure of Tityrus; for the Servian locution quietly suggests that, precisely by *denying* unfairness, Virgil has secretly invoked it. These mildly subversive inferences are confirmed in the commentary on Meliboeus's later lament for his farm (1.70), for Servius declares that by using the strong term *impius,* the antithet of Aeneas's Roman ethics, Virgil "injured Octavian; nevertheless he followed the truth" ("hic Vergilius Octavianum laesit; tamen secutus est veritatem"). In other words, Servius was not naive in his primary identification of Tityrus as the poet's own persona; the reproach conveyed by these glosses suggests instead that Virgil was speaking *sub persona* in *both* the fortunate and the unfortunate shepherd, and, insofar as the protégé's actual condition was closer to his own than the exile's, that the self-enclosed and insensitive presentation of *otium* was irony at his own expense.

But the word insofar raises, of course, the problem of the relation of the first eclogue to the ninth, where the restoration of the lost lands is brought into question. Again, it is impossible to determine how poetic sequence relates to a reified chronology of the expropriations and Virgil's possible involvement in them. What matters for subsequent interpretation is that Servius here perceived an expression of Virgil's fears for the survival of poetry in time of civic or national violence, that the poem makes at best a provisional statement of the chances for a cultural renewal under Octavian. Thus Servius explains that when Lycidas refers to the songs of Menalcas (another of Virgil's personae) as *solacia* (line 18), comforts, "obliquely he blames the times of Augustus, in which songs were not for delight, but for consolation, as he inures himself to unhappiness." And the Daniel text, for good measure, comments suggestively on the meaning in this poem of quotations and song-fragments. On the lines "Nunc oblita mihi tot carmina, vox quoque Moerim / Iam fugit ipsa" ("Now all my songs are forgotten, and his very voice flees from Moeris," lines 53–54), the gloss reads:

> et ostendit Moerin nullum suum, sed omnia Menalcae carmina retulisse . . . his verbis ostendit, vigorem cantandi, quem prius habueret, perdidisse (se). et per allegoriam obsessum malis animum demonstrat.

And he shows that Moeris has retained nothing of his own, but all his songs derive from Menalcas; in these verses he shows that he has lost the power of song that once he had, and, through allegory, that his mind is obsessed with loss.

Not so great a distance, after all, divides this account of Virgilian nostalgia from what we find in one of the most perceptive of twentieth-century readers: "The sense of irony and limitation in this poem is unquestionable. . . . Yet the sound of our voices may not be so hollow after all. . . . Echoes that are explicitly of other songs may be enough to sustain us."[31] The effect of these glosses is to drive home the message that Eclogues 1 and 9 are connected by more than the theme of the lost lands, for they both speak to the fragile relationship between art and its political supports, whether they be seen as national peace, an intelligent system of patronage, or unbroken ties between the intellectual and the land, his native soil. Moeris's inability to sing a continuous song is thus connected to that of Meliboeus ("carmina nulla canam," 1.77), a connection that Servius himself does not make, though he notes that Lycidas echoes (9.50) what Meliboeus has spoken "invidiose" about the pointlessness of planting *his* pear trees (1.73).

This, then, is the mainframe of Servian commentary on the *Eclogues.* In redescribing it, I have tried to mediate between the dangers of selectivity and an assumption that the majority of readers have a limited appetite for Latin glosses. Yet surely enough has been shown to throw into question the negative assessments cited earlier in this chapter and those that can readily be found in standard accounts of the classical heritage. It is hard to reconcile the evidence presented above with the statement, for example, by R. R. Bolgar, that in Servius

> one cannot fail to be struck by the almost complete absence from the notes of any discussion on the wider problems of aesthetics and literary form. . . . A similar narrowness of approach can be observed in his treatment of historical and cultural material. Though it would be pointless to criticize him for falling short of standards imposed by the mental habits of a later age, a comparison between his interests and those of modern scholarship is nevertheless instructive. Servius does not make the slightest attempt to reconstruct the personal or cultural background of his poet or of the period in which the action of the poem is ostensibly set. His explanations deal exclusively with matters of detail which he discusses in a spirit of antiquarian curiosity.[32]

[31] Paul Alpers, *The Singer of the Eclogues: A Study of Virgilian Pastoral* (Berkeley, Los Angeles, London, 1979), pp. 151, 153.

[32] R. R. Bolgar, *The Classical Heritage and Its Beneficiaries* (Cambridge, 1954; reprinted New York, 1964), pp. 41–42.

But it would be equally pointless to criticize Bolgar for *his* perspective, produced, in part, by an exclusive focus on the *Aeneid*.[33] It was the *Eclogues* that elicited from Servius the kind of analysis that deserves the term *cultural,* statements that, however elliptically, locate the act of writing in a complex set of relations. For what is truly remarkable about the Servian readings is the sense they manage to give of the interpenetration in Virgil's text of different, yet not after all conflicting, objectives: the intention of imitating Theocritus, and the Roman causation, the reason for writing such poems at such a time; the necessity of paying his respects to Octavian and other leading survivors of the civil war, and the imperative of personal independence, expressed *latenter* as a series of reproaches to Octavian. As Virgil *sub persona* appears and disappears in Servian commentary there emerges the composite idea of the cultural spokesman, speaking, if not with many tongues, polysemously, and with the authority of more than one language behind him.

What Thomas Greene recognized as the highest form of imitation, that which "dramatizes a passage of history," which "assumes historical responsibilities, one which remembers, preserves, resuscitates, and recreates" is certainly represented by Virgil's rewriting of Theocritus, as Servius and Petrarch recognized. For precisely by remembering Theocritus and by making him the sign of a lost innocence that only survives in echoes and memorable Greek names—Tityrus and Amaryllis, with which the woods can still be made to echo ("formosam resonare doces Amaryllida silvas," 1.5)—Virgil established the principle that genuine imitation, especially of pastoral, always remakes its object in a new historical context. Given the need to develop a definitively Roman culture that would erase the "sceleris vestigia nostri" (4.13), the old crimes that included those against the Greek city-states, Virgil decided to make his peace with Greek culture by incorporating it into the Roman present. What Servius recognized as "urbanity" or poetic sophistication, therefore, and as Virgil's distinctive difference from Theocritus, was actually the equivalent of what Greene called "transitivity," the historical transaction with the past that only writing, the artificial form of memory, can ever attempt.[34]

There also emerged out of Servian hermeneutics the recognition that culture is not only necessarily cumulative but also necessarily implicated with political power. It is much too simple to say, as is often said, that Virgil deformed the pastoral idea by politicizing it. What Servius recognized in

---

[33] For more sympathetic accounts of Servian interpretation, though also focused exclusively on the *Aeneid,* see Michael O'Connell, *Mirror and Veil: The Historical Dimension of Spenser's "Faerie Queene"* (Chapel Hill, 1977), pp. 24–31; Michael Murrin, *The Allegorical Epic: Essays in Its Rise and Decline* (Chicago, 1980), pp. 32–45.

[34] Greene, *The Light in Troy,* p. 41.

Virgil was a self-conscious admission of the problems faced by all writer-intellectuals, who must weigh their need for survival and recognition against the demands of personal freedom and interiority. The result was a founding myth of authorial presence and motive, and a viable and far from reductive model of a metaphorical pastoral, a paradigm of self- and societal representation. It was such an interpretive system, I submit, that Petrarch recognized in Servius, for his own inspiration having it encapsulated, in both verbal and visual form, on the first page of his most precious manuscript.

Historical transactions have two terms. Each new interpreter of Virgil brought to the task his own historically conditioned set of priorities and preoccupations, needs and pressures that brought to the surface of the text as he meditated upon it meanings partly located outside the text, in his own cultural environment. In the case of Servius, whose lifetime can be only conjecturally dated, the contexts of his thought must be reconstructed in the most tentative and general terms. Yet such projections are nonetheless instructive. The conditions of life in the late Roman Empire, in broad terms, were established in the third century and not much changed, except for the worse. There was, first, the replacement of the military anarchy of the late third century by a ruthless and socially insensitive bureaucracy, which reduced almost all classes except the senatorial rank to a form of political servitude. Diocletian's "reforms," which were completed by Constantine, were particularly disastrous for agriculture.[35] According to Samuel Dill, unjust taxation and property seizures reduced farmers and shepherds to a state of brigandage.[36] And Rostovtzeff pointed out that what looked like a stabilizing measure, the reorganization of the land-ownership system into inseparable units of *iuga* and *capita*, effectively "made the *colonus* a serf," by denying him freedom of movement.[37] In the meantime the senatorial class was permitted to amass huge private estates. More important still as a determinant of intellectual life was the redefinition of the emperor as absolute monarch; all pretense of constitutional government was abolished, along with political freedom of expression. The conversion of Constantine, by which Christianity was not merely guaranteed toleration but recognized as the official imperial religion, actually facilitated the cult of the emperor by removing one vast source of subversion; while this improved life for the Christians, it worsened the situa-

---

[35] M. Rostovtzeff, *The Social and Economic History of the Roman Empire*, 2 vols. (Oxford, 1926), 1: 447–77.
[36] Samuel Dill, *Roman Society in the Last Century of the Western Empire* (London, 1898), pp. 200—201, 220–27.
[37] Rostovtzeff, *Social and Economic History*, p. 472.

tion of those who, like Servius apparently, remained committed to the old religion, now residual and resistant in Rome.

Whether we regard Servius as having actually been a contemporary of Praetextatus and Symmachus, with whom (in Macrobius's *Saturnalia*) he discussed Virgil in about 384, it is clear that he shared with them (as with Macrobius) an intense concern for ancient Roman customs and rituals. Taken together with the absence of any trace of Christian exegesis in his commentary, this essentially conservative and pagan approach is, at the very least, not incompatible with the ideology of the pagan party in Rome, who campaigned unsuccessfully against Christian suppression of the ancient institutions.

Even to write a major commentary on Virgil, emphasizing its Roman historical origins, must be seen as an act of ideological significance at almost any stage in the late fourth century, when the empire was not only divided between East and West, but even the Western emperors had abandoned Rome for Milan, and the Church Fathers were united in their attacks on the ancient city. Such a project might easily have been conceived in the wake of Symmachus's appeal to Valentinian in 384 or during the consulship of Flavianus in 394, when the altar of Victory was restored to the Curia; it would have been inconceivable after the fall of Rome to Alaric in 410.

It is not difficult to imagine, therefore, how from conditions like these might have arisen the characteristic preoccupations of Servian commentary: the sense of the imperial presence as controlling the culture; the belief in the ancient idea of Rome as Virgil had definitively articulated it; the strange focus on the issue of land ownership; and the concept of compulsion and necessity as components of authorial motive. In such a context Servius's gloss on *libertas*, to the effect that by using that term Virgil "covertly blames the times, in which there is no liberty except in the city of Rome," takes on an additional resonance.

It may even be that the characteristic *structure* of Servian commentary, that of the syncretic variorum, which for scholars of our own era has seemed to undermine his authority, had certain benefits particularly germane to the late fourth century. Not only did the variorum preserve what Servius thought needed to be preserved of early Virgilian interpretation; it was thanks to Servius, after all, that the commentary of Donatus, who was teaching Jerome at Rome during the brief reign of Julian the Apostate, survived in any form. But the variorum also, as Jerome himself pointed out, enabled the commentator, to some extent, to conceal his own opinions. In the *Contra Rufinum*, significantly Jerome's self-defense against the charge of having written heresy into his commentary on Ephesians, we have in effect a contemporary definition of the fourth-century commentary as a genre:

What is the function of commentators? They expound the statements of someone else; they express in simple language views that have been expressed in an obscure manner; they quote the opinions of many individuals and they say, "Some interpret this passage in this sense, others, in another sense"; they attempt to support their own understanding and interpretation with these testimonies in this fashion, so that the prudent reader, after reading the different interpretations and studying which of these many views are to be accepted and which rejected, will judge for himself which is the more correct. . . . Will the person, who has quoted the interpretations of many individuals in a work that he is expounding, be held responsible for the different interpretations and contradictory views? [38]

And for the proof of this statement Jerome referred his own reader to various commentators on the classics, including "praeceptoris mei Donati aeque in Virgilium." This is only one of the many ironies in the story of Jerome's relation to Roman culture, so deeply embedded in his boyhood consciousness that even as he defended himself against the charge of citing secular literature the phrase that served his turn was a quotation from the *Georgics* 2.272: "adeo in teneris consuescere multum est" ("so strong is habit in the tender years"). [39]

Petrarch's Pastorals: Imitation as Interpretation

We can now begin to see, perhaps, in what deep channels the course of Virgilian interpretation flowed from Servius to Petrarch, bringing with it an idea of Rome and an imperative to conserve that idea. In Petrarch, facing the physical and ideological ruins of Rome, that imperative had, rather, to be expressed as archeological reverence and a lifetime commitment to salvage. We can gather from Petrarch's notes in the Virgil manuscript how hostile to that program he perceived his own cultural environment to be. On the first folio he wrote:

Poeta. Tibi permissum est Rome ustoriam et quicquid libet scribere, nobis non sic immo liquimus fines patriae, id est ustoriam Rome que nostra atque omnium communis patri est. et dulcia arva id est studia et

---

[38] *Saint Jerome: Dogmatic and Polemical Works,* trans. J. N. Hritzu (Washington, D.C., 1965), pp. 79–80. The significance of this passage was noted by Anthony Grafton, "On the Scholarship of Politian and Its Context," *Journal of the Warburg and Courtauld Institutes* 40 (1977): 187–88.

[39] *Against Rufinus,* in Hritzu, trans., *Saint Jerome,* p. 100.

carmina nostra in quibus agricolarum more poete exercentur laborando, excolendo.[40]

Poet: you are permitted to write the history of Rome and whatever you wish; for us it is not so. We are always outcasts from our country, that is, the history of Rome which is our common patrimony, and the sweet fields, that is, our studies and our songs, in which, after the custom of farmers, poets are employed in labor and cultivation.

In this crucial *translatio* to his own circumstances of the opening lines of Virgil's first eclogue, Petrarch took upon himself the melancholy persona of Meliboeus the exile. In this one private gesture the entire pastoral construct was translated into a metaphor for the condition of the intellectual, the humanist scholar and poet in the middle of the fourteenth century, and, because he perceived that condition to be perilous, Petrarch extended the Servian hermeneutic beyond the boundaries that Servius himself set for it.

What Petrarch's pastorals share with his notes on the *Eclogues* is, obviously, the commitment to allegory. But in the preface to his *Epistolae sine nomine,* a small collection of letters of such polemical character that he chose not to publish them during his lifetime, he explained the principle of the *Bucolicum carmen:*

Cum semper odiosa fuerit, nunc capitalis est veritas. Crescentibus nempe flagitiis hominum, crevit veri odium, et regnum blanditiis ac mendacio datum est. Id me sepe dixisse, interdum etiam et scripsisse memini: sed dicendum sepius scribendumque est. Non ante fletus desinet quam dolor. Ea me pridem cogitatio induxit ut *Bucolicum Carmen,* poematis genus ambigui, scriberem quod paucis intellectum plures forsitan delectaret. Est enim nonnullis corruptus adeo gustus ingenii ut eos notus sapor, quamvis idem suavissimus, offendat, ignota omnia, licet asperiora, permulceant.

Though truth has always been hated, it is now a capital crime. It is a fact that the hatred of truth and the kingdom of flattery and falsehood has increased in proportion to the growing sins of mankind. I remember often having said this, and sometimes even writing it, but it ought to be said and written more often. The lament will not cease before the grief. This idea led me some time ago to write the *Bucoli-*

---

[40] The Latin was transcribed by Wulff, *Deux Discours sur Pétrarque,* p. 17.

cum Carmen, a kind of cryptic poem which, though understood only by a few, might possibly please many; for some people have a taste for letters so corrupt that the well-known savor, no matter how sweet, offends them, while everything mysterious pleases them, no matter how harsh.[41]

And he added that it was precisely because the letters *Sine nomine* were not, like the *Bucolicum carmen,* covered by a veil of ambiguity that they were to be jealously guarded from circulation during his lifetime, whereas the eclogues had once fallen into the hands of "some high-ranking personages" who were themselves represented in them but who were unable to decipher those dangerous allusions.

Making due allowance for the revisionary effects of reminiscence (a letter to his brother at the beginning of the project suggests a more therapeutic motive for turning to pastoral in 1346,[42] and the eclogues were composed over a six-year period, during which Petrarch became increasingly pessimistic), this statement is nevertheless of central importance. As compared to the elliptical Servian premise of necessity, which served to justify and qualify the theme of emperor worship, Petrarch's allegorical method in his pastorals is *primarily* subversive. It is, therefore, not merely occasional and "in certain places," but ubiquitous, involving every pastoral character and event and extending to the smallest details of landscape, weather, and gesture. The result was a text substantially more enigmatic than its model, in which the reader was required to make informed guesses about what *else* was being said. Petrarch therefore confronted the central paradox of the hermeneutics of censorship, that the more effectively a text is encoded for the writer's self-protection, the greater the danger it runs of not being able to communicate at all. Petrarch himself felt this difficulty; for his first and fifth eclogues he supplied a personal key, sending the first to his brother Gherardo and the fifth to the revolutionary leader Cola di Rienzi. Among Petrarch's first readers the *Bucolicum carmen* quickly generated its own commentary tradition, creating a forest of competing and obfuscating suggestions,[43] and even the modern translator of Petrarch's eclogues, after struggling to make them accessible, advised us "to look beyond the mediaevalism, not allowing our eye to be distracted by the gargoyles of the allegory."[44]

---

[41] *Sine nomine: Lettere polemiche e politiche,* ed. Ugo Dotti (Rome, 1974), pp. 2, 4; trans. Norman P. Zacour, *Petrarch's Book without a Name* (Toronto, 1973), p. 27.

[42] *Epistolae familiares* 10.4. See Thomas G. Bergin, ed. and trans., *Petrarch's Bucolicum Carmen* (New Haven, 1974), pp. xiv–xv. All my citations from Petrarch (and much other valuable information) derive from Bergin.

[43] See Antonio Avena, ed., *Il Bucolicum carmen e i suoi commenti inediti* (Padua, 1906).

[44] Bergin, *Petrarch's Bucolicum Carmen,* p. xv.

Yet, as I have already argued, such language begs the central question of the character and motives of Petrarch's enigmas. Petrarch's pastoral allegories were conceived in the same spirit as that which informs the Virgil frontispiece. Taken together, the twelve eclogues articulate a humanist ideal, a dream of Italy united once more under a strong and stable central government, located in the city of Rome and blending the old principles of constitutional government and civic liberty with the transcendent principles of Christianity. Petrarch confronted, in actuality, an empire divided between the authority of the papacy and the so-called Holy Roman Emperor; the church hopelessly corrupted by secular power, as a result of the Donation of Constantine; the papal see removed to Avignon; the city of Rome left without central authority, and reeling from the feuds between the two great houses of the Colonna and the Orsini; and the Hundred Years' War between France and England, which deferred any resolution of the question of Italian unity. It was not impossible to see an analogy between Virgil's objectives at the end of the civil war and Petrarch's own hopes for a regenerate empire that would be in reality both Roman and holy, but as his perception of the present was infinitely more pessimistic than Virgil's, in the vast gap between nascence and decadence Petrarch's strategy diverged from his model. His referentiality became obsessive; his tone alternated between elegy and vituperation; and, most important for later evaluation, he utterly forfeited, in the service of maximum emphasis, all sense of poetic economy.

It is all too easy, therefore, to overlook the precision and the acuity that distinguish Petrarch's Virgilianism in its details. The text of the *Bucolicum carmen* is not only a palimpsest of quotations from the *Eclogues,* a form of rearrangement that even the most mechanical imitator could manage, but it is studded with incisive rewritings and redeployments of the original. This is true even of the eclogues in which Petrarch apparently deviated furthest from Virgilian themes: the sixth and seventh, those that definitively fused the secular and the church's meanings of *pastoral* and that introduced into the genre, for better or worse, the theme of anti-clerical satire. In the first of these paired poems Petrarch established a debate between Pamphilus, as St. Peter, symbol of true spiritual leadership, and Mitio, as Clement VI, the decadent Avignon pope. But they also represent, as it were, the hard and soft versions of pastoral. So Mitio insults Pamphilus by calling him "Crude senex," in distortion of Virgil's "Fortunate senex," and explaining that his "sors" or lot in Christian history is to carry the cross and suffer the fetters of repression; whereas Mitio identifies himself, again by Virgilian quotation, as a perverted Corydon:

Dulcem cantando nactus amicam,
Formosus fieri studio; solemque perosus

Antra umbroso colo. . . .
Speculum Corydon bizantius istud,
Quo michi complaceo dono dedit.

(lines 142–45)

Since by my singing I have found a fair friend, I study to make
myself beautiful; and avoiding the sunlight I seek out a shady
cave. . . . Byzantian Corydon gave me this mirror as a gift, in
which I pleasure myself.

This ingenious allusion to the Donation of Constantine is also an original
contribution to Virgilian interpretation; the proposal that Corydon, in the
second eclogue, is narcissistic in his passion and that Virgil had thereby
equated the self-reflexiveness of Theocritean pastoral with self-deception
("si numquam fallit imago," 2.26) and representational failure.

But Petrarch's importing of church politics into the genre was, in fact,
compatible with his Roman-historical reading of Virgil and not to be confused with other procedures for christianizing the pastoral. In a discussion
of prophecy in his treatise on the *Repose of the Monks* Petrarch carefully
qualified the patristic view of the messianic eclogue, by distinguishing, in
historicist terms, between Virgil's conceivable intentions and the recon-
structions that Christian exegesis might desire. Starting with the premise
that even pagans might contribute to messianic prophecy, though ignorant
of what they spoke ("quid dicerent ignorantes"), Petrarch stated his own
historicist compromise on the fourth eclogue:

> Huc enim et illa trahi possunt que Virgilius in *Bucolicis* de alio loquens
> ait: "Iam redit et Virgo redeunt Saturnia regna, / iam nova progenies
> caelo demittitur alto." . . . Que quidem religiosus et pius lector,
> quamvis de Cesare dicta, ad celestem potius trahet imperatorem, cuius
> in adventum toto orbe signa precesserant, que audiens poeta neque
> altius aspirans ad imperatoris romani, quo nil maius noverat, reflexit
> adventum.[45]

> There is a text of the *Bucolics* which speaks of how the Virgin returns,
> the reign of Saturn returns, and a new race descends from heaven. . . .
> Although it is merely Caesar who is referred to, a pious and devout
> reader might think it was the emperor of the heavens, whose advent
> on earth had been announced by universal prophecies. The poet,
> who knew of these, did not attempt to soar as high: he thought of
> the coming of a Roman emperor, unable to conceive of anything
> greater.

---

[45] *Il De otio religioso*, ed. Giuseppe Rotondi (Vatican City, 1958), pp. 28–29.

So, too, Petrarch adapted to his own humanist preoccupations the Servian premise that pastoral is a form of self-representation and that it articulates the dilemmas of literary ambition and vocation. His first eclogue is predominantly an expression of vocational anxiety, a rewriting of Virgil's first eclogue in terms of a choice between secular and spiritual writing. Although the date of the poem's composition is somewhat disputed, it was undoubtedly one of the first Petrarch wrote and connected to a visit he made in 1347 to his brother Gherardo, a recluse in the Charterhouse of Montreux. In this version the role of the happy shepherd Monicus, whose life is fixed and secure, is taken by Gherardo, and that of the unhappy wanderer Silvius by Petrarch himself:

> Monice, tranquillo solus tibi conditus antro,
> Et gregis et rurus potuisti spernere curas;
> Ast ego dumosos colles silvasque pererro.
> Infelix!

> Monicus, hidden away alone in your tranquil cave, you have been able to reject the cares of the flock and the pastures; but I go wandering over thorny hills and woods. Unhappy!

What follows, as Petrarch himself explained, is a debate in which the rival claims of sacred and secular pastoral are fully and equally articulated, for the first time in Western cultural history. Silvius expresses his admiration for the "generosus pastor" (Theocritus) who spoke a different language and was the source from which Virgil drank, and he describes how his own poetry has been received by his contemporaries: the learned, themselves sources or "fountains" applauding him, the uneducated dryly repeating his words like barren echoes. Monicus recommends that instead of continually subjecting himself to the tensions of ambition and emulation, Silvius should enter the cave (the monastic life) and listen instead to poetry of a different ontological order:

> Dulcius hic quanto media sub nocte videbis
> Psallere pastorem! Reliquorum oblivia sensim
> Ingeret ille tibi.

(lines 55–57)

> Here in the depths of the night you will see a shepherd sing psalms of greater sweetness. In time he will cause you to become oblivious of everything else.

We hardly need Petrarch's gloss in the letter to tell us that the psalmist is David, who always reminds us of the inhabitants and the humble walls of Jerusalem ("Cives et menia parve / Sepe Jerosolime memorat," lines 72–73), whereas the authorities to whom Silvius turns sing of Rome and Troy and kingly conflicts ("Hi Roman Troiamque canunt et prelia regum," line 75). If Virgil ambiguated the choice between Tityrus and Meliboeus, so Petrarch leaves the choice of sacred or secular poetry unsettled for the time being, pending the completion of the *Africa,* to which the final lines of the eclogue are devoted. Yet in terms of Virgilian interpretation, the effect of the entire eclogue is to confirm the hypothesis, only inferential in Servian commentary, that one could read the *Eclogues,* in particular the first, as a dramatized poetics, or at least that branch of poetics that deals with authorial motives and with poetry's sanctions and functions.

Another adaptation of the Servian theme of patronage and one equally tightly connected to Virgil's first eclogue is Petrarch's eighth, the *Divortium* or *Separation,* where he expresses as dramatic debate his parting in 1347 from his Avignon patron, Cardinal Giovanni Colonna. An old friend in Parma had invited Petrarch to return to Italy, but his acceptance of the invitation was probably also motivated by a desire to return to Rome, recently rendered attractive by the new regime of Cola di Rienzi. Petrarch here presented his residence in France as aberrant, as an exile forced upon him as a child by his father, who carried him away from the land of his forefathers and abandoned him in the marshes ("Huc genitor profugus me ruris aviti / Finibus infantem rapuit, ripaque palustri / Exposuit miserum," lines 86–88), and declares his determination to return to his origins. Few statements in Petrarch's canon can be more culturally resonant than this, wonderfully impossible to translate: "Levis est ad prima recursus / Principia," lines 85–86); for the return to first principles, or sources, may bring happiness, but it was not, as Petrarch the philologist certainly knew, a light or easy matter. Equally subtle was Petrarch's appropriation for his own autobiographical purposes of Virgil's tendentious *libertas,* as well as of Servius's gloss upon it. For two decades, Petrarch reminded Colonna, he had served him faithfully, "nor is the love of liberty, surely, an injury" ("nulla est iniuria iustus / Libertatis amor"). Using the very phrase, "libertatis amor," that Servius had employed to suggest the presence of Virgilian ambiguity, Petrarch explicitly identified the language of the *ingenuus,* the man born free, with his own proposed emancipation from the duties of clientage; and in the context of Cola di Rienzi's revolution, however short-lived, it certainly also carried intensely republican connotations.[46]

There was, of course, another major theme in this rewriting of the

---

[46] See Mario Emilio Cosenza, *Francesco Petrarca and the Revolution of Cola di Rienzi* (Chicago, 1913), especially for the letter (pp. 16–44) that Petrarch wrote to Cola in June 1347, which was essentially a paean to republicanism, with Cola recognized as the third Roman Brutus. Cola's revolution lasted for less than a year, from May to December 1347.

eclogue as cultural autobiography, one that is more familiarly attached to Petrarch's name and that has occasioned more respect than other parts of his pastoral subtext. I refer to the presence of Laura in this third eclogue, a courtship dialogue between Stupeus (Petrarch) and Daphne (Laura); in his ninth eclogue, the *Querelus* or *Lamentation,* occasioned by Laura's death in the plague in April 1348; and in his tenth eclogue, *Laura occidens,* where, as Bergin justly remarks, both the personal and the Virgilian motives are completely overshadowed by the excessively long and insufficiently justified roll-call of poets, a list to which Petrarch continued to add names for several years. Yet the very structual and conceptual inadequacies of this poem point to the other great leap in "translation" accomplished by Petrarch—the recognition that the theme of love in Virgil, which Virgil himself had represented, through Corydon and Gallus, as at best solipsistic and at worst self-destructive, could itself be redeemed by *translatio,* that is to say, by transforming sexual love into a metaphor for something beyond itself without abandoning the literal fact. Thus Laura, as everyone knows even if they have read barely a word of Petrarch, was both a real person to whom Petrarch was passionately committed and a symbol of his vocation, the laurel tree or the laurel crown of poetic preeminence. It is a telling fact that we can prove her historical existence primarily because Petrarch himself recorded her death on the flyleaf of the precious Virgil manuscript.[47]

"In the Shade": Metaphors of Patronage

The last significant item of Petrarch's reading of Virgil that we shall examine here, significant in that it too created its own mini-tradition within the larger trajectory of pastoral, is connected to the Laura eclogues via the symbolism of trees. Calling himself Silvius within his pastoral discourse, Petrarch alerted his readers to the role that trees played in his personal iconography, and in the tenth eclogue he arrives at an Arcadian landscape where stand side by side the green laurel of Petrarch's personal love and ambition and the towering beech offering its shade to the flocks and the shepherds ("Optatamque gregi gregis ac ductoribus umbram," line 285) and creating an appropriate setting for Augustus. In this poem Petrarch slides over the signifying gap that was leaped in Servian commentary, whereby the beechen shade (*umbra*) under which Tityrus reposed was virtually equated with imperial protection; put in its starkest form, as Servius

---

[47] See de Nolhac, *Pétrarque et l'humanisme,* 1: 119; but compare F. A. Wulff, *La Note sur le Virgile de l'Ambrosienne* (Uppsala, 1901), who questioned the authenticity of the autobiographical notes on the added first folio.

Danielis has it, *umbra* meant "allegorice sub tutela Imp[eratoris] Aug[usti]." But in the second eclogue, the *Argus,* the tree metaphor grows considerably larger and in the process shows us exactly how Petrarch understood its cultural ramifications.

The *Argus* is Petrarch's response to Virgil's *Daphnis* and shares its model's cryptic and disputed referentiality. Petrarch did, however, supply his own partial gloss. In January 1347 he sent a copy of the poem to Barbato de Sulmona with a letter in which he explained that it was an elegy for "our most sainted king," that is, Robert of Naples, who had died in January 1343. In order to grasp what Robert signified to Petrarch, and hence the structure and strategy of the elegy, it is pertinent to know that despite the internecine struggles for power in Italy and despite Robert's interventions on behalf of the Guelph party, his kingdom had by the time of his death acquired an ideal reputation as the territory of peaceful government and enlightened patronage of the arts. As Benedetto Croce put it in his *History of the Kingdom of Naples,* "the times of 'the wise King Robert,' 'the new Solomon,' were long harked back to; a song written half a century later celebrates the peace and plenty of his reign, the just laws, festivities, games, tournaments, music, and love songs, while another poem recalls it as 'something like paradise.'"[48] Moreover, Robert was for Petrarch the monarch to whom he had presented himself for examination and who in 1341 had crowned him poet laureate.

There are, therefore, no interpretive problems or even questions of appropriateness about the second half of the elegy, in which Robert is celebrated as Argus, the shepherd of manifold vision, whose death has left the other pastoral protagonists desolate. But the elegy proper is preceded by a different kind of symbolism, one that Petrarch's letter leaves unglossed. The eclogue begins with a description of a fearful storm, suddenly interrupting a period of unusual calm:

> Nec nemorum tantam per secula multa quietem
> Viderat ulla dies: passim saturata iacebant
> Armenta et lenis pastores somnus habebat;
> Pars teretes baculos, pars nectere serta canendo
> Frondea, pars agiles calamos; tum fusca nitentem
> Obduxit Phebum nubes, precepsque repente
> Ante expectatum nox affuit; horruit ether
> Grandine terribili; certatim ventus et imber

---

[48] Benedetto Croce, *History of the Kingdom of Naples,* ed. H. Stuart Hughes, trans. Frances Frenaye (Chicago, 1965), pp. 51–52. Croce also cited Dominicus of Gravina's *Chronicon de rebus in Apulia gestis,* which looked back with nostalgia to the time when the Neapolitans enjoyed the long peace under Robert ("qui dudum peractis annis tranquillo pacis statu gaudebant sub regno Regis Reoberti et progenitorum suorum"). See L. A. Muratori, *Rerum italicarum scriptores* (Milan, 1751), sec. 22.

Sevire et fractis descendere fulmina nimbis,
Altior, ethereo penitus convulsa fragore,
Corruit et colles concussit et arva cupressus.

. . . .

. . . Ingentis strepitu tremefacta ruine,
Pastorum mox turba fugit, quecunque sub illa
Per longum secura diem consederat umbra.

(2–13, 19–21)

For no day for many centuries had seen so great a calm in the groves:
on all sides gentle sleep possessed full-fed flocks and shepherds;
some as they sang constructed wooden staffs, or leafy garlands, or
fluent reed-pipes; when a dark cloud obstructed the shining sun,
and suddenly and without warning night descended on us; the sky
shuddered with a terrible hailstorm; rain and wind contested and
lightning descended through the cloud-fissures. Standing higher than
the rest, deeply smitten by a thunderbolt, the cypress fell headlong,
shaking the hills and the fields on impact. . . . Trembling in the great
crash of its ruin, a crowd of shepherds took flight who had formerly
through the long day sheltered in its secure shade.

In this intense vision of a shattered idyll, Petrarch expanded the Servian
reading of the pastoral *umbra* into a drama of its loss; and in this instance
his tendency to rhetorical plenitude rather than thrift works to advantage.
The value of *umbra* as a term is denoted both by its being withheld so long
in the grammatical and rhetorical construction—until, indeed, it no longer
exists—and by the conceptual frame of peaceful continuity, expressed as
repetition: "Per longum secura diem" looks back regretfully at "per secula
multa quietem . . . ulla dies."

The most natural understanding of this great and fallen shade-tree
would be to associate it with Robert of Naples, a contemporary Augustus,
the stability of his thirty-four-year reign, from 1309 to 1343, certainly
qualifying as a "long day in the secure shade." In the elegy proper, it is said
that the woods were always safe under his rule ("semper sub principe
tuta") and that peace crowned his brow ("pax inerat fronti," lines 100–
101). Yet thanks to Petrarch's early commentators, later ones have seen in
the fall of the cypress a reference to the murder of Andrew of Hungary,
husband of Robert's granddaughter Joan, who was suspected of complicity
in the murder but eventually "cleared" by Clement VI.[49]

It is hard to see how Andrew's brief and pathetic career could have in-

---

[49] Bergin, *Petrarch's Bucolicum Carmen*, pp. 220–21, following Piendibeni da Monte-
pulciano and an anonymous commentator; see Avena, *Il Bucolicum carmen*, pp. 175–78,
254–55.

spired this *translatio* of Virgil's resonant and multifoliate shade. A far less
problematic solution is to see the *Argus* as exploring the death of Robert of
Naples through two different but parallel structures; the first, an expansion
of Servian commentary on the protected posture of Tityrus; the second, an
imitation of Virgil's fifth eclogue, governed by the premise that the Daphnis
of that poem was Julius Caesar. Structurally far more powerful, the poem
so understood also functions as an emblem of Petrarch's pessimism. For
Virgil there were two political persons to be celebrated as gods, one dead,
the other very much alive and the site of cultural optimism, but in this
poem, as befits the pastoral of Rome's dismemberment, the two Caesars
converge and are buried in a single ritual. The closest Petrarch comes to an
apotheosis for Argus is to imagine him looking down from a peak high
above and observing "our cares and tumults" (lines 117–18). Considering
that the laurel of *Laura occidens* is also felled by a thunderstorm (lines
381–93), we may infer that this metaphor was indeed central to Petrarch's
poetics as well as his emotional life. It was unlikely to have been expended
on a comparatively insignificant victim of those same tumults.

In the subsequent history of this metaphor, however, it was not the
specific reference that mattered. On the contrary, it was what Petrarch had
done to Virgil's protective *umbra* that gave his fallen tree roots in the culture, or perhaps we should say branches.[50] What Petrarch had done, driven
by his own pessimism, was to collate the sheltering beech of Eclogue 1.1
with the lightning-struck oaks of 1.17, glossed in Servian commentary as a
symbol of the wrath of Octavian; and Petrarch himself in his own interlinear gloss had identified the lightning with Caesarian decree. In his version, therefore, the location of power and protection is deeply ambiguous,
subjecting the tree of patronage to forces that the ruler does not control;
while the tree itself is transferred from the territory of idyll to that of elegy.
It was this move that dozens of later writers would find irresistible, and the
species of the tree would vary according to local and temporal circumstances. In 1504 Jacopo Sannazaro, in exile from Naples which had been
invaded and divided between France and Spain, built into the twelfth book
of his *Arcadia* a vision of a great orange tree (*arangio*)—clearly symbolic of
the house of Aragon, now uprooted, with all its leaves and fruit scat-
tered—and lamented, "Where then shall I repose? Under what shade shall
I sing my verses?"[51] And toward the end of the century, from the perspec-

---

[50] On the rich semantics of *umbra* in Virgil, see P. L. Smith, "*Lentus in Umbra*: A Symbolic Pattern in Vergil's *Eclogues*," *Phoenix* 19 (1965): 298–304; Michael Putnam, "Virgil's
First Eclogue: Poetics of Enclosure," *Ramus* 4 (1975): 81–104. On the shadow of the laurel
and Petrarch's "umbrageous consciousness" see Greene, *The Light in Troy*, pp. 131–46; and
on the polysemy of *umbra* in antiquity, see Julie Nováková, *Umbra: Ein Beitrag zur dich-
terischen Semantik* (Berlin, 1964).

[51] Jacopo Sannazaro, *Arcadia,* ed. Michele Scherillo (Turin, 1888), pp. 274–75: "Ul-
timamente un albero bellissimo di arangio et da me molto coltivato, mi parea trovare tronco

tive of an English Protestant, Sir Philip Sidney noted, "How Holland hearts, now so good townes be lost, / Trust in the shade of pleasing Orange tree," an allusion to the protective role of the Dutch house of Orange in northern Europe.[52]

The topos was particularly accessible in England, and following it gives a remarkably sharp and memorable series of images (indeed, some of them were visual) of the ideological shifts in English public affairs and the discourses they produced. In 1552 the great Tudor and Protestant patron of letters Thomas Seymour, who was executed in the reign of Edward VI, was privately lamented in a poem entitled *The Hospitable Oake,* ingeniously constructed out of Virgilian allusions. The tree, "Beneath whose shade did gladsome shepherds hie," "Outstretch'd in all the luxurie of ease," originally grew "in Arcadia's londe" and supplied its protégés not only with acorns, the food of true Arcadian primitivism, but also with the "honey dew" that in *Georgic* 1.131 is said to drop naturally from the leaves of trees ("mellaque decussit foliis"). Its fall is not through divine wrath but through envy; "'twas bruited all around, / This goodlie tree did shadowe too much grounde"; and Jove "aloud in thunder spoke" to express his anger at its fate.[53]

By the middle of the seventeenth century the metaphor of the protective oak had been transferred to Charles I, a notion perhaps most graphically represented by James Howell's *Dodona's Grove: or, the Vocall Forest,* an extended tree-fable of the civil war in which the poet appeared in person (Fig. 1) under the shade of the British oak; a Latin epigraph, "Tutus obumbror," alluded simultaneously to the situation of Tityrus and the allegorical mode of representation that Howell, for safety's sake, elected. In 1658 Andrew Marvell represented the death of another "protector," Oliver Cromwell, as the fall of the "sacred oak" of the Puritan revolution:

> When angry Jove darts lightning through the aire,
> At mortalls sins, nor his own plant will spare;
> (It groanes, and bruises all below that stood
> So many yeares the shelter of the wood.)[54]

---

da le radici con le frondi e i fiori e i frutti sparsi per terra. . . . Ove dunque mi riposero io? sotto qual ombra homai cantero i miei versi?" On the relation between Sannazaro's *Arcadia* and Virgil, see David Quint, *Origin and Originality in Renaissance Literature* (New Haven, 1983), pp. 43–69; and William J. Kennedy, *Jacopo Sannazaro and the Uses of Pastoral* (Hanover, 1983), pp. 28–37.

[52] Sir Philip Sidney, *Astrophil and Stella* 30: 7–8.

[53] See *Nugae Antiquae,* ed. Henry Harington, 2 vols. (London, 1804), 2: 330–32; and John N. King, *English Reformation Literature: The Tudor Origins of the Protestant Tradition* (Princeton, 1982), pp. 240–41.

[54] Andrew Marvell, "A Poem upon the Death of O.C.," *Poems and Letters,* ed. H. M. Margoliouth, rev. Pierre Legouis, 2 vols. (Oxford, 1971), 1: 136.

Figure 1. Claude Mellan, portrait of James Howell, from *Dodona's Grove* (London, 1650), facing p. 286. By permission of the British Library.

Figure 2. Funeral medal for Oliver Cromwell. By permission of the British Library.

And the nation took, as it were, official cognizance of the tree-metaphor in a form precisely adapted to Oliver Cromwell, for the funeral medal issued for 3 September 1658 showed on one side an image of the Protector and on the other a tree under whose shade resides a shepherd with his sheep (Fig. 2). The legend explains the tree's species and its connection to the moment: "Non deficient oliva" ("Let them not lack the olive"), a motto derived from *Aeneid* 6.143–44 ("Primo avulso non deficit alter aureus") or the magically self-restoring Golden Bough.[55]

[55] The Virgilian motto had already acquired dynastic connotations in Medici Florence. See Janet Cox-Rearick, *Dynasty and Destiny in Medici Art: Pontormo, Leo X and the Two Cosimos* (Princeton, 1984), pp. 44–49.

In 1783 George Crabbe, who claimed in *The Village,* his supposedly realist poem on eighteenth-century country life, to have rejected all Neoclassical pastoral imitation, nevertheless himself sought help from the ancient trope when faced with the task of writing a public elegy to commemorate the youngest son of his patron, the marquess of Granby. Shot in a naval battle against the French, Lord Robert Manners went down

> As the tall oak, whose vigorous branches form
> An ample shade and brave the wildest storm,
> High o'er the subject wood is seen to grow,
> The guard and glory of the trees below;
> Till on its head the fiery bolt descends,
> And o'er the plain the shatter'd trunk extends;
> Yet then it lies, as wond'rous as before,
> And still the glory, though the guard no more[56]

To show, finally and more profoundly, how deeply the pastoral shade tree was embedded in the cultural history of Europe, I have chosen an example from the period of high Romanticism, from Germany, and from the visual arts. In 1822 Caspar David Friedrich produced for the consul Joachim Heinrich Wilhelm Wagener a painting now known variously as *Village Landscape, The Lonely Tree,* or *The Solitary Oak* (Plate 2). None of these titles does justice to the fact that this is a pastoral, and that it carries iconographical significance intelligible only in the context of pastoral tradition. The painting offers, clearly, a version of the tree that has in the past protected or failed to protect the artist, and beneath it a diminutive shepherd with his sheep, dwarfed, as the commentators are united in observing, by the majesty of the landscape. But this sense of nature's sublimity, typical of Romanticism and, as in Romanticism's central documents, marked by the presence of mountains, is complicated by the tree's own structure, by the damage it has sustained, perhaps by lightning. Here is a central ambiguity, on which the critics disagree. For Helmut Börsch-Supan, the oak "meets the contours of the mountains at precisely the point on its trunk where it is beginning to wither," a sign of life's transience that is echoed by other withered branches in the background and by the ruined castle.[57] For Linda Siegel, the painting needs to be read as the last of a *political* series, landscapes in which the oak stands, as in Hölderlin's *Die Eichen* (1792), for the spirit of Germany. From 1806 to 1814, Friedrich was obsessed by the French domination and devastation of his country,

[56] George Crabbe, "The Village," in *Poems,* ed. Adolphus Ward, 3 vols. (Cambridge, 1905), 1: 133.
[57] Helmut Börsch-Supan, *Caspar David Friedrich,* trans. Sarah Twohig (New York, 1974), p. 130.

and during the German wars of liberation in 1812–13 his studio became a center for the anti-French nationalists in Dresden, a group that included Kleist and Schubert. The series of paintings that chart his feelings over these years runs from the desolate and wintry *Abbey in the Oak Forest* (1810) through the *Oak Tree in Snow* (1821), where the central tree shows some green foliage to herald the coming of spring, to *The Solitary Oak,* where the foliage is richer, despite the tree's dead summit, and spring has given place to summer.[58]

It is the presence of the sheltered shepherd with his sheep, however, that definitively marks the transition to cultural optimism, qualified by the Romantic premises of human isolation and insignificance. What remains ambiguous is the new optimism's source. Does it come, as is usually said of Friedrich, from the loss of his passionate patriotism and its transcendence by natural supernaturalism and religious mysticism? Or is his mature pastoral (so confidently beautiful that it is used for the cover of this book) a memorial not only of his own earlier oaks but of all the pastoral texts that had previously spoken of art's contested relation to freedom and of its need for protection? There is no record in his notebooks to suggest that Virgil's "woods worthy of a consul" entered Friedrich's mind as he worked on his commission for the German consul; the coincidence remains remarkable.

Ruins in the Realm of Thoughts

Since we will eventually follow the *Eclogues* into the twentieth century, it is appropriate to close this chapter by returning to its opening epigraph and unfolding its relevance here. Walter Benjamin was one of the first writers of the twentieth century to attempt to recuperate allegory from the biases of Romantic and post-Romantic aesthetics and one of the few to perceive its philosophical connections to historical consciousness. Although his focus was not medieval but Baroque allegory, the terms in which he made his plea for the value of the arcane are astonishingly germane to the series Virgil-Servius-Petrarch. Unlike the Romantic conception of the symbol as that which transcends time by an instantaneous fusion of image and perception, for Benjamin allegory was from its origins realistic in the face of change and mortality:

> And in this guise history does not assume the form of the process of an eternal life so much as that of irresistible decay. Allegory thereby declares itself to be beyond beauty. Allegories are, in the realm of

---

[58] Linda Siegel, *Caspar David Friedrich and the Age of German Romanticism* (Boston, 1978), pp. 71, 75–77, 108–9.

thoughts, what ruins are in the realm of things. . . . The legacy of antiquity constitutes, item for item, the elements from which the new
whole is mixed. Or rather: is constructed. For the perfect vision of this
new phenomenon was the ruin. The exuberant subjection of antique
elements in a structure which, without uniting them in a single whole,
would, in destruction, still be superior to the harmonies of antiquity,
is the purpose of the technique which applies itself separately, and ostentatiously, to realia, rhetorical figures and rules. Literature ought to
be called *ars inveniendi.* The notion of the man of genius, the master of
the *ars inveniendi,* is that of a man who could manipulate models with
sovereign skill.[59]

In this profound redefinition of classical imitation as the bravest form of
contemporaneity (and of the grammarian's art as a commitment to realism) Benjamin speaks for Servius and Petrarch as well as for the writers of
the German *trauerspiel* of the seventeenth century.

Benjamin's perception that allegory expresses "a deep-rooted intu-
ition of the problematic character of art" was connected to his plea, in the
Epistemo-Critical Prologue, for some transaction between art and political
life. The use of allegory, he suggested, is one of the signs that in certain
periods "men of letters who . . . live their lives in a sphere cut off from the
active national feeling of the people" become passionately resistant to that
isolation.[60] It is very much to my point that Benjamin's own runic criticism, with its implicit political allegory (and its explicit analogy between
the decadence of Germany in the 1920s and that of the final period of the
Roman Empire) should have itself acquired the status of a cultural ruin.
Written in 1924–25, with the fratricidal tendencies of the Weimar Republic amid the terrifying rise of the National Socialists in full evidence,
the *Ursprung des deutschen Trauerspiels* became, as George Steiner has
pointed out, an "extinct work . . . one of a fascinating group of writings
and works of art assigned to oblivion by National Socialism and the consequent dispersal or destruction of the German-Jewish community."[61] Benjamin himself died a hunted fugitive. It was only by chance that a few
copies of his work survived in the hands of friends, to be subsequently preserved in modern editions and translations.

Yet at almost the same time as the fate of Benjamin's *Ursprung* was
proving the truth of his aphorisms in one way, the fate of Petrarch's precious manuscript was making another, less melancholy demonstration. The
mere fact of its survival (even after having been stolen from Petrarch) and

---

[59] Benjamin, *The Origin of German Tragic Drama,* pp. 178–79.
[60] Ibid., pp. 176, 55.
[61] George Steiner, Introduction to Benjamin, *The Origin of German Tragic Drama,* p. 7.

of its superb preservation in the Ambrosian library in Milan is an emblem of humanism's continuity. And considering Petrarch's reputation as the first *literary* critic of the papacy, it is one of history's more generous ironies that the man responsible for the superb facsimile edition of Petrarch's manuscript, which makes it accessible to hundreds of scholars internationally, was Achille Ratti, formerly director of the Ambrosian library but better known as Pope Pius XI. However one interprets the dealings between Pius and Mussolini and the consequent signing of the Lateran Accord, the pope was identified as a spokesman for peace and as a critic of Mussolini's brand of Italian nationalism.[62] In the preface to the Virgil facsimile, written in Latin and addressed to the international community of scholars, we can hear, perhaps, the voice of pastoral care convergent again with the voice of humanism, much as Petrarch would have wished.[63] We are reminded that although Virgil and Petrarch were separated by so many centuries, they were joined by such great love and esteem that their names are intertwined in the pages of the Ambrosian codex *ad aeternitatem;* that the whole current of Italian poetry flows from this source; and we are invited to join in a Virgilian celebration. The year was 1930, the bimillennial anniversary of Virgil's birth, an event that, as we shall see again in Chapter 5, was celebrated by European intellectuals with an unusual poignancy and self-consciousness, because of the political shadow that hung over them.

[62] See, for example, Lillian Browne-Olf, *Pius XI, Apostle of Peace* (New York, 1938), pp. 163, 174–75, 206–7. This study, though hagiographic and apologetic, effectively contrasts Mussolini's cynicism about the Lateran Accord with the pope's Christmas message to the cardinals in 1930 (the year in which the Ambrosian Virgil was issued in facsimile).

[63] The preface (in a separate fascicle) was written not by Pius XI but by Giovanni Galbiati, also the author of *Il libro che il Petrarca ebbe più caro* (Milan, 1957).

2
VERSIONS OF
RENAISSANCE HUMANISM

> "Long-winded arguments are always meant to
> conceal something, especially when . . . they try
> to establish themselves on time-wasting philologi-
> cal arguments."
> "This is no philology, Octavian."
> "But it sounds like a commentary that you
> should add to the *Aeneid*."
> "Yes, it might be so described."
> "A commentary by Virgil on his own work!
> Who would want to miss that!"
>
> Hermann Broch, *The Death of Virgil*

By the end of the fourteenth century, as Petrarch demonstrated, the potency of the *Eclogues* as a master-text in the cultural imagination had already been understood. Seen through the lens (or veil) of Servian commentary, now permanently in place for all subsequent interpreters, they
offered far more than an introduction (later to be relinquished) to the vast
civic themes of the *Aeneid*. Rather than merely a test and display of crafts-
manship preparatory to a major work of cultural definition, the *Eclogues*
were themselves, it appeared, a matrix of social, political, and aesthetic
thought, however delicately and interrogatively recorded. And as later
writers meditated on the Servian "notes towards a theory of representation," they were found to enable a wide range of ideological activity, whose
center was the concept of the writer-intellectual at work *sub umbra*, defin-

ing himself and his responsibilities in relation to the power structures of his own place and time.

This chapter will reapproach the huge subject of Virgilianism in the Renaissance, which may fairly be said to have been initiated by Petrarch and may be conveniently rounded off, at the end of the sixteenth century in England, by the publication of Spenser's *Shepheardes Calender,* along with its formal imitation of Servian commentary. Because Virgil was omnipresent in the Renaissance, we shall inevitably be constrained here to a ruthless selectivity, attempting to contract into a single chapter a panorama whose enormous scale and detail have already been mapped. Giuliano Mambelli's checklist of Renaissance editions of Virgil registers 275 editions of the complete works of Virgil, and 75 of the *Eclogues* alone.[1] Most of these contained some form of commentary. Under the leadership of Virginia Brown, a team of scholars are compiling the Virgil volumes of the *Catalogus Commentariorum et Translationum,* which, it is estimated, will contain some 200 items, in both printed and manuscript form. Among the more important commentators who can only be named here were Josse Bade (Badius Ascensius), Ermanno Torrentino, Domizio Calderino, Antonio Mancinelli, Jacopo Pontano, Filippo Beroaldo, Philip Melanchthon, Pierre de la Ramée (Peter Ramus), Thomas Farnaby, and Jean Luis de la Cerda. During the late fifteenth and the early sixteenth century, Italy, as one would expect, dominated the field, but the enterprise soon spread to French, German, Dutch, and English philologues and pedagogues. The stronger the philological or pedagogical motives, in fact, the weaker became the genre as a vehicle of cultural information. The vast majority of such commentary added little to the story of interpretation, which passed, rather, into other forms; and as Petrarch's own eclogues constituted an act of interpretation by creative imitation, so the various pastoral ventures of Renaissance poets, whose numbers we know from the giant surveys of Enrico Carrara, Vladimiro Zabughin, Alice Hulubei, W. W. Greg, and others, continued the project of rediscovering Virgil's *Eclogues* for such distinctive cultures as Medicean Florence, early post-Reformation France, and Elizabethan England.[2]

The focus of this chapter will be divided between formal commentaries and the poetry of exegesis, selecting only examples where the writer's response to Virgil is both sharply distinctive and fully intelligible only in terms of contemporary circumstance. In Quattrocento Italy, the most significant scholarly issues, both textual and extratextual, are on striking display in the different kinds of commentary developed by Cristoforo Lan-

[1] Giuliano Mambelli, *Gli annali delle edizioni Virgiliane* (Florence, 1954).

[2] Enrico Carrara, *La poesia pastorale* (Milan, 1909); Vladimiro Zabughin, *Virgilio nel Rinascimento Italiano,* 2 vols. (Bologna, 1921); Alice Hulubei, *L'Eglogue en France au seizième siècle* (Paris, 1938); W. W. Greg, *Pastoral Poetry and Pastoral Drama* (London, 1905; reprinted New York, 1959).

dino and Angelo Poliziano. In contrast to these stands, the illustrated edition of Virgil produced by Sebastian Brant at the turn of the sixteenth century is both an example of how visual illustration was another important form of commentary and a strong instance of how northern European humanism distinguished itself from that of Italy. Different again, both formally and ideologically, is the mid-century commentary on the *Eclogues* produced by Ludovico Vives, Spanish-born but alienated by circumstances and internationalist by conviction, while the cultural implications of neo-Virgilian pastoral are dramatically demonstrated by the linked figures of Clément Marot and Edmund Spenser—French and English versions, respectively, of the post-Reformation intellectual.

By a certain argumentative thrift, therefore, the chronological scope and the major locations of the Renaissance in Europe will be represented. It is very much to the point that these exemplars can also be said, though with marked diversity, to embody Renaissance humanism. It will be a by-product of the larger argument, therefore, to recall how polyvalent, indeed how contentious, the term *humanism* has become, and possibly to recover for it some congruity of meaning by reconnecting it to the concept of the intellectual and his habit—by the Renaissance already long-standing—of pastoral self-definition. But by the same token, the possibility of grouping together as versions of Renaissance humanism such widely divergent sets of ideas and principles as Florentine neo-Platonism and German popularism is instructive in proportion to its difficulty. The apparent disparity between Landino's appeal to the select community of the Platonic Academy at Careggi and Brant's outreach to the *indocti,* or between the internationalism of Vives (however anti-Italianate) and Marot's determined Francophilia (however harassed), is the measure of the power of the language they have in common: the Virgilian language of writerly self-recognition, embedded with historical meaning several strata deep, whose allure was less of origins than continuity and which therefore both incited and restrained the perception of historical difference.

The Commentary Tradition

VIRGIL FOR THE MEDICIS: LANDINO AND POLITIAN

In 1487 Cristoforo Landino published the text of Virgil with his own commentary and that of Servius. Addressing the project to Pietro, a son of Lorenzo de' Medici, he explained the relationship of this commentary to his far more famous *Disputationes Camaldulenses,* that great repository of Florentine neo-Platonism, indicating that he regarded the earlier work, completed in the early 1470s, as his main contribution to a Virgilian hermeneutics and that the edition would concern itself primarily with points of grammar and rhetoric.[3] While this distinction was, as we shall see, neither precisely adhered to nor exactly what it seemed, it is important to realize how strongly, in theory, Landino distinguished between two different approaches to the text of Virgil or between two rival conceptions of the Virgilian commentator and interpreter. The first, articulated in his lectures to the Florentine Studium and in their final product, the 1487 edition, was defined according to the model of the scholiasts of late antiquity, especially Servius; the second was the new model of the philosopher-critic, made possible by the rediscovery of Plato and the work of Marsilio Ficino.

In his preface to the third book of the *Disputations,* addressing Federigo of Urbino, Landino had explained the superiority of the philosophical method he was now following. What you are seeking, he tells his audience, is much nobler than anything so far explained in the commentary tradition, "something which lies more hidden in obscurity and has never been revealed in its own sequential order by anyone, as far as I know, up to this point. Neither grammarian nor rhetorician knows this, but it must be brought to light from the deepest secrets of philosophy [*intimis philosophiae arcanis*], for you wish to know what Virgil intended [*voluerit*] in his enigmas concerning the wanderings of Aeneas and the departure of that man to Italy." Landino was sardonic on the subject of authorial intention, as typically handled in an *accessus:* "But if you ask them [the grammarians] what Virgil wanted to accomplish in the poem, they will affirm that he proposed for himself the imitation of Homer."[4] But he clearly felt the need to defend himself against the charge of having willfully imagined the great allegorical account of the quest for the *summum bonum* that he was about to discover in the *Aeneid.* And he justified what was coming in advance, as a privileged esotericism designed for an interpretive community of the elite. Not only poets, Landino suggested, but all who engaged in a major literary project have been wise enough to veil their statements with various fictions and figurative discourse ("variis figmentis, variis figurarum integumentis obscurarent").

> Putabant enim . . . si negotium difficilius redderent, ut et quae scripsissent maiorem essent dignitatem auctoritatemque habitura et qui

[3] *P. Vergilii opera cum commentario Christophori Landini* (Florence, 1487). The explanation occurs in the third prefatory address to Pietro, which immediately precedes the *Aeneid.*

[4] Cristoforo Landino, *Disputationes Camaldulenses,* ed. Peter Lohe (Florence, 1980), pp. 117–18. In translating this section of the *Disputations* I have consulted, and partially followed, Thomas Stahel, "Cristoforo Landino's Allegorization of the Aeneid," Ph.D. dissertation, Johns Hopkins University, 1973, a translation of the third and fourth books of the *Disputations.*

percepissent, quoniam non sine labore atque industria id assequeren-
tur, ea pluris esse facturos maioremque inde voluptatem percepturos,
si quae ipsi tenerent minime sibi cum indoctis communia essent. Hac
igitur ratione a sanctis sacrisque rebus profanos arcebant non invidia
moti, sed ut aliquod inter sollertem atque inertem discrimen apparent,
cum non idem otiosus quod studiosus assequeretur. Sic enim et prae-
mia quae doctis debentur solis illis proponebantur. . . . Difficultate
enim et inopia rei mortalium ingenia acuuntur: vincitque omnia la-
bor/improbus et duris urgens in rebus egestas.

(pp. 113–14)

For they thought that if they rendered the matter more difficult, not
only would the things they had written take on great dignity and
authority, but also those who heard them (because they would not
fully attain them without labor and industry) would make more of
them; and that they would take greater pleasure from them if those
things which they learned were not in the least shared with the ignorant. In this way they kept the profane away from holy and sacred
matters, not motivated by envy, but so that there might be some
distinction between the clever and the idle man. Because the idle
man does not achieve as much as the studious one, thus the rewards
due to the learned were held out to them alone. For men's minds are
sharpened by difficulty and scarcity: *vincit omnia labor/improbus et
duris urgens in rebus egestas*.

There was nothing casual or unthought in Landino's quotation here of
the ethos of labor from Virgil's *Georgics* 1.145–46, a quotation that transformed Virgil's selective critique of pastoral into a defense of the intellectual in one of his most sheltered manifestations. For this was a hermeneutic
well adapted to the social situation in which it was produced, the circle of
scholars with Lorenzo de' Medici at its center that constituted the Florentine Academy. As Janet Cox-Rearick has demonstrated, Laurentian culture
was characterized in part by a self-endorsing fusion of pastoral and georgic,
not only in such idyllic settings as the Villa Careggi but also by an iconography devised by and for Lorenzo the Magnificent that derived ultimately
from Virgil. Much of the Laurentian iconography was an expression of
Golden Age idealism based on the fourth eclogue; but the first eclogue
also provided a whole series of verbal and visual allusions to the ruler as
shade-tree, now identified, in compliment to Laurentian rule, as the laurel,
symbol of peace, immortality (through its imperviousness to lightning),
and literary accomplishment. The second eclogue yielded material for a
cult of Pan Medicus, symbol of the numinous powers of the house of Medici

and definitively attached to Lorenzo by Luca Signorelli's *Realm of Pan,* painted about two years before Lorenzo's death in 1492.[5] At the beginning of Lorenzo's regime the poet Naldo Naldi had dedicated to him eleven eclogues constituting a history of the house of Medici from Cosimo to the present and concluding with dynastic allegory and prophecy, and in his *Rusticus* Poliziano presented his patron with an updated version of the *Georgics,* especially the "happy man" passage at the end of Virgil's second book.[6]

Landino's definition of his Camaldolese hermeneutics as the georgics of the mind was, therefore, consistent with Laurentian mythology, creating for the early 1470s a generative vocabulary of the intellectual life and its responsibilities. But the alignment of the *Georgics* with the Platonic Academy at Careggi had also to be supported by a discreet but ingenious manipulation of Eclogue 1, where Virgil's doubts about the sheltered life had been registered. It can hardly be a coincidence that the status of the *indocti,* that large and amorphous group whom the *docti* need to posit in order to establish their own claims to privilege, are here delimited by words—*otiosus* and *iners*—that Virgil associated with Tityrus, and Servius with the Augustan protégé, while Meliboeus's disclaimer that he did not envy ("non equidem invideo") his neighbor's superior fortune here serves to protect the intellectual against the charge of selfishness.

This passage is obviously connected to the opening sections of the *Disputations,* where Landino describes how a group of "litteratissimi" with Lorenzo at their head arrived in the Camaldolese woods to seek respite from the summer heat and the cares of the city, "where in a flowery meadow a spreading beech [*patula fagus*] covered with its extended branches a clear fountain" (p. 10), an environment deliberately recalling the opening of Virgil's first eclogue. But as articulated by Alberti, who will lead the discussions, the primary associations of this "pastoral" environment (the word is his) are with Socrates under his plane tree, and beyond that to the image of Mary sitting quietly at the feet of Christ while her sister Martha

---

[5] Janet Cox-Rearick, *Dynasty and Destiny in Medici Art: Pontormo, Leo X and the Two Cosimos* (Princeton, 1984), pp. 18–19. For Signorelli's painting, which was destroyed in the Second World War, see Cox-Rearick, pp. 83–86. The cult of Pan was grounded in Eclogue 2.33 ("Pan curat oves oviumque magistros") and its mystic interpretation by Servius as a complex figure of cosmic unity and harmony. For Servius, the literal translation of the Greek name ("everything") blended with a figurative translation of the god's appearance, "formed in the image of nature," horned like the moon, goat-footed (and hence sure-footed) to "show the solidity of the earth," and with a pipe of seven reeds to match the notes in the heavenly diapason.

[6] For Naldi, see Cox-Rearick, *Dynasty and Destiny,* pp. 76, 84–85, and Alice Hulubei, "Naldo Naldi: Etude sur la Joute de Julien et sur les Bucoliques dédiées à Laurent de Medici," *Humanisme et Renaissance* 3 (1936): 169–86, 309–26. The *Rusticus* of Poliziano (henceforth anglicized as Politian) was published in 1483.

busied herself with household duties. This biblical image of the two lives, active and contemplative, will be the most unanswerable defense of Laurentian pastoral and neo-Platonic reclusiveness. And it was, as Roberto Cardini has argued, ideologically worlds apart from the work of the first generation of Florentine humanists such as Salutati and Bruni. It was certainly the effect and perhaps also the intended function of the Florentine Academy, however loosely structured and however variegated its membership, to transform the ethical and civic emphases of the early Quattrocento into a literary and poetic version of humanism.[7]

The response of later readers to this development has inevitably diverged along ideological lines, however blurred by scholarly process. Florentine neo-Platonism has had many distinguished devotees, but to those influenced by Hans Baron's studies of Florentine civic humanism,[8] or generally suspicious of any principate, let alone one that masked itself as republicanism, the school of Ficino has been viewed as an instrument of Medicean hegemony. There is something of a compromise in J. G. A. Pocock's suggestion that members of the Academy might have been as troubled by Lorenzo as Cavalcanti had been by Cosimo, faced with the contradiction between Cosimo's exemplary success as de facto head of state, achieved largely by backroom politics, and Florentine ideals of equality and participatory citizenship, which had demonstrably failed to produce a working social system. The recall of Cosimo from exile in 1434 and the complicity of the *ottimati* in Medicean ascendancy were themselves political compromises. And the philosophical emphases of Laurentian culture, Pocock thought, "may be read as attempts to restore that harmony and control in a non-civic form."[9] The ambivalences that Pocock discerned in Cavalcanti's writings about Cosimo may well have been present in Landino himself, who, as Arthur Field has noted, advised his students to separate themselves from the distractions of politics while himself attempting to become chancellor of Florence, and served as secretary to the Guelph party while completing *De anima,* his treatise on spiritual reclusiveness.[10]

We should therefore pay more attention to the formal presentation of the *Camaldolese Disputations* in time as well as in place. While the last two books were based on lectures on Virgil delivered in 1462–63, it is now

[7] Roberto Cardini, *La critica del Landino* (Florence, 1973), p. 1. See also Eugenio Garin, *Italian Humanism: Philosophy and Civic Life in the Renaissance,* trans. Peter Munz (New York, 1965; orig. pub. 1947), pp. 84–88. Garin's emphasis on the Quattrocento's intellectuals' transition from civic humanism to Platonism has conditioned all subsequent scholarship.

[8] Hans Baron, *The Crisis of the Early Italian Renaissance: Civic Humanism and Republican Liberty in an Age of Classicism and Tyranny* (2nd ed. Princeton, 1966).

[9] J. G. A. Pocock, *The Machiavellian Moment* (Princeton, 1975), pp. 97–98.

[10] Arthur Field, "The Beginning of the Philosophical Renaissance in Florence, 1454–1469," Ph.D. dissertation, University of Michigan, 1980, p. 200.

believed that the whole work was put together in 1473–74 and dedicated to Federigo of Urbino before the autumn of 1474.[11] That fact alone—the dedication to someone other than Lorenzo—might bear inspection; but the matter becomes more complicated by the backdating of the dialogue to the period between Cosimo's death and that of Piero the Gouty, when Lorenzo was still only the heir apparent. As Alberti puts it to Lorenzo at the beginning of the first discussion, "Videtis enim universam rei publicae molem propter ingravescentem parentis vestri morbum iam vestris humeris sustinendam" ("You see the whole weight of the state, on account of your father's growing sickness, already having to be supported on your shoulders," p. 10). And if this places the dialogue not later than the summer of 1469, it has also been argued that its other temporal boundary is set by a reference to "this recent war against Bartolomeo Bergamense" (p. 98), that is to say, the Colleone war of 1467–68.[12] It is impossible to be certain whether such a glancing reference was utterly cunning and precise or a chronological slip, but what was certainly deliberate was the location of Lorenzo in a pastoral world of *adolescentia,* however precocious. Indeed, Landino goes out of his way to stress the trope of youthfulness, which is mentioned more often than would seem to be required for a nineteen-year-old, especially one who had already been visible in Florentine diplomacy and whose savoir faire had recently helped to save his father from assassination.[13]

What can this have meant? The question can be approached on various levels. The first and most innocent explanation is that Landino, who had been Lorenzo's teacher, had conceived of a fictional structure that would allow him, indirectly, to continue in that role. The *Camaldolese Disputations* would thereby take their place at the head of a long list of Renaissance *enchiridia* for princes; by such a view, the dedication to Federigo of Urbino

---

[11] For the chronology of Landino's lectures, see Cardini, *La critica,* pp. 16–17, and Field, *Philosophical Renaissance,* pp. 205–6, 463–74. See also Field's report on his discovery of a manuscript related to the 1462–63 lectures, "A Manuscript of Cristoforo Landino's First Lectures on Virgil, 1462–63 (Codex 1368, Biblioteca Casanatense, Rome)," *Renaissance Quarterly* 31 (1978): 17–20. Apart from this manuscript, a student draft of the commentary on the first seven books of the *Aeneid,* the traces of Landino's Virgilian pedagogy that survive are (1) a prefatory oration delivered in the Florentine Studium in 1463 which announces a course of lectures for the coming year; (2) a second inaugural oration, perhaps for a course of lectures in 1467–68; and (3) some notes by Bartolomeo della Fonte indicating that Landino had lectured on the *Eclogues* by 1468. See Cardini, *La critica,* pp. 294–308, and his *Cristoforo Landino, scritti critici e teorici,* 2 vols. (Rome, 1974), 1: 5–15; Arthur Field, "An Inaugural Oration by Cristoforo Landino in Praise of Virgil," *Rinascimento* 2nd series, 21 (1981): 235–45.

[12] Peter Lohe, "Die Datierung der 'Disputationes Camaldulenses' des Cristoforo Landino," *Rinascimento* 2nd series, 9 (1969): 291–99.

[13] See *Disputationes,* ed. Lohe, p. 10 line 27, 11 line 25, 12 line 22, 35 line 30, 254 line 3, 262 line 21.

(along with the allusion to his management of the Colleone war) served a double purpose, both complimenting an outstandingly successful head of state and providing a model for the one who would shortly (or already had) become the ruler of Florence. A second and more disturbing scenario emerges when we stop to consider what had actually occurred in the interval that the fictional time scheme elides. In the two years between the time when Lorenzo was asked by a delegation of leading citizens to assume the position of *primus inter pares* he had reconstructed the voting system in Florence so that, in effect, all magistracies were under his control; and in June 1472 he had ruthlessly suppressed and sacked the commune at Volterra.[14] It could hardly have escaped the readers of the *Disputations* that this campaign also was commanded by Federigo of Urbino. The effect of the fictional time scheme, then, was to situate both the explicit and the implicit dedicatee in an earlier phase of decency and innocence, while permitting Landino to remain laudatory throughout.

But there may be yet a third reading of the temporal strategy, not incompatible with either the first or the second. For all the emphasis on the ultimate superiority of the contemplative life, Landino managed to incorporate into the debates a substantial amount of political commentary. The source is usually Alberti, who for Cardini and others functioned as a link between Landino and the earlier tradition of civic humanism. It is Alberti, for example, who introduces the long praise of Cicero that appears toward the end of the second book and functions as the chief example of civic virtue, especially in Cicero's attempts, so dangerous to himself, to restore constitutional government ("libertatem iam diu intermissam vel potius amissam civitati restitueret") after Julius Caesar's assassination (p. 43); and it is also Alberti who, in the process of proving that honor cannot be the *summum bonum,* remarks that it is typical of tyrants, "quot enim tyrannos, cum durissimum servitutis iugum patriae cervicibus imposuerint, iis titulis iisque insignibus honestatos videmus, quae libertatis auctoribus debentur" ("when they have imposed the hardest yoke of servitude upon their country's neck, to make themselves respectable with the titles and insignia that belong to the authors of liberty," p. 83).

The ideological pastoralism of the *Disputations,* in other words, cannot simply be dismissed as utter unworldliness or, on the contrary, political opportunism. The dialogues are more evenhanded than is indicated even by Alberti's conclusion that the Mary and Martha principles must continue to

---

[14] Even the most neutral of historians of the Volterra episode concluded that it was intended as a show of strength by Lorenzo at the beginning of his regime. See Enrico Fiume, *L'impresa di Lorenzo de' Medici contro Volterra (1472)* (Florence, 1948), p. 171. The cruelty of the sack was in striking contrast to the clemency with which Piero had treated the members of the Pitti or Neroni conspiracy in 1466.

be recognized as sisters, "ambae bonae" (p. 47). And if the dialogue admits of a small but still audible republican voice, it is easier to understand what we find in Landino's Virgil edition, a decade and a half later.

Before turning to that project, we must enter the testimony of another Virgilian property of the Medici circle, the illustrated manuscript of Virgil's works now in the Biblioteca Riccardiana at Florence.[15] This is the most lavishly illuminated manuscript of Virgil in the period, with a full-color scene at the foot of every page of the *Aeneid,* and one each at the opening of the *Eclogues* and of the *Georgics.* The format evinces some knowledge of and desire to imitate the illustrated codices from late antiquity, especially in their contribution to exegesis, by identifying the figures in each scene by name. The scribe has been identified as Niccolò Ricci, who produced at least ten manuscripts of classical Latin texts, six of which indicate their commission by a member of the Medici family. The illustrations, which are incomplete, running only through the second book of the *Aeneid,* have been definitively attributed to Apollonio di Giovanni, otherwise known as the "Dido master," and the artist of two Virgilian cassoni in the Jarves collection at Yale University.[16] Apollonio died in 1465; the manuscript is now thought to date from the early 1460s. The association of the manuscript with some member of the Medici family is to be assumed not only from the practices of Niccolò Ricci, but from the rather remarkable presence, in several of the illustrations for the *Aeneid,* of the Medici palace in Florence (Figs. 3 and 4).[17]

The representation of the Medici palace has been contested, if not precisely denied, by Ernst Gombrich, the art historian chiefly responsible for settling the questions of attribution and date. In refuting Schubring's thesis about the date and his theory that the Virgil manuscript preceded Apollonio's success as a painter of cassoni,[18] Gombrich complained that his predecessor had mistakenly identified the images of Carthage in construction as allusions to the building of the Medici palace, more or less completed by 1452. Not only was such a hypothesis rendered obsolete by the subsequent identification of the scribe, born in 1433, but, argued

[15] *Virgilius Opera Bucolica Georgica Aeneis,* Biblioteca Riccardiana ms. 492; ed. in facsimile by B. Maracchi Biagiarelli (Florence, 1969).

[16] See E. H. Gombrich, "Apollonio di Giovanni," *Journal of the Warburg and Courtauld Institutes* 18 (1955): 16–34. The identification rests in part on a poem in Ugolino Verino's *Fiammetta,* "De Apollonio Pictore insigni," a *paragone* between the sister arts, in which the "tuscus Apelles" or Apollonio is described as having surpassed Virgil in representing all the major scenes from the first three books of the *Aeneid.*

[17] Versions of the Medici palace appear in the manuscript on folios 72r, 72v, 74v, 77v, 79r, 80v, 82v, 83r, 84r, 85r, 85v, 86r, 86v. On other folios there are additional rusticated structures which do not otherwise resemble the Medici palace in either general structure or detail.

[18] Paul Schubring, *Cassoni* (Leipzig, 1915), pp. 430–37.

Figure 3. Apollonio di Giovanni, "The Siege of Priam's Palace," Riccardiana ms. 492, fol. 85r. By permission of the Biblioteca Riccardiana, Florence.

Figure 4. The Medici Palace in 1478, from *Angelo Politiani Conjurationis Pactianae . . . Commentarium, Documentis, Figuris, Notis,* ed. Joannis Adimari (Naples, 1769), p. 85. By permission of the Folger Shakespeare Library, Washington, D.C.

Gombrich, the entire argument was based on the faulty art-historical premise, common to the scholars of Schubring's generation, that Quattrocento painters were concerned with the representation of "real life." On the contrary, according to Gombrich, "Quattrocento art offers no reportage of the places and persons of the time, for it operates with types and patterns, not with individualistic portrayals." He produced as evidence that the Medici palace was not the building specified by Apollonio a "somewhat" analogous structure in a painting by Gentile da Fabriano. "In bringing this formula up to date for the representation of buildings—both complete and incomplete—in the noble city of Carthage," Gombrich concluded, Apollonio "may well have made use of the type of the Medici Palace, but this does not turn his miniatures into topographical views. Least of all need we think that the degree of incompleteness of Carthage allows us to refer back to the building history of Florence." [19]

Behind this disagreement lie contrasting biases similar to those that inform the criticism of Florentine neo-Platonism: both are structured by divergent principles of art's relationship to society. Other art historians, even of Gombrich's own generation, have believed that the type of architecture in question, denoted by the status symbol of heavily rusticated stone blocks on the first story, was recognized as having been established by Michelozzi as a symbol of the Medici and imitated on a grander scale by the Pazzi as a deliberate political statement. [20] But even those who take for granted that the Medici palace was intended by the miniaturist to be recognized have not queried that intention in its most problematic aspect: namely, that the scenes in which the palace is most clearly recognizable refer not to Carthage but to Troy, and that the Medici palace stands for Priam's palace under siege. What could it have meant to the Medicis in the early 1460s to have their own architectural symbol in Florence identified first as Carthage (which would later in Roman history be destroyed and its lands sown with salt), and then as Troy, whose immolation Apollonio graphically insisted upon? It is hard to agree with Biagiarelli that the allusion would have been seen as simply complimentary to the dynasty; [21] we might, rather, align the manuscript with the ambivalences of Landino's dialogue, as presenting a historical warning to the house of Medici, precisely lest the analogy come home to them.

---

[19] Gombrich, "Apollonio di Giovanni," p. 19. See also Ellen Callman, *Apollonio di Giovanni* (Oxford, 1974), pp. 7–11, who agrees with Gombrich on the Medici palace but dissents from his view that the work was interrupted by Apollonio's death, arguing that he frequently left work to be finished by others.

[20] See Ludwig H. Heydenreich and Wolfgang Lotz, *Architecture in Italy 1400 to 1600,* trans. Mary Hottinger (Harmondsworth, 1974), pp. 22–23.

[21] Biagiarelli, ed., *Virgilius Opera,* p. xiii, proposed that the allusion would have been seen as complimentary to the Medici because their coat of arms, a black eagle on a field of gold, appears on the palace on folio 85r, suggesting "il simbolo della potenza imperiale, trasmesso a Roma dal fondatore della stirpe italica."

In the light of this argument, the illustration of the *Eclogues* (Plate 3) is exceptionally interesting. It offers a vision of pastoral dominated by the first eclogue, with the contrast between Tityrus and Meliboeus central to an understanding of the whole. As compared to the corresponding scene in the Romanus Virgil (Plate 4), which is assumed to have classical iconography behind it, Apollonio's shepherds are realistically costumed as medieval peasants; indeed, they articulate a vocabulary of realism in detail that was to leave its mark on Virgilian illustration for decades to come. As in the Romanus, Tityrus is seated under a tree playing his pipes, while Meliboeus stands in the position of a transient, holding the horns of the goat who will accompany him into exile; but in place of the rhetorical gesture of speaker to viewer he holds the traveler's staff, and, surprisingly, turns his back on the viewer in a gesture that keeps his complaint private. The props, as it were, are historically specific—notably, the conical straw hat on the head of Meliboeus giving the traveler protection from the sun, and the bagpipes or zampogna on Tityrus's lap in striking contrast to the flute in the Romanus.[22]

But what distinguishes the miniature as a statement for its own time goes beyond a local realism of detail. Claiming the viewer's primary attention is the central figure: an attractive youth, inexplicable in purely illustrative terms, in aristocratic costume, and with an elegant little dog at his feet. No other miniature contains a character who cannot be accounted for by the text, and the young man's presence is the more intriguing for the absence here of the name that elsewhere identifies each of the figures. These anomalies make it entirely plausible, as Biagiarelli suggests, that the boy was an idealized representation of Lorenzo de' Medici, who was thirteen years old in 1462, the year that Cosimo endowed the Platonic Academy at Careggi, and whose presence as an adolescent in that pastoral world between 1464 and 1469 was so carefully delineated by Landino. The peaceful presence of the patron in the center of the culture, then, is visually dominant. But behind the protagonists, in the background, are two other images that, however minimalized, require interpretation: in the upper left, a smaller seated figure *is* playing the flute, plausibly a visual allusion to the eclogue's classical origins; and in the upper right, a figure with raised stick threatens another, a reminder that a history of violent dispossession links the first and ninth eclogues. The far from idyllic version of pastoral, then, that this manuscript offered to the Medici was recognizably in the tradition of Servian commentary.

The enterprise represented by Landino's Virgil edition of 1487, despite the contrasts he wished to draw between it and the products of the Academy, is not unrelated to what we have just seen. While the commen-

---

[22] On the bagpipes in medieval iconography, see V. A. Kolve, *Chaucer and the Imagery of Narrative* (Stanford, 1984), pp. 76–77, 402–3.

tary itself, the product of Landino's earlier lectures in the Florentine Studium, followed the line-by-line approach of Servian tradition, its preface was markedly different in form from a grammarian's *accessus* with its sharply demarcated topics, its emphasis on the poet's life and motives, on problems of intentionality, on models and metrics, all intended to explain and justify the actual nature of the detailed commentary that completed the scholarly exercise. Landino's preface begins with a humanist praise of Virgil, as the "princeps" of all who have taught us "both to speak seriously and ornately, and to live well and blessedly," but more than half of it is devoted to a history of the Medici family, addressed to the son of Lorenzo de' Medici while the father was still in control of Florence. The entire volume was thereby explicitly located in the context of Florentine politics, and while there is certainly no overt contradiction between the content and tone of this history and the picture of the Medicean hegemonist developed by Cardini, the mere fact of its presence here supports those intimations in the *Camaldolese Disputations* of a sustained political concern.

We need to consider why such a history should have been addressed to Lorenzo's heir at such a moment, and especially why Landino chose to remind Pietro (who was in four years to succeed his father, and in two more to be personally responsible for the expulsion of the dynasty) of the dangers and difficulties faced and overcome by his Medici predecessors. In particular, the history seems to problematize its laudatory premise by dwelling at considerable length on the Pazzi conspiracy of 1478, in which Lorenzo had narrowly escaped being stabbed to death and in which his brother Giuliano had in fact been assassinated. As a document, therefore, the 1487 preface invited comparison with the statements of other leading Florentine intellectuals in the aftermath of the Pazzi conspiracy. In a climate of expression suddenly polarized, the two extreme positions had been significantly represented, as Landino certainly knew, by Politian's polemic against the Pazzi and by Alamanno Rinuccini's dialogue *De Libertate,* written in 1479.[23] Rinuccini had been one of Landino's philosophical discussants, but the *De Libertate* explicitly identified the pastoral recluse as he who has abandoned civic life precisely because the Florentines, in submitting to the Medicis and allowing the conspiracy to fail, have abandoned the principles of the ancient republic. And while Landino's preface might seem to align

[23] Angelo Politian, *Della Congiura dei Pazzi,* ed. Alessandro Perosa (Padua, 1958); for a translation, see "The Pazzi Conspiracy," in Renée Neu Watkins, ed. and trans., *Humanism and Liberty: Writings on Freedom from Fifteenth-Century Florence* (Columbia, S.C., 1978), pp. 171–83; for a discussion of its hegemonic implications, including its final association of Lorenzo with Octavian via a quotation from *Georgics* 1.500, see Ida Maier, *Ange Politien: La Formation d'un poète humaniste (1469–1480)* (Geneva, 1966), pp. 358–71. For the text of Rinuccini's dialogue see *Dialogus de libertate,* ed. F. Adorno, *Atti e memorie dell'Accademia toscana di scienze e lettere 'La Colombaria'* 22 (1957): 270–303; and for a translation, see Watkins, ed., *Humanism and Liberty,* pp. 193–224.

him with Politian, there are aspects of the commentary itself that seem to lead in the other direction.

It is much to the point that this occurs in Landino's commentary on the *Eclogues,* and that it partly depends on his reading of Servius. His preface indicates a scrutiny of Servius's introduction to the *Eclogues,* and its central distinction between Virgil and Theocritus. "For what do you find in Theocritus," Landino asked,

> if you take away that propriety of speech, which the Greeks call Idiom, which he perfected with both pastoral mores and diction, what else will you find in which the Latin poet may be thought conquered by the Sicilian? Yet this I admire in Virgil as I desire it in Theocritus if it is missing. . . . For by the fiction he so concealed greater matters, that however much he did not depart from the pastoral persona, nevertheless he concealed beneath that vulgar surface another sense more excellent by far, so that the work was adorned with a double argument, and that which was obvious, he observed, and that which was hidden, he perfected.

And it certainly shows Virgil's divine nature, Landino concluded, that "he concerned himself with humble characters from the first age, so that, now and then, he both conceived those great matters intellectually and, as matters went, to some degree incorporated them in the text, in such a way that he managed to honor the generic boundaries of the pastoral."

If we glance back at the Servian distinction between writing *simpliciter* and *allegorice,* it certainly looks as though Landino was appropriating that critical vocabulary to different ends. Servius's insight into the strategic discontinuity of Virgilian allegory—"hic necessitate compulsus aliquibus locis miscet figuras" ("Compelled by this necessity, *in certain places* he mingles figures")—appears in Landino as the mysterious operation of genius, over which the only real compulsion is that of generic boundaries. Landino's repeated emphasis on the term *persona* is assimilated to the concept of pastoral decorum, rather than functioning, as it does in Servius, as a central term in a historical and biographical approach to the pastoral metaphor: "Et hoc loco sub persona Tityri Virgilium debemus intelligere" ("And in this place, under the persona of Tityrus, we ought to understand Virgil"). And in the "maiora illa," those great conceptions that Landino found in Virgil but not in Theocritus, we undoubtedly hear the language of the *Camaldolese Disputations.* Yet when it comes to the commentary Landino by no means managed, or intended, to emancipate himself from the old Roman historical patterns of exegesis, and the glosses exhibit a strange and uncertain fluctuation between philosophical and political explanation.

So the commentary on the first eclogue avoids any reference to the patronage system with its rewards and punishments and manages to slip in a gratuitous note to the effect that the host in Christian worship is so called because it overcomes our adversary the devil (A11r). Yet the gloss to the opening of the second eclogue clearly compromises between a Roman historical reading and a neo-Platonic one. Landino accepted the Servian premise that the seemingly immoral burning referred to in the opening line was really a metaphorical statement of Virgil's admiration, as Corydon, for Caesar, as Alexis. But where Servius had glossed the opening word, *Formosum,* as pertaining to Caesar "in operibus et gloria," Landino proceeded to a neo-Platonic dissertation on the nature of beauty and the distinction between *forma* and *materia* (A1v). So, too, on the fourth eclogue Landino omitted Servius's militaristic introduction of Pollio and all explanation of what it meant to Virgil to sing woods worthy of a consul. He took note of the Christian tradition, represented by Augustine, that the poem prophesied the birth of Christ, but he firmly declined to endorse the presence of Christian hieroglyphics in the poem, remarking that Virgil was "ignorant of such theology," and he concluded that the poet was "referring this happiness to Octavian" (B11v). With respect to the *puer* whose loss is mourned in the fifth eclogue, Landino again eschewed a Christian or otherwise mystical reading, finding no difficulty with the identification of Daphnis as Julius Caesar, and remarking of the disparity in their age that "Nam allegoricus sermo huius sermo huiuscemodi mutationem non aspernatur" ("allegory does not reject this kind of mutation," B5r).

Landino's account of the second eclogue includes an expansive gloss on Pan as the principle of order and harmony in nature; he remarked that Servius "has most elegantly interpreted the countenance of the god" (A5r). He therefore potentially associated his own commentary with the Laurentian iconography of Pan Medicus. This may also be the reason for a long, unprecedented, and unnecessary gloss on the name Daphnis in Eclogue III as a synonym for the laurel. Yet Landino's reminders that the laurel is an "arbor pacifera" (B1r), perpetually green, and beloved of Apollo, in fact derive directly from Pliny's account in the *Natural History* 15.40. In the process of quoting directly from Pliny Landino had cause to recall the figure of Lucius Junius Brutus, that great emblem of Roman republicanism, and how "quoniam ibi libertatem publicam is meruisset lauriferam tellurem illam osculatus" ("he won freedom for the people by kissing the famous plot of earth that bore the laurel").

But the most pertinent of these adjustments to any account of Landino's ideology occurs in the long gloss provided for the word *libertas* at Eclogue 1.27. Here something extremely interesting happened, proving among other things that Landino had deeply considered his own relationship to Servian commentary. Where Servius had written of the distinction in *language* between a slave and a man freeborn ("et aliter dicit servus, . . . aliter ingenuus") on the subject of freedom and had concluded from the lexical choice that here Virgil spoke under the persona of Tityrus about his own love of liberty, Landino converted this distinction to something more directly relevant to his Florentine audience: "aliter servus: aliter civis optat libertatem" (AIIr). A slave and a citizen would *choose* different forms of liberty, for a slave chooses manumission from his bonds, a citizen seeks to live with equal rights ("aequo jure") within the state, so that his opinions may be free ("ut libera sint judicia"). No one, unless he be in the role of magistrate, is to be served ("nemini nisi qui sit in magistratu sit serviendum"). What makes this gloss still more remarkable is Landino's move to the analysis of liberty as an abstraction, for what we expect from the philosopher at this point, that is to say, an articulation of how the intellectual may be freed from worldly concerns, does *not* appear. Instead, we hear:

> Dicitur praeterea libertas excellentia & magnitudo animi cum nullo metu coherci possumus: quin freti optima conscientia apertis verbis honestati aequitatique & publicae utilitati favemus.

> Liberty, furthermore, is a term for excellence and greatness of spirit, when we cannot be coerced by any fear. Nay rather, relying on a good conscience, with free speech, we promote that which is honest and lawful and in the public service.

The result of this meditation on liberty is only apparently to transcend the civic and historical by generalization and sublimation, for the "superior" liberty is not after all reclusive, but boldly committed to the civic and rhetorical mode of self-expression.

In this extraordinary republican moment, Landino seems to have discovered his own historical correlative to the Servian proposition that Virgil, merely by using the term *libertas,* so indecorous in the mouth of a slave, implicitly ("latenter") blamed the times. More to the point, Landino echoed the language and concerns of Florentine civic humanism. While *libertas* itself was, as Rubinstein has remarked, an ambivalent concept in Florentine usage, simultaneously connoting republican practice at home and independence from foreign rule,[24] its appearance here is controlled by vocabulary and concerns unmistakably those of the civic humanists—freedom of speech and equality of access to political office. As Poggio had written in a letter to the duke of Milan in 1438, "neither individual citi-

---

[24] Nicolai Rubinstein, "Florentine Constitutionalism and Medici Ascendancy in the Fifteenth Century," in Rubinstein, ed., *Florentine Studies: Politics and Society in Renaissance Florence* (London, 1968), p. 449.

zens nor the aristocrats rule the city, but the entire people are admitted with equal rights [*aequo jure*] to public offices; as a result of which high and low, noble and non-noble, rich and poor alike are united in the service of liberty [*conspirent in causa libertatis*]," and Rubinstein has documented the intense and frequent discussions of freedom of speech in the Parlamento of 1458 and the November councils of 1465.[25]

Landino's return to the *Eclogues,* in other words, and his close attention to the import of Servian interpretation seem to have given him another kind of freedom. His neo-Virgilian *libertas* seems to have turned into a noble echo of Bruni's *History of Florence,* in which, as Nancy Struever has argued, "*Libertas* . . . is not merely the slogan of the Florentine commune and the Guelph party; history becomes the story of liberty; the development or decline of public freedom is the strand of meaning on which all political history is made to depend."[26] It was also, of course, the subject of Rinuccini's dialogue, and Landino was surely informed that the rallying cry of the Pazzis, in the heat of the assassination attempt, had been "Libertà." We have, then, a remarkable collaboration between two kinds of linguistic selection and foregrounding: on the one hand, a body of historical facts that charge a particular word with ideological intensity; on the other, the formal procedure of selection and emphasis provided by the commentary tradition.

The entire gloss, therefore, stands as eloquent testimony to Landino's old loyalties, and a counter, however unobtrusive, to his more familiar argument that the reading of Virgil leads a man away from the active life, with all its agitations, into contemplative serenity. But what it must surely also counter, or at least complicate, are the expressions of unequivocal support for Medicean politics that Landino inserted into his prefatory address to Pietro. These included the statements that the Pazzis, in their attempt on the life of an innocent young man who had offended no one, were prepared to betray simultaneously both him and Florentine liberty ("illum simul & libertatem nostram") and that by Lorenzo's subsequent foreign policy the liberty of the republic had been snatched out of the jaws of its enemies and restored to its former splendor (*IIv). By addressing himself once again to the Medici heir apparent, Landino might again have hoped to influence the future of Florence without implying a criticism of the present. By again choosing to work by indirection—by letting Virgil's text and its interpretive tradition speak for his own earlier convictions—Landino suggested that (as Cardini said of Alberti in the same environment)

[25] Poggio Bracciolini, *Epistolae,* ed. T. de' Tonelli (Florence, 1859), p. 183, cited in Rubinstein, "Florentine Constitutionalism," p. 448; ibid., pp. 456–58.

[26] Nancy S. Struever, *The Language of History in the Renaissance* (Princeton, 1970), pp. 116–17.

his sympathies would no longer allow him to submit the intellectual's function in society to the constraints of political clientage.[27]

But we should not forget the role that commentary, as a genre, played in this process or what it signified that Landino incorporated into his edition and into his own glosses the hypotheses of Servius, whom he had admitted, even in the *Disputationes,* to be "diligentissimus omnium grammaticorum" (p. 190). In this procedure Landino not only allowed himself a certain latitude of political inference but suggested another kind of ideology, that which defines the scholarly profession and its ethos. By collaborating with Servius, Landino in effect located himself near the head of a tradition of humanist scholarship which was seen as cooperative and cumulative; this, at least, is what happened, as Landino's commentary was incorporated into subsequent editions of Virgil that carried more than one commentary. The effect of such publishing practices, of the lists of learned names featured on the title pages and of the various typographical strategies for disposing scholarly contributions around the Virgilian text, was to represent the exegetical project as a sort of permanent colloquium.

An illustration from a Venetian edition of 1508 (Fig. 5) provides another visual representation of this process: here the dynamic exegetical role of the commentator as conceived by Simone Martini for Petrarch has been replaced by a rather sober-sided community of the well-informed. Beneath the structure of patronage within which Virgil's canon was developed had grown up another structure, dependent upon the first—the structure of the academy. In this representation of the scholarly tradition, the ancient grammarians Servius, Donatus, and Probus (whose commentary was published for the first time in Venice in 1507) share the stage with the early Renaissance humanists Domitizio Calderino, Antonio Mancinelli, and Landino himself.

Indeed, Landino seemed to have anticipated and welcomed such a development, even in the *Camaldolese Disputations*. Addressing himself to the problem of intention, Landino abandoned any claim to having delivered a definitive reading of the *Aeneid,* inviting others to complete what he had begun. When more learned men, he suggested, perceive that we have not been able to do everything ("cum nos non omnia potuisse intelligent") they will both be able to correct the errors and add whatever is missing. Landino is not only willing to be emended but earnestly prays that those who are qualified to improve on his work should do so (p. 115). The disclaimer sounds sincere, and Landino framed it in terms of a quotation from Virgil's eighth eclogue, which would shortly become one of the figures of humanist discourse:

[27] Cardini, *La critica,* p. 140.

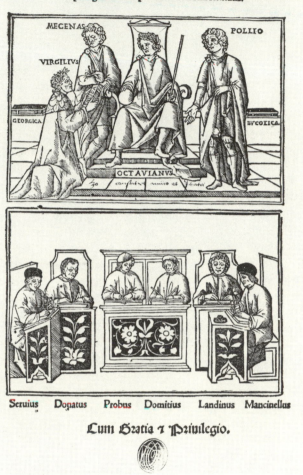

P.V.M.Omnia opera:diligenti caſtigatione exculta:aptiſſimiſeꝗ ornata figuris:
cōmentantibus Seruio:Donato:Probo:Domitio:Landino:Antonioꝗ Man
cinello uiris clariſſimis.Additis inſuper in Seruium multis:quæ dee=
rant:græciſꝗ dictiōibus:& uerſibus ꝗplurimis:qui paſſim cor=
rupte legebantur:in priſtinum decorem reſtitutis.

MECENAS   POLLIO

VIRGILIVS

GEORGICA   BVCOLICA

OCTAVIANVS

Seruius   Donatus   Probus   Domitius   Landinus   Mancinellus

Cum Gratia ⁊ Priuilegio.

Figure 5. Virgil, *Opera* (Venice: Bernadino de Portesio, 1510), frontispiece.
By permission of Princeton University Library.

Haec Damon; vos, quae responderit Alphesiboeus,
dicite, Pierides; non omnia possumus omnes.

So sung Damon; to which Alphesiboeus replied, tell me, Muses: we
cannot all do everything.[28]

In his masterly account of the scholarship of Politian, Anthony Grafton
argued that the commentary tradition inherited from Servius was rightly
displaced by Politian's own more rigorous philological method. Noting
that the line-by-line commentaries inherited from late antiquity had certain advantages, functioning both as encyclopedias of ancient culture and
as classroom tools "accessible even to students of mean intelligence or poor
preparation," Grafton nevertheless objected, as Politian had done, to the
triviality of much of the annotation, "the donkey-work of listing syn-
onyms—which is all that thousands of the humanists' short glosses amount
to," and the suppression of individuality that the method required. In what
he defined as a period of intense literary competition, the cumulative principle in the commentary tradition "made it impossible for its author to
shine."[29] This is, obviously, the obverse of the phenomenon I have just interpreted more positively as the institutional form of collaborative scholarship; the effect of such an argument on Landino's 1487 edition would be
to declare it a dinosaur.

It was Politian's desire for uniqueness, Grafton argued, that caused
him to abandon the line-by-line commentary on a classical text and replace
it with a new scholarly manifest, the separately published volume of annotations.[30] The move is all the more striking in view of the fact that Politian had earlier created for his own use what was in effect a line-by-line
commentary, working (in much the same way that Petrarch had annotated
his personal Virgil manuscript) in the margins and blank leaves of a copy of
the works of Virgil published in Rome in 1471.[31] This extraordinary document, once in the library of Fulvio Orsini and now in the Bibliothèque
Nationale in Paris, was described by Pierre de Nolhac as "a fine testimonial
of Politian's love for Virgil and an important monument, in more ways

---

[28] Compare Erasmus writing to Maarten Lips in 1518 about editorial practice: "Augustine declares that he has actually been helped by the difference between copies, since what
is obscure in one version is more clearly rendered in another; we cannot do all things." *The
Correspondence of Erasmus: Letters 8442–992, 1518 to 1519*, trans. R. A. B. Mynors and
F. F. S. Thomson, annotated by Peter G. Bietenholz (Toronto, 1982), in *Collected Works*, 6: 6.

[29] Anthony Grafton, "On the Scholarship of Politian and its Context," *Journal of the Warburg and Courtauld Institutes* 40 (1977): 150–88; see also his *Joseph Scaliger: A Study in the
History of Classical Scholarship*, 2 vols. (Oxford, 1983–), 1: 9–44.

[30] I.e., the *Miscellaneorum centuria prima* published in Florence in 1489.

[31] Virgil, *Opera* (2nd ed., Rome, 1471); Bibliothèque Nationale Inc. res. gr. Yc. 236.

than one, of fifteenth-century Virgilian scholarship."[32] While many of the notes, crammed into tiny spaces as Politian returned several times to the same page, are virtually indecipherable, it is possible to reconstruct in general terms the focus and purpose of this elaborate personal commentary.

If we assume that Politian acquired the *Virgil* soon after its publication, when he himself was eighteen, we could associate it with his own education. Alternatively, it may have been his preparatory text for the course of lectures he gave in the Florentine Studium in 1482–83 on Virgil's *Eclogues* and the *Idylls* of Theocritus.[33] One of the first stages of annotation was, clearly, the insertion, alongside Virgil's text, of the appropriate passages from Theocritus. The margins soon developed into a palimpsest of information derived from classical or late antique authors: Junius Philargyrius, Probus, Macrobius, Donatus, Servius, Pliny, Priscian, Aulus Gellius, Cicero, Caesar, Suetonius, Plutarch, Horace, Pausanias, and others. In some instances Politian indicated by the sign "Ang." that a gloss was his own contribution. The first eclogue included a long allegorical note on the nurturing aspects of the beech tree and an interlinear comment to the effect that *lentus*, the word that defines Tityrus, is to be understood as *securus*. In the fourth eclogue Politian glossed Apollo as Augustus, and, in the ninth, Menalcas as Virgil himself. Included among Politian's exegetical principles, then, was a core of commitment to the older tradition of how the *Eclogues* came to be written and what they meant as a metaphor of Virgil's own career.

This had already been unmistakably established on the blank pages that precede the *Eclogues* in this spaciously printed edition. Here Politian inserted, first, the *accessus* of Probus, which included a brief account of the historical cause behind the *Eclogues*, the expropriation of the lands of Cremona and Mantua to pay Octavian's veterans after Philippi, and the statement that while Tityrus and Meliboeus were both personae derived from Theocritus, the *Eclogues* as a whole were to be understood allegorically ("totus liber per allegoriam intelligitur"). Politian followed this with an anthology of classical authors who had spoken with reverence of Virgil: Macrobius; Quintilian (*Institutes* 1.8.5 and 10.1.85–86); Horace (*Satires* 1.10.45); Ovid (*Amores* 1.15.25: "Tityrus and the crops and the arms of Aeneas will find their readers while Rome is capital of the conquered earth"); the story in Pliny's *Natural History* 7.114 of how Augustus contravened the instructions in Virgil's will that the manuscript of the *Aeneid* was to be burned; and the still more significant story in Tacitus's *Dialogue on Oratory* 12.13 illustrating the veneration in which Virgil was held at

---

[32] Pierre de Nolhac, *La Bibliothèque de Fulvio Orsini* (Paris, 1887), p. 212.
[33] These lectures survive as rudimentary notes recorded by Politian's student Pietro Crinito, now in the Munich Staatsbibliothek, ms. Clm. 754.

Rome by the occasion on which, "hearing a quotation from the *Eclogues* in the course of a theatrical performance, the audience rose to their feet as one man, and did homage to the poet, who happened to be present at the play, just as they would have done to the emperor himself." Politian cited this passage at length, including its idealization of *otium:*

> Ac ne fortunam quidem vatum et illud felix contubernium comparare timuerim cum inquieta et anxia oratorum vita. Licet illos certamina et pericula sua ad consulatus evexerint. . . . malo securum et quietum Vergilii secessum, in quo tamen neque apud divum Augustum gratia caruit neque apud populum Romanorum notitia.

> Nor should I hesitate to contrast the poet's lot in life and his delightful literary companionships with the unrest and anxiety that mark the orator's career. For my part I would rather have the seclusion in which Virgil lived, tranquil and serene, without forfeiting either the favour of the sainted Augustus, or popularity with the citizens of Rome.[34]

But there is another side to this careful reconstruction of Virgil's own cultural environment. For Politian also carefully transcribed the text of Martial's cynical epigram to Domitian (8.56) and the preface to Sidonius's panegyric to Maiorianus, delivered in 458 in the aftermath of an insurrection in which he himself had been implicated. Martial, utterly without conviction, had recalled the image of Tityrus and the lost lands in order to remind Domitian that only patronage would produce the kind of poets that Augustus could count on; he concluded, "Ergo ego Vergilius, si munera Maecenatis / des mihi? Vergilius non ero, Marsus ero" ("Shall I then be a Virgil, if you give me the gifts of Maecenas? I shall not be a Virgil, but I will be a Marsus").[35] And Sidonius, no doubt with comparable irony, had opened his appeal to Maiorianus's clemency with an appropriation of the first eclogue that stressed imperial anger:

> Tityrus ut quondam patulae sub tegmine fagi
> volveret inflatos murmura per calamos,
> praestitit adflicto ius vitae Caesar et agri,
> nec stetit ad tenuem celsior ira reum; sed
> rus concessum dum largo in principe laudat,
> caelum pro terris rustica Musa dedit;

---

[34] Tacitus, *Dialogue on Oratory,* trans. Sir William Peterson (Cambridge, Mass., 1914), p. 49.

[35] Martial, *Epigrams,* ed. and trans. Walter C. A. Ker, 2 vols. (London, 1920), 2: 45.

That Tityrus of old under the canopy of a spreading beech might pour forth his warblings breathed into the reed, Caesar vouchsafed him in his hour of distress the right to live and possess his land, and the wrath of majesty endured not against an humble offender. But the rustic Muse, praising thus a bounteous prince for a farm restored, gave in return for that earthly boon a place in heaven.[36]

The material added by Politian to his copy of Virgil, then, created a personal preface to the canon, one that approached the work by way of the *Eclogues,* and the *Eclogues* by way of meditation on the archetypal poetic career. And he updated that model by historical extension into the first and fifth centuries, reminding himself and his friends that the patronage relationship was as continuous and as protean as the classical text.[37] We might reasonably infer that he constructed this document at the beginning of Lorenzo's primacy, when the roles of princely patron and writer-intellectual were being redefined in Medici Florence, and that its construction was connected to his version, in the *Stanze,* of Virgil's pastoral *umbra* and Servian commentary upon it:

E tu, ben nato Laur, sotto il cui velo
Fiorenza lieta in pace si riposa,
ne teme i venti o 'l minacciar del celo
o Giove irato in vista piu crucciosa,
accogli all'ombra del tuo santo stelo
La voce umil.

And you, well-born Laurel, under whose veil happy Florence rests in peace, nor fears the winds or the threats of heaven or angry Jove in his fiercest manifestation, in the shade of your sacred trunk receive my humble voice.[38]

It was prophetic of Politian's later career that his early Virgilian annotations do *not* include a gloss on the tendentious *libertas* of Eclogue 1, while in his *Manto,* dedicated to Lorenzo in 1482 and connected to his

---

[36] Sidonius, *Poems and Letters,* ed. and trans. W. B. Anderson, 2 vols. (Cambridge, Mass., 1963–65), 1: 59. Sidonius had been caught up in the chaotic reversals of power that characterized the late empire and had imprudently involved himself in a failed rebellion of Gallo-Romans.

[37] For a parallel example, compare his *Commento inedito alle Stanze di Stazio,* ed. L. Cesarini Martinelli (Florence, 1978), p. 51.

[38] Politian, *Stanze cominciate per la Giostra del Magnifico Giuliano de' Medici,* trans. David Quint (Amherst, Mass., 1979), p. 3. The *Stanze* were begun in 1475 and broken off with Giuliano's assassination in 1478.

lectures on Virgil for that year, a four-line paraphrase of the first eclogue conspicuously omits all reference to Meliboeus.[39] Such moves are consistent with the narrowing of political perspective that informs Politian's unqualified propaganda on the Pazzi conspiracy, as well as with his later concentration on the science of textual reconstruction. In the development of editorial practice, the value of Politian's innovations is unquestionable. It is also worth noting Grafton's remark that Politian erected such barriers of learning around the ancient texts that only a tiny minority of specially trained scholars might hope to engage with them; a form of esotericism that was probably as much a disincentive to civic humanism as neo-Platonic "nonsense."[40]

VIVES AND VIRGILIAN ESCHATOLOGY

Beyond philology, other scholarly revolutions were brewing. In 1519 the Spanish scholar Ludovico (Juan Luis) Vives, moved to exasperation by the outmoded Aristotelianism of the University of Paris, gave his own definition of classical humanism as he hoped to see it advancing through Europe. In the *In pseudo-dialecticos* Vives described the advent of the new learning as the restoration of intellectual freedom, significantly described in the classical language of republicanism:

> Erigunt enim se se apud nationes omnes clara, excellentia, libraque ingenia, impatientia servitutis, et jugum hoc stultissimae ac violentissimae tyrannidis ex cervicibus suis animose depellunt, civesque suos ad libertatem vocant, vindicabuntque totam prorsus litterariam civitatem in libertatem longe suavissimam.[41]

> For there arise among all nations clear, excellent, and free minds, impatient of servitude, and they are boldly shaking from their necks the yoke of this stupid and violent tyranny and calling their citizens to liberty, and they will straightaway emancipate the whole republic of letters, returning it far and wide to the sweetest of freedoms.

It was no accident that this gifted Spaniard of Jewish origin but Christian convictions would commit himself to a concept—the republic of letters and an international community of scholars—that we most readily associate with the name of Erasmus. Already, at twenty-seven, alienated

---

[39] See Politian, *Opera* (Paris, 1519), folio 85r.

[40] Grafton, "On the Scholarship of Politian," p. 183.

[41] Vives, *Opera omnia*, ed. Gregorio Mayáns y Siscár, 8 vols. (Valencia, 1782; repr. London, 1964), 3: 62.

from the country that had formally expelled the Jews in 1492 and whose Inquisition would execute his father in 1524, Vives had gone to Paris in search of intellectual independence and found nothing but rigid conservatism.[42] The language of Florentine civic humanism was, therefore, converted by Vives to the cause of educational reform, which in the minds of Erasmus and his circle would ideally transcend local political boundaries and objectives. Yet Vives would not be able to remain indifferent to the course of European politics. If the tensions perceptible in Landino's responses to Virgil may be defined as competition between two versions of early European humanism or between two ideologically distinct definitions of the intellectual in his relation to classical culture, the same may certainly be said of Vives. And it may also be said that the competing constructs were once again civic functionalism and moral transcendentalism. But the stakes had now been raised and their locale widened dramatically. By 1537, when Vives published his commentary on Virgil's *Eclogues,* the social, political, and intellectual structures of Europe had been radically transformed by the centripetal forces of nationalism and the leveling effects of the Reformation. Unlike the relatively autonomous and secure circle of clientage within an Italian principate, the intellectuals of Vives's generation could not avoid at least taking cognizance of a much larger and more disturbing field of operations.

What Vives witnessed was, first, an unseemly struggle for power among Francis I of France, Henry VIII of England, and the Holy Roman Emperor Charles V, as well as the various incumbents of the Holy See. This resulted in the Hapsburg-Valois wars over Italy during which the French king was taken prisoner by the emperor, and the disastrous conflict between Charles and the second Medici pope, Clement VII, as a consequence of which the city of Rome was sacked by Charles's German and Spanish mercenaries. In the meantime, the doctrines of Martin Luther were spreading throughout northern Europe, and from the southeast the Turks advanced across the Mediterranean basin, invading Hungary in 1526 and wiping out the army of the young king Louis II. The international confusion of values was most acutely represented by the sack of Rome in 1527, which struck at the center both of the classical Renaissance and of institutional Christianity. While Lutheran mercenaries in the imperial army defaced Raphael's *Triumph of the Holy Sacrament* in the Vatican, the pope's abandonment of the Holy City was lamented in the language of Virgil's first eclogue, as responsive as ever to shifting circumstances:

---

[42] See Carlos G. Noreña, *Juan Luis Vives* (The Hague, 1970), pp. 16–22. Noreña was the first biographer to recognize the significance of Vives's Jewish origin. His most reliable predecessor was A. J. Namèche, "Mémoire sur la vie et les écrits de Jean-Louis Vives," *Mémoires couronnées par l'Académie Royale des sciences de Bruxelles* 15 (1841).

Trist' Amarilli mia: donq'è pur vero
Che di Titiro tuo si stranamente
Vada la grege errante e li dolente
Lassi'l bel Tevere e Vaticano altiero.

Poor Amaryllis, it is thus true indeed that the flock of your Tityrus
wanders away so strangely, and sadly he leaves the beautiful Tiber
and mighty Vatican.[43]

Most shocking to humanists, whatever their nationality, was the fact that
Italian scholars had to flee for their lives and that irreparable damage was
done to libraries. At stake, then, was not only the quality of the intellectual
life but its very survival. While Vives shared with Erasmus a dislike of Ital-
ianate culture and the self-assumed superiority of Rome in its relationship
with the classical past, he also shared with men of letters all over Europe a
horror at this multiple sacrilege. His response to the sack would be expressed partly in terms of Virgil's first and ninth eclogues, the poems that
had first thematized the fragility of culture and its dependence on political
stability; and in one of his last projects, the *In Bucolici Vergilii interpretatio,* he
gave an interpretation of the *Eclogues* that was dominated by cultural and vocational anxiety, for which the only solution was to translate Virgil's own
optimism, centered in the fourth eclogue, into Christian apocalypticism.

In order to understand Vives's response to the *Eclogues,* we need to
recall certain aspects of his previous career. His relationship to England
and to English politics in the years immediately preceding Henry VIII's
break with Rome brought Vives a sharp personal awareness that the scholarly life carried with it no immunities. Invited to England by Henry in
1523, Vives spent much of the next five years there, either at court as the
tutor of the princess Mary or in residence at Corpus Christi College, Oxford, where he lectured on philosophy and rapidly became a leading authority on educational reform. In 1527 he found himself in an impossible
situation, opposed in principle to Henry's plans for divorce from Catherine
of Aragon, yet unwilling to defend the queen before the judges appointed
to pronounce on the legitimacy of her marriage. The result was the withdrawal of the small pension he received from the queen, and six weeks of
house arrest at the order of Cardinal Wolsey, from which Vives was only
released on his promise of immediate departure from the country.

Possibly there occurred to Vives at this early stage the relevance to his
own situation of Virgil's first and ninth eclogues. At any rate, both these

---

[43] André Chastel, *The Sack of Rome, 1527,* trans. Beth Archer (Princeton, 1983), pp. 92,
23. See also pp. 123–28, "The Despair of Men of Letters."

texts were to figure in what was surely his most ambitious contribution
to internationalism, his treatise *De concordia et discordia,* addressed to
Charles V. Vives's dedication to the emperor was dated from Brussels on
1 July 1529. Anticipating by just over a month the treaty of Cambrai—
otherwise known as the *paix des dames,* negotiated by Charles's aunt, Margaret, and by the French queen mother, Louise of Savoy—which brought
to conclusion the Hapsburg-Valois wars, the treatise was unquestionably
designed to influence Charles in the direction of peace. In the third book
of the *De concordia,* as part of the argument that Christian princes should
not engage in internecine warfare but should instead unite against the
Turks, Vives quoted Meliboeus's complaint against civil war: "En quo discordia cives / Perduxit miseros" (5.275). Later in the same book, in explaining the necessary relationship between culture and political stability,
he leaned on the language of Virgil's Moeris in the ninth eclogue:

> Nor can the voice of the wise man be heard in the meeting-places,
> when everything is thrown into confusion by warfare, and there is
> much tumult. "But our songs," said the Poet, "are of no more avail
> among weapons than, as they say, the doves of Chaonia among eagles."
> Nor can anything be heard inwardly, and understood, when a great
> tempest is blowing in the spirit and great shouts confound all, in those
> tumultuous conflicts in which the mind is prevented from hearing any-
> thing spoken in truth and wisdom. (5.306)

Where Virgil had permitted a moment of skepticism about Octavian's
settlement, Vives discovered for sixteenth-century Europe an entirely cir-
cular and more deeply pessimistic application. Men of letters will not be
heard, will not even be able to think clearly, when nations are at war; therefore their writings, which should lead the way to a more civilized state of
affairs, will be of no avail. Despite this sense of the writer's inefficacy, it was
to Vives's credit, especially given his recent expulsion from England, that
he tackled Charles on the subject of his attack on Rome, comparing it to
the earlier sack by the Visigoth Alaric in 410 and reproaching the emperor
(although somewhat obliquely) for a comparable destruction of libraries,
"by which studies and arts of all kinds received an indescribable wound"
(5.306–7).

     When the Virgil commentary appeared, it too was presented in terms
of a larger conception of the intellectual life. The commentary was preceded by a preface in which Vives defended the cultural significance of poetry, citing Aristotle and Greek culture as his authority and blaming the
Latins of recent history for their exclusive attention to philosophy and neglect of the Muses. Presumably Vives referred in this vague and unjust

statement to the Italians of the late fifteenth and the early sixteenth century, but his motives seem rather defensive than offensive, designed to protect his own image as a serious scholar. Having Aristotle behind him, he will himself "not hesitate to mingle such sweet remissions of the mind with severer studies, and to comment somewhat upon the festive Muses." But the chief justification for studying the *Eclogues* lies in what he has found in them, "many more sublime meanings than were recognized by the crowd of Grammarians":

> Neque enim si nihil subesset magis recondituum, quam quod verba prae se ferunt, opus ille fuisset triennali expolitione, mutuanti praesertim pleraque omnia a Theocrito Siculo. Adde quod maximiis Romanorum ingeniis illa elaborabat Cor. Gallo, Asinio Pollioni, Varo, Tucae, ipsi quoque principe Augusto, qui leviculis rebus et pastoricii sine altiore alique sententia, haud facile fuissent capti. . . . Accedit huc, quod res ipsae plerisque in locis satis testantur, non simpliciter dici, sed figurate; quo magis miror, Servium Honoratum nullas allegorias admittere, nisi de agris deperditis: quae aliis multis de rebus manifestissimae sunt. . . . Poetae etiam reddemus mentis suae scopum, et ostendemus non in rebus leviculis consumtos illi esse tot versus; et quae pastoriciae sensu Theocritus rudiori seculo cantasset, ea ipsum ad Romanos transtulisse, et quasi fecisse sua, cum intelligentia eruditis auribus digna. Non dubito quin allegoriam aliquibus versibus aptaverim, de qua Poeta ne cogitarit quidem.
>
> (2.2)

> For if Virgil had not concealed more in his subtext than the words overtly carry, he would not have taken three years to complete the work, especially given that he borrowed a great deal of it from Theocritus the Sicilian. Add to this that he addressed these matters to the greatest Roman minds, Cornelius Gallus, Asinius Pollio, Varus, Tucca, as also the prince himself Augustus, men who would never have been so taken with light and pastoral subjects without the presence of some higher meaning. Further, things themselves in many places sufficiently testify that they are not spoken simply, but figuratively, which makes me wonder the more that Servius Honoratus would admit of no allegories, except those connected with the lost lands, allegories which are most evident concerning many other matters. We shall therefore restore to the poet the full scope of his mind and show that so many verses were not reduced to triviality, and that what Theocritus had sung in a pastoral sense to a primitive age, Virgil transferred to the Romans, making them, as it were, his

own, with an intelligence worthy of learned ears. Nor do I doubt but that I have fitted to certain verses an allegory of which the Poet himself had no conception.

We may recognize in this statement a fully self-conscious and historicized hermeneutic, with something of the triple structure articulated by Petrarch. For Vives, the pastoral tradition began with Theocritus singing to a primitive age ("rudiori seculi") and was transformed by Virgil into a medium appropriate both to the Roman historical moment and for the consideration of the Roman intellectual elite, including the emperor himself; in the third stage of development, for which Vives takes personal responsibility, what was left unseen or unstated by Servius the grammarian will be revealed to the learned of contemporary Europe. The proof that an allegorical subtext is present in the *Eclogues* is both textual ("res ipsae plerisque in locis satis testantur") and contextual (those clever and important Romans must have been given something more important than pastoral songs). So the humanist scholar justifies his venture by positing an interpretive community comparable to the one he wishes to address and, in so doing, implicitly defines that later community as being made up of those with political power. Vives is clearly aware of the principle of authorial intention and realizes that his own contribution to Virgilian interpretation will sometimes be in breach of that principle, but he is also possessed of a rudimentary grasp of the counter-principle that *all* interpretation is to some degree in breach of "original" meaning and that the interpreter properly translates the text into his own cultural terms, "making it his own."

The effect of this principle on Vives's commentary is perhaps predictable. It becomes the vehicle of a Christian humanist pacificist, who reads the fourth and fifth eclogues as Christian documents. Setting aside historicist scruples as to whether Virgil could conceivably have understood the Sibylline verses as Augustine and Eusebius did or whether he was an unconscious medium of Christian prophecy, Vives declares that there is no plausible historical candidate for the wonderful child in Eclogue 4: "And therefore everything pertains to Christ, and we will interpret them accordingly. . . . Let the unbelievers be silent; for even in the simple sense of the words, utterly without any allegories, what is spoken here can certainly be understood as applying to no one other than Christ" (2.32). In the fifth eclogue Vives adopted the less absolute position that Virgil had indeed prophetically lamented the Crucifixion and the Resurrection, inspired by other Sibylline verses, but that he had mingled with them some matters of his own, out of ignorance of the true sense, so that he could square the prophecy with his own application. So the natural sympathy for Daphnis's death ("montesque feri silvaeque loquuntur," 5.28), is "an allusion, perhaps," to the portents that in Matthew 27:51 marked the moment of

Christ's expiring, when "the veil of the temple was rent in twain . . . and the earth did quake, and the rocks rent."

Vives's own intentions are especially manifest in his gloss on lines 60–61: "Wolves lay no ambush for the flocks, no nets wait to betray the deer: Daphnis loves peace." This refers to the "pax Christi," by which "exuperat omnem sensum superiorum cum inferioribus, ferocium cum mansuetis, astutorum cum simplicibus, exaequante omnia caritate, et reddente tuta omnia et secura" ("he overcomes all sense of things higher with things lower, of the fierce with the gentle, of the clever with the simple, leveling all things in charity and returning things into a state of safety and security," 2.43). Through eschatological vision and revision, therefore, Vives arrives at the ultimate justification for Christian allegory, for what was originally proposed as higher meaning is now, by the logic of Christian paradox, revealed as absolute (and omnipotent) abasement. Simplicity, demoted in Servian commentary on the *Eclogues* in favor of poetic urbanity, can be reinstated by the new dispensation as the "true" meaning of pastoral nostalgia.

Yet Vives's commentary is by no means consistently religious. Personal experience of the vagaries of patronage informs his commentary on the first eclogue with unusual emotional intensity: "Felicitas autem haec est, quod in omnium trepidatione sit quietus ipse ac securus, in periculo tutus" ("But this is happiness, that in all tumult he himself may be quiet and secure, safe from danger," 2.6). Later interpreters, especially in England, would make similar connections between *lentus* and *tutus*, giving the latter a specifically political resonance, as they made themselves safe beneath the pastoral fiction. But for Vives *otium* is only proleptically available at the end of Christian time: for the time being, his own persona is more likely to be Meliboeus. That, at least, is the effect of his gloss on "En quo discordia cives," expanded to adumbrate "not only the civil wars of Rome as a state, and in the whole empire, but even intestine to individual cities." There is also an unusually complicated and threatening gloss on the lightning-stricken oaks: Meliboeus "effugere licuisset tantam calamitatem, si quum primum viderunt fulgure ictas quercus, hoc est Brutos, Cassium, et alios Caesaris percussores proscriptos victosque, in quorum partibus Cremonenses erant, longius discessissent a contagio viciniae, tamquam a pestilentia, aut victorem conciliassent sibi aliqua oratione" ("would have been able to flee that calamity, if when they had first seen the oaks struck by lightning—that is to say, Brutus, Cassius, and the others proscribed and conquered by Caesar, on whose side the people of Cremona had fought—they had left far behind that contagion, as if it were a plague, or had managed to conciliate the victor by some speech," 2.7). The revealing slippage from singular to plural transfers these local incidents of Roman history to a larger constituency; while the ironical question of Meliboeus, "En quis consevimus agros?" becomes a lament for any situation in human experience when the fruits of our labors are enjoyed by those who are unworthy of them. An added allusion to Solomon is surely to Ecclesiastes 2:18–23: "Yea, I hated all my labour which I had taken under the sun: because I should leave it unto the man that shall be after me. And who knoweth whether he shall be a wise man or a fool? yet shall he have rule over all my labour wherein I have laboured, and wherein have shewed myself wise under the sun."

The most recent biographer of Vives has amply documented the melancholy fact that the last phase of his career, from the time of his expulsion from England to his death in 1540 at the age of only forty-eight, was a period of isolation, illness, and disillusion. This did not prevent him, as Noreña and others have recognized, from doing his most significant work in the analysis of culture and the philosophy of mind. But the admiration generated by his *De Disciplinis* (1531) and the *De Anima et Vita* (1538) has obscured his commentary on the *Eclogues,* which Noreña dismisses as probably having been written at the request of Dona Mencia, wife of Henry of Nassau, whose education Vives supervised at the court of Breda from 1537 until his death.[44] Yet the work shows no trace of adaptation to the theme of women's education with which Vives had concerned himself earlier; its strangely defensive preface shows, rather, every sign of having been wrested out of his own experience. The mere fact that he came back to the *Eclogues* at the end of his career suggests the seriousness with which he approached that project, but the preface, by explaining its address to the ears of the most learned, including "the prince himself, Augustus," places the *Interpretatio* in the same arena as the *De concordia* and makes it, as well as an elegy for Vives himself, an appeal for international accord.

SEBASTIAN BRANT: ILLUSTRATION AS EXEGESIS

Sebastian Brant (1458–1521) was a humanist-scholar of many competencies. Trained in classics and law at the University of Basel, Brant later lectured in jurisprudence there and practiced law in his native city of Strasbourg. While his satirical poem *Das Narrenschiff* won him considerable standing as a writer, his role in the transmission of Virgil to the Renaissance was at least as important. In 1502 he and the Strasbourg printer Johannes Grüninger produced a major edition of Virgil's works, along with Donatus's *Life* and the commentaries of Servius, Landino, Mancinelli, and Calderini, with more than two hundred woodcut illustrations. A Latin poem, "Sebastian Brant ad lectorem operis," indicates at least a collabo-

---

[44] Noreña, p. 111; and see, for example, H. A. Mason, *Humanism and Poetry in the Early Tudor Period* (London, 1959), in which Vives, "one of the greatest, most distinguished minds among the Humanists" (p. 263), is seen as an important intellectual influence on Ben Jonson.

rative effort between editor and engraver: "has nostras quas pinximus ecce tabellas" ("Lo, we have painted these little pictures"). This is the second of two introductory poems in which, together with a quatrain at the end of the volume, Brant explained the relationship between the text and the illustrations. While the commentary is designed for the learned, the volume is equally, through the illustrations, accessible to the unlearned: "Hic legere historias commentaque plurima doctus: / Ne minus indoctus perlegere illa potest." And the pictures were added so that we, the readers, might also see without veils, for no one has ever shown us these things so clearly before ("Charas tu quoque habere velis. / Has tibi nemo ante haec tam plane ostenderat usquam").[45] The veil obscuring Virgil's meaning is here to be withdrawn by a new, visual form of commentary, and the achievements of ancient painters—Parrhasius, Zeuxis, Apelles—are cited as authorities for the intellectual dignity and social usefulness of painting:

> Nobilis imprimis opifex: qui pingere mores
> Novit: & outinam viveret idem hodie:
> Quo pueris nostris: senibus quoque virginibusque
> Matribus ac: mores pingeret ipse bonos.

> Noble was the first artificer who discovered how to paint behavior. Would that he were alive today, so that he could paint good customs for our boys, our old men, and also our girls and matrons.

While continuing to assert his membership in a learned community, then, Brant also conceived of his *Virgil* as a revolutionary document in the dissemination of the classics, one that embodied an anti-elitist ethics of production. In this respect his program might be compared to the *biblia pauperum,* bibles crudely illustrated with woodcuts and used primarily by the *pauperes praedicatores* in Germany and the Low Countries for pedagogic purposes.[46] But while the *biblia pauperum* were in a sense anticipatory of the Reformation, Brant's own ideology, it seems, was a mixture of social and religious conservatism, combined with the broadest possible critique of abuses in both church and state.[47] In the *Narrenschiff* he inveighs against the holding of multiple benefices and the ordination of unfit, worldly priests; yet he combines under the heading of Antichrist both

---

[45] *Publii Virgilii Maronis opera cum quinque vulgatis commentariis: Expolitissimisque figuriis atque imaginibus nuper per Sebastianum Brant superadditis* (Strasbourg, 1502), folio A5v.

[46] See Max Sander, *Le Livre à figures italien depuis 1467 jusqu'à 1530,* 6 vols. (Milan, 1942), 1: xxi–xxii: "pour les illettrés, l'image devait remplacer le texte comme intermédiaire de la compréhension."

[47] For Brant's ideology and a bibliography, see *The Ship of Fools,* trans. Edwin H. Zeydel (New York, 1944), pp. 1–19, 45–54.

those preachers who take it upon themselves to interpret Holy Writ (using it, for instance, as the basis for attacks on the commercialization of penance) and the printers who make their reformist arguments accessible. Arguing against financial corruption, Brant reminded his readers, "Das Rom von hyrten gbuwen sy / Von armen burne lang regiert / Dar noch durch richtum gantz verfuhrt" ("Rome was founded by shepherds, long ruled by poor peasants, and then through riches quite undone," Section 83). Yet the most powerfully argued section in the *Narrenschiff* (Section 99: "Of the Decline of the Faith") is a defense of the Holy Roman Empire, of which his own German monarch became leader in 1486. Like Vives, but from a pre-Reformation perspective, Brant was clearly oppressed by conflicting values, his northern version of humanism a precarious compromise between the classicist's veneration for the idea of ancient Rome and his rationalist perception that all was not well with the Roman church; while a sense of menace stemming from the advances of the Turks to the outskirts of Italy, and the insidious internal invasions of Lollards and Beguines, was apparently sufficient to inhibit any coherent reformist program.

How, then, are we to understand the *Virgil*, with its explicit appeal to the intellectually underprivileged? It has been established that Brant's illustrations do indeed accomplish what he claimed for them, that they constitute a running gloss on the text of Virgil by providing a visual equivalent, in either narrative or symbolic form, for as many elements of the text as the artist could manage to incorporate into any single design.[48] As in the surviving illustrated *Virgils* from late antiquity, the characters are identified by name, clearly a pedagogic device; the designs are often erudite, including details that can only be accounted for by one of Servius's glosses; and they also sometimes "give visual articulation to images that appear in the poems as imaginary images, thus organizing mental space as real space."[49]

But if the intellectual content of the woodcuts is agreed to be sophisticated, their aesthetic status has been disputed. Their medievalism, especially in their use of "anachronistic" contemporary costume, has been deplored as being inferior to the "realistic" traditions of illustration deriving from Italy; realistic, that is to say, in the handling of anatomic detail and the disposition of landscape according to true perspective.[50] *Realism* is, however, a notoriously unstable term: one could equally well argue that Brant's designs are realistic in another sense, especially (and this is crucial

[48] See the pioneering essay on Brant by Theodore K. Rabb, "Sebastian Brant and the First Illustrated Edition of Vergil," *Princeton Library Chronicle* 21 (1960): 187–99, and the brilliant but unreliable one by Eleanor Winsor Leach, "Illustration as Interpretation in Brant's and Dryden's Editions of Vergil," in *The Early Illustrated Book: Essays in Honor of Lessing J. Rosenwald*, ed. Sandra Hindman (Washington, D.C., 1982).

[49] Leach, "Illustration," pp. 178–79.

[50] This is the prevailing argument of Rabb's essay; see also A. F. Didot, *Essai typographique et bibliographique sur l'histoire de la gravure sur bois* (Paris, 1863), where it is claimed (p. 98) that antiquity is "bizarrement travestié" in the Brant woodcuts.

Figure 6.   Sebastian Brant, "Eclogue 1," from Virgil, *Opera* (Strasbourg, 1502), fol. A1v. Lessing J. Rosenwald Collection, Library of Congress, Washington, D.C.

to the volume's intentions) in the *Eclogues,* which are unique in this early period in being given a woodcut apiece. Realism, in this sense, inheres in the attention lavished on details of costume and setting, on what we might call local color. This is especially true of the woodcut for the first eclogue (Fig. 6), where Tityrus and Meliboeus are represented in peasant costume, the former seated under a tree playing the bagpipes, the latter, in a conical straw hat and carrying a traveler's staff, in the wanderer's stance. We have seen these details before, in the Codex Riccardianus in Florence, the manuscript associated with the Medici.

The Riccardianus is in fact one of the sources of Brant's designs. We can be sure that this is so, astonishing though it seems, by noting that Brant has also followed the Riccardianus in most of the designs for the first book of the *Aeneid*.[51] His characteristic procedure was to turn to that manuscript for guidance as to what details in the text required illustration, sometimes copying actual images, especially for what I have called props, but altering the larger design so that its origins are partially obscured. He frequently condenses two or sometimes three of the Riccardianus scenes into one; thus his scene of the Trojans' arrival at Carthage after the storm combines Apollonio's representation of the ships in harbor with the subsequent portrayal of their meal on the beach. There are unmistakable debts to Apollonio, however, in Brant's representation of the three goddesses in the Judgment of Paris (Figs. 7 and 8), in the storm scenes, dominated by the puffing heads of the winds, and in Dido's feast for Aeneas (Figs. 9 and 10), where the row of pots on the shelves is only the most obvious of his imitations. Yet this imitation ceased abruptly *before* Apollonio himself ran out of time. There are no discernible connections between Brant's conception of the siege of Troy and Apollonio's Medicean translation; so that along with the unanswerable question of how Brant or his engraver got access to that manuscript goes the equally mysterious problem of why he stopped where he did.

For the first eclogue, then, Brant derived from the Riccardianus his Virgilian protagonists and their appurtenances, excluding, of course, the figure of the youthful patron; and from this point onward, because of the extraordinary success of his woodcuts, an illustrated *Virgil* is likely to include one or more of his speaking details. Thus the bagpipes and the walking staff are featured in the Venice edition of 1507 by Bernardino Stagnino, and the straw hat in the illustrated *Compendium* of the *Eclogues* produced by Crispian Passaeus in Utrecht in 1612 (Fig. 11). The last is particularly entertaining in its choice of hats, Tityrus's rustic headpiece being clearly recognizable and yet just as clearly transformed into a rakish fedora adorned with flowers; while the cityscape behind the two figures reveals another important feature of Brant's influence.

Brant's visualization of the first eclogue began with the Riccardianus, but it made a number of significant changes of greater ideological import and of equal influence on subsequent illustrators. Most striking, perhaps,

---

[51] Rabb, concerned to show that Brant approached the task of illustration "uninfluenced by a previous method" ("Sebastian Brant," p. 195), actually contrasted the Brant woodcuts with the illuminations in the Riccardianus in point of realism of perspective, without noticing the specific debts.

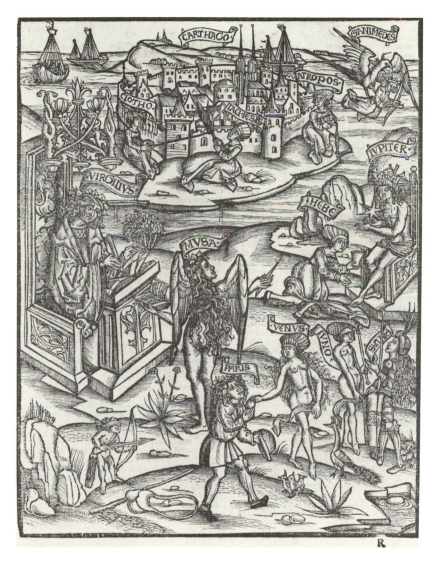

Figure 7. Sebastian Brant, "The Judgement of Paris," from Virgil, *Opera* (Strasbourg, 1502), fol. CXXI. Lessing J. Rosenwald Collection, Library of Congress, Washington, D.C.

is the visible increase in the pathos of Meliboeus's situation, his exhaustion and the distance he has traveled already manifest, while down in the left-hand corner are the two newborn kids he has had to abandon (1.15). The other marked alteration is in Brant's treatment of the background, not, to be sure, a naturalistic landscape receding according to true perspective,

Figure 8. Apollonio di Giovanni, "The Judgement of Paris," Riccardiana ms. 492, fol. 61v. By permission of the Biblioteca Riccardiana, Florence.

Figure 9. Sebastian Brant, "Dido Feasting Aeneas," from Virgil, *Opera* (Strasbourg, 1502), fol. CLI. Lessing J. Rosenwald Collection, Library of Congress, Washington, D.C.

but a representation of the two cities, Rome and Mantua, contrasted by Tityrus (1.19–25), which represent, as Eleanor Leach observed, "the political consciousness of the poem."[52] How important they are to Brant's conception of the eclogue may also be discerned in the formal arrangement of the images, for Meliboeus's newly central position in the design provides literally a pointer, his conical straw hat leading the eye upward to the other pointed forms, particularly the thatched roof of the barn

[52] Leach, "Illustration," p. 182. The cities are not, however, labeled, as Leach states they are.

Figure 10. Apollonio di Giovanni, "Dido Feasting Aeneas," Riccardiana ms. 492, fol. 75r. By permission of the Biblioteca Riccardiana, Florence.

Figure 11. Crispin Passaeus, "Eclogues 1, 2, 3," from *Compendium operum Virgilianorum* (Utrecht, 1612). By permission of Princeton University Library.

immediately above his head. Surely the inference to be drawn is that the two cities represent two different worlds, the one rustic, associated with Meliboeus and hence with the underprivileged, the other a symbol of the power to which Tityrus has access; yet both are essential to any understanding of Virgilian pastoral, with its dialectical structure and its Roman-historical origins. To judge from the *Narrenschiff*, Brant would also have expected his audience to translate this choice of environment and allegiance into an attitude toward Rome and the empire at the turn of the sixteenth century and to recognize in the plight of Meliboeus the costs of maintaining a unified and Christian Europe. The domed buildings of his Rome suggest not only, as Leach proposed, "a more foreign species of architecture," but the outlines of a Christian basilica.[53]

One other detail in this first woodcut might seem totally mysterious: the image between the two cities of a woodcutter with lifted axe about to demolish a tree. A different kind of wit than Brant's might suggest that this is a visual allusion to the illustrator's medium, the woodcut! But if we recall the Codex Riccardianus we find a better clue in the background figure brandishing a stick and threatening another, in reference to the context of violence "behind" the first and ninth eclogues. In Brant's design, civic disruption has apparently been further encoded, by way of the tradition that blended the tree of patronage with the smitten oaks that stood, in Servian commentary, for the defeated republican leaders. This dead tree, echoing in its shape the tree of patronage under which Tityrus sits, a sign of a sign, speaks something inarticulate to Brant's audience about living and dead traditions, and, perhaps, of how scholarship endeavors constantly to make the latter the former.

For the remaining illustrations to the *Eclogues* Apollonio provided no guidance. But the second eclogue especially seems to have benefited from a certain ideological spillover from the first. Leach read this woodcut (Fig. 12) as "a deliberate evocation of the lover's extravagant state of mind";[54] yet along with the presence of the courtesan-like Nympha from Corydon's fantasy, the figure who lays most claim to the spectator's attention is Thestylis, placed, like Meliboeus, in center stage. Thestylis is Virgil's agent of a quiet but ironic critique of Corydon, for it is only through *his* mention of *her* that we can recognize the contrast between the pastoral of idle solipsism and that (as represented by Meliboeus) that borders on georgic. It is through the medium of Thestylis that the activity of the harvesters can be brought to Corydon's and our consciousness, and then only in the form of a dependent clause: "Thestylis et rapido fessis messoribus aestu / alia serpyllymque herbas contundit olentis" (2.10–11). Thestylis

[53] Ibid., p. 182.
[54] Ibid., p. 181.

Figure 12. Sebastian Brant, "Eclogue 2," from Virgil, *Opera* (Strasbourg, 1502), fol. XXXIII. Lessing J. Rosenwald Collection, Library of Congress, Washington, D.C.

pounds thyme and garlic, pungent herbs, for the heat-exhausted reapers, and to Corydon she has no more significance than the green lizards hunting for shelter from the heat. But Brant's woodcut places her in the central spot from which the spokes of the composition radiate, and to emphasize her georgic and ethical function he added the reapers themselves. The point becomes clearer if we consider what items of this imaginative landscape Brant chose *not* to represent: neither Pan, nor Corydon regarding his image in the water, nor all the flowers and fruits that have so engaged the affection of twentieth-century readers. Again, Brant started an illustrative tradition. His reapers appear, for example, in the 1612 *Compendium* and also in Franz Cleyn's engraving for John Ogilby's *Virgil* of 1654; while in Aert Ortkens's manuscript drawing (Fig. 13), the whole of Brant's composition has been translated into the artistic vocabulary of late sixteenth-century Dutch realism and transformed into an allegory of labor versus luxury.[55]

The woodcuts for the remaining eight eclogues are ideologically less distinct and apparently without subsequent influence. For the fourth eclogue Brant eschewed all representation of the Golden Age and instead presented a straightforward reading of the poem as compliment to Pollio on the birth of his son Saloninus, both of whom are carefully identified. His fifth eclogue avoids both a Roman-historical reading and Christian allegorization. There is no sign of the apotheosis that turns the poem back toward optimism and that would later be brilliantly exploited by Franz Cleyn; instead the audience is faced with a bleak and massive sarcophagus, inscribed with the Virgilian epitaph "Daphnis ego in silvis." It would not be unreasonable to conclude that Brant's reading of Virgil was considerably starker than that of Apollonio di Giovanni, however important the original point of contact and however he may have intuited a subtext in the visual language of clientage. Brant's eclogues are anti-idyllic and unsentimental to a degree unprecedented in Virgilian illustration, as they were also unprecedented in discriminating *between* their different versions of pastoral.

The *Eclogues* therefore carry unusual weight in the volume as a whole—an effect that Brant surely intended, for at the end of his edition he explained once more, and in highly significant language, the relation of image to text, of his own edition to previous conventions of pedagogy:

Virgilium exponant alii sermone diserto
Et calamo pueris tradere et ore iuvent.
Pictura agresti voluit Brant atque tabellis
Edere eum indoctis rusticolisque viris.

---

[55] Aert Ortkens, manuscript drawing, Ashmolean Museum, Catalogue Parker 1938, I no. 65. Ortkens, also known as Aert van Ort, began his career in Anvers in 1513.

Figure 13. Aert Ortkens, "Virgil, Eclogue 2," ink drawing. By permission of the Ashmolean Museum, Oxford.

> Let others explain Virgil in eloquent speech and be pleased to hand him down to boys both in written and spoken form; Brant wished to publish him for unlearned and peasant folk in rustic pictures and drawings.

The entire program, then, can be understood retrospectively as a version of pastoral, which Brant defined as the language of the common people and which he read in a way that was peculiarly sympathetic to them. Reading Virgil's *Eclogues,* we might say, brought out in Brant the popularist and reformist instincts that were also present in the *Narrenschiff* but were there in conflict with religious and political conservatism.

In conclusion to this sketch of the commentary tradition, we may note how Brant responded to the iconographic challenge of the *Georgics*, which in the Codex Riccardianus was simply represented by a gentle scene of ploughing. Although many of Brant's illustrations to the *Georgics* similarly derive from medieval books of hours, the woodcut that initiates understanding of the *Georgics* is once again demonstrably symbolic. In the center of the radial composition are the competing gifts to mankind of Neptune and Pallas Athene, respectively the horse, symbol of war, and the olive, tree of peace and georgic prosperity. It was, of course, Servius who had glossed the brief mention of Neptune's horse in *Georgics* 1.13–14 with a full-scale account of the *fabula* of divine contest, adding the statement that "Minerva iacta hasta olivam creavit, quae res est melior conprobata et pacis insigne" ("Minerva by casting her spear created the olive, which has proved to be a better thing, and sign of peace"). It is no coincidence that this gloss, with its natural affinity to pastoral theory and cultural history, should reappear in one of the glosses to Spenser's *Shepheardes Calender,* which was, as we shall see, indebted to Brant in more ways than one, and not least, I think, in the conception of the pastoral woodcut as that which speaks to the people, however the poet himself must have access to education and its privileges.

Reopening the Green Cabinet: Clément Marot and Edmund Spenser

The "green cabinet" is surely the most celebrated of the quotations from Clément Marot that Edmund Spenser built into *The Shepheardes Calender.* Its presence in the "December" eclogue signifies that that closing poem is largely a paraphrase of Marot's *Eglogue au roy, soubz les noms de Pan & Robin,* where Marot, as Robin, addresses Pan, or Francis I, in his "vert cabinet." Now *The Shepheardes Calender* is the book that in English literary history most closely resembles Virgil's *Eclogues.* Its presentation as a coherent "eclogue-book," its elaborate provision of glosses by a certain E.K., its woodcuts at the head of each of the twelve eclogues: all suggest a holistic attempt to replicate in English the cultural phenomenon that Virgil's text had become, a phenomenon that combined the aesthetics of book production, the politics of self-representation, and a historically constituted system of textual exegesis. Clément Marot left no such structure. Yet the poem that had pride of place in his first collection of poems was his translation of Virgil's first eclogue, and the echo of his "vert cabinet" is only one of many indications in the *Calender* that Marot stood for Spenser as an intermediary between himself and Virgil. As E.K. put it in a characteristically obfuscating gloss to "January," even Spenser's pastoral pseudonym, Colin Clout, has a complicated precedent that includes Marot along with the native Skelton: "But indeede the word Colin is Frenche, and used of the French Poete Marot (if he be worthy of the name of a Poete) in a certain Æglogue. Under which name this Poete secretly shadoweth himself, as sometime did Virgil under the name of Tityrus."[56]

I propose here to reconsider the Virgilianism of Marot and Spenser, for several reasons. First, they each and together represent a version of Renaissance humanism that would have been inconceivable and unnecessary without the Reformation and that shows how elastic our conception of humanism in the sixteenth century must necessarily be. Second, the connection between them has not been interrogated hitherto with any persistence, in part because Marot's English reputation has been regarded as insignificant and as accurately reflected in E.K.'s condition, "if he be worthy of the name of a Poete."[57] Instead, I shall argue, Marot's status as an early supporter of the Reformation in France virtually guaranteed him Spenser's admiration, both for his verse paraphrases of the Psalms for the Geneva psalter and for his personal history as a Lutheran exile. Beyond this, it was the connection made by Marot between his Protestantism and his reinterpretations of Virgil that made him for Spenser a challenging and provocative model, one that affected the whole emotional tone of the *Calender*, giving it its melancholy and wintry aspect. Finally, as my readers will no doubt already be wondering what relation such an argument might bear to Thomas Rosenmeyer's *The Green Cabinet*, this argument will come to terms both with Rosenmeyer's essentially modernist and idealist position and with its most strenuous competitor in post-modernist theory of pastoral, that of Louis Adrian Montrose.[58] Both these powerful critics have produced views of the *Shepheardes Calender* that will have to be adjusted in the light of the series Virgil-Marot-Spenser and of Renaissance Virgilianism as already surveyed here.

Our key term, *cabinet*, is a word by no means innocent or transparent, despite E.K.'s (dis)ingenuous gloss to the effect that it is merely the diminutive of "cabin." One of its connotations was, certainly, a rustic summer-

---

[56] *The Poetical Works of Edmund Spenser*, ed. J. C. Smith and E. de Sélincourt (Oxford, 1912), p. 422.

[57] See Anne Lake Prescott, *French Poets and the English Renaissance* (New Haven, 1978), pp. 1–36. Being dependent on actual references to Marot in England, Prescott's careful influence study did not report inferences, and she therefore concluded that his "reputed Protestantism" failed to win him sympathy in England. Such analysis as there is of Spenser's debt to Marot is perhaps typified by Nancy Jo Hoffman, *Spenser's Pastorals* (Baltimore, 1977), who argued that Marot only understood Virgil "remotely" and that Spenser echoed Marot only to dissociate himself from the pastoral of state (pp. 34–40).

[58] Thomas Rosenmeyer, *The Green Cabinet: Theocritus and the European Pastoral Lyric* (Berkeley and Los Angeles, 1969), Louis Adrian Montrose, "Of Gentlemen and Shepherds: The Politics of Elizabethan Pastoral Form," *ELH* 50 (1983): 415–59, and Montrose, "'Eliza, Queene of shepheardes,' and the Pastoral of Power," *English Literary Renaissance* 10 (1980): 153–82.

house or bower, as in Spenser's designation of Guyon's mission against the Bower of Bliss: "their cabinets suppresse."[59] Yet even here there is a trace of contamination by other meanings, senses in which artfulness, privacy, or secrecy may be present, separately or together. As a private chamber of the privileged, for reading, writing, or keeping one's treasures, we find it in Rabelais's *Gargantua* (1532), in a context suggestive of the artful confusion of art and nature, inside and outside: "Toutes les salles, chambres et cabinetz, estoient tapissez en diverses sortes, *selon les saisons de l'année*. Tout le pavé estoit couvert de *drap verd*" ("All the rooms, chambers and cabinets, were hung with tapestries varied *according to the seasons of the year*. All the floor was covered with green carpet," chap. 55; italics added).[60] These green cabinets are recreational; as a private place for conducting business, especially of state, *cabinet* could acquire a more tendentious meaning. In Francis Bacon's essay "Of Counsels" we find a critique of "the doctrine of Italy, and practice of France in some Kings' times," the introduction of "cabinet councils" for the sake of secrecy, a remedy, Bacon added in 1627, "worse than the disease."[61] Yet for Agrippa d'Aubigné, one generation younger than Marot, the word could also stand for human mental space:

> La memoyre heureuse qui leur faict
> Ses contemplations metre en son cabinet
> Leurs resolutions, chose qui rend facile
> Pour mediter souvent la chose difficile.[62]

> Benign memory, who produces thoughts, stores their essences in her cabinet, a process that often makes the most difficult material available for meditation.

I have selected these instances of polysemy not only to show how exclusive was E.K.'s gloss, but also because this is a plausible collocation of meanings in which pastoral already had a special interest. Indeed, in d'Aubigné's configuration of the terms *memory, contemplation,* and *meditate* as operations which define the human mental cabinet, we see something of the semantic potency that resides in Virgil's *umbra, meditaris, resonare,* thoughts, echoes, figures, shadows, all the lexical apparatus by which we try to catch the mind at work: "souvent la chose difficile."

---

[59] Edmund Spenser, *The Faerie Queene* II: xii: 83. Note that Spenser's victim of the Bower is named Verdant.

[60] François Rabelais, *Gargantua,* in *Oeuvres complètes,* ed. Jean Plattard, 4 vols. (Paris, 1955), 1: 185.

[61] Francis Bacon, *Essays,* ed. S. H. Reynolds (Oxford, 1890), p. 148.

[62] Agrippa d'Aubigné, *Oeuvres complètes,* ed. E. Reaume and F. de Caussaude, 6 vols. (Paris, 1873–92), 3: 440.

How much of this was conceivable to Marot in 1538, when he addressed his *Eglogue au roy* to Francis I, with the salient request, "Escoute ung peu, de ton vert cabinet, / Le chant rural du petit Robinet?"[63] The clearest, if not necessarily the most direct, route to an answer is by way of Marot's biography, from the moment he entered the household of Francis's sister, Marguerite of Angoulême, later queen of Navarre, in 1519, to the period of his second exile, when he fled to the protection of Calvin in Geneva. For what marks the career of Marot as a writer, what gives his Virgilianism its resonance, is the way circumstances and his own behavior shuffled him from one side to another of the Virgilian pattern of "lots," fortunate and unfortunate shepherd, protection and exile. In many ways his career strikingly predicted that of d'Aubigné, who narrowly escaped the massacre of Protestants on St. Bartholomew's Day in 1572 and who in 1620 also fled to Geneva for protection from the consequences of his publications. While Marot never achieved the range and power of d'Aubigné as an analyst and critic of the French wars of religion, his eclogues do have a sociopolitical cause and the color, however cautious, of dissent.

As a member of Marguerite's staff, Marot began his career under the protection of an educated woman known to be sympathetic to the reformist, if not to the schismatic, elements of Lutheranism.[64] But in 1525 the Medici pope Clement VII (en route to his own disaster) addressed a letter to the Parlement of Paris, urging them to combat the spreading heresy, and the queen mother, Louise of Savoy, ordered the papal bull to be put into execution. In March 1526 Marot was arrested and imprisoned, perhaps on the pretext that he had eaten meat in Lent, a gesture perceivable as symbolic defiance of the Catholic church and as support for the anti-ritualist preacher Aimé Maigret.[65] This experience produced Marot's first major critique of the ecclesiastical establishment, *L'Enfer*, in which he represented himself as a prisoner at the bar in the underworld and presenting, in self-defense, an account of himself and his beliefs. Central to this credo was wordplay on his personal signatures. Marot explored ironically the relationship between the given name, Clément, he shared with the persecuting pope, and its latinate meaning, clemency. As for his surname:

Il tire à cil du Poete Vergille,
Jadis chery de Mecenas à Romme:
Maro s'appelle, & Marot je me nomme,
Marot je suis, & Maro ne suis pas;

[63] *Clément Marot: Oeuvres lyriques*, ed. C. A. Mayer (London, 1964), p. 343.
[64] P. Jourda, *Marguerite d'Angoulême* (Paris, 1930); P. M. Smith, *Clément Marot: Poet of the French Renaissance* (London, 1970), pp. 49–51.
[65] C. A. Mayer, *Clément Marot* (Paris, 1972), pp. 83–131, esp. p. 130; P. M. Smith, *Clément Marot*, pp. 71–73.

Il n'en fut oncq' depuis le sien trespas;
Mais puis qu'avons ung vray Mecenas ores,
Quelcque Maro nous pourrons veoir encores.[66]

It derives from the poet Virgil, whom Maecenas formerly cherished
in Rome: Maro he was called, and I am named Marot, Marot I am,
and Maro I am not; after death he was no more; but since we have
now a true Maecenas, we may hope to see again some other Maro.

We should not underestimate the importance for Marot of this symbolic nominalism, this recognition of a patronymy, in both senses, that is
embedded genetically in the structure of his language, in what French culture has inherited from Roman culture. In his dazzling study of onomastics
in the French Renaissance, François Rigolot remarked that "Marot's du-
plicity discovers in the similarity between names a *syntax* that, it is claimed,
rules the world." But while he applauded the panache of the gesture,
Rigolot, from the perspective of a post-Saussurian critic, declared it a sign
of a contest in Marot's mind between words and things, "une querelle entre
le nominaliste et le réaliste."[67] I believe it to have been, rather, a sign of the
special character of Marot's humanism, in which his budding Protestantism, his ideals of learning and respect for antiquity, his interest in interpretation (which would eventually lead him to translate the Psalms), and
his commitment to the French language all coalesce in an intense focus on
words, a textuality that is never oppressed by the incapacity of words to
mean, even though, with the help of "la duplicité marotique," they may
mean more than one thing at a time. And in a present tense that assumed
what he desired, Marot appealed to Francis I to reincarnate Augustus: "O
Roy heureux, soubs lequel sont entrés / (Presque périz) les lettres & Let-
trés!" ("O happy king, under whom are returned [almost eradicated] both
letters and lettered men!").[68]
  Released from prison through the influence of Marguerite, Marot succeeded to his father's place in the king's household, to enter on a period of
royal favor such as he proleptically described in *L'Enfer,* which was in the
meantime discreetly withheld from publication. It was from this secure
position that he launched his first collected edition of poems, the *Adolescence Clémentine,* precisely dated 12 August 1532. The first item in this
volume was Marot's translation of Virgil's first eclogue, stated in the au-

[66] *Clément Marot: L'Enfer, Les Coq-à-l'âne, Les Elégies,* ed. C. A. Mayer (Paris, 1977),
p. 16.
  [67] François Rigolot, *Poétique et onomastique* (Geneva, 1977), pp. 66, 67.
  [68] *Clément Marot: L'Enfer,* ed. Mayer, p. 16.

thor's preface to have been "translatée (certes) en grande jeunesse," an assertion that has been taken completely at face value by subsequent readers.[69] Yet if we wonder why Marot seems so insistent ("certes") upon the youthfulness of his translation, the answer may be that he had come to see it, whenever produced, as having a special pertinence to his situation in 1532, for Marot's situation now resembled that of Tityrus, while others suspected of Lutheranism, such as Jacques Le Fevre, were already in exile. Moreover, in March 1532 Marot had again been charged by the ecclesiastical authorities with eating meat in Lent and had again been saved from prison by Marguerite's intervention. As one of the lucky ones, Marot must have known that he held his place precariously; with a peculiar mixture of bravado and caution, he published the eclogue and held back *L'Enfer.* "Amour de liberté," that which had propelled his Tityrus to Rome, restricted Marot to protest by allusion, while the trope of juvenilia, of prematurity, was invoked to give him another kind of protection.

Yet the volume clearly contained poems that no stretching of the term *adolescence* could contain. His elegy for Louise of Savoy, who died in 1531, when Marot was thirty-four, was the first formal eclogue in French literature, and everything about it registers it as an expression of French vernacular humanism, including the strenuous wordplay by which the Arcadian landscape and topoi are literally translated into France. Thus the "francs Bergers, sur franche herbe marchans" are free/French shepherds who walk on fresh/French grass, a statement which was not intended to be merely playful.[70] The two pastoral speakers named in the eclogue's elaborate title are "Colin d'Anjou & Thenot de Poictou"; it is worth noticing, too, that Colin (whom E.K. assumed to be Marot's persona) lists his own place of origin among the French locales whose response to the death of Louise is expressed in puns on their names. Amboise, the king's residence, "en boyt une amertume extreme" ("drinks a deep bitterness"), but Anjou, oddly, "faict jou" ("plays games"), as does Angoulême, birthplace of Marguerite (lines 160–61). The play on names, crucial to French nationalism in the same sense that Francis I signifies his country, permits the expression of local divisions of feeling. *Jouer sur les mots* means to equivocate. As premier poet of the French court, Marot was now in a situation of having to formalize the lament for a woman who had been largely responsible for the persecution of himself and his fellows. Anjou plays games indeed, using the convenience of a ready-made system of reference in which ideals of liberty were culturally embedded, alongside and perhaps in tension with ideals of peace. The real claim of Louise to Marot's regard was that she had negotiated the peace treaty of Cambrai that permitted her to be described

---

[69] *L'Adolescence Clémentine de Clément Marot,* ed. V. L. Saulnier (Paris, 1958), p. 14.
[70] *Oeuvres lyriques,* p. 329.

in Augustan terms as "la Bergère de Paix" (line 240); but in the tradition of writing *latenter* about Octavian's injustice Marot also played on the right of the French to freedom, a right built into their name as a nation.

According to Mayer, Marot's elegy for Louise went directly back to the Greek sources of the pastoral elegy and took from Virgil "only a few of the least important details."[71] One of these details, however, an unmistakable quotation from Virgil's first eclogue, may be more important than it seems. When Colin speaks of the portents that should have warned him of the queen's death, he speaks in the superstitious voice of Meliboeus:

> Ha, quand j'ouy l'autrhyer (il me souvient)
> Si fort crier la Corneille en ung Chesne,
> C'est ung grand cas (dis je lors) s'il n'advient
> Quelcque meschef bien tost en cestuy Regne.
>
> (lines 181–84)

Ah! now I remember how I heard the other day the raven crying so loudly in an oak; it will be by great luck (I said then) if we don't have some mischance, very soon, in this kingdom.

On the one hand, to recall the voice of Meliboeus was to invoke Lutheran exiles like Jacques Le Fevre; on the other, it was to quote his own Virgilian translation and hence to reveal, not its naïveté, but its cultural self-consciousness:

> Ha Tityrus (si j'eusse esté bien sage)
> Il me souvient que souvent, par presage,
> Chesnes frappez de la fouldre des cieulx
> Me predisoient ce mal pernicieux:
> Semblablement la sinistre corneille
> Me disoit bien la fortune pareille.[72]
>
> (lines 37–42)

Ah, Tityrus, if I had been wise, I would have remembered, as a portent, how often lightning-struck oaks foretold this pernicious evil: likewise the sinister raven told me truly of a similar fate.

The very question of priority and origin is here literally inscribed, in the relation between *sage* and *présage*, *dire* and *prédire*, along with the depen-

---

[71] *Clément Marot, Oeuvres lyriques,* ed. Mayer, p. 26.

[72] *L'Adolescence Clémentine,* p. 18. I find the translation more knowing than did Alice Hulubei, *L'Eglogue en France au seizième siècle,* p. 50; it is unfortunate that Mayer, who grouped together all the other eclogues in his edition of the *Oeuvres lyriques,* should not have included the translation among them.

dence of a sense of origin on an act of memory ("Il me souvient"). What this chain of linguistic echoes also tells is that not only texts but *fortunae*—career-patterns and real experience—often recall (*souvent/souvient*) each other. In the mirror of the translation, the elegy for Louise intensifies its relationship to Virgilian tradition and permits a more complicated meditation on the cultural effects of her death.

As it turned out, the intermittent campaign against the Lutherans was not coterminous with Louise, in part because the more extremist reformers seemed determined to provoke confrontation. In October 1534, pamphlets were distributed in the streets of Paris and Amboise, where the king resided, attacking the ceremony of the mass. The enraged Francis was easily persuaded to take extreme measures against all suspects. Officers were sent to Marot's home at Blois. He escaped to Navarre, but his books and papers were seized, and in January 1535 his name was listed in a royal proclamation of those condemned to banishment from French territory. He did not return to Paris until 1537, having finally taken advantage of the general amnesty offered by Francis to all who would formally abjure their Protestantism and promise to live in future "comme bons & vrays catholiques." Marot's formal abjuration has, of course, considerably obscured his ideological trail.

A new edition of the *Adolescence Clémentine* had appeared in 1536, an exile's edition, published in Antwerp and containing an outspoken *Epistre au Roy, du temps de son exil a Ferrare*. In this poem, our key term *cabinet* appears as the meeting-place of two concepts which, we may infer, had governed his poetics hitherto: the idea of poetic immunity from censorship, and the ideal of intellectual liberty of interpretation, a direct consequence of the Lutheran approach to scriptural exegesis. Marot complained to the king about the seizure of his books and papers at Blois:

> . . . o juge sacrilege,
> Qui t'a donné ne loy ne privileige
> D'aller toucher & faire tes massacres
> Au cabinet des sainctes Muses sacres?
> Bien est il vray que livres de deffence
> On y trouva; mais cela n'est offence
> A ung poëte, a qui on doibt lascher
> La bride longue, & rien ne luy cacher,
> Soit d'art magicq, nygromance ou caballe;
> Et n'est doctrine escripte ne verballe
> Qu'ung vray Poëte au chef ne deust avoir
> Pour faire bien d'escripre son debvoir.[73]

---

[73] *Clément Marot: Epîtres*, ed. C. A. Mayer (London, 1958), pp. 202–3.

> O sacrilegious judge, who gave you the legal right or privilege to go
> tampering and wrecking in the cabinet of the sacred Muses? It is true
> that they found forbidden books there; but that is no offense in a
> poet, who should be allowed a long rein and have nothing hidden
> from him, whether it be magic, necromancy, or cabalism; there is no
> doctrine, written or spoken, that a true poet should not understand
> in order to do his duty as a writer.

The cabinet sacred to the Muses, then, is a symbol both of intellectual privacy and of artistic liberty. For General Chambor, who wrote his own epistle
in response, Marot's defense of "la liberté de scavoir" was tantamount to an
admission of heresy,[74] and indeed it was immediately followed, in the *Epistre au Roy,* by an argument for the right of the Christian intellectual to
judge for himself between good and bad books, true and false doctrine, by
testing his "sens d'eslire" against the "sacre sens" of "l'escripture."

The enclosure of these statements in a poem seems partially to have
gained Marot's point about poetic immunity; for he received back his place
as the king's *valet de chambre* and was once again recognized as the official
poet of the French court. The most palpable signs of his acceptance were a
new edition of his *Oeuvres,* published in 1538 by special royal privilege,
and the royal gift of a house near St. Germain. It was in response to this
royal generosity that Marot composed the *Eglogue au Roy, soubz les noms de
Pan & Robin,* his third French eclogue,[75] and the one in which the cabinet
reappears with a different coloring (green)—defined now as the pastoral
center, or shrine of Pan, that is to say, the court, or perhaps the privy chamber, of Francis I.

Like the pastoral elegy for Louise of Savoy, the *Eglogue au Roy* is an
anthology of pastoral quotations, but in selecting his pretexts Marot was
once again going beyond mere textual archeology. It opens with a subtle
synthesis of Virgil's first and second eclogues:

> Ung pastoureau qui Robin s'appelloit
> Tout à par[t] soy nagueres s'en alloit
> Parmy fousteaulx (arbres qui font umbraige);
> Et là tout seul faisoit, de grand couraige,
> Hault retentir les boys & l'air serain,
> Chantant ainsi: O Pan dieu souverain,

---

[74] *Epistre de general Chambor, le printemps de l'humble esperant* (Paris, 1536), cited by
Mayer, ed., *Epîtres,* p. 203.
[75] He had written an intermediate pastoral to celebrate the birth of Renée de France's
third child in 1535.

Qui de garder ne fuz oncq paresseux
Parcs & brebis & les maistres d'iceulx.[76]

A shepherd named Robin lately went wandering in isolation among
beeches (trees that provide shade) and there all alone, with great
courage, made the woods and the air echo, singing like this: O Pan,
sovereign god, who never wearies of protecting folds and flocks and
their masters.

The setting, in the shade of beech trees, and the song that makes the woods
echo identify the speaker as Tityrus; his isolation, signaled by repetition
("Tout à part . . . tout seul"), aligns him also with Corydon; the address to
Pan as he who guards folds and flocks and those in charge of them is a
direct translation of 2.33, "Pan curat oves oviumque magistros." Such
echoes are appropriate to a poem whose first level of significance (which is
already a second level) is an expression of gratitude to a royal patron. But
this does not remain a poem of security unquestioned. Transforming the
seasonal structure of Mantuan's sixth eclogue into a sociopolitical argument for change rather than a metaphor for the natural unavoidability of
sorrow, Robin appeals to Pan to protect him from the coming of a winter
of discontent. Birds of harsh voice now threaten the approach of the cold
season, "triste yver, qui la terre desnue," (1.222); his flocks huddle together and seem to beg the poet to appeal to Pan on their behalf. If Pan
will continue his protection, promises the poet, his pipe, which has been
hung up on an oak ("a ung chesne pendue") will be taken down again, and
he will sing again, in security ("a seureté"). For poetry's continuance the
poet needs to be assured that the favor he now enjoys will not be taken
from him.

Marot's response to the Virgilian dialectic, in other words, was sufficiently alert to its cultural transferability to produce a new story, in which
the lots of the fortunate and unfortunate shepherd might alternate in a
single life (or the life of a nation, perhaps). On the basis of this perception
we can better understand the function of his other major quotation from
Virgil in the *Eglogue au Roy*. In the center of his paraphrase from Jean
Lemaire de Belges,[77] and in the process of merging the paternal shepherd
with old Janot (his real father, Jean Marot), Marot inserted his own version
of the Virgilian idyll in its purest and only possible form: hypothesis. Virgil made this the most poignant contribution of Meliboeus—the capacity

---

[76] *Oeuvres lyriques*, p. 343.
[77] Jean Lemaire de Belges, *Oeuvres*, ed. J. Stecher, 4 vols. (Louvain, 1882), 1: 133–52.

to describe for all time the value of what one cannot have. In Marot's poem this responsibility is transferred to the father-figure, who proposes that idyll is attainable, again under certain conditions. Worship Pan, so went the paternal advice, and teach the landscape to echo ("rechanter") his name:

> Car c'est celluy par qui foisonnera
> Ton champ, ta vigne, & qui te donnera
> Plaisante loge entre sacrez ruisseaulx
> Encourtinez de flairans arbrisseaulx.
> Là, d'ung costé, auras la grande closture
> De saulx espes, où, pour prendre pasture,
> Mousches à miel la fleur sucer iront,
> Et d'ung doulx bruit souvent t'endormiront:
> . . . .
> T'esveillera aussi la colombelle,
> Pour rechanter encores de plus belle.

(lines 85–102)

For it is he who will make your field, your vine, bear harvest, and who will give you a pleasant dwelling among the sacred streams surrounded by sweet-smelling shrubs. On the one side you will have the great enclosure of thick willows, where the bees go to suck the flowers, and with their sweet noise often lull you to sleep; and the dove will waken you, to sing again all the more sweetly.

One could argue that by framing this passage as a promise of goods within the tactful poet's reach Marot had eliminated (or failed to understand) the ironies of its presentation in the original. But in fact the language of his translation suggests the opposite. "La grande closture" is his addition, a phrase which illuminates the enclosed status of the passage as a premise rather than a promise. The repetition of "rechanter" at beginning and end also bespeaks both boundaries and echoes. These elegant lexical adjustments (no translation can do justice to the syntactical ambiguity of that "encores") suggest that classical imitation has become its own theme. The Virgilian echo is itself doubly nested in French culture, within the remembered speech of Marot's father inside a quotation from Jean Lemaire de Belges.

This reading of the *Eglogue au Roy* must be strengthened by the fact that after Marot's death there was discovered among his papers its companion piece. *La Complaincte d'un Pastoureau Chrestien*, published in Rouen in 1549, announces in the remainder of its title that the Pan of this poem is God himself.[78] Its opening lines, however, establish a clear intertextual relationship to the *Eglogue au Roy*:

---

[78] *Oeuvres lyriques,* p. 56. It was first attributed to Marot in a Paris edition of 1558.

Un pastoreau n'agueres je escoutois,
Qui s'en alloit complaignant par les boys,
Seul, & privé de compagnie toute,
N'ayant en luy de plaisir une goute.[79]

Lately I heard a shepherd who went lamenting through the woods, solitary, and quite deprived of companions, nor having the slightest pleasure in himself.

The sad shepherd in this poem has therefore to be understood in terms of Marot's habit of self-quotation, but he is also to be seen as a correction of Virgil's. However initially solitary, he laments primarily on behalf of others, his "compaings," unmistakably the Lutheran exiles, who have suffered "pareille amertume" (lines 220–23) and who are now "peregrins en region loingtaine" (line 49). His references to his own exile, leaving behind his wife and infant child ("ton humble bergerette, / Et du petit bergeret qu'elle alaicte," lines 103–4), are offered in order to establish his claim to the role of witness. The poem's object is to enable Pan to observe the injustices taking place in his realm; then, promises the complaining shepherd, "Mon flageolet, à un chesne pendu, / Sera aussi proprement despendu" (lines 295–96).

The opening and closing connections between the *Complaincte* and the *Eglogue* would seem to settle the question of Marot's authorship of both.[80] It follows that, no matter when the *Complaincte* was written, the period of exile referred to was that of 1534, when Marot did leave behind a newly married wife. If he wrote it in 1534 and withheld it, its quotation in the *Eglogue* has the effect of making that already subtle construct more subtle still, giving body to those premonitions of a winter of discontent and explaining his most significant change in its Virgilian opening, for "umbraige," as a rhyme, was there significantly modified by "couraige," the solitary voice in the shade of the pastoral metaphor daring to speak out, but only so far as the convention of literariness will permit.

If, however, the *Complaincte* was written after the *Eglogue*, the most likely date for its composition was during Marot's third and final exile. In August 1542, Francis set out letters patent for a hunt for Lutherans. Marot's *Trente Pseaulmes* had been authorized for publication by the Sorbonne, but in early 1542, Etienne Dolet, perhaps overconfident, had issued the first French edition of *L'Enfer*. Whether or not this was the cause, by the end of that year Marot had taken refuge in Geneva under the protec-

---

[79] *Oeuvres lyriques*, pp. 390–91. Mayer, however, separates the poems by consigning the *Complaincte* to an appendix.

[80] Mayer, *Oeuvres lyriques*, p. 57, declared that it was equally impossible to prove it authentic or apocryphal.

tion of Calvin; the next edition of his Psalms carried a preface by Calvin. From that moment Marot's identification with radical Protestantism was unavoidable. When he wrote from exile an adaptation of Virgil's fourth eclogue on the birth of the Dauphin, he represented himself explicitly as "l'infortuné Berger," the only excluded celebrant at an occasion "dont la Gaule est si gaye."[81]

By the middle of the century, then, the pastoral *marotique* had taken a significant step in reconceiving Virgilian tradition, uniting the pastoral of state with the strain of anticlerical satire derived from Petrarch, Boccaccio, and Mantuan. By revealing the dilemma of a Protestant humanist who believed in an ideal of vernacular Neoclassicism and in an Augustan environment for the arts, yet who found those ideals unsupported by his own Catholic monarchy, Marot had updated the already capacious dialectic of Virgil's first eclogue and rendered it even more eloquent to the post-Reformation reader. What particularly distinguished Marot's Virgilianism was his subtle and continuous meditation on the first eclogue, with its opportunities for insight into the ethical problems of dependency and privilege. His grasp of pastoral as the language of exile he shared with Petrarch and Sannazaro, but he added to it a personal gloss on the inevitable predicament of the intellectual, the problem of mediation between the self "tout seul" and the community, particularly the community at risk. And he especially exceeded his Italian predecessors by his fix on the ontology of imitation itself, his sense of the memorial and reflective function of quotation as echo.

What, then, did Marot as a model mean to Spenser when not only the "vert cabinet" but the whole of the *Eglogue au roy* attracted his attention? It is not always noted that "January," as well as "December," bears the imprint of Robin's address to Pan, framing the poem in a cold wind blowing from the continent. References to Marot also figure prominently in E.K.'s commentary, which despite (or because of) their imprecision suggest a larger influence still. Marot is the only French poet mentioned in E.K.'s epistle, along with Theocritus, Virgil, Mantuan, Petrarch, and Sannazaro. The "November" elegy for Dido is stated to be an "imitation of Marot his song, which he made upon the death of Loys the frenche Queene," although the textual resemblance there is marginal when compared to that between "December" and the *Eglogue au roy,* about which E.K. says nothing at all. No mention is made of the fact that the emblem of this poem, "La mort ny mord," was the motto under which Marot published his *Oeuvres* of 1539. And the use of the name Roffy in "September" is ex-

[81] *Oeuvres lyriques,* p. 354. Georges Guiffrey suggested that the prophetic text so resecularized concealed an ironic subtext supporting the claim of his Genevan psalter to be restoring the golden age of *sacred* verse, and that Marot had chosen the Virgilian model precisely because its interpretive history could suggest such a critique while protecting him from its consequences. See his *Les Oeuvres de Clément Marot,* 5 vols. (Paris, 1876–1911), 1: 546.

plained as "the name of a shepehearde in Marot his Ægloge of Robin and the Kinge," when in fact it occurred in the elegy for Louise. At the very least, this unreliable commentary seems designed to drive the reader back to Marot's work, where a certain initial puzzlement might have led to further inquiry.

We can safely assume that Spenser accepted Marot as a model for constructing the pastoral of state, or, more precisely, for adapting to the needs of a modern European nation the Virgilian strategy of address to those in power. So the "Romish Tityrus," as E.K. himself put it, "by Mecaenas means was brought into the favour of the Emperor Augustus" (p. 459). We must also now recognize that Marot represented a more problematic example of that process than even Virgil himself, one that considerably extended the terms of confrontation within the forms of accommodation. Spenser would certainly have been informed of Marot's reputation as a figure of embattled Protestantism, by virtue of his own involvement in Van der Noot's *Theatre for Worldlings*, his first literary venture.[82]

We should also take into account the current state of English-French relations, a context to which another of E.K.'s glosses makes significant allusion. In commenting on the fable of the fox and the kid in "May," E.K. underlined the topical meaning of its anti-Catholic satire: "the morall of the whole tale . . . is to warne the protestaunt beware, howe he geveth credit to the unfaythfull Catholique: whereof we have dayly proofes suficient, but one most famous of all, practised of Late yeares in Fraunce, by Charles the nynth." He spoke, of course, of the massacre of the Huguenots on St. Bartholomew's Day in 1572, that hideous breach of contract for which the French house of Valois, and specifically Charles IX under the influence of his mother, Catherine de Medici, was held responsible. In 1562 the English had signed the treaty of Hampton Court with the Huguenot rebels and had themselves been driven out of Le Havre a year later; yet at the time Spenser was constructing *The Shepheardes Calender* Elizabeth was negotiating marriage with a member of that fatal dynasty, Francis, duke of Alençon, Charles IX's brother. It would be fair to say that these negotiations were creating the first major rift between Elizabeth and her public. Sir Philip Sidney, to whom the *Calender* was dedicated, wrote a bold letter to the queen advising against the match.[83] Even as the *Calender* was being completed, the country saw a striking example of what hap-

---

[82] Six of the sonnets that Spenser contributed to Van der Noot's *Theatre for Worldlings* (1569) were translations of Marot's translations from Petrarch. On Van der Noot's Protestantism see Carl Rasmussen, "'Quietnesse of Minde': *A Theatre for Worldlings* as Protestant Poetics," *Spenser Studies* 1 (1980): 3–27. The Protestantism of the *Calender* has been scrupulously defined by David Norbrook, *Poetry and Politics in the English Renaissance* (London, 1984), pp. 59–90.

[83] *A Discourse of Syr Ph. S. to the Queenes Majesty Touching Hir Marriage with Monsieur* survives in a number of manuscripts but was first published in 1663. See *The Complete Works of Sir Philip Sidney,* ed. A. Feuillerat, 4 vols. (Cambridge, 1912; reprinted 1969), 3: 51–60.

pened to those who spoke out publicly against the French connection. On October 13, 1579, John Stubbs, author of *The Gaping Gulf, Whereinunto England Is Like to Be Swallowed by Another French Marriage,* his publisher, and his printer were all tried for seditious libel and sentenced to lose their right hands. The printer, Hugh Singleton, who somehow escaped this punishment, then proceeded to publish the *Calender.* By citing a French poet as one of his major models, then, but by choosing one whose ideology set him retroactively more clearly among the victims than the protégés of the French monarchy,[84] Spenser placed himself in a position with respect to the pastoral of state that was consistent with his choice of patron (Sidney) and his connections (through Singleton) with the oppositionist press.

The precise nature of that stance was to be defined primarily by the structure of the *Calender* itself, in which the contrasting eclogues, the pseudo-Servian commentary, the woodcuts, and the seasonal structure all played a part. The reader who opened *The Shepheardes Calender* in 1579 would have known instantly that the strange composite work he held in his hand, whatever it was, was ideologically complex.[85] E.K.'s opening epistle seems to address both international humanists and linguistic nationalists, courtiers and the general public. The presence of the commentary, scholarly to the point of pedantry, contrasted with the woodcuts, which were reminiscent not only of popular almanacs but also of Sebastian Brant's great *Virgil,* with its double audience of the learned and the unlettered. The new poet's persona, as defined in the opening gloss to "January," also looked two ways, for if Marot was an authority in the new genre of Protestant poetry, the "ragged" rhymes of Skelton's *Colin Clout* had served, among other clerkly purposes, to defend the Catholic church against the invasions of Lutheranism.[86] The very structure of the *Calender* was presented from the first as something about which rational persons could have different positions, the debate on the January versus the March opening of the year serving, among other things, to alert the reader to the choice here made and its historical and aesthetic consequences.

---

[84] We might note particularly Spenser's *avoidance* of another French pastoral model, that of Ronsard. In 1565 Ronsard had responded to Catherine de' Medici's overtures of friendship toward Elizabeth by dedicating to the English queen his *Elégies, mascarades et bergeries* and by explaining its function as a tribute to the "amitié et fidelité tresassurée" of the two monarchs. See Francis M. Higman, "Ronsard's Political and Polemical Poetry," in *Ronsard the Poet,* ed. Terence Cave (London, 1983), pp. 275–82.

[85] Ruth Samson Luborsky, in "The Allusive Presentation of *The Shepheardes Calender,*" *Spenser Studies* 1 (1980): 29–68, sees it as alluding to the mixed precedents of Renaissance editions of Virgil, Aesop's fables, and the *Kalendar and Compost of Shepherds,* Bruce R. Smith, "On Reading *The Shepheardes Calender,*" *Spenser Studies* 1 (1980): 69–93, sees it as a merger of classical eclogue, medieval almanac, and Renaissance pastoral romance.

[86] Skelton attacked those members of the clergy who were "somewhat suspect / In Luther's sect" or who talk of that "heresiarch / Called Wicliffista." See *The Complete Poems of John Skelton Laureate,* ed. Philip Henderson (London, 1931: rev. 1948), p. 266.

A similar but more exacting balance appears to have been struck in the *Calender* between two versions of nationalism: that which could be expressed in whole-hearted appreciation of Elizabeth, and that which admitted the anxieties of the Protestant activists grouped around Sidney, Leicester, and Walsingham, whose power at court and even whose access to Elizabeth had been severely encroached upon by the French marriage negotiations. Spenser's response to this division in his loyalties is articulated in the symmetrical relationship, asserted by several intertextual echoes, between the "April" and "November" eclogues. The first was a simple eulogy to Elizabeth, unmistakably glossed as such by the woodcut, which showed the queen surrounded by ladies of her court playing musical instruments, an identification further confirmed by the poem's "argument." The elegy for Dido in "November," however, was presented by E.K. as the most enigmatic and profound poem in the series: "he bewayleth the death of some mayden of great bloud, whom he calleth Dido. The personage is secrete, and to me altogether unknowne, albe of him selfe I often required the same." And, remarking that this poem was an imitation of Marot's elegy for Louise of Savoy, E.K. added that it is "farre passing his reache, and in myne opinion all other the Eglogues of this book." The suggestion implicit in this comment is that "November" concerns the death of a queen, and in 1961 it was in fact so interpreted. In a systematic attempt to uncover the topical significance of the *Calender,* to which E.K.'s comments give such provocative presence, Paul McLane read "November" as an allegorical expression of grief at the prospect of the French marriage, by which, it was argued, the queen would to all intents and purposes be dead to the nation. McLane adduced in support of his hypothesis the Virgilian equation between the names Dido and Elissa, suggesting that the "April" and "November" eclogues were the two sides of Spenser's ambivalent view of his sovereign.[87]

From the perspective of Spenser's Virgilianism, McLane's hypothesis deserves more respect than it has generally achieved.[88] For it is only if we consider Dido as a dark foreboding of what Elizabeth might become that the formal structure of the *Calender,* and indeed the entire project that it represents, becomes fully intelligible. That is to say, the contrast between "April" and "November" represents two views of the English cultural situation, with the more somber one, given the circumstances of 1579, prevail-

---

[87] Paul E. McLane, *Spenser's Shepheardes Calender: A Study in Elizabethan Allegory* (Notre Dame, Ind., 1961), pp. 27–60. The contemporary identification of Dido with Elizabeth was confirmed at her death by John Lane, whose pastoral *Elegie upon the Death of the High Renowned Princesse, Our Late Souveraigne Elizabeth* combined obvious quotations from "April" and "November." See Helen Cooper, *Pastoral: Mediaeval into Renaissance* (Ipswich, 1977), p. 209.

[88] I refer solely to the context of the French marriage. McLane needs to be read selectively. Much of his allegoresis is over-detailed and hence fallible; and note the objection of Norbrook, *Poetry and Politics,* p. 61, to McLane's argument for Spenser's religious conservatism.

ing. For Spenser to function as the second English Tityrus (with Chaucer as the first) he needs not only a Maecenas but an Augusta. In the "April" eclogue (significantly the fourth in the series, in imitation of Virgil's "Pollio") Elizabeth is given the primary qualification for that role, namely, that she has brought her country peace, symbolized by her crown, not of flowers, but of olives: "Olives bene for peace, / When wars doe surcease: / Such for a Princesse bene principall," Spenser commented. For good measure E. K. added his own version of the Servian gloss on *Georgics* 1.11–13:

> The Olive was wont to be the ensigne of Peace and quietnesse, eyther for that it cannot be planted and pruned, and so carefully looked to, as it ought, but in time of peace: or els for that the Olive tree, they say, will not growe neare the Firre tree, which is dedicate to Mars the god of battaile, and used most for speares and other instruments of warre. Whereupon it is finely feigned, that when Neptune and Minerva strove for the naming of the citie of Athens, Neptune striking the ground with his mace, caused a horse to come forth, that importeth warre, but at Minervaes stroke sprong out an Olive to note that it should be a nurse of learning, and such peaceable studies.

Yet as the *Calender* moves on through the seasonal cycle, this spring-like optimism is replaced by an increasingly gloomy cultural prognosis. The "October" eclogue which presents to Cuddie, as "the perfecte patterne of a Poete," the stages of Virgil's model career for him to follow, also declares that it cannot be replicated:

> But ah Mecaenas is yclad in claye,
> And great Augustus long ygoe is dead:
> And all the worthies liggen wrapt in leade,
> That matter made for Poets on to play.

> (lines 61–64)

"November" offers an example of one such "worthy," whose formal relationship to Eliza is marked by the substitution of a different kind of wreath: "The water Nymphs, that wont with her to sing and daunce, / And for her girlond Olive braunches beare, / Now balefull boughes of Cypres doen advance" (lines 142–44). "December" closes the cycle by returning to Marot's *Eglogue au Roy* and accepting from it only what is unrelievedly depressing. In "January" Colin breaks his pipe; in "December" he hangs it upon a tree, unconditionally. And at precisely the point where Marot had incorporated into his conditional praise of Francis/Pan an echo, suitably ironic, of Tityrus's idyll as conceived by Meliboeus—including the hypothesis that *otium* will be accompanied by nature's lullabies—Spenser translated the dream into nightmare:

> Where as I was wont to seeke the honey Bee,
> Working her formall rowmes in Wexen frame;
> The grieslie Todestoole growne there moght I see
> And loathed Paddocks lording on the same.
> And where the chaunting birds luld me a sleepe,
> The ghastlie Owle her grievous ynne doth keepe.

(lines 67–72)

In the English winter, poetry is effectively discontinued.

Here again the woodcuts contribute to the argument, directly but subtly. It has been recognized for some time that the woodcuts for the *Shepheardes Calender* must owe something to earlier traditions of Virgilian illustration and specifically to Sebastian Brant.[89] And while some question has been raised as to how to relate the comparatively small and simple cuts of the *Calender* to Brant's large and complex designs, there is at least one contemporary translation of Virgil's *Eclogues* that provides an intermediary stage of reduction and simplification. In a 1540 *Oeuvres de Virgile* produced in Paris, containing the earlier translation of the *Eclogues* by Guillaume Michel, the first eclogue is illustrated by a small woodcut (Fig. 14) that clearly reverses and condenses Brant's, retaining what the artist understood as the crucial semantic items: the contrasting figures of leisure and exile, the two cities in the background, and the mysterious woodcutter.

In Spenser's "January," also (Fig. 15), there are versions of the two cities, Rome on the left having recovered two of its pointed towers but also having gained, unmistakably, a section of the Colosseum; but the woodcutter has disappeared, only to reappear in a slightly different posture in "February" (Fig. 16). While this visual quotation is not without significance for Spenser's fable of the oak and the briar, its chief importance for this argument is in showing how closely Spenser too was working with the dialectical structure of Virgil's first eclogue. While his Colin is identified as Tityrus by virtue of his possession of the broken bagpipes, his *stance* in "January" identifies him also as Meliboeus: upright, leaning on a crook which resembles the exile's walking staff, beneath a leafless tree which can afford him no protection, Spenser's shepherd is one whose happy days are over, whose journey is about to begin. Poised uncertainly between Tityrus and Meliboeus, between the poetics of accommodation and the poetics of dissent, Spenser presented himself (anonymously) to the English public as a mutant in the Virgilian tradition mediated by Marot, and in self-fulfilling

---

[89] Smith, "On Reading *The Shepheardes Calender*," pp. 80–84.

Figure 14. "Eclogue 1," from Virgil, *Oeuvres* (Paris, 1540). By permission of Princeton University Library.

prophecy he predicted the great paradox of his later career—that the greatest representation of Elizabethanism as a national ideology should be offered to the country by the exile who had promised to sing no more.

As Spenser's Augusta, Elizabeth's beneficent influence is limited in the *Calender,* partly because she must reincarnate both Caesars, the rising star of Eclogue 4 and the dead shepherd, however apotheosed, of Eclogue 5, but also because her relationship to English culture must be inferred from the relationship of Spenser's pastoral practice to Marot's. By choosing Marot's *Eglogue au roy* as his frame, Spenser demanded from his readers an ability to translate one metaphorical system into another, a personal explanation of Colin's melancholy into a national one. By going significantly beyond his French model in pessimism, Spenser also showed how well he understood the special character of Marot's Virgilianism, its network of internal pressures and anxieties that were specific to French culture at the very beginning of the Reformation. And in his later knowledge of Marot's own career and his sense of how that career fitted into the recent history of French/English relations, Spenser proceeded in his rewriting of Virgil still further in the direction that Marot had shown him. It may be true that "La mort ny mord" and that the meaning of Colin's missing emblem (why is it missing?) in "December" is that "all thinges perish and come to theyr last

Figure 15. Edmund Spenser, "January," *The Shepheardes Calender* (London, 1579), fol. 1. By permission of the Henry E. Huntington Library, San Marino, California.

Figure 16. Edmund Spenser, "February," *The Shepheardes Calender* (London, 1579), fol. 3. By permission of the Henry E. Huntington Library, San Marino, California.

end, but workes of learned wits and monuments of Poetry abide for ever."
But it is also true that the first significant English pastoral of state (for that
is what the *Calender* surely was) is dominated by the unhappy, and not the
fortunate shepherd.

The French marriage question was not the only issue on which the
Calender might seem to have been taking a dangerous position, however
cautiously. Spenser's position on the character and government of the English church is also, unmistakably, part of his subtext and goes considerably beyond the generalized anti-Catholic satire of "May," disclosing itself
in "August" as a marked sympathy for the reformist and radical wing of
English Protestantism. In "May," "July," and "August" the authority deferred to is no longer either the Romish Tityrus or the English one, but the
figure of Algrind, whom Thomalin cites as a major critic of worldly and
ambitious ecclesiastics. It has long been recognized that Algrind is a barely
concealed representation of Edmund Grindal, archbishop of Canterbury,
and that his alarming fate when an eagle drops a shellfish on his head, so
that "now astonied with the stroke, / he lyes in lingring payne" (lines 227–
28), refers to his punishment by Elizabeth for refusing to suppress the
radical "prophesyings" or unauthorized meetings of ministers to discuss
the interpretation of biblical texts.[90] In other words, by keying his anti-
clerical eclogues, "May," "July," and "September," to a local confrontation
between Elizabeth and her senior bishop, Spenser provided a contemporary and national equivalent to both the pre-Reformation critiques of the
Roman church by Petrarch, Boccaccio, and Mantuan and the early embattled Protestantism of Marot.

The first Elizabethan pastoral of both church and state, then, was distinctly equivocal in structure and expression, and nothing is more equivocal in the *Calender* than its own commentary, that peculiar mutant of the
familiar commentary of Servius. Where Servius had preeminently explica-
ted Virgil's meanings and motives, while at the same time observing that
Virgil had criticized Octavian's policies *latenter,* the prefatory epistle and
notes to the *Calender* serve mainly to alert the reader to the presence of
mystery and enigma. "Now as touching the generall dryft and purpose of
his Æglogues," wrote E.K., "I mind not to say much, him selfe labouring
to conceale it" (p. 418). In his account of the "generall argument of the
whole booke," E.K. follows his famous classification of the poems into

---

[90] John Strype, *The History of the Life and Acts of . . . Edmund Grindal* (London, 1710),
Appendix 3, pp. 74–85. Strype's biography was, however, intended to recuperate Grindal's
reputation and thus deemphasizes any "Inclination in him towards a Discipline in this Church
different to what was established" (p. iii). Compare Patrick Collinson, *Archbishop Grindal
1519–1583: The Struggle for a Reformed Church* (Berkeley and Los Angeles, 1979), pp. 18–
19, for Strype's own political contexts and the connection of his work on Grindal to the notorious Sacheverell trial of June 1710.

plaintive, moral, and recreative by the statement that "to this division may every thing herein be reasonably applyed: A few onely except, whose speciall purpose and meaning I am not privie to." Comments of the same provocative kind appear throughout the *Calender* in both glosses and arguments, climaxing in the already cited argument to "November" and augmented by a gloss which insists again that Dido's identity, as that of the "great shepheard" who chiefly mourns her, are "unknowen and closely buried in the Authors conceipt." It need hardly be said that these are the strategies of a discourse that cannot risk either full transparency or incomprehensibility, and that the new function of the commentator in the native pastoral of state is *not* to explain but, on the contrary, to incite the reader to interpretive speculation.

It was precisely this quality of enigma and discretion that was emphasized in Elizabethan pastoral theory (such as it is) that followed the *Shepheardes Calender*. The earliest comments came from a person with an obvious interest in the *Calender*, Sir Philip Sidney himself. In his *Defence of Poesie,* probably written in 1580, Sidney built into his cumulative defense of the poetic genres an account of pastoral that was not only Virgilian in focus and political in inference but peculiarly limited to the first eclogue and its dialectical structure:

> Is the poor pipe disdained, which sometimes out of Meliboeus' mouth can show the misery of people under hard lords or ravening soldiers? and again, by Tityrus, what blessedness is derived to them that lie lowest from the goodness of them that sit highest; sometimes, under the pretty tales of wolves and sheep, can include the whole consideration of wrongdoing and patience.[91]

The sociopolitical force of this passage resides in the connection between living "under hard lords" and writing *under* a pastoral veil, a less benign explanation for the pastoral of state than is found in contemporary French criticism.[92] So too the primary emphasis on Meliboeus suggests repres-

---

[91] *An Apology for Poetry,* ed. Geoffrey Shepherd (London, 1965), p. 116. See also my *Censorship and Interpretation* (Madison, 1984), pp. 29–30, for Sidney's theorization of pastoral in the two versions of his *Arcadia*.

[92] Compare Thomas Sebillet, *Art poétique françoys,* ed. Félix Gaiffe (Paris, 1910; reprinted 1932), pp. 159–61, where the eclogue is defined as that which treats "under a pastoral premise and language deaths of princes, calamities of the times, alterations of republics, happy successes and events of fortune . . . under so clear an allegory that the designs . . . are made clearly visible, as a painting is perceived under its glass" ("soubz propos et termes pastoraus, mortz de Princes, calamitéz de temps, mutations de Republiques, joyeus succés et evenements de fortune . . . soubz allégorie tant cláre, que lés desseins . . . lés facent voir clérement, comme s'apperçoit la peinture soubz le verre"). The Servian veil of political allegory has here been made perspicuous, crystallizing to a "verre" that needs no withdrawal. For Sebillet, apparently, a political subtext is not seen as threatening to the system or the poet.

sion, and even the elliptical account given of Tityrus suspiciously connects his "blessedness" to his capacity to keep a low profile.

A decade after the *Calender* was published, when the vogue for Elizabethan pastoral of all kinds was at its height, an *Arte of English Poesie* was published by an anonymous author, later agreed to be George Puttenham. He offered a definition of pastoral that was even more clearly than Sidney's an updating of the Servian hermeneutic:

> the poet devised the Eglogue . . . not of purpose to counterfait or represent the rusticall manner of loves and communication; but under the vaile of homely persons, and in rude speeches to insinuate and glaunce at greater matters, and such as perchance had not bene safe to have disclosed in any other sort, which may be perceived in the Eglogues of Virgill, in which are treated by figure matters of greater importance then the loves of Titirus and Corydon.[93]

Puttenham's emphasis on what "had not bene safe" is threatening from the points of view of both the poet and the state, suggesting that the political subtexts of Elizabethan pastoral were more likely to have been seen as subversive than as legitimating.

This account of the *Shepheardes Calender,* it will by now be apparent, runs considerably athwart of two other powerful impulses in the pastoral theory of our own century. The first is modernism, which has been on the whole hostile to, or at least depreciatory of, any version of pastoral that takes its primary valence from sociopolitical cause and content. This brings me back to Thomas Rosenmeyer, one of the most influential exponents of a modernist theory of pastoral. In his preface to *The Green Cabinet* Rosenmeyer explained the origins of his title:

> Theocritus does not, as a rule, call his pleasance green, nor does he think of it as an enclosure. But "green cabinet" caught my eye when I read it in Spenser's "December," as "*vert cabinet*" had caught Spenser's eye when he found it in Marot's "Eglogue au Roy." It is the sort of phrase which is at home on a title page. And, with a bit of squeezing, it can be made to fit the *locus amoenus* of Greek pastoral poetry.[94]

It is perhaps unfair to catch a critic in a confidential moment and hold him to its consequences. Yet this accidental catching of the eye is revealing, connecting the green cabinets of Marot and Spenser with an account of pas-

[93] George Puttenham, *The Arte of English Poesie* (1589), ed. G. D. Willcock and A. Walker (Cambridge, 1936), pp. 38–39.
[94] Rosenmeyer, *The Green Cabinet,* p. vii.

toral tradition dominated by the concept of "green thought" or world-avoidance, as Marvell encapsulated that concept in *The Garden*. And in fact the squeezing that goes on in *The Green Cabinet* extends beyond the choice of title, for Theocritus is made the norm of pastoral theory and all non-Theocritean pastoralists, especially Virgil, are moved as far as is possible by redescription in the direction of that norm. It is stated in the final chapter that Theocritus and Virgil are *alike* in avoiding allegory, in avoiding any form of representation that has designs on the reader. "Neither the poet nor the poem is in the business of therapy, or social adjustment or ideological conversion" (p. 280).

This credo produces, on the one hand, negative evaluations of early Renaissance pastoral, of Petrarch, Boccaccio, and Mantuan, for creating "closet poetry, esoteric and inbred, a development . . . which makes a sham of the original mandate of the genre" (p. 274), and, on the other, wishful thinking. The writers of the High Renaissance, according to Rosenmeyer,

> went back to the pre-Virgilian writers and discovered Theocritus' combination of detachment and immediacy. Sannazaro, Montemayor, Sidney, even Spenser, yearn for the pure air of pastoral innocence, doctrinal or ideological innocence, that is. In spite of the satire of the church in "May," "July" and "September," the pastoral art of the *Calender* is relatively free of the pervasive symbolisms that we associate with the Middle Ages.
>
> (p. 273)

Wherever ideological innocence may reside, it is not here, in these statements. And if we squeeze firmly in the other direction, by putting less emphasis on the significance of "green" and more on the semantics of "cabinet," we can come closer to the actual texture of the *Calender* as I have described it. "How our Poete is seene," E.K. reminds us, depends on whether the reader is "privie to his study" (p. 466). And the cabinet, in one sense, is Spenser's study, the space filled with books, the place pastoral as he understood it could be written. The *Calender* and its glosses are the record of a considerable education. But the second meaning of the cabinet is, surely, that it is "privie," a place of secrets. The function of E.K.'s apparatus is not only to present the English "eclogue-book" and its producers as "the equal to the learned of other nations" (p. 418), but also to reveal *by failing to reveal* the mysteries of the text. A modernist reading can take no notice of such strategies, lest attention be drawn thereby to another structure of meaning less innocent of ideological commitment.

There is a third meaning of "cabinet" relevant to this argument, one conveniently suggested by Puttenham's *Arte*. In discussing successful relationships between poets and monarchs Puttenham mentioned not only Virgil and Augustus but how "Frauncis the Frenche king made . . . Clement Marot of his privy Chamber for [his] excellent skill in vulgare . . . Poesie" (p. 16). Here is the cultural space to which any serious poet might aspire, the place of "cabinet councils," though not quite in the Baconian sense. And it is this space which has been most interesting to the criticism that followed modernism, a criticism which sees pastoral, once again, as primarily a discourse of power relations.

In the case of Elizabethan pastoral, the leading exponent of this position has been Louis Adrian Montrose, who fastened upon the *The Arte of English Poesie* as the key. For Montrose, working out of but beyond the Marxist premises of Raymond Williams in *The Country and the City*, the precondition of Elizabethan pastoral was the erasure of all genuinely rural or agricultural concerns, despite the fact that statistically England was still a country of sheep-farmers, and the reinscription of "country" values within a court ideology. The result, according to Montrose, was a reinvented genre available for the discussion, in symbolic terms, of royal power and courtiers' ambitions. Connecting Puttenham's emphasis on the "vaile" of pastoral to his peculiarly institutionalized definition of allegory as "the Courtly figure . . . when we speake one thing, and thinke another," Montrose elevated the *Arte of English Poesie* to the status of a complete semantics of power relations in the last quarter of the sixteenth century. And because Elizabeth herself happily embraced the pastoral metaphor as one element of her personal mythography and iconography and enjoyed such social rituals as the Sudeley entertainment of 1591, which featured shepherd speakers and allusions to Virgil's fourth eclogue, Montrose produced a holistic account of Elizabethan pastoral that assimilated all its witnesses to Spenser's "April" eclogue.

From my own perspective, which is certainly no less historically and socially conditioned than any other described here, Montrose's position seems considerably nearer the mark than the modernist one, at least as a description of Elizabethan pastoral lyric. Yet an argument that makes Spenser's "April" eclogue definitive of the *Shepheardes Calender* as a whole is at best, it should now be clear, only a partial reading. In a curious way it reinstates the idealism of the earlier twentieth-century criticism, by suggesting that the heart of the *Calender* is a rewriting of Virgil's messianic eclogue to the poet's and the monarch's mutual benefit. While it is certainly true that the *Calender,* as the first systematic reinterpretation of Virgil's *Eclogues* in England, has as one of its subjects the poet's power "to create illusions which sanctify political power,"[95] and his natural ambition to be rewarded for doing so, its other subject, to which Spenser gave more than equal time, is the poet's responsibility to suggest *latenter* what is wrong with the system,

---

[95] Montrose, "'Eliza, Queene of shepheardes,'" p. 168.

and the dangers he may incur by so doing. Marot's appeal to Pan in his green cabinet was a form of advice to his monarch that drew much of its strength from that statement from Marot's other life, the withheld and only posthumously published *Complaincte* of the poet of exile. It is a tribute to Spenser's intelligence and his courage that he conceived a way to say, as it were, both things at once, to publish the unspeakable criticism alongside the celebration; and although he did not exactly get away with it (he spent the rest of his life in cultural exile in Ireland), the product was a text so peculiarly equivocal that even now it remains possible for readers to see in the *Calender* only what they choose.

A postscript: if it was felt that the English pastoral of state in Elizabeth's reign was *more* oppressed by the need for equivocation, for dark conceits, than was the case in sixteenth-century France, Spenser may have left us a late statement of those feelings and their cost. In the last book of *The Faerie Queene,* where the idea of pastoral is incarnate (and feminized) in Pastorella, Spenser introduces a character whose career-profile derives from Tasso's *Gerusalemme liberata* but whose name and significance come rather from Virgil's first eclogue. Pastorella's supposed father is old Meliboee, a symbol of pastoral's by now confused paternity; he is also, like the Colin Clout of "January," a fusion of the happy and unhappy shepherd. "Certes," cries Calidore, "I your happinesse envie" (6:9:19), negating the *denial* of envy by the original Meliboeus. But his envy need not last. Enter the brigands, the descendants of Virgil's barbarous soldiers, "A lawlesse people . . . That never usde to live by plough nor spade" and who "spoyld old Melibee of all he had, / And all his people captive led away" (6:10:39–40). It has often been remarked that here Spenser rendered in narrative symbol the fragility of the pastoral idea, yet this very way of formulating the issue obscures by its sentiment the historically specific story about pastoral that, I would argue, Spenser means to tell. For Pastorella herself is imprisoned underground in a world of darkness, lighted only by candles "which delt / A doubtfull sense of things" (6:10:42). In this ethical obscurity she has to come to terms with the brigand leader, "sith in his powre she was."

> She thought it best, for shadow to pretend
> Some shew of favour, by him gracing small
> That she thereby mote either freely wend,
> Or at more ease continue there his thrall:
> A little well is lent, that gaineth more withall.

>   (6:11:6)

This, surely, is Spenser's story of Elizabethan pastoral, constrained by power to two unacceptable modes of survival; either an underground and subversive discourse or a show of favor to the holders of power to buy some personal freedom. This insight cannot but inform with irony the tale's romantic solution, when Pastorella is rescued from brigands only to be returned to the court, whose child, it emerges, she has been all along. In the 1590s, pastoral denied its ancient heritage and was fully absorbed into the hegemony, whose need for poetic support increased as the queen aged and herself grew bitter. Who are we to blame the poet of exile for this last act of submission? The *Faerie Queene* ends with an allusion to "a mighty Peres displeasure," and a fin de siècle resolution:

> Therfore do you my rimes keep better measure,
> And seeke to please, that now is counted wisemens threasure.
>
> (6:12:41)

3

GOING PUBLIC

Pastoral versus Georgic:
The Politics of Virgilian Quotation

Renaissance humanism, however different its manifestations, tended toward a relationship with pastoral that stressed above all its capacity to stand as a metaphor for the condition of the writer-intellectual, whether that condition was seen as a privileged status or, on the contrary, one of extreme dependence and vulnerability. As such, it tended to be a semi-private vocabulary, for the expression of vocational goals and anxieties, or a self-protective one, for the articulation of otherwise dangerous opinions. This chapter focuses almost exclusively on the reception of the *Eclogues* in England in the seventeenth century. The pastoralism of this period differed from that of Petrarch, Landino, Marot, and Spenser in that the impulse to recall and transvalue the *Eclogues* for one's generation was not archeological reverence or the need to articulate the role of the intellectual in society. Nor was the value of the master-text located, as it had been for the humanists, in its capacity to embody ideals of free speech and free thought in a hostile cultural environment,[1] although there continued to be instances of writing *latenter* under the pastoral metaphor in the interests of personal safety. Instead, as a direct result of the policies of the early Stuarts and their reincarnation under the late ones, the Virgilian code and the ideological possibilities it represented passed out of the cabinet of the lone intellectual, isolated and besieged, into the terrain of politics proper and became widely disseminated as a public language.

Also, a rearrangement occurred in the ideological possibilities themselves. The relationship between culture and national or international peace, so important to Vives, became under the Stuarts virtually synonymous with pastoral; but an issue that had not concerned the humanists and that Vives had found obsessive in Servian commentary did indeed become central. What Servius called the "necessity of the lost lands" reappeared in seventeenth-century England as an ideology of landownership and land use, to which were annexed the central issues of political representation and franchise and the class implications of enclosures versus common land, and hence, ultimately, the class system itself. At this point, therefore, the cultural history of pastoral becomes truly inseparable from georgic. Because of the events which divide in fortune the shepherds in Eclogue 1 and unite in anxiety those in Eclogue 9—the expropriations of farmland in Mantua for the purpose of rewarding Octavian's veterans—Virgilian pastoral would have indicated its liminal status on the borders of georgic even if the *Georgics* had never been written. Meliboeus was as much farmer as shepherd, and the question of culture's relationship to agriculture was therefore inscribed in the same master-text that appeared, if read from a certain perspective, to privilege leisure. This was particularly well understood in England in the seventeenth century, when the relationship between the two genres became, in effect, a sign-system for other sets of relationships and arguments.

We can begin by looking in some detail at a writer, Sir Francis Bacon, whose work has already been recognized as deeply organized by the idea of georgic as a metaphor. By making that argument more precise and by relat-

---

[1] A counter-example who yet proves the point was Michael Drayton, whose *Pastorals*—published in three editions, 1593, 1606, and 1619—were delayed expressions of Renaissance humanism. The Jacobean editions contain a critique of James as the shepherd Olcon who "forsakes the Heard-groome and his Flocks" and a tribute to "that old Winken de Word," simultaneously the sixteenth-century humanist printer whose *Bucolica Virgilii* was published in 1514 and Drayton's own grammar-school teacher Leonard Cox. The 1619 edition explicitly endorses and revises the Servian hermeneutic: "The most High, and most Noble Matters of the World may bee shaddowed in [pastorals], and for certaine sometimes are: but he who hath almost nothing Pastorall in his Pastorals, but the name (which is my Case) deales more plainly, because *detracto velamine,* he speakes of most weightie things." See *Works,* ed. J. W. Hebel, K. Tillotson, and B. H. Newdigate, 5 vols. (Oxford, 1931–41), 2: 561, 546, 517.

ing it directly to its Virgilian sources, we can begin to see the structure of the code that Bacon and his contemporaries took for granted. At the same time we will see in Bacon a contract between pastoral and georgic as social forces that the history of the seventeenth century would abrogate. In 1605 Bacon recognized a new century and a new English monarch by proposing a program of intellectual husbandry, whose fruits should be great advances in the proximate fields of ethics and politics. In the second book of the *Advancement of Learning,* a text aimed indirectly at the vanity and administrative indolence of James I, Bacon suggested classical precedent for the type of advice he was offering his sovereign, remarking that "the poet Virgil . . . got as much glory of eloquence, wit, and learning in the expressing of the observations of husbandry, as of the heroical acts of Aeneas." Here he quoted *Georgics* 3.289, and continued:

> And, surely, if the purpose be in good earnest not to write at leisure that which men may read at leisure, but really to instruct and suborn action and active life, these Georgics of the mind, concerning the husbandry and tillage thereof, are no less worthy than the heroical descriptions of Virtue, Duty, and Felicity.[2]

In accordance with this program (which explains and governs the many images of agriculture and gardening in the text)[3] Bacon incorporated into the *Advancement* certain central statements from the *Georgics,* subjecting them to highly original application. Into the service of the new science he pressed the famous lines from the second georgic (490–93) where Virgil distinguished between two kinds of happiness, that of the simple rustic and that of the Stoic philosopher who uses knowledge to acquire intellectual repose:

> Virgil did excellently and profoundly couple the knowledge of causes and the conquest of all fears together, as *concomitantia:*
>
> Felix, qui potuit rerum cognoscere causas,
> Quique metus omnes, et inexorabile fatum
> Subjecit pedibus, strepitumque Acherontis avari.
>
> (3: 315)

But in Bacon's conceptual system, where "causes" are determinately secondary and material, Stoic recessiveness has been replaced by the language

---

[2] Francis Bacon, *Works,* ed. J. Spedding, R. L. Ellis, and D. D. Heath, 14 vols. (London, 1857–74), 3: 419. Compare James S. Tillman, "Bacon's Georgics of Science," *Papers in Language and Literature* 11 (1975): 357–77.

[3] As recognized by Brian Vickers, *Francis Bacon and Renaissance Prose* (Cambridge, 1968), pp. 187–98.

of psychological and even physiological amelioration. What his happy man gains are "the particular remedies which learning doth minister to all the diseases of the mind; sometimes purging the ill-humours, sometimes opening the obstructions, sometimes helping digestion, sometimes increasing appetite, sometimes healing the wounds and exulcerations thereof, and the like" (3: 315).

So too in his discussion of invention Bacon recalls the Hesiodic theogony of the first georgic, that version of the Fall in which the products of hardship and need are human effort and inventiveness. Highly congenial to Bacon as a general proposition, the theogony serves to underline his point that the instrument of invention is not logic but experience:

> Neither is the form of invention which Virgil describeth much other: "Ut varias usus meditando extunderet artes / Paulatim." For if you observe the words well, it is no other method than that which brute beasts are capable of, and do put in ure; which is a perpetual intending or practising some one thing, urged and imposed by an absolute necessity of conservation of being.
>
> (3: 386)

The central principle of the *Georgics,* then, "Labor omnia vincit / Improbus, et duris urgens in rebus egestas," is used by Bacon not as a reproach to pastoral's "Omnia vincit Amor" but as a rejection of Aristotle. Even the grammarian's move ("observe the words well") acquires a new epistemological status, reproaching the philosophy of the past for its resistance to the advancement of learning: "Add then the word *extundere,* which importeth the extreme difficulty, and the word *paulatim,* which importeth the extreme slowness, and we are where we were, even amongst the Ægyptians' gods" (3: 386–87).

It was, however, essential to Bacon to enclose the practicalities of georgic within the intellectualism for which the *Eclogues* had grown to stand. The *Advancement* begins with a reminder that Cain and Abel, respectively farmer and shepherd, represent the rival claims of action and contemplation and that from the beginning "the favour and election of God went to the shepherd, and not to the tiller of the ground" (3: 297). Bacon needed a counterargument capable of restoring to the activist the enabling innocence of Abel. He found it in, or constructed it out of, that other scripture to which the Renaissance had given canonical status, discovering in Virgil's canon not an antipathy between pastoral and georgic but their interdependence, their meeting, so to speak, in the head.

For instance: the most political section of the *Georgics,* the instructions for bee-keeping in the fourth book, appears in the *Advancement of Learning* with its emphasis on statecraft suppressed. Instead, Virgil's instructions for the setting up of the hives (4.8) are presented by Bacon as a metaphor for the institutionalization of learning, "foundations and buildings, endowments with revenues, endowments with franchises and privileges, institutions and ordinances for government; *all tending to quietness and privateness of life*" (3: 323; italics added). And the bees themselves as collectors of honey, *coelestia dona,* are an image of "how the mind doth gather this excellent dew of knowledge . . . distilling and contriving it out of particulars natural and artificial, as the flowers of the field and garden" (3: 387). The almost lyrical language sweetens the reader's perception of what is actually being defined here, that is, inductive method, the cornerstone of Baconian science. But if quotations from the *Georgics* are rendered idyllic, echoes from the *Eclogues* appear in oddly scientific contexts. The would-be black magic of the woman in Eclogue 8, who plans to recover her lover by firing both a clay and a wax image of him, appears in the *Advancement* to support a principle in physics. "Fire," wrote Bacon, somewhat comically, "is the cause of induration, but respective to clay; fire is the cause of colliquation, but respective to wax" (3: 354). More profoundly, Bacon transformed the theme of echo in the *Eclogues,* Virgil's metaphor for the sympathy between man and nature, into an argument for the authenticity of the new science. If it was true for the shepherd that all the woods responded to his songs ("respondent omnia sylvae," 10.8), then "the voice of nature will consent, whether the voice of man do or no" (3: 363).

Finally, and most poignantly (especially in the light of our afterknowledge of how long it took for that consensus to develop and how incomplete Bacon's great instauration would remain when he died), he built into the penultimate section of the *Advancement* an echo of Virgil's second eclogue, remembering that moment of comic self-congratulation when Corydon considers his own reflection:

> Thus have I concluded this portion of learning touching Civil Knowledge; and with civil knowledge have concluded Human Philosophy; and with human philosophy, Philosophy in General. And being now at some pause, looking back into that I have passed through, this writing seemeth to me *si nunquam fallit imago* as far as a man can judge of his own work, not much better than that noise or sound which musicians make while they are tuning their instruments: which is nothing pleasant to hear, but yet is a cause why the music is sweeter afterwards.
>
> (3: 476)

Given the Servian gloss on Corydon's *imago* (2.27) ("for nothing is so deceptive as the image; for everything shows in reverse in a mirror, and we see the oar as it were fractured in the water"), we can guess how much this echo meant to Bacon, on the threshold of a skeptical phenomenology.

What looks at first sight, then, to be merely a chance scattering of memories of Virgil, the misused traces of a type of education that Bacon himself believed obsolete, becomes on closer investigation a principled synthesis of two conceptual structures, a synthesis which is, for all its minor and deliberate distortions, not untrue to either of them. A pastoralized georgic, or vice versa, as a program for the intellectual development of the seventeenth century could have served his contemporaries extremely well. Had it taken hold, and particularly had it been given royal or institutional support, it might well have protected England from the polarization that followed, with all its political consequences. What happened instead, as the policies of James I and Charles I became increasingly unpopular and hence on the defensive in terms of their cultural expression, was a split on class lines between intellectuals (a group increasingly conceived in aesthetic terms) and those involved in "work," whether commercial or agricultural. It has been persuasively argued by Anthony Low that georgic became the form either of radical scientific thought or of social protest, while pastoral became the exclusive terrain of an aristocratic and later royalist elite.[4] Low's argument is itself a restatement, however differently documented, of the position established by Stephen Orgel, that Stuart pastoralism as expressed in the court masque was one of the major illusions of power, creating and supporting a myth of peace and prosperity and protecting its primary audience, the monarch, from hearing the increasingly numerous and coordinated voices of the opposition.[5]

This explanatory model has actually been reinforced by its mirror image in Marxist criticism. Raymond Williams and James Turner have laid bare the deceptions and evasions of Jacobean and Caroline literary representations of country life, their pastoralization of georgic which erased from cultural consciousness the facts of rural labor. As Williams observed in his pioneering essay on Ben Jonson's *To Penshurst,* a "magical extraction of the curse of labour is achieved by a simple extraction of the existence of labourers"; and Turner greatly expanded the documentation of a cultural conspiracy, by which "rural poetry defends an imaginary England, green and pleasant, from which all hardness and extortion has been banished."[6]

---

[4] Anthony Low, *The Georgic Revolution* (Princeton, 1985). Minor exceptions to Low's thesis were Joseph Aylett's *Thrift's Equipage* (1622), which blended biblical and Virgilian georgic and defended James I as promoting "a true Idea of high labour" (p. 38); and Peter Heylyn's *Historie of that Most Famous Saint and Souldier of Christ Jesus, George of Cappodoccia* (1633), which attempted to appropriate the georgic ethos for Charles I by way of the Spenserian etymology ("George" = husbandman).

[5] Stephen Orgel, *The Illusion of Power* (Berkeley and Los Angeles, 1975), especially pp. 49–52.

[6] Raymond Williams, *The Country and the City* (New York, 1973), p. 32; James Turner, *The Politics of Landscape: Rural Scenery and Society in English Poetry 1630–1660* (Cambridge, Mass., 1979), p. 135.

Rural poverty is concealed by an emphasis on the landowner's charity and hospitality; peasants are presented as subhuman, incapable of thought, and ontologically inseparable from farm instruments. In such a hegemony, pastoral is fully appropriated to the defense of landed property. On the one hand, its tropicality, its insistence, since Virgil, that "shepherds" are not really what they seem, contributed to the general fictionality of the Stuart cultural myth; on the other, the landscape of literary pastoral bore an actual and, for some, shocking relationship to the landscape produced when mixed agricultural terrain was subjected to enclosure: "Nothing remaines but a champant wildernesse for sheepe, with a Cote, a pastorall boy, his dogge, a crooke and a pipe." [7]

My own procedure and conclusions will diverge, however, from both the illusionist and Marxist models, by blurring the edges of class conflict and allowing for a wider range of responses to the feud, if that is what it was, between pastoral and georgic. First, instead of subsuming under pastoralism any reference to country life or landscape I shall follow more narrowly the historical traces of Virgil's *Eclogues* as a text; and because that text arrived in seventeenth-century England already potent with ideology and was generally understood to be so, it follows that those traces will constitute a deliberately chosen political vocabulary, rather than the workings of the political unconscious.

Second, while I do not intend to challenge in its broad outlines the premise that seventeenth-century pastoral was ideologically the property of the most privileged class, and never more so than during their temporary defeat, I hope to show that the story of the *Eclogues* as political discourse is rather more complicated than a strictly partisan analysis can produce. Neither the illusionist nor the Marxist model will account, for instance, for Andrew Marvell's use of the *Eclogues* in the service of the Commonwealth, or the enigmatic case of Milton's 1645 *Poems,* whose relationship to Virgilian pastoral defeats all attempts at explanation in terms of class conflict. There is also a whole range of eccentric responses *within* the hegemonic corpus, intimations of doubt, criticisms of self or of the monarch or of the sociopolitical system, that may be generated either by some temporary alienation of the writer from his privileged environment or by some deeper affinity with Virgil's profound open-mindedness. It is well to bear in mind, therefore, the potentially liberating alternative model defined

[7]Turner, *The Politics of Landscape,* p. 163. The quotation is from Robert Powell, *Depopulation Arraigned, Convicted, and Condemned* (London, 1636). Powell's attack on enclosure was presented as praise of Charles I, under the premise that the king *wished* to enforce the anti-enclosure laws, and it defined the "future reformation" of English agriculture as the fulfillment of Virgil's credo in *Georgics* 2.458: "O fortunatos nimium, sua si bona norint / Agricolas" ("O happy husbandman, too happy, if they would recognize their blessings") (pp. 116–17).

by Bakhtin, in which the principle of heteroglossia, multi-languagedness, is constantly at work throughout cultural history. Whenever, in Bakhtin's terms, "a sealed-off interest group, caste or class . . . becomes riddled with decay or shifted somehow from its state of internal balance and self-sufficiency" it becomes theoretically vulnerable to penetration by the sound of other voices, the recognition of otherness that leads to genuine self-consciousness or "novelization." "It is necessary," wrote Bakhtin (though thinking primarily of what conditions are productive of the novel), "that heteroglossia wash over a culture's awareness of itself and its language, penetrate to its core, relativize the primary language system underlying its ideology and literature and deprive it of its naive absence of conflict."[8] It will be part of my argument here that the seventeenth century in England, with which Bakhtin does not directly concern himself but which was in almost every respect a century of novelization, manifests the force of cultural heteroglossia almost from the beginning, not merely by the explosive sectarianism of the revolution itself. And because to read one's own culture in terms of Virgil's was inevitably to expose oneself to another language, to historicity and difference, even the most conservative of writers who did so, thinking thereby to align themselves with "tradition," became participants, willy-nilly, in the dialogic imagination.

Third, I shall argue that we have here a particularly useful test of the concept of what Michel Foucault has called discursive practice, a concept fashionable to discuss but remarkably difficult to document.[9] We know, to begin with, how widely this code was disseminated, because it was actually taught in the schools. When John Brinsley produced his grammarian's translation of the *Eclogues* "chiefly for the good of Schooles" in 1620, he justified his choice "as being the most familiar of all Virgil's workes, and fittest for childrens capacities."[10] It was already familiar, part of the culture, and therefore a suitable text on which to practise one's grammar. But at the same time Brinsley hoped, somewhat contradictorily, that "happie experience" of the kind his translation offered would "in time drive it, and all like it, utterly out of the schooles and into the minds of all." He was partially right on both counts. And in fact the Virgilian semiotics was so well and so widely known, in the same decade that Brinsley's book entered the schools, that it became a kind of public shorthand. Because the conceptual structure of this language was so well understood, its units could be used

---

[8] M. M. Bakhtin, *The Dialogic Imagination,* ed. Michael Holquist, trans. Caryl Emerson and Michael Holquist (Austin, 1981), p. 368.

[9] In *Language and Political Understanding: The Politics of Discursive Practices* (New Haven, 1981), p. 131, Michael Shapiro points out that although Foucault had not addressed himself specifically to political discourse or behavior, he envisioned this extension of his theory. See Michel Foucault, *The Archeology of Knowledge* (New York, 1972), p. 194.

[10] John Brinsley, *Virgils Eclogues, with His Booke De apibus, concerning the Government and Ordering of Bees . . . Translated Grammatically* (London, 1620), folio A1vv.

elliptically, without, as it were, the syntax showing. Brief quotations could stand for larger arguments or even for an entire ideology, and the text could be splintered into what, borrowing a phrase from Fredric Jameson, we might call *ideologemes*.[11] As writers, statesmen, and even kings grasped the capacity of the original to contribute to their own debates, fragments of the *Eclogues* became nodes of political theory or policy, articulating issues such as the nature of liberty or the value of English isolationism from Europe. We have, therefore, a rare instance of a discursive practice that permeates the culture while being fully intelligible to those who practiced it at the time.

For instance: in 1612 Sir John Davies published a pamphlet apparently in support of James I and his policy for Ireland. Certainly its title leads one to suppose that this was his intention: *A Discoverie of the True Causes Why Ireland Was Never Entirely Subdued, nor Brought under Obedience of the Crowne of England, untill the Beginning of His Maiesties Happy Raigne*. Yet the *Discoverie* consists largely of an account of the stupid and cruel mistakes perpetrated in Ireland by previous administrations, and in a section on taxation of "Mansmeate, Horsemeat, & Money . . . at the will and pleasure of the soldier" (p. 173), something rather extraordinary happens. "This Extortion was originally Irish," wrote Davies,

> for they used to lay *Bonaght* upon their people, and never gave their soldiers any other pay. But when the English had Learned it, they used it with more insolency, and made it more intollerable. . . . This extortion of Coyne and Livery, did produce two notorious effects. First, it made the Land wast; Next, it made the people, ydle. For, when the Husbandman had laboured all the yeare, the soldier in one night, did consume the fruites of all his labour. . . . Had hee reason then to manure the Land for the next yeare? Or rather might he not complaine as the Shepherd in Virgil:
>
> Impius haec tam culta novalia miles habebit?
> Barbarus has segetes? En quo discordia Cives
> Perduxit miseros? En queis consevimus Agros?
>
> (pp. 173–75)
>
> Shall the impious soldier possess these well-tilled grounds? A barbarian possess these crops? Where has fighting brought our miserable countrymen? For whom have we sown our fields?

Not only is that passage isolated by its classical quotation, unique in this pamphlet, but its emotional force works directly against its supposedly heg-

---

[11] Fredric Jameson, *The Political Unconscious* (Ithaca, 1981), p. 76.

emonic function. Was it the Virgilian text, we may ask, or something unspoken in Davies's own experience that moved him to so deep an identification with the social and political Other, the Irish peasantry who are here
dignified by the Roman term *cives,* citizens, while it is the English standing
army who are registered as barbarous?

The ideology of landownership is more than merely an undercurrent
in another Jacobean work that made its relationship to Virgilian pastoral
both central and problematic. William Browne of Tavistock had begun by
publishing a set of seven eclogues, *The Shepheards Pipe,* in 1614, gesturing
toward the Virgilianism of the previous century by stating that they contained "Things of a higher fame . . . / Vaild in a Shepheards name." But his
major contribution was made not in eclogue form but in *Britannia's Pastorals,* a generic blend of pastoral, georgic, epic, and allegorical romance.
Declining to "tune the Swaines of Thessaly / Or, bootlesse, adde to them of
Arcadie," [12] Browne declared in his opening lines that his theme was British
nationalism, which throughout the poem is identified with the golden age
of Elizabethan naval eminence. His aim is to make his own West Country
as famous "as Mantua by her Virgil's birth"; and it is no coincidence that
the West Country was also the homeland of Sir Francis Drake, whose name
functions as the sign of a generic boundary—of what the poem might have
been had Browne lived a generation earlier. Introducing Plymouth Sound
to his readers, Browne remembers a more heroic age, when the English
navy made Spain tremble; but under James I, and his dreams of becoming
the peacemaker of Europe, Britannia is now locked into a pastoral stasis,
which ironically permits a parody of georgic prosperity:

> But now our Leaders want; those Vessels lye
> Rotting, like houses through ill husbandry;
> And on their Masts where oft the Ship-boy stood,
> Or silver Trumpets charm'd the brackish Flood,
> Some wearied Crow it set; and daily seene
> Their sides instead of pitch calk'd o're with greene:
> Ill hap (alas) have you that once were knowne
> By reaping what was by Iberia sowne.
> By bringing yealow sheaves from out their plaine,
> Making our Barnes the store-house for their graine:
> When now as if we wanted land to till,
> Wherewith we might our uselesse Souldiers fill:

---

[12] William Browne, *The Whole Works,* ed. W. Carew Hazlitt, 2 vols. in 1 (Hildesheim and
New York, 1970), 2: 219; 1: 34. The first book of *Britannia's Pastorals* was published in 1613,
the second in 1616; both were reissued, significantly, in 1625, when James's foreign policy
was in crisis.

Upon their Hatches where halfe-pikes were borne,
In every chinke rise stems of bearded corne

(2: 4; pp. 65–66)

Reversing the lament of Meliboeus, Browne also rebuts the lament of *Georgics* 2.506–8: "Our lands, robbed of the tillers, lie waste, and the crooked pruning-hooks are forged into stiff swords." Green slime and wild oats reproach the "idle times" of Jacobean pacificism, and even the crow is otiose.

But for Browne husbandry is not only a metaphor, nor only negatively conceived. Rather, he proposes the proper national use and cultivation of both land and sea, neither of which is flourishing under James. And in a digression on the causes of famine in England, Browne identifies with shocking clarity the negative georgic implications of the English system of landownership:

Here should they finde a great one paling in
A meane mans land, which many yeeres had bin
His charges life, and by the others heast,
The poore must starve to feed a scurvy beast.

. . . .

There should they see another that commands
His Farmers Teame from furrowing his lands,
To bring him stones to raise his building vast,
The while his Tenants sowing time is past.

. . . .

The Countrey Gentleman, from's neighbours hand
Forceth th'inheritance, joynes land to land,

. . . .

The griping Farmer hoords the seed of bread,
Whilst in the streets the poore lye famished:
And free there's none from all this worldly strife,
Except the Shepherds heaven-blest happy life.

(2: 1; 188–90)

This is not only a parody of the "happy man" section of the second georgic, a passage that Browne imitated closely elsewhere,[13] but also a refutation of the idealizing Jacobean country-house poem, of which Ben Jonson's *To Penshurst*, published in the same year as this passage, was the supreme ex-

---

[13] Browne, *The Whole Works*, 2: 3, pp. 32–39.

ample. In Browne's view, for all James's proclamations requiring the country gentlemen to return to the country and cultivate their lands, Britannia is disabled by a false pastoral premise; and it will take the analytical vision of the true pastoral, in all its generic complexity, to make the darker vision perceptible. Presumably, the shepherds who alone in Jacobean society are not complicit in the general exploitation are not real rustics, but Virgilian writer-intellectuals whose autonomy sets them "free." And far from exploiting the pastoral to support Jacobean policy, whether national or international, Browne allows it to reveal to the monarch, should he care to look, the topography of social injustice.

These connections between pastoral and Jacobean foreign policy can help to explain the next example of Virgilian quotation, which occurred in a more dramatically public form. In the winter of 1623–24 a group of young troublemakers appeared in London, under what was obviously a code name. As Walter Yonge wrote in his diary:

> The beginning of December, 1623, there was a great number in London, haunting taverns and other debauched places, who swore themselves in a brotherhood, and namd themselves *Tytere tues*. . . . There were divers knights, some young noblemen and gentlemen of this brotherhood, and they were to know each other by a black bugle which they wore, and their followers to be known by a blue ribbond. There are discovered of them about 80 or 100 persons, and have been examined by the Privy Council; but nothing discovered of any intent they had. It is said, that the king hath given commandment that they shall be reexamined.[14]

The political context of this episode, so badly in need of official interpretation, was the public unrest created in England by the loss to Spain of the Palatinate, briefly the possession of James's daughter Elizabeth, Queen of Bohemia. James had refused to intervene in Europe on behalf of his ousted son-in-law Frederick, the Elector Palatine, and pursued instead his conciliation of Spain. Other contemporary comments make it clear that the Tityre-tues, those living quotations, were perceived as antagonistic to James's policies, at least at the level of ritual embodiment of an argument. Richard Brathwaite remarked that in the current mood of suspicion and unrest, wearing a blue ribbon, however innocently, could get one arrested as "a Tityre-tu; / An enemy to th' State."[15] And Robert Herrick congratu-

---

[14] Walter Yonge, *Diary at Colyton and Axminster, 1604–1628* (London, 1848), p. 70. See also *Calender of State Papers Domestic* for 6 and 19 December 1623, pp. 56, 125.
[15] Richard Brathwaite, *An Age for Apes* (London, 1658), p. 247. Though published late in the Protectorate, Brathwaite's satires were written mostly in 1623–24.

lated himself on the peace of a country Christmas, in contrast to what had been going on in London. In Devon, there was

> No noise of late spawn'd Tittyries:
> No closset plot, or open vent,
> That frights men with a Parliament[16]

This conservative's response to the threat of a parliament points forward to the defeat of Jacobean pacificism as a political program, when in February 1624 James was forced to recall the recalcitrant parliament he had dissolved in a rage two years earlier and to receive their advice in favor of war with Spain.

Why should such a situation have been presented in terms of Virgil's first eclogue? The answer is both obvious in its outlines and elusive in its details. Whether we take the Tityre-tues as standing for the voice of Meliboeus or as an entry-code to the whole eclogue, the issues so addressed, *in the circumstances of 1623–24,* were the advantages of peace versus the ethical weakness of Tityrus's position, at ease in the shade while others suffered expropriation and exile. The relevance of Virgil's dialectic to the German wars was created not only by analogy (the selfish pacificism of England, the expropriation of the Palatinate and exile of James's daughter and her husband) but also by the king's adoption of the ethos of Tityrus, or a version of it, to authenticate his own position. On 26 March 1621, James had opened a new parliament with a defense of his style of government presented as a version of *otium:*

> And now I confesse, that when I looked before upon the face of government I thought . . . that the people were never so happy as in my time . . . and for peace, both at home and abrode, I may truely say more setled, and longer lasting than ever before, together with as great plenty as ever: so as it was to be thought, that every man might sit in safety under his own vine, and his owne figge-tree.[17]

The adaptation, as was only to be expected of the British Solomon, was by way of I Kings 4:24, 25: "And [Solomon] had . . . peace on all sides

---

[16] Robert Herrick, "A New-Yeares Gift to Sir Simeon Steward," *Poetical Works,* ed. L. C. Martin (Oxford, 1956), p. 126. The writ recalling parliament was signed on 28 December 1623. See also Ben Jonson's allusion in *The Fortunate Isles* (1624) to the poet Skelton as the "Tityre-tu" of Henry VIII's court (lines 306–8); and Richard Brome's later parody of the allusion in *The Weeding of Covent Garden,* ed. Donald S. McClure (New York, 1980), p. 109 (III: 1, lines 61–62) where Clotpoll remarks, "So, now I am a Blade, and of a better row than those of Tytere tu, or Oatmeal Hoe."

[17] *His Majesties Speach in the Upper House of Parliament, on Munday, the 26 of March, 1621* (London, 1621), folio B3v.

round about him: And Judah and Israel dwelt safely, every man under his own vine and under his fig-tree." Yet the classical origins of the pacifist shade remained clearly apparent, and were often reinforced by other writers as James's speech, which was promptly published, entered the cultural spectrum.[18]

James in the meantime had himself confirmed the Virgilian origins of his language, if not of his thinking, in a contribution to another political controversy arising from his foreign policy. Closely connected to the question of nonintervention in the fate of the Palatinate was James's plan to marry his son to the Spanish Infanta. In 1623 this highly unpopular project exploded in a wave of public anxiety when it was learned that Charles and Buckingham, impatient at the slowness of the marriage negotiations being conducted by the Earl of Bristol, had taken matters into their own hands and left in disguise for Spain to do the royal wooing in person. James's response to the public dismay at this development, which put the heir to the throne literally in Spanish hands, was to write, of all things, a pastoral poem, a poem whose echoes of Virgil's fifth eclogue, the lament for Daphnis, could scarcely have been unconscious:

> Whatt: suddayne Chance hath darkt of late
> the glorye of th'Arcadian State
> the ffleecye fflockes, reffuse to feede
> the Lambes to playe the Ewes to breede.
> > The Altars smoak the Offringes Burne
> > that Jacke and Tom, may safe Returne.
>
> The Springe neglects his Course to keepe
> the Ayre contynual stormes doth weepe
> The pretty Byrdes, disdayne to singe
> the Meades to smyle, the Woodes to springe
> > The Mountaynes droppe the ffountaynes mourne
> > tyll Jacke and Tom, doe safe Returne.

---

[18] See, for example, William Loe, *Vox Clamantis* (London, 1622), an appeal for peace addressed to the "Three-Thrice honourable Estates of Parliament," p. 23; Samuel Buggs, *Miles Mediterraneus: The Mid-Land Souldier* (London, 1622), pp. 2–3; Philip Massinger, *The Maid of Honour* (1621–22), *Plays and Poems*, ed. Philip Edwards and Colin Gibson, 5 vols. (Oxford, 1976), 1: 126, lines 164–69. The topos was subsequently applied to Charles I and his decision, in 1628, to return to the pacificism of his father. See Massinger, *Believe as You List* (1630), *Plays and Poems*, 3: 351; William Habington, *The Queene of Aragon* (1640), folio c4v; Francis Quarles, *The Shepheards Oracles: Delivered in Certain Eglogues* (1646), "To the Reader." For retrospective applications of the topos to both Jacobean and Caroline pacificism, see Richard Brathwaite, "Solomon's Reign," in *The History of Moderation* (London, 1669), p. 112. The most poignant of all such appearances of the peaceful shade must surely be in Charles's own speech of defense at his trial in 1649: see Charles Petrie, ed., *The Letters, Speeches and Proclamations of King Charles I* (London, 1968), p. 270.

What maye they bee that move this woe
whose want afflicts Arcadia soe
The hope of Greece the propp of Artes
was prencely Jack the joye of hartes,
    And Tom, was to our Royall Pan
    his truest Swayne and cheiffest Man.

. . . .

Kinde Sheappeardes, that have lov'd them longe
bee not soe rashe, in Censuringe wronge
Correct your ffeares, leave off to murne,
the Heavens will favour there returne,
    Remitt the Care, to Royall Pan
    of Jacke his Sonne, and Tom, his Man.[19]

However modified by previous Renaissance imitations of the elegy, the parodic traces of Virgil's text must have been visible to the Jacobean audience, and they may have wondered whether James was intelligent enough to argue thereby that the public outcry over the prince's absence was in excess of its cause. That there was an audience for this poem is indicated by the fact that copies of it were quickly handed about and discussed in contemporary correspondence. On 21 March 1623 John Chamberlain sent a copy to Dudley Carleton in Paris, and the next day the Reverend J. Mead wrote from Cambridge to Sir Martin Stateville that he *would* have sent him a copy did he not assume that he had already been "prevented by others." [20] In other words, the king's eclogue was an extremely hot item on at least such circuits. The meaning of the entire episode was clear and matched the inferences of the king's message to parliament: England was Arcadia, and its government could safely be left in the hands of the ruling deity, "Royall Pan."

Caroline Arcadianism was, if anything, more explicit and more pervasive as cultural statement, due in large part to Henrietta Maria's famous preference for pastoral as the expression of *her* personal style, and the encouragement she gave to writers to articulate that style. The result was the suppression, during the so-called halcyon days, and in court masques, plays, poems, of most of the Virgilian dialectic, all interpretations of or responses to the *Eclogues* that might have interrogated the myth of peace and prosperity. Yet the suppression could not be absolute; and although from a distance Caroline pastoral seems to be merely Caroline propaganda, a

[19] *The Poems of King James VI of Scotland,* ed. James Craigie, 2 vols. (Edinburgh, 1958), 2: 192–93.
[20] Ibid., 2: 266.

closer inspection often reveals that the ideological power of the model remained intact, producing even in writers assumed to be court apologists interesting signs of tension and complexity.

The gentleman poet Richard Fanshawe, for instance, called on to support the royal proclamation of 1630 "Commanding the Gentry to reside upon their Estates in the Country," responded by writing an ode in praise of both foreign and domestic policy, connecting England's isolation from the Thirty Years' War to a program of agriculture reform, which was in turn to produce cultural benefits:

> And if the Fields as thankfull prove
> For benefits receiv'd, as seed,
> They will, to quite so great a love,
>   A Virgill breed;
>
> A Tytirus, that shall not cease
> Th' Augustus of our world to praise
> In equall verse, author of peace
>   And Halcyon dayes.[21]

Yet the poem not only begins with eight stanzas of heroic language describing the wars in Europe, and among them the achievements of Gustavus Adolphus of Sweden "Revenging lost Bohemia," but it is also perversely structured along a trail of blood. From the "bloudyer rage" of the German wars, the "Spanish bloud" spilled by Gustavus Adolphus, and the "blouds boyling in the North" among the Poles and Russians, Fanshawe turns to proclaiming that the return of the landed gentry to their lands will be the resurgence of "The sapp and bloud o' th' land" to its heart; and in the last section, ostensibly a defense of the innocent country life, the word *blood* appears four times, in a way that makes the mental act of washing one's hands more difficult to perform than might have been possible *without* the poem:

> Nor Cupid there lesse bloud doth spill,
> But heads his shafts with chaster love,
> Not featherd with a Sparrowes quill
>   But of a Dove.
>
> There shall you heare the Nightingale
> (The harmelesse Syren of the wood)
> How prettily she tells a tale
>   Of rape and blood.

---

[21] Richard Fanshawe, *Il Pastor Fido: The Faithfull Shepheard, with an Addition of Divers Other Poems* (London, 1648), p. 227.

. . . .
The Lillie (Queene), the (Royall) Rose,
The Gillyflowre (Prince of the bloud),
The (Courtyer) Tulip (gay in clothes),
                    The (Regall) Budd,

. . . .
Plant Trees you may, and see them shoote
Up with your Children, to be serv'd
To your cleane boards, and the fair'st Fruite
                    To be preserv'd:

And learne to use their severall gummes,
" 'Tis innocence in the sweet blood
"Of Cherryes, Apricocks and Plummes
                    "To be imbru'd.

                                        (p. 229)

Such wresting of *blood* from its normal connotations might well remind us of *Macbeth,* a play in which the numerical frequency of its use is underscored by the determination (and hence the failure) of its two protagonists to erase it from their minds. As Macbeth himself put it, such imaginative strain merely results in "making the green one red." Nor can it have been unintentional that Fanshawe's final instructions to the gentry to "Plant Trees . . . and see them shoote / Up with your Children" recalls both the injunction of Meliboeus to himself to graft his pear trees (1.73) and its echo in the ninth eclogue ("Plant your pear trees, Daphnis, your offspring will enjoy the fruits," 9.50). But by blending the two together, Fanshawe's quotation denies both the sarcasm of the first and the uncertain status of the second, one of the half-remembered fragments ("oblita carmina") of cultural uncertainty.

Fanshawe's entire construct rests also on another partially hidden quotation from Meliboeus anticipating the pains of exile in a country as distant to his imagination as England ("penitus toto divisos orbe Britannos," 1.66). This had already become a commonplace of English political discourse. In the debates in parliament in 1628, for example, as the grievances caused by the wars against France and Spain led to the unprecedented discussions of the constitution and ultimately to the Petition of Right, Sir Edward Coke reminded his audience of the uniqueness of England in her dependence on the common law. "No other state is like this: we are *divisos ab orbe Britannos.*" [22] The classical definition of Britain as a savage place be-

---

[22] *Commons Debates 1628,* ed. Robert Johnson et al., 3 vols. (New Haven, 1977), 2: 555; cited by Conrad Russell, *Parliaments and English Politics 1621–1629* (Oxford, 1979), p. 358. The Virgilian aphorism had been interpreted as a compliment to England, in Giordano

yond conceptual reach was thus reversed and turned to a praise of an ancient national heritage of law. After the wars, Fanshawe took this transvaluation a stage further. What was in Virgil's text a sign denoting the very
opposite of pastoral security became a defense of Caroline Arcadianism:

> Onely the Island which wee sowe,
> (A world without the world) so farre
> From present wounds, it cannot showe
>   An ancient skarre.

(p. 226)

The most frequently cited document of Caroline pastoralism is probably Thomas Carew's *Answer of an Elegiacal Letter, upon the Death of the
King of Sweden, from Aurelian Townshend, Inviting Me to Write on That Subject.* Written in 1632, the poem celebrates Charles's version of the *pax Augusta,* resolving the dialectic of Virgil's first eclogue in favor of an unmiti-
gated idyllicism and arguing explicitly the connection between peace and
artistic activity. As in Fanshawe's ode, the German wars are invoked for
contrast with the English situation; but while they still carry epic connotations, they are dismissed from consideration with an easy negligence:

> Then let the Germans feare if Caesar shall,
> Or the United Princes, rise, and fall,
> But let us that in myrtle bowers sit
> *Under secure shades,* use the benefit
> Of peace and plenty, which the blessed hand
> Of our good King gives this obdurate Land.
>
> . . . .
>
> These harmlesse pastimes let my Townsend sing
> To rurall tunes; not that thy Muse wants wing
> To soare a loftier pitch, for she hath made
> A noble flight, and plac'd th'Heroique shade
> Above the reach of our faint flagging ryme;
> But these are subjects proper to our clyme.

Bruno's *Eroici furori,* published in London in 1585 under a false Paris imprint, in the dedication of that work to Sir Philip Sidney (*6v), and in Ben Jonson's *Masque of Blacknesse* (1605);
and as a compliment to James I in Sir Thomas Craig's *De unione regnorum Britanniae trac-
tatus,* not published in his lifetime but dating from the first decade of James's reign. See the
edition and translation by L. Sanford Terry (Edinburgh, 1909), p. 350. The motto would
reappear on the seal of Charles II, represented as the ruler of the sea, "et penitus toto reg-
nantes orbe Britannos." See Edgar Wind, *Pagan Mysteries in the Renaissance* (New Haven,
1958), p. 182, who asks: "But could that proud emendation have been designed to supplant
the memory of Virgil's verse? Did its effect not rather depend on evoking it: That *divisos* was
the clue to *regnante* was not too esoteric a lesson for Charles's minister [Halifax]."

Tourneyes, Masques, Theaters, better become
Our Halcyon days. *What though the German Drum*
Bellow for freedome and revenge, the noyse
Concernes not us, nor should divert our joyes;
Nor ought the thunder of their Carabins
Drowne the sweet Ayres of our tun'd Violins;
Beleeve me friend, if their prevailing powers
Gaine them a calme securitie like ours
They'l hang their Armes up on the Olive bough,
And dance, and revell then, as we doe now.[23]

The selfishness of Tityrus is here given formal approval, "lentus in umbra" loses its potential for irony, and even the problematic "libertas" is devalued by being tied to revenge; yet the fact remains (and is insisted upon in the cumbersome title) that Carew's poem is presented as an "Answer" to a request for a very different generic response to contemporary events. The other side of the unspoken dialogue is intimated solely in the telling reference to "this obdurate land." Behind that phrase lie Charles's struggles with the parliament of 1628–29, and immediately before it impends the conflict between the court and its puritan critics over "the queen's pastoral," the production of Walter Montague's *The Shepheardes Paradise* and the trial for sedition of William Prynne.[24] It is important to remember that the queen's fixation on pastoral drama was one of the factors that exacerbated class conflict and disputes over economics. When the crisis came in 1640, pastoral ideology had incorporated a new and local credo: that the opponents of idyllicism or Arcadianism were also the opponents of poetry, the theater, and the arts in general.

During the civil war the pastoral myth of the halcyon days was undoubtedly recognized for precisely what it was, a proposition designed to ratify the behavior and circumstances of the ruling class. Included in that recognition was a renewed sense of its Virgilian origins, its social dialectic, and especially its reversibility. Many royalists, of course, now found themselves in the position of Meliboeus, and if they themselves were not actually in exile in France, their estates were frequently "sequestrated" (confiscated) by the Long Parliament. It was hardly surprising, therefore, that the public practice of allusion to the *Eclogues* continued. In 1643, Francis Quarles placed on the title page of his *Loyal Convert* the same motto that thirty years earlier had served to focus the sympathies of Sir John Davies for the Irish peasants: "Improbus haec tam culta novalia miles habebit? /

---

[23] Thomas Carew, *Poems,* ed. Rhodes Dunlap (Oxford, 1949), pp. 75–77 (italics added).

[24] See my *Censorship and Interpretation* (Madison, 1984), pp. 105–7.

Barbarus has segetes?" Now it denoted the plight of the royalist supporters of Charles who found their estates sequestered by the Long Parliament. In the same year a broadside *Letter from Mercurius Civicus to Mercurius Rusticus* carried on its title page the epigraph "En quo discordia Cives? [*sic*] / Perduxit miseros" (1.71–72). In this reinterpretation of the dialogue between fortunate and unfortunate (now contrasted as countryman and citizen) the positions are ingeniously rearranged so that Civicus, the Londoner, is both the victim of civil war and its cause:

> I cannot but congratulate your happinesse that breathe in so free an ayre, wherein it is lawfull to heare and speak truth. . . . Your sad stories of the Ruine and devastation of the Country are ecchoed in our Streets, and though we beare it out in a Vaunting way, as if these things concerned not us, yet I assure you there are many soules that mourne in private, (for in publique we must be as mad as the rest . . .) knowing how justly we stand charged with all those Calamities, which the sword of Rebellion hath brought upon you. . . . But you may aske, Is there any evill in the Countrey, and the City hath not done it? You have made us Rich and Populous, and we in foule Ingratitude have prodigally powerd out both our Wealth and Strength to make you and our selves miserable.
>
> (pp. 1, 3)

The Virgilian "quotations" show an equal freedom of application, built on and counting on a profound familiarity with the original. In a different way, a small volume published in 1649 (the year of the king's execution) tackled head-on the related questions of interpretation and reception that such a politics of quotation engendered. The anonymous translator of La Mothe le Vayer's *Of Liberty and Servitude* placed on its title page a crucial question and answer from the first eclogue:

> Melib. Et quae tanta fuit Romam tibi causa videndi?
> Tit. Libertas: quae sera, tamen respexit Inertem.
>
> (A2r)
>
> Meliboeus: "And what gave you so great a reason for going to see Rome?" Tityrus: "Liberty: who, though late, nevertheless remembered me, the idle one."

He thereby tapped a reservoir of ancient and Renaissance commentary on these lines which had explained them in terms of some attitude toward republican theory; but precisely because of their traditional association with republicanism, this commentator added a long explanatory epistle "To Him that reads," which urgently sought to reorganize the reader's response:

> This free subject, coming abroad in these Licentious times may happily cause the World to mistake both the Author, and the Translator; neither of whom by LIBERTY do understand that impious *Impostoria pila,* so frequently of late exhibited, and held forth to the People, whilst (in the meane time) indeed, it is thrown into the hands of a few private Persons. By FREEDOME is here intended that which the Philosopher teacheth us: . . . not that Platonique Chimaera of a State, no where existant save in UTOPIA. . . . And of this truth we have now had the experience of more than five thousand yeeres, during all which . . . never was there either heard, or read of a more equal & excelent form of Government than that under which we our selves have lived, during the Reign of our most gratious Soveraignes Halcion daies. . . . If therefore we were once the most happy of Subjects, why do we thus attempt to render our selves the most miserable of Slaves?
>
> (A9–10)

Rejecting a literal *translatio* of Tityrus's term *libertas* into the political structure of the 1640s, the anonymous author insists instead on converting it into a philosophical abstraction. Freedom cannot mean the manumission of the slave, far less any general principle of democratic egalitarianism, a principle which has in his recent experience been invoked only in order to mask the transfer of power to an ambitious oligarchy; rather, it must now be understood as the stoic principle of self-knowledge and self-sufficiency, the state of mind of the superior, philosophic "felix qui" of the second georgic.

The appropriation of Virgil to their own cause was not unique to the royalists. A few educated men who supported the revolution clearly felt the need to challenge their opponents' monopolization of pastoral, and all it could stand for. So in 1654 Richard Flecknoe dedicated his pastoral romance, *Love's Dominion,* to Cromwell's daughter, Lady Elizabeth Claypole, and asserted in its preface the right of the "Anti-Pastoral party" to have pastorals of their own.[25] More directly to the point, Andrew Marvell celebrated in 1657 the marriage of Cromwell's third daughter Mary by naming her "Menalcas' daughter" and proposing Cromwell himself, as Menalcas, as a figure of cultural plenitude:

---

[25] Richard Flecknoe, *Love's Dominion* (London, 1654), folio A5r. Flecknoe adds that he chose pastoral romance because he "thought it necessary there first to apply the Remedy, where the harm was most universal, . . . and there begin the Reformation of the State, where its abuse was most frequent" (folio A6v).

Fear not, at Menalcas' Hall
There is Bayes enough for all.
He when Young as we did graze,
But when old he planted Bayes.[26]

These were private compliments, but three years earlier Marvell's Latinity had been brought into the service of the commonwealth, providing a Virgilian distich to accompany Cromwell's portrait as a diplomatic gift to Queen Christina of Sweden:

Haec est quae toties Inimicos Umbra fugavit,
At sub qua Cives Otia lenta terunt

(1:108)

This shadow-picture is that which absolutely
puts enemies to flight, but beneath which
citizens enjoy peaceful leisure.

In one deft reordering of the value-bearing fragments of Virgil's first eclogue, he reattributed to Cromwell the protective shade of Caroline idyll, while making it clear that the peace of the Commonwealth was based on military activism. At the same time, as one would expect from Marvell, the term *umbra* is made to reflect back upon itself, as that which connotes the gap between the icon and the original, political effectiveness inseparable from representational inadequacy.

Marvell was also deeply interested in Virgil's second eclogue, and characteristically urbane in his response. In *Damon the Mower* he identified his overheated and clumsy rustic, who ends by running his scythe into his own leg, as Virgil's Corydon, marking the connection by quotation. Virgil's "nec sum adeo informis: nuper me in litore vidi . . . si numquam fallit imago" reappears as Damon's irresistible country narcissism:

Nor am I so deform'd to sight,
If in my Sithe I looked right;
In which I see my Picture done,
As in a crescent Moon the sun.

(1: 46)

Yet the match between their personalities should only emphasize the difference in their occupations, Marvell's Damon being unmistakably a worker,

---

[26]Andrew Marvell, *Poems and Letters*, ed. H. M. Margoliouth, rev. Pierre Legouis, 2 vols. (Oxford, 1971), 1: 128.

a georgic figure, whose "Sweat" the sun "licks off" and who deliberately contrasts himself to the "piping Shepherd" (line 49). He is therefore socially a correction of his Virgilian prototype, whose *otium* was signified by his own mention of "reapers weary in the consuming heat," a point that had been visually established for the last century and a half by illustrated editions that derived from Sebastian Brant's.

These inferences are more than confirmed in *Upon Appleton House,* where the scene of haymaking in the meadows has long been recognized as a metaphor for the civil war. There is no doubt of Marvell's intentions in the main shape of the analogy:

> The Mower now commands the Field;
> In whose new Traverse seemeth wrought
> A Camp of Battail newly fought:
> Where, as the Meads with Hay, the Plain
> Lyes quilted ore with Bodies slain:
> The Women that with forks it fling,
> Do represent the Pillaging.

(1: 75, lines 418–24)

But there is also another kind of sociopolitical referent here, embodied in the figure of Thestylis. In Virgil's second eclogue, especially as interpreted by Brant (see Fig. 12), Thestylis is part of the reminder that Corydon's complaint is made against a background of rural labor; and the fact that in Brant's woodcut Thestylis became the center of the composition leads surely to her strange centrality in Marvell's poem. As the basket on her head in which she brings, as Marvell puts it, "the mowing Camp their Cates" (line 402) signifies her participation in real life and work, so her obtrusiveness in Brant's design becomes in Marvell's consciousness a vivid interruption of the imaginative process, cutting into the poet-tutor's reverie and breaking down his self-enclosure. When the mowers, whom he has silently compared to the Israelites crossing a green sea, accidentally slice up a meadow-bird, Thestylis becomes the voice of peasant realism mocking his metaphors. "Greedy as Kites," she pounces on the bird "And forthwith means on it to sup." But she also, mysteriously, cries aloud:

> he call'd us Israelites;
> But now, to make his saying true,
> Rails rain for Quails, for Manna Dew.

(lines 403–8)

By identifying himself with Corydon and by identifying Thestylis with an actual and brutal rusticity, Marvell took elegant cognizance of a double dialectic: that between pastoral leisure and rural labor, as in the Virgilian original; and that between Cavalier contempt for the rustic laborer and the voice of genuine social protest, most clearly heard in the programs of the Levellers and Diggers.

It is usually assumed that Marvell was hostile to such voices.[27] Yet as tutor to Sir Thomas Fairfax's household, he cannot have been unaware of the social paradoxes becoming apparent in the revolution. As Margaret James pointed out, the record of the Long Parliament on agrarian policy was conservative at best, involving the suppression by force of anti-enclosure riots, the dispersal of the Diggers from St. George's Hill in Surrey, and, most ironically, the acquisition by leaders of the revolution of large estates that had been confiscated from the royalists.[28] In 1647 Fairfax received, by parliamentary ordinance, land to the value of five thousand pounds, a very considerable estate;[29] and two years later it was to Fairfax that Winstanley and Everard presented the case of the Diggers. As Winstanley informed Fairfax in a published letter, the agrarian policy of the revolution required him to answer a fundamental question: "whether the earth with her fruits, was made to be bought and sold from one to another: and whether one part of mankind was made Lord of the land, and another part a servant, by the law of Creation before the fall?" Wielding a biblical rather than classical authority, Winstanley asserted that "Abel shall not alwaies be slain, nor alwaies lie under the bondage of Cains cursed propriety"[30]—which brings us back full circle to Bacon, and those beginning-of-the-century hopes for a reconciliation between pastoral and georgic as cultural models. In *Upon Appleton House,* Marvell quietly admits how wide the gap has grown between pastoral and georgic, between the intellectual and the worker; and while placing himself, as poet-tutor, inevitably on one side of the gap, he allows for considerable irony at his own and his employer's expense.

Such indirection, with Virgil at its center, is typical of Marvell. We do not normally associate it with Milton, at least not with the Milton of the civil war period. Yet in 1645, the man who had resisted a literary appearance in Caroline culture chose to publish his first collection of poems

[27] On the basis of the hostile comment in *The First Anniversary of the Government under O.C.:* Cromwell is compared to the olive in Jotham's fable in Judges 9 : 8–15, and his opponents to the ambitious brambles who "without a timely stop, / Had quickly Levell'd every Cedar's top" (1: 115). The comparable allusion in *Upon Appleton House,* however, describing the recently flooded meadows as a "naked equal Flat, / Which Levellers take Pattern at" (1: 76), is socially ambiguous, for it is here that "The Villagers in common chase / Their Cattle."

[28] Margaret James, *Social Problems and Policy during the Puritan Revolution 1640–1660* (New York, 1966), pp. 80–96.

[29] *Journal of the House of Commons,* 5: 162.

[30] Gerrard Winstanley, *Works . . . with an Appendix of Documents Relating to the Digger Movement,* ed. G. H. Sabine (Ithaca, 1941), pp. 289–90.

under an epigraph from Virgil's seventh eclogue, the lines spoken by Thyrsis as the beginning of his singing match: "Baccare frontem / Cingite, ne vati noceat mala lingua futuro" ("Wreathe his brow with ivy, lest evil tongues harm the future bard," 7.27–28). Louis Martz has argued that the function of the quotation was to draw attention to the "rising poet," while at the same time defining the limitations of the *Eclogues* as model. The *Poems of Mr. John Milton,* with its English and Latin poems separated into twin volumes and its tissue of quotations from the *Eclogues,* especially in *Lycidas* and the *Epitaphium Damonis,* presented in effect an account of a poetic apprenticeship and suggested his farewell to the pastoral genre. So Milton's "vos cedite silvae" in the Latin elegy is, as Martz points out, an echo of the "concedite silvae" with which Gallus bids farewell to Arcadian pleasures (10.63), while his threat to leave his pipe dangling on some ancient pine tree, far away and forgotten ("Tu procul annosa pendebis, fistula, pinu / Multum oblita mihi") revises Corydon's boast in Eclogue 7.24–25. In other words, the volume is a retrospective arranged at the age of thirty-seven with the wisdom of hindsight, and its purpose was to formalize Milton's "farewell to the pleasures and attitudes of youth."[31]

As well as a statement of personal evolution, the 1645 volume functions as a record, enigmatic but nonetheless telling, of the social history of pastoral in the Caroline era. In the *Hymn on the Morning of Christs Nativity,* a pacific poem composed as Charles was in the process of negotiating his own peace with Spain, Milton produced his own "messianic" poem; yet for all its reference to "the age of gold" the poem firmly demotes its own pastoral content:

> The Shepherds on the Lawn,
> Or ere the point of dawn,
>   Sate simply chatting in a rustick row;
> Full little thought they than,
> That the mighty Pan
>   Was kindly come to live with them below;
> Perhaps their loves, or els their sheep,
> Was all that did their silly thoughts so busie keep.[32]

If the primary argument here is the disproportion between pastoral metaphor and Christian content—a denial, in effect, of the traditional reading of Virgil's fourth eclogue—there would have been a secondary inference available to the reader in 1645, that the pastorals in which Caroline poets

[31] Louis L. Martz, *Poet of Exile: A Study of Milton's Poetry* (New Haven, 1980), pp. 34, 37.
[32] *The Works of John Milton,* ed. Frank Allen Patterson, 18 vols. (New York, 1931–38), I: i: 4–5.

had celebrated the various births of the king's children had trivialized the form and rendered it useless for devotional poetry. And in *Lycidas,* written in 1637, and appearing in 1645 with a defiant headnote identifying the author as an opponent of Laud and the Anglican prelates,[33] the overt homage to Virgil's first eclogue was accompanied by the suggestion that even in secular pastoral the genre had been betrayed by the Caroline focus on the ethos of Tityrus:[34]

> Alas! What boots it with uncessant care
> To tend the homely slighted Shepherd's trade,
> And strictly meditate the thankles Muse?
> Were it not better don as other use,
> To sport with Amaryllis in the shade . . . ?

(I: i: 79)

The origins of this famous moment of vocational doubt are not only Virgil's *meditaris* and *lentus in umbra,* but also Cavalier lyrics (or pastoral drama) in which the erotic potential of pastoral, encapsulated in the name of Amaryllis, was strategically exaggerated. Carew's *A Rapture,* for instance, cited in the Long Parliament as an instance of royalist decadence, created alongside his *Answer* a diptych of Caroline pastoral ideology and iconography. Beaumont and Fletcher's *The Faithful Shepherdess* had been revived in 1634 as a "smooth Pastorall" for Henrietta Maria's entertainment.[35] The latter was unquestionably at the back of Milton's mind in 1634 when he constructed his own pastoral entertainment, *A Masque at Ludlow,* and made its argument partly turn on the contrast between the attendant spirit and Comus, *both* disguised as shepherds. The viewer's task was to discriminate between a lawful metaphor indigenous to pastoral tradition and an unwarrantable appropriation of the genre: on the one hand, the artist (Henry Lawes as Thyrsis) enacting his own cultural function as good shepherd of the country's morals; on the other, the aristocratic spendthrift Comus, pretending pastoralism only to betray.

---

[33] In 1645 the poem, with hindsight, "foretells the ruin of our corrupted Clergy then in their height."

[34] Compare J. W. Saunders, "Milton, Diomede and Amaryllis," *ELH* 22 (1955): 254–86. For a similar argument with respect to *Comus,* see Maryann McGuire, *Milton's Puritan Masque* (Athens, Ga., 1983). Yet *Comus* had been published in 1637 with a Virgilian pastoral epigraph, "Eheu / quid volui misero mihi! floribus austrum / Perditus," a self-deprecatory identification with Corydon which disappears from the 1645 *Poems* only to be replaced by the equally peculiar emphasis on "mala lingua." Both epigraphs suggest that Milton was unsure of his ground.

[35] See *The Dramatic Works in the Beaumont and Fletcher Canon,* ed. Fredson Bowers, 5 vols. (Cambridge, 1976), 3: 498; and my *Censorship and Interpretation* (Madison, 1984), pp. 172–74.

This splitting of the model suggests that Milton was heteroglot in his response both to pastoral and to the ideological issues for which it was currently serving as a language. It is one of the oddities of the 1645 *Poems* that Milton's portrait appears on the frontispiece, with a pastoral scene in the background visually reinforcing the message of the volume's network of quotations from the *Eclogues,* but *also* representing the poet in Cavalier dress and hairstyle. The title page defers ostentatiously to "Mr. Henry Lawes Gentleman of the Kings Chappel, and one of His Majesties Private Musick"; and as Martz pointed out, Moseley's preface associated Milton with Edmund Waller, recently exiled for a royalist plot against the Long Parliament. It is difficult to accommodate these gestures to the John Milton whose stance at the beginning of the civil war had been unmistakably revolutionary, at least with respect to the question of church government. And there are signs in his earliest poems that Milton, who suffered all his life from a conflict between radicalism and elitism, found support in the idea of pastoral for the doctrine of his own intellectual superiority, a doctrine that was clearly incompatible with social reform. His Lady, in the *Masque,* is not only herself an aristocrat, performing a courtly ritual, but she draws a *class* distinction between herself and another kind of pastoral performance:

> me thought it was the sound
> Of Riot, and ill manag'd Merriment,
> Such as the jocond Flute, or gamesome Pipe
> Stirs up among the loose *unletter'd* Hinds,
> When for their teeming Flocks and granges full
> In wanton dance they praise the bounteous Pan,
> And thank the gods amiss. I should be loath
> To meet the rudeness.

> (I: i: 91; italics added)

It is true that the noise she hears is that of Comus and his revelers; but her instinctive elitism is confirmed at the end of the masque, when the "Swains" on her father's estate are first permitted to dance in celebration of her escape and then dismissed to their normal occupation: "Back Shepherds, back, anough your play, / Till next Sun-shine holiday" (I: i: 121). The social vision is that of *L'Allegro,* the man who sees country life as a storehouse of his own pleasures, who is confident that rural laborers enjoy their work as much as he enjoys its contemplation:

> While the Plowman neer at hand,
> Whistles ore the Furrow'd Land,
> And the Milkmaid singeth blithe,

And the Mower whets his sithe,
And every Shepherd tells his tale
Under the Hawthorn in the dale.
Streit mine eye hath caught new pleasures.

(I: i: 36–37)

It was this strain in Milton's thought, utterly at odds with the populist aims of Brant's approach to the "unletter'd" or even with Spenser's more complicated populism, that blended the 1645 volume into Caroline culture, apparently with Milton's approbation. The distinction that Milton sought to make between Thyrsis and Comus was in some fundamental way unmakable by him. Beside Marvell he seems comparatively unself-knowing. On the one hand his Virgilian allusions suggest a critique of the complacencies of Caroline pastoral and a return to a "strict" conception of the genre as the basis for a serious and reformed national culture; on the other, the frontal royalist associations suggest a resistance to the anti-literary tendencies of the revolution, and a temporary realignment with an aristocratic culture that, for all its faults, was at least in favor of the arts. It may be that these contradictions were themselves manifest to Milton as he compiled the 1645 volume, and that their irreconcilability was another motive, beyond maturation, for saying goodbye to pastoral.[36]

The story of the politics of Virgilian quotation in seventeenth-century England clearly cannot be completed here. Yet we need to follow Milton with one last example of how the Virgilian metaphor of shade served both to identify an ideological position and to imply the structure and purpose of a poetic collection. We run in this some risk of bathos, for the writer in question, Mildmay Fane, earl of Westmorland, was a minor poet at best and at worst an execrable one. Nevertheless, the issues raised by his *Otia Sacra*,[37] a two-part anthology of pastoral poetry published in 1648, are paradigmatic of English culture at mid-century and will lead us directly into another aspect of Virgilian interpretation, that of the wholesale translation. Fane's volume, published at a crucial moment in English political history, when the nation had more or less abandoned faith in Charles I, a moment marked by the Vote of No Addresses, presented itself under two Virgilian epigraphs, one for each section of the volume. The first title page featured a pillar of faith, thereby converting its quotation from Eclogue 1.6, "Deus nobis haec Otia fecit," "A god gave us this leisure," to Christian functionalism. The second offered a pastoral landscape (Fig. 17) with a slight misquotation of 1.2 and 4: "tutus in Umbra / Silvestram tenui

---

[36] Milton returned to pastoral, of course, in its most absolute form, in the Edenic scenes of *Paradise Lost*.

[37] Mildmay Fane, *Otia Sacra* (London, 1648), ed. Donald M. Friedman (New York, 1975).

Figure 17. William Marshall, second frontispiece to Mildmay Fane's *Otia sacra* (London, 1648), p. 124. By permission of the British Library.

Musam meditatus avena." The substitution of *tutus* for *lentus* is only the most explicit stage in the process of interpretation we have marked from Servius through the humanists to the Caroline idyllicists, but in this instance Fane translated it into a structural principle. The first part of his volume contained almost nothing except devotional poems. In the poem which explains the presence of a second part, this preliminary religiosity is explained as strategic: it "bears a stamp Divine, / And so may pass for currant Coin" (p. 125). In other words, it may pass the scrutiny of the Presbyterian divines now in charge of the licensing system. Meanwhile, in the second part, the work will "swim under a shade / Of such Security" as the pastoral metaphor provides, a protected space "where no times rage or thunder / Shall blast or scorch those [who] so lie under." There is even an allusion here, it seems, to the Servian gloss on the blasted oaks of Eclogue 1.17. And thanks to the tradition of writing *latenter,* Fane could now convert the Virgilian *umbra* into a private language for the use of royalists, a code in which the king's servants could express their "modest Loyaltie; / such as the Hils, and Groves, and Brooks / Afford the Fancy."

The facts suggest precisely how modest Fane's loyalty was. The records show him host to the king in 1639, contributing to his army fund in 1642, and in the same summer appointed as one of his Commissioners of Array. They also show him complaining about ship-money assessments, and hesitating about putting his military charge into effect.[38] Fane's hesitation did not preserve him. In August 1642 he was arrested and sent to the Tower; he was one of the first Cavaliers to compound with the Long Parliament for the release of his estate from confiscation. *Otia Sacra* is, therefore, the statement of a man who has already had his convictions tested and has discovered the prudential limits to his royalism. The second part of his volume, accordingly, witnesses to an unusually unsettled pastoral ethos. Poems of Stoic retreat modeled on Horace and on Virgil's second georgic alternate with comments on the political situation, past and present. The most astonishing poem in *Otia Sacra* is one in which Fane, disguising himself as a female pastoral figure (Chloris), appears to make a public apology for his compounding:

> My Kalendar yet marks out spring,
> Disgust may shake, not blast the Blossoming.
>   And therefore as I roav'd astray,
> 'Tis reconciling Truth points now the way
>   In which I would be thought as farr
> From variation, as the fixedst Starr;

---

[38] See Clifford Leech's edition of two of Fane's unpublished plays, "Raguallo D'Oceano" and "Candy Restored, 1641" (Louvain, 1938), pp. 12–14.

But with a constant shining thence,
Serve King and Countrey by my Influence.

(p. 130)

The interest for us in this eccentric procedure lies less in what it tells us about Fane's uneasy conscience than in what it implies about his understanding of the *Eclogues,* and the choice that they initiated for the intellectual between self-preservation and sociopolitical principle. What are the responsibilities of a writer in a period of civil war, or under a hostile regime? Is it better to suffer the hardships of political exile and silence, to sing no more ("carmina nulla canam"); or is it better to survive in the shade and keep the lines of communication open, to continue, in Fane's phrase, to "serve King and Country by [one's] Influence," by exerting more subtle pressures on the culture? These questions were inevitably reiterated throughout the revolutionary period, but never more intensely than in the years immediately after the execution of the king, and in the aftermath of the battle of Worcester in 1651, when any further possibility of a military restoration of the Stuarts was abandoned.

"Making Them His Own": The Politics of Translation

It is often said that any translation is an act of interpretation, and no one any longer doubts that all translation is culturally determined. The mere fact that the classical texts, in particular, seem to require a new translation for each major shift in aesthetic, philosophic, or social premises proves the point, notwithstanding the possibility of contemporary and rival translations in very different styles, yet intended for the same audience. For the purposes of this study, translations of Virgil's *Eclogues* are particularly instrumental in documenting both cultural history in general and in particular the ideological factors in the reception of that text: a close comparison of how certain crucial passages were rendered from one translation to the next can exert an unusually precise control over our own interpretive assumptions. In the remainder of this chapter we will examine three different English translations of the seventeenth century, created for three markedly different cultural situations: the first, a semi-anonymous translation produced for the Caroline court at the very beginning of the halcyon days; the second, a document of the Protectorate era, but unmistakably designed for a royalist audience; and the third, Dryden's translation of the turn of the century, which both records the political experience of the previous half-century and, in its style and stated aesthetic, anticipates what we call Neoclassicism.

In 1628, at a turning point in Charles's reign, there appeared a new translation of Virgil's *Eclogues,* to replace the by then obsolete Elizabethan version of Abraham Fleming and the literal, schooltext version of John Brinsley.[39] The Stationers' Register for 17 July 1628 refers to "A booke called Virgills Egloges in English with a glosse by Master Latham gentleman." This was undoubtedly the volume published sometime in 1628 by W.L., which has subsequently been attributed to William L'Isle, once a groom in James's household and now in his sixties a gentleman-scholar at Cambridge with a reputation for pioneering in Anglo-Saxon scholarship. Yet there is nothing to attach this translation to L'Isle in defiance of the Stationers' Register except those initials; they may well belong to the William Latham who matriculated at Emmanuel College, Cambridge, in 1591.[40]

Whoever he was, this translator was either ill-informed or disingenuous, since he claimed, not that he was superseding his predecessors, but that his translation had no forerunner:

> I am the first, that have met my Countrymen with these dainty Æclogues, in our English tongue: which (beeing like Riddles, wrapt up in a Mask, and under a clowd of reserved sense, & a double Meaning,) I have sent abroad with a Gloss borrow'd from divers learned Authors, as strangers with a guide to direct them in an unknown way.[41]

But in fact the "Gloss" is "borrow'd" entirely from Ludovico Vives, a debt that Latham admits by proceeding also to translate, as a second introduction, Vives's own preface:

> I will never make nice to intermixe these so pleasing and sweet remissions, and unbending of the minde, with the severity of my more serious studies, and to comment upon the merry Muses, as now of late I have done upon Virgils *Bucolickes,* out of which I have picked a deeper sense in many places, than the vulgar common Grammarians can conceive. For, did these Aeglogues containe in them no farther hidden matter, than the very bare barke of the words makes shew of, I cannot thinke that the Author had needed to have taken three yeares time to have brought them to perfection, especially borrowing the greatest part of the whole subject out of Theocritus the Sicilian Poet.
>
> (pp. 9–10)

[39] A[braham] F[leming], *The Bucoliks of Publius Virgilius Maro, Prince of the Latine Poets, Otherwise Called His Pastoralls, or Shepeherds Meetings* . . . (London, 1589).
[40] John and J. A. Venn, *Alumni Cantabrigienses,* 10 vols. (Cambridge, 1922–54), 3: 49.
[41] *Virgils Eclogues Translated into English* (London, 1628), fols. 7v–8r.

A reader familiar with Brinsley might well have noted the coincidence, that here was an approach to Virgil beyond the reach of "vulgar common Grammarians"; instead of grammatical fluency in Latin, with the structure of the language laid bare in an ungainly word-for-word translation, it is now the allure of interpretive difficulty that is offered as the incentive.

But there was also in Vives, we remember, a strong implication that the chief audience for the *Eclogues* were the leaders of the state:

> Adde hereunto, that he undertooke this taske to present the greatest wits of Rome withall, namely Cornelius Gallus, Asinius Pollio, Varus, Tucca, yea the Prince himselfe Augustus; all which (excellently learned men themselves, and much conversant and accustomed in the best and chiefest writers, both in Greeke and Latin) would doubtlesse never have been so taken, and infinitely delighted, with such kindes of light matter as Pastoralls, had they not affoorded some hidden meaning and sense of a higher nature.
>
> (p. 10)

And if Latham intended his translation for a similar audience, his choice of Vives as an interpreter was indeed prophetic. For this was exactly the hermeneutical stance likely to appeal to a court that would shortly create a new, neo-Platonized version of pastoral romance, in which higher meanings were to be the justification for the vast amounts of attention and money lavished on court theatricals.[42]

The translation of Vives's preface shows how easily a translator can alter the cultural resonance of a text, even while hewing faithfully to his original:

> Againe, . . . it is to be thought that Virgil, under these sporting passages of pastorall verse, did finely and neatly as it were, inlay, and couch many things tending to their praise and commendation, . . . which being understood rightly, might affect the Readers mindes; like the elegant and artificiall Pictures, which lay secretly hidden under the statue of the Sileni. . . . The matter itselfe and subject of this worke doth plainly witnesse in sundry places, that it is not simply, but figuratively spoken, under a shadow: . . . wherefore I have thought good, to signifie to the world, that I have trimmed up these Allegories for their use, and behoofe, who are delighted with the reading of Virgil (as

---

[42] See Louis Carlane, *L'Influence Française en Angleterre au XVIIᵉ siècle* (Paris, 1904); George Sensabaugh, "Love Ethics in Platonic/Court Drama," *Huntington Library Quarterly* 1 (1938): 277–304; Sensabaugh, "Platonic Love and the Puritan Rebellion," *Studies in Philology* 37 (1940): 457–81.

who is it that is not?) to the end that the finest wits might have a certaine repast, and delicate foode fitting their taste, and might be drawne
to mount higher than the simple sense of the very bare letter. Moreover I shall hereby restore the Poet to the true scope and aime of his
meaning, and shew, that his purpose was not to consume so much precious time, and exquisite verses in triviall light matters of no moment;
and that those things which Theocritus in a ruder barbarous age, did
sing in a Pastorall plaine sense, Virgil here doth apply to the Romans,
making them his owne, under a mysticall understanding, worthy the
eares of the most learned: notwithstanding I make no doubt but I have
fitted some of his verses with such an allegory and explication, as the
Author himselfe never dreamed of.

(pp. 10–12)

Faithfully reproduced here are Vives's eclectic historicism and hermeneutical candor, his recognition that as Virgil engaged in "applying" Theocritean pastoral to the needs of his Roman audience the enigmas he created
remained open to later and quite different interpretive needs; and without
doing anything more than writing like a Caroline gentleman, this translator in effect demonstrated the accuracy of Vives's perception. For "obtex-
isse," the Caroline reader found "did finely and neatly, as it were, inlay, and
couch." Where Vives had written "ut habeant praestantiora ingenia, velut
pastum quendam sibi congruentem," the translation offers "to the end that
the finest wits might have a certaine repast, and delicate foode fitting their
taste." The difference seems marginal; but what happens nonetheless (given
the interpretive community to which this text was addressed) was an aes-
theticization of the text, the imposition of a courtly code on a humanist one.

It is also noteworthy that Latham's treatment of Vives's glosses (which
is highly selective) particularly favors those with a strong pacificist emphasis. One of the longest notes replicates that of Vives on "si numquam fallit
imago" in Eclogue 2:

In the time of the last peace, when in the cessation of warres, every
man betooke him to his owne home, laying by their Armes, and all
tumults remooved, that so it may appeare, that they were at leisure, to
make a true estimate of me; For as quiet still water, doth receive the
resemblance of the face, and so presents it back againe; so when the
mind is quiet, it gives right judgement, which being troubled, and full
of agitation it is not able to perform. The Poet here very fitly names
Italy the sea, and the Windes the troubles of wars.

(p. 34)

And on the cry of Meliboeus, "En quo discordia civis / produxit miseros" (1.71–72), the gloss reads: "Civill warres, not onely in Rome, the head of the Empire, but also intestine broyles in every hamlet and tributary towne; And this is a sentence, full of weight, and grave indignation: *describing herein the maine reason and ground of the subversion, and alienation of all Kingdomes, to proceede from mutinous and envious distractions, amongst the people of the same Nation*" (p. 24). The passage in italics is entirely his own addition. We therefore need to recall that in 1628 Peter Paul Rubens was in London to negotiate on behalf of Spain for a peace settlement, and that by the end of July rumors were rife in London that peace was imminent.[43] In other words, Latham was imitating Vives also in being a lobbyist for the peace that would later be celebrated by Fanshawe and Carew. But his reference to "intestine broyles" (like Fanshawe's admission that the land was "obdurate") would also have reminded his audience that throughout 1628 the king had been locked in a struggle with parliament about how the war was to be funded and over Buckingham's misconduct of the campaign, and in early June fears were expressed in the Lords that Charles would prorogue the parliament in order to proceed unilaterally in his dealings with Spain. These fears were well founded; parliament was prorogued on 26 June.

These facts may also explain the remarkable emphasis that Latham gives in his commentary to the ever-tendentious *Libertas* of Eclogue 1. Vives had set the direction with a gloss that took issue with Servius's grammatical approach to subversion, denying that *libertas* was a locution unlikely to be used by a shepherd, but arguing nevertheless that Virgil intended this *speciosus titulus* to be taken ironically. But Latham expands this gloss so far beyond the five lines of the original that it takes on a disproportionate importance; unless we perceive that the emphasis so produced was proportionate, rather, to occurrences outside the translation. In the citation that follows, the sections in brackets are Latham's additions:

> A specious tittle, and a very reasonable pretext, and such as might easily pierse the simple mind of a Shepheard; [it being even imprinted in the disposition of all creatures as well reasonable, as others, naturally to affect freedome: which principle is found most true by daily experience, in such birds and beasts, as by mans art are reclaimed, how loath they are to yeeld unto bondage; and being subdued, if never so little left to themselves, how soone they apprehend their first estate and freedome, and how warily they preserve themselves from being en-

---

[43] On 31 July 1628, Sir Francis Nethersole told Conway to discuss the rumors of peace with Spain with Elizabeth, Queen of Bohemia. See Russell, *Parliaments and English Politics*, p. 390.

thralled againe.] Againe Virgil could not have devised to have flattered
more artificially, than by confessing to have gained liberty by his
meanes, who was suspected to have aimed at the destruction and usur-
pation of the generall liberty and immunities of Rome: moreover in
acknowledging Caesars favour, for restoring him to his estate and liberty: he yet mentions his libertie in the first place, [as the most excellent benefit, worthy to bee preferred before all other blessings what-
soever, as a Jewell of most incomparable value; which caused another
Poet to cry out, as being rapt with admiration thereof: *O bona libertas,
pretio, pretiosior omni:* Deere Liberty, a gemm beyond all price.]

(p. 19)

It would have been impossible to read this passage in England in 1628
without attempting to correlate its emphasis with the debates in the House
of Commons and *their* focus on the liberty of the subject as the counter-
principle to royal prerogative. Latham's translation, therefore, cannot simply be understood as a document whose pacifist ethos supported the
king's new direction in foreign policy; for despite the attempt, as it were,
to expand the idea of liberty by making it equally accessible to men and
animals, the political origins of the gloss survive and are recorded with (for
Latham) unusual clarity. We do not find here what we shall later find in
Wordsworth, a concept of "natural" liberty that the shepherds of his Lake
District memories are supposed to have possessed in defiance of social
facts, of their actual working conditions. Instead, the concept is rendered,
by expansion, an undebatable human right and value. Latham's motives in
translating this text and this commentary at this time must, therefore, have
been not merely pacifist but mediatorial, conciliatory of the two forces
whose conflict at home made a mockery of peace abroad; and his selection
of Vives as the foundation of his own enterprise was, given the earlier
scholar's contributions to the theory of concord, remarkably acute.

The ultimate cost of the halcyon days was the civil war. And it is perhaps not surprising that the next major translation did not appear until the
war was over, in the period known to some as the Protectorate and to
others, depending on their political sympathies, as the Interregnum. There
is considerable evidence, however, that whatever the ideology of the survivors, both sides decided that the time had come for accommodation. On
the one hand, Cromwell himself embarked on a campaign of moderate reform combined with limited conciliation of the royalists (until the Penrud-
dock rising of 1655 convinced him that such leniency was dangerous); on
the other, the disaster at Worcester persuaded the various factions of royalists in exile to return to the policy of the moderates, conceived by Edward
Hyde, later Earl of Clarendon, and expressed in terms of the wisdom of
patience. In place of the Western Association, the militant at-home con-

spiracy that had supported the 1651 invasion, the new policy passed for execution to the Sealed Knot, a group of six selected by Hyde himself and directly authorized by Charles II.[44] Their mandate was as follows:

> As they would not engage in any absurd and desperate attempt, but use all their credit and authority to prevent and discountenance the same, so they would take the first rational opportunity, which they expected from the divisions and animosities which daily grew and appeared in the army, to draw their friends and old soldiers who were ready to receive their commands together, and try the utmost that could be done with[out] the loss or hazard of their lives.[45]

It is in this context of engagement politics and a new, accommodationist version of royalist conspiracy that we can best understand the achievement of John Ogilby, in the first outstanding translation of Virgil produced in England.

If John Ogilby's name is recognized at all today, it is probably in reference to his translation of Aesop, or to his Restoration role as Charles II's cosmographer.[46] His reputation as a translator of Virgil has been completely eclipsed, in our century, by that of Dryden, for reasons that themselves bear reinvestigation. Few of Dryden's admirers care to discuss the fact that the impressive engraved plates in his 1697 *Virgil,* designed by Franz Cleyn and executed by Hollar, Lombart, and Faithorne, were actually created for Ogilby's folio edition of 1654. By merely changing the dedications at the foot of those plates, Dryden was able to use them to fulfill his obligations to his own subscribers, while at the same time he inherited for his own translation the prestige that Ogilby's had hitherto maintained.[47]

The disteem in which Ogilby's *Virgil* is now usually held is partly to be accounted for by the *Dictionary of National Biography,* where the original culprits are identified. "Ogilby's name," we are informed, "thanks to the ridicule of Dryden in *MacFlecknoe* and of Pope in the *Dunciad,* has become almost proverbial for a bad poet." Ogilby's reputation as a translator, in

[44] See David Underdown, *Royalist Conspiracy in England, 1649–1660* (New Haven, 1960), pp. 30–51, 73–96.

[45] Quoted by Underdown, *Royalist Conspiracy,* p. 87, from the *Life of Edward Earl of Clarendon* (Oxford, 1857).

[46] The most complete account of Ogilby's career is by Katherine S. Van Eerde, *John Ogilby and the Taste of His Times* (Folkestone, 1976). See also Marion Eames, "John Ogilby and His *Aesop,*" *Bulletin of the New York Public Library* 65 (1960): 73–88; and Margret Schuchard, *John Ogilby, 1600–1676: Lebensbild eines Gentelman mit vielen Karrieren* (Bern, 1973).

[47] As is indicated in the title of L. Proudfoot's *Dryden's Aeneid and Its Seventeenth-Century Predecessors* (Manchester, 1960).

other words, has been largely determined by the sneers of Dryden and Pope, each of whom might well have had a personal interest in depreciating a translator whose versions of Virgil and Homer they hoped to replace with their own. The *Dictionary* completed its evaluation by observing that Ogilby also wrote an epic poem, the *Carolies,* in honor of Charles I, in twelve books, all of them "fortunately burnt in the fire of London."

But within the longer perspective of Virgilian reception and inter-pretation, Ogilby's accomplishment reappears as the landmark it undoubt-edly was in 1649 and especially in 1654, when the small octavo version of the translation was replaced by a sumptuous folio edition, provided with an elaborate series of marginalia, in the best commentary tradition, and ornamented by "sculptures," or finely engraved illustrations, individually dedicated to members of the aristocracy and gentry.[48] As Anthony à Wood remarked, "it was the fairest Edition that till then the English Press ever produced," and was "reserved for libraries and the Nobility."[49] Wood's comment underlines the unique cultural status effected by this production. As the choice of Virgil spoke specifically to the educated mind and to the literary imagination, which during the revolution were assumed for the purposes of propaganda to be the property of the royalists,[50] so the address to an economic and cultural elite was expressed in the cost of the volume and the individual dedications, which made the volume visibly the prop-erty of the beleaguered upper class.

What Wood did not mention was the significance of the family par-ticularly selected for eminence. Ogilby's 1649 *Virgil* was dedicated to William Seymour, Marquess of Hertford, head of the great Seymour fam-ily in the west. The first six plates of his 1654 *Virgil* (and hence of the *Eclogues*) were dedicated to William Seymour, to his son, Henry, Lord Beauchamp, and to other members of their family. It can scarcely have been a coincidence that Beauchamp was head of the Western Association, whose crushing defeat at the battle of Worcester in 1651 was in effect framed by Ogilby's two *Virgils*; and his special form of address to them was certainly part of the new interpretive context that he brought to the text, and that his pre-selected and self-selected audience was expected to under-stand. It seems highly likely that it was the failure of the 1649 text to make its message sufficiently clear that led, along with more orthodox financial and careerist motives, to the 1654 production.

The powerfully historicized nature of Ogilby's reading of Virgil was already apparent in the 1649 octavo, even if his medium for expressing it was not yet fully developed. It is apparent already in the "Argument" he

---

[48] There were actually two separate octavo editions: one in 1649, printed by T. R. and E. M. for John Crook, and one in 1650, printed by Thomas Maxey for Andrew Crook.

[49] Anthony à Wood, *Athenae Oxonienses* (London, 1691), 2: 263.

[50] See P. W. Thomas, "Two Cultures? Court and Country under Charles I," in Conrad Russell, ed., *The Origins of the English Civil War* (London, 1973), pp. 168–93.

supplied for the first eclogue, four lines which inevitably shape a reader's first impressions:

> Sad Meliboeus banished declares
> Those miseries attend on civill Wars,
> But happy Tityrus, the safe defence
> People enjoy, under a setled Prince.
>
> (p. 1)

While there is nothing here that had not been anticipated in Virgilian commentary since Servius, the connections among "civill Wars," "safe defence," and "a setled Prince" were striking, inviting seventeenth-century readers to align the civil wars of Rome and of England and to consider where the condition of Tityrus was discoverable in the English half of the analogy; was it during the halcyon days of the Caroline era, or, now that the king was dead, was it only an ideal for the future, dependent on the restoration of Charles II? The pressure of topicality upon the text becomes unmistakable when the translation begins, and Meliboeus expresses the contrast between his neighbor's good fortune and his own, in a formula that carried a particularly local significance:

> I envie not, but wonder th'art so blest
> Since all with *Sequestrations* are opprest.
>
> (p. 2; italics original)

The term *sequestration,* normally used to express a chosen seclusion or withdrawal, perhaps from public life, is here clearly used in the peculiar and technical sense it had acquired in the proceedings of the Long Parliament, to refer to the confiscation of the estates of those royalists who had been judged "delinquent," active and dangerous in their support of the king.

In the 1654 folio, these innuendoes become considerably more explicit. The marginal annotations to the first eclogue provide the traditional accounts of Virgil's motives as defined by Servius, but the phrase with which Ogilby chose to begin that story gives it a different emphasis: "Amongst those who took part with the Conspirators and Murtherers of Caesar, was the City of Cremona" (p. 1). The effect is to shift the emphasis from the long chain of historical causes that in Servius and Donatus led to the creation of the *Eclogues,* and to focus on the criminality of Julius Caesar's assassination. As for the term *sequestration,* the commentary includes a specious little note which, like many apologies, serves rather to heighten the liberties taken:

> Though in literal construction the word will not square with the original, yet, since by *turbatur agris* is meant the Civil distractions that fol-

low'd the Defeat of the Brutian and Cassian Party, in which Sequestrations were frequent and violent, the Version may very well by rational consequence be admitted.

(p. 2)

What Ogilby means here by "rational consequence" is clearly more than the replacement of a general term by a historically specific one. He implies, rather, the whole process of cultural transvaluation, in which analysis of the past alone permits one to comprehend and articulate the shape of one's own society. Further, when the text was reproduced after the Restoration, this gloss had been significantly augmented to bring it still further up to date. It now referred to the "Civil distractions . . . in which, as in our Times of the late Rebellion, Sequestrations were frequent and violent."[51]

The shape of the future is, however, also under discussion in Ogilby's *Eclogues*. Upon Meliboeus's expression of superstition ("Oft, thunder-strucken Oaks I call to mind"), the 1654 gloss offers an explanation that takes the reader far out of the territory of rustic beliefs:

Under this Augural Praemonition is contein'd an Historical Allegorie, by thunder-strucken Oaks intending Brutus and Cassius defeated by the Emperor: Meliboeus therefore implies his and his Countrymens unhappiness in not being deterr'd by the sufferings of Caesar's Murtherers, (who fell under the just revenge of Augustus) from adhering to their unfortunate cause.

(p. 2)

Given the principle of "translation" from Roman history to English, the "just revenge of Augustus" cannot yet have occurred, its correlative in English history being the expected return of Charles II from his exile in France to deal at last with his father's executioners. For the perfected "fell" the English reader was therefore encouraged to read the predictive "will fall"; by a more complicated adjustment of syntax and chronology, he was also required to disentangle the implications of "not being deterr'd . . . from adhering to their unfortunate cause" and perceive it as a warning to the revolutionaries and perhaps the compounders of the present. The cause of the revolution *will* be "unfortunate" when the king's son returns for his just revenge; but the royalists of Ogilby's day are theoretically ca-

---

[51]There were three Restoration editions of Ogilby's "second" Virgil; a 1668 reissue of the 1654 folio; an octavo edition, issued in 1675, dedicated to Princess Mary, daughter of James, Duke of York, and illustrated with inferior copies of the Cleyn designs; and a still cheaper and more spatially condensed edition of 1684. Van Eerde, *John Ogilby*, p. 47, was mistaken in reporting that the 1675 edition contained a different (and hence a third) translation.

pable of being deterred *now* from adherence to that cause precisely because they are, alerted by the Roman historical analogy, capable of prediction.

In Ogilby's translation, therefore, Meliboeus's complaints have a most ambiguous status. On the one hand they raise the question (through the gloss and its deft manipulation of the commentary tradition) of what will happen to the regicides if historical precedent holds true; on the other they illustrate, and demand sympathy for, the sufferings *already* experienced by royalists who have lost their estates through sequestration or have accompanied their royal master into exile. The second meaning is surely dominant in the first eclogue, not least because of the natural analogy between its two shepherds and two kinds of royalist writers, the exiles represented by Fanshawe and William Davenant, the safe survivors represented by those who chose to stay in England, including Ogilby himself. The poem has added to its long chain of interpretive possibilities the power to speak to the circumstances of engagement politics, circumstances unique to the years 1649 to 1655, and indeed significantly different after the battle of Worcester from what they had been in 1649. It speaks now as it had always spoken about the ethical costs of accommodation to those in power; but the selfishness of Tityrus has now to be understood also in terms of contemporary debates as to whether long-term royalist loyalty (and policy) was compatible with *temporary* submission to the *force majeure*.

Where does Ogilby's translation locate itself in these debates? A partial answer appears in the first of the "sculptures" included in the 1654 edition (Fig. 18). It shows clearly the contrast between the fortunate and unfortunate shepherd, and in the background a scene of distant violence, the Mantuan expulsions of the original "occasion" and the "sequestrations" of the present. Extending the iconography popularized by Sebastian Brant (compare Fig. 6), the Cleyn engraving clearly expands the role of Meliboeus at the expense of Tityrus. A figure of strength rather than pathos, he absorbs the center of the scene, and Tityrus, seated awkwardly at the side, looks flaccid and ineffective by comparison.[52]

It is also possible to determine what Ogilby's version of the first eclogue does *not* suggest. In Latham's translation, the gloss on the "thunderstrucken Oaks" also explained them as referring metaphorically to Brutus and Cassius "and others the murtherers of Caesar." But in 1628 it was possible to suggest that these lines imported political prudence:

When I saw them banished, and overthrowne, and all that tooke their part. . . . I might have escaped that calamity, if I had departed; and

---

[52] For a similar reading of this plate, see Eleanor Winsor Leach, "Illustration as Interpretation in Brant's and Dryden's Editions of Vergil," in *The Early Illustrated Book: Essays in Honor of Lessing J. Rosenwald*, ed. Sandra Hindman (Washington, D.C., 1982), p. 185. While full of insights, Leach's treatment of Cleyn's plates is confused, recognizing that they were designed for Ogilby's Virgil but describing them as if they were made for Dryden, in conformity with a later aesthetic.

Figure 18. Franz Cleyn, "Eclogue 1," from *The Works of Virgil,* trans. John Ogilby (London, 1654), facing p. 1. Rare Books and Special Collections, Library of Congress, Washington, D.C.

avoided the contagion of my neighbours, (that is, their treason and conspiracy) and had by some meanes made my peace with the Conquerour, and procured him to be my friend.[53]

If something like this had appeared in Ogilby's gloss in 1654, it would surely have suggested collaboration; but Ogilby's adjustment of the gloss carefully avoids the disloyalty of which Abraham Cowley, for one notorious example, was about to be accused.[54]

Like Vives, Ogilby partly read the *Eclogues* as a more general discussion of the role of the intellectual in the culture of his day. His argument for the second eclogue relates it to the complaints of "learned men" hampered by ungrateful or unreceptive patrons; and that for the seventh (Milton's paradigm for the 1645 *Poems*) offers two different versions, one for 1649 and one for 1654, of why it is that in song contests the best man seldom wins. In the earlier version the fault is said to lie with the "Vulgar," who "make their choice / Not from best Language, but the loudest voyce" (p. 25). In the later, the blame is laid conversely on the "Prejudice" of "proud Cities, and Phantastick Courts" (p. 35). But if Eclogues 2 and 7 speak to the complaints of the intellectual, Eclogue 5 speaks, rather, to his responsibilities. In both 1649 and 1654 this poem carried a fully politicized and updated preliminary argument:

Since Kings as Common Fathers cherish all,
Subjects like Children should lament their fall:
But Learned men, of Grief should have more sense,
When violent Death seizeth a gracious Prince.

(1654: p. 23)

In the 1654 marginal annotation Ogilby noted the range of identifications of Daphnis to be found in the commentaries; but the engraving (Fig. 19) unmistakably shows Julius Caesar's apotheosis. The visual image thus selects the desired Roman reference, while the inferences available from the first Eclogue, that Julius Caesar may be recognized as the historical prototype of Charles I, is here reinforced by the language of the argument, with its emphasis on "kings." The translation suggests, then, that Englishmen could safely mourn for Charles under the pastoral fiction; but it also

---

[53] W. L., *Virgils Eclogues Translated*, p. 14.

[54] The cause was the notorious preface to Cowley's *Poems* of 1656, in which Cowley recommended that since "the unaccountable Will of God has determined the controversie, and . . . we have submitted to the conditions of the Conqueror, we must lay down our Pens as well as our Arms, we must march out of our Cause itself, and dismantle . . . all the Works and Fortifications of Wit and Reason by which we defended it." See A. H. Nethercot, *Abraham Cowley: The Muses' Hannibal* (Oxford, 1931), pp. 188–91.

Figure 19. Franz Cleyn, "Eclogue 5," from *The Works of Virgil,* trans. John Ogilby (London, 1654), p. 22. Rare Books and Special Collections, Library of Congress, Washington, D.C.

proposes, more subtly, that the remembrance promoted by "Learned men" should differ in kind from the childlike laments of the common people.

Just how it might differ is illustrated in the formal composition of the engraving. Instead of history in the background, we are shown superimposed meaning in the heavens, a reading of the lament for Daphnis that is in more than one sense over the heads of the shepherds whose grief gives rise to it. The structure of levels of understanding, reminiscent of Simone Martini's design for Petrarch's *Virgil* (compare Plate 1) is both a visual statement of the Servian distinction between reading *simpliciter* and *allegorice* and a message of special application to the sophisticated readers of the mid-seventeenth century. The role of "learned men," Ogilby suggests, is to interpret with "more sense" than the common people. Not only should they be able to read Virgilian pastoral as a metaphor of their own historical experience, but they should also be capable of approaching that history with an analytic rather than an emotional response. To focus on the ruler's apotheosis will be to acquire insight into the symbolic nature of rule and the role of memory in supporting it, the legend of power and the power of legend. Thoughtful men, Ogilby's icon suggests, will be able to translate their Caesar's departure into an ideal of patient conservation, where what survives for the use of his true successor is the idea of kingship in its purest conceptual form.

The role of memory in pastoral and the importance of waiting were of course already the subject of Eclogue 9, in its textual emphasis on fragments of songs recalled from the past, its allusions to the expected return of Menalcas, and in the Servian hypothesis that that poem, too, referred to the loss of Virgil's patrimonial estate. In the margin of his 1654 edition Ogilby repeated that old story almost word for word:

> When in the distribution of the Country beyond Padua . . . by the order of the Triumviri, Virgil amongst the rest was turn'd out, he went to Rome, where he was so much favour'd, as to be reinstated in his own Land: But Arius the Centurion, to whose lot it had faln, was so much displeas'd with his endevours thereof, that he had almost kill'd him; . . . Virgil for redress of these insolencies, repairs once more to Rome, leaving order with his servant to comply with Arius till his return.
>
> (p. 49)

But in addition to this venerable message, Ogilby wished his readers to understand the poem as another stage in his rationale for a temporary accommodation to the Commonwealth. In both stages of his translation the preceding "argument" reads (without any authorization from the commentary tradition):

Best Princes peace affect, and more delight
Their subjects to preserve, than their own right;
But those who follow war, no power can aw;
Swords make oppression just, and madness law.

(1654: p. 49)

The two halves of this argument offered a double message to the royalists. In the first part, the injunction to "best princes" to prefer their servants' safety to the repossession of their patrimonial estates was clearly an endorsement of the policies of Hyde and, after 1650, of the Sealed Knot. In the second part, a genuine ambiguity affects the application of the aphorism that might makes right, since it is both an indictment of the militarist factions among the royalists and a statement (whose tone cannot be determined) of the revolutionary proposition that sovereignty can be ratified by conquest. But the text of the eclogue eventually resolves that ambiguity. In 1649 the poem's conclusion read:

Shepherd, no more, let's do what next remaines,
When our chiefe comes wee'le fancie better straines.

And even though the 1654 version revised this slightly toward prudence, "to Menalcus we'll sing better strains" (p. 52), the emotional (and syntactical) clarity of "Carmina tum melius, cum venerit ipse, canamus" remains, functioning as a promise that all the waiting and the remembering *will* be rewarded, that the Restoration *will* surely come.

The message of the *Eclogues* as a whole, then, was for quietism without collaboration. It was a remarkable achievement for this man, who began life as a dancing master, who had worked in Strafford's household in Ireland as a member of his guard and master of the revels, who had lost his job with the outbreak of the civil war and arrived completely destitute in Cambridge, and who within a decade of that disaster had acquired a scholar's mastery over the Virgilian tradition, and a perspective on the political situation that was almost as broad as that of Hyde himself. It is surely significant that Ogilby had, by 1654, made such connections in royalist circles that he could count one hundred members of the aristocracy and gentry among his audience, specified by name; and of all the namings that ground his volume in a class culture he had somehow made his own, none is more extraordinary than those at the beginning of the *Eclogues* to the Seymour family. For if Ogilby's message was quietist, since the Seymour family were at the head of the Western Association, a family shattered and to some extent discredited by the events of 1651, when Henry, Lord Beauchamp, was captured and imprisoned in the Tower, the message that he brought them was doubly consoling and restorative. What we cannot know for certain is

Plates

1. Simone Martini, frontispiece to Petrarch's manuscript of Virgil. Biblioteca Ambrosiana, Codex A.49. inf. By permission of the Biblioteca Ambrosiana, Milan.

2.   Caspar David Friedrich, "The Solitary Tree." By permission of the Nationalgalerie Staatliche Museen Preussischer Kulturbesitz, Berlin.

3. Apollonio di Giovanni, "The Eclogues," Riccardiana ms. 492, fol. 1r. By permission of the Biblioteca Riccardiana, Florence.

4. Vergilius Romanus, Codex Vaticanus Latinus 3867, fol. 1r. "Eclogue 1." By permission of the Biblioteca Apostolica Vaticana.

MELIBOEUS ▪ TITYRUS

MELIBOEUS

Tityre, tu patulae recubans sub tegmine fagi
Silvestrem tenui musam meditaris avena ;
Nos patriae fines et dulcia linquimus arva ;
Nos patriam fugimus ; tu, Tityre, lentus in umbra
Formosam resonare doces Amaryllida silvas.

2

5. Jacques Villon, "Meliboeus," from *Les Bucoliques de Virgile,* trans. Paul Valéry (Paris, 1953), p. 2. Lessing J. Rosenwald Collection, Library of Congress, Washington, D.C.

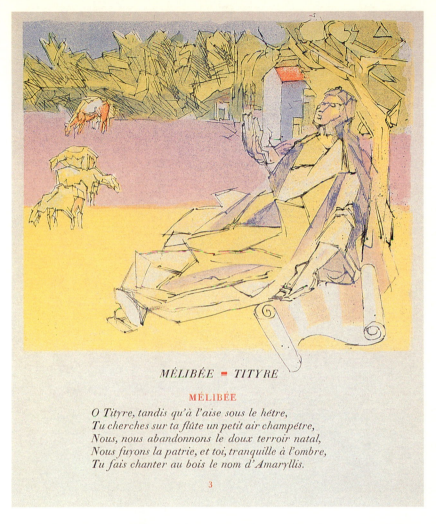

MÉLIBÉE ▪ TITYRE

MÉLIBÉE

O Tityre, tandis qu'à l'aise sous le hêtre,
Tu cherches sur ta flûte un petit air champêtre,
Nous, nous abandonnons le doux terroir natal,
Nous fuyons la patrie, et toi, tranquille à l'ombre,
Tu fais chanter au bois le nom d'Amaryllis.

3

6. Jacques Villon, "Tityrus," from *Les Bucoliques de Virgile,* trans. Paul Valéry (Paris, 1953), p. 3. Lessing J. Rosenwald Collection, Library of Congress, Washington, D.C.

whether the illustration dedicated to Beauchamp, the one for the fifth eclogue with its vision of Caesar's apotheosis, acquired for Ogilby its final level of meaning before the volume left the press; for at the beginning of April 1654 Beauchamp died, and Charles and Hyde were lamenting his loss to the royalist cause.[55]

We can scarcely forget, however, that Ogilby's message to his countrymen did not stop with the *Eclogues* and that it would undoubtedly have been complicated, and to some extent qualified, by what they found in his *Georgics* and *Aeneid*. That argument will have to be almost completely evaded here; but it is worth noting proleptically that his treatment of the most pastoral moment of the *Georgics,* the "happy man" passage, is no less lexically current than his treatment of the first eclogue, and strikingly different in tone from the versions of Jacobean and Caroline poets:

> Happy is he that hidden causes knowes,
> And bold all shapes of danger dares oppose,
> Trampling beneath his Feet the cruell Fates,
> Whom Death, nor swallowing Acheron amates:
> And he is blest who knowes our Country Gods,
> Pan, old Sylvanus, and the Nymphs aboads;
> He fears not Scepters, nor aspiring States,
> Nor treacherous Brethren stirring up Debates;
> Nor Dacians Covenants at Ister's streams;
> Nor Rome's affairs, and nigh destroyed Realms;
> Or Poor men pitties, or the Rich envies.
> What nourishment the bounteous field supplies,
> What Trees allow, he takes: nor ever saw
> Mad Parlements, Acts of Commons, nor Sword-Law.

(p. 110)

Once again, the marginal gloss drew attention to the contemporaneity of his lexical choices: on the phrase "Acts of Commons," which so clearly relocates Virgil's "insanum forum, aut tabularia" in English revolutionary discourse, Ogilby commented: "Tabularium was the place where the Publike Acts and Instruments of the People were kept, and may here Figuratively be taken for the Acts themselves." The engraving that supports Ogilby's reading of this passage is also an example of how "illustration" may be taken "Figuratively," of how a single composition can both combine for representation fragments of the text that, as text, were conceptually separated, even contrasted, and also display in them, in their recombination, previously invisible meaning. The engraving shows a dignified

---

[55] Underdown, *Royalist Conspiracy,* p. 87.

community watching two young men *preparing* to hurl their javelins at a target, an illustration of the rural sports ("velocis jaculi certamina") of *Georgics* 2.530. Behind them in the background can be seen Roman ruins, physically embodying the "insanum forum" and the "tabularia" on which this same rural community turns its back, thereby ensuring their own stability and peace of mind. Yet for the seventeenth-century audience, already trained to incorporate this *Virgil* into their own experience, the contrast between background and foreground could have carried another message, the ruins suggestive of a collapsed political system, of what lies behind them in a historical sense, the athletes in the foreground allowing nonetheless a glimpse of poised strength, of muscular readiness, their weapons harmless in this context yet pointing inevitably toward the *Aeneid*.

And what was to be thought of the *Aeneid* itself? The tone in which it was to be approached was not, we may be fairly sure, one of unthinking heroism. The vision that introduces Ogilby's *Aeneid* is one of extreme violence, loss, and fear, inextricably blended with divine supervision; the "sculpture" in which these themes were visually articulated was dedicated to William Wentworth, Strafford's heir, son of Ogilby's first great patron, and therefore one of those second-generation royalists who had to grapple with feelings of loss and instincts of revenge. In the anguished figure of Aeneas, the center of a great shipwreck, a seventeenth-century reader would have recognized all of those travelers who in one sense or another would have much to suffer before the state could be refounded in pastoral peace. When Charles II came home in 1660 he was celebrated as Aeneas. That he did not come at the head of an army and at the cost of another generation of young men was attributable to the policy of Hyde and the moderates. Among them, and selected to inaugurate the iconography of the Restoration, was John Ogilby, the old dancing master made good. He was entrusted with the "poetical part" of the coronation rituals; by 1665 he was firmly established under the king's patronage; and a royal proclamation ensured that for fifteen years no one might reproduce his engravings. We may infer from this that, unlike Cowley, his career as a writer during the Protectorate had been widely perceived as supportive of the king's cause.

There is one further context in which we can locate Ogilby's *Virgil* as a physical object and historical event; for the conception of the 1654 volume seems, like so much that determined English culture in the later seventeenth century, to have come from France. In Ogilby's 1649 dedication to Seymour he spoke already of a second edition: "it may live to be received (when time shall ripen more ornament of Sculpture and Annotations) with none of the meanest attempts of this nature." He surely had in mind the prose translation of Virgil published in Paris in 1649 by Michel Marolles, abbot of Villeloin. For in two remarkable ways Marolles anticipated the conception and execution of Ogilby's grander project. One is the deliberate relocation of Virgil in contemporary political history. Marolles's preface had insisted upon the reader's coming to terms with what the date of publication of his *Virgil* meant for the world of letters:

> Tandis que les armes victorieuses de nostre jeune Monarque . . . adjoustent de jour en jour des Provinces entières à tant de conquestes . . . que beaucoup de peuples n'ont point de passion plus violente, que de r'entrer en la jouissance de leurs héritages perdus; & ceux qui cherchent en peu de nom dans les Lettres, ne semblent s'occuper qu'à un loisir peu glorieux; j'ay fait cette Version d'un Ouvrage excellent, que j'ay dediée au Roy.[56]

> While the victorious arms of our young monarch day by day reconciled whole provinces by so many victories . . . that many people had no more violent desire than to joyfully recover their lost patrimony; and those who sought something of a name in the world of letters, only seemed to be engaged in an inglorious leisure, I produced this translation of a masterpiece, which I have dedicated to the king.

Yet the actual printing of the *Virgil,* we are told, was interrupted for three months during "un temps calamiteux," the revolt of the Fronde, which placed all of Paris in arms; and the volume appears just as their Majesties, "having received assurances of the fidelity and obedience of Parlement and the people of Paris, have agreed to certain articles for the peace of the realm, which they have signed at the Conference of Ruel, the eleventh day of March of this present year, 1649." The translation was, then, to be read simultaneously as a tribute to the young Louis XIV, as an expression of French monarchism that would indeed be prophetic of the style of government, centrist and absolutist, developed by Louis in the 1650s, and as an expression of optimism for French culture in the wake of the revolution. Along with the epic and imperialist resonance of the preface, Marolles also recalled the *Eclogues,* in his reference to "héritages perdus," which are clearly both actual estates and literary territories; while the "loisir" which may be inglorious is an echo of Georgic 2. This application of Virgil in the service of French royalism after a revolution could hardly have escaped the attention of English royalists, many of whom, of course, were currently in political exile in France; and it is no coincidence that Marolles's preface makes passing mention of "les troubles d'Angleterre & d'Ecosse."

The second attention-getting feature of the Marolles *Virgil* was its magnificent format. A royal folio, not only was it dedicated to the young

---

[56] *Les Oeuvres de Virgile traduites en prose; enrichies de figures, tables, remarques, commentaires, éloges, & vie de l'autheur. Par Michel de Marolles, abbé de Villeloin* (Paris, 1649), n.p.

king but it opened with a fine engraved portrait of him by Melan, followed
by one of Marolles, while the text itself was lavishly illustrated. And the
designer of the illustrative engravings identified himself as F.C., surely
Franz Cleyn, who would shortly be commissioned to illustrate Ogilby's
Virgil.[57] The style and composition of these 1649 plates are both strikingly
similar to those of 1654 and completely different from any Virgilian illustrations produced in Europe hitherto. In contrast especially to the narrative-
symbolic organization of Brant's woodcuts, which dominated sixteenth-
century perceptions of Virgil, both sets of Cleyn's plates relocate Virgil
decisively in the world of early European Neoclassicism, with their emphasis on realistically modeled figures in the foreground, and a landscape background in scientific perspective. But the very resemblance, in style, between the two sets of engravings enables us to perceive the conceptual
difference between them. In the 1649 series, Cleyn produced only five illustrations for the *Eclogues,* grouping them in pairs, but choosing (or being
instructed) to address the second member of the pair rather than the first.
The result was to subordinate the theme of expropriation and exile in the
"Tityrus" to that of lamenting love in the "Corydon" (Fig. 20), to suppress
the political implications of the "Daphnis" in favor of the more genial "Silenus" (Fig. 21), and generally to blur the Virgilian dialectic, rendering the
entire sequence equally and vaguely idyllic. But in the 1654 plates designed for Ogilby's edition, Cleyn had obviously responded to a request
for a more precisely interpretive style of illustration, which (in terms of objectives, if not of execution) harks back to the Brant program. Instead of
grouping the eclogues in pairs, each is given its own sharply differentiated
design; the emphasis falls on tonal and ethical contrasts; and, as we have
seen, the visual elements themselves are endowed with not merely narrative, emotive, or thematic force, but actually become the formal signs of
interpretive process, a visual hermeneutics. A scene of violence in the background means not only that the artist has mastered visual perspective, but
that the audience is to place the eclogue in the historical perspective of Roman and English history; a vision above the heads of the shepherds in
Eclogue 5 stands for the process of reading pastoral symbolically, and
making it speak of matters above a common understanding.

Lastly, there is, even in the arrangement of the volumes, an implied
difference of tone, intention, and circumstance, all of which are inseparable
from one another. Instead of the massive emphasis on royalty which defines the Marolles production, Ogilby's volume addresses itself, as we now

---

[57] Cleyn's contribution to the Marolles *Virgil* seems to have gone unrecorded; yet he did
sometimes sign his designs F.C. The chief source for his biography is Horace Walpole, *Anecdotes of Painting in England*, 4 vols. (London, 1828), 2: 291–92. He was summoned to England in 1623 by Prince Charles and employed by James to design tapestries at Mortlake. On
Charles's accession he received denization and a pension of one hundred pounds a year, which
was cut off by the civil war.

Sous ce hestre touffu, Melibée et Tityre,
Disent de leur Destin le sort Capricieux.
Corydon a l'escart ouure son Cœur aux Cieux
Il se plaint d'Alexis, et conte son Martyre.

1 et 2.me Eglogue

Figure 20. F(ranz) C(leyn), "Eclogues 1 and 2," from *Les Oeuvres de Virgile,*
trans. Michel de Marolles (Paris, 1649). By permission of Princeton University
Library.

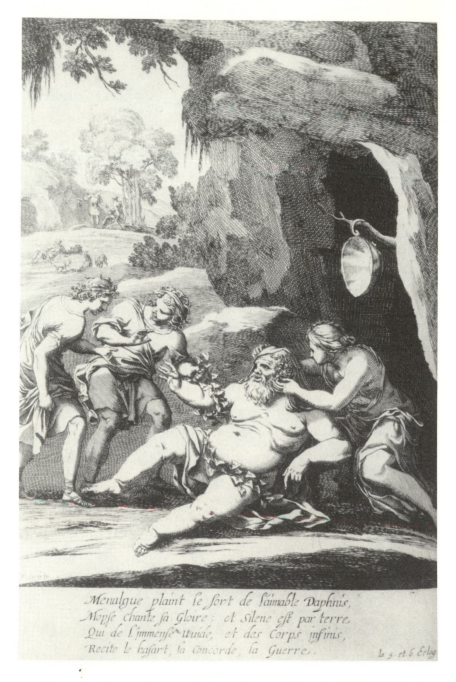

Menalgue plaint le fort de l'aimable Daphnis,
Mopfe chante fa Gloire : et Silene eft par terre
Qui de l'immenfe Uniае, et des Corps infinis,
Recite le hafart, la Concorde, la Guerre.

L. 5. et 6. Eclog

Figure 21. F(ranz) C(leyn), "Eclogues 5 and 6," from *Les Oeuvres de Virgile,* trans. Michel de Marolles (Paris, 1649). By permission of Princeton University Library.

know, to aristocracy whose royal leaders are missing. Instead of the imperial beginning, fulfilled by placing the *Aeneid* first and by representing to
Louis XIV that Aeneas is the model he should follow, Ogilby's volume begins with the *Eclogues* and qualifies heroism with strategic quietism. Marolles's *Virgil* is consistent with the move in French culture after the Fronde
to emphasize the authority of the crown at the expense of the nobles;[58]
Ogilby's is consistent with English royalist policy during the Protectorate to define the aristocracy as the keepers of the flame, those on whose
loyalty would depend the regeneration of the monarchy from its virtual
annihilation.

We come, then, to John Dryden's close-of-the-century *Virgil,* the only
re-presentation of the master-text that has hitherto been given serious attention, and almost all of that attention having been directed to Dryden's
translation of the *Aeneid.* Yet the entire volume is, as a cultural document,
as a visual and textual emblem of historical and aesthetic change, extraordinarily rich, and not least in its adoption and adaptation of Ogilby's plates
to an entirely different set of premises. Unlike the reappearance of Sebastian Brant's woodcuts in later sixteenth-century editions of Virgil, the decision of Dryden's publisher Jacob Tonson, and of Dryden himself, to recycle
Cleyn's designs almost half a century later is rich in ideological import. We
have on record Dryden's letter about his quarrel with Tonson as to where
the volume was to stand in the politics of the 1690s. Was it to be dedicated
to William, and thus represent the last phase of Dryden's own accommodation to the principle of stability and the power of success? Or was the volume to stand in uneasy relationship to a government (and hence a religion)
that Dryden, after *The Hind and the Panther,* could never regard as his or
his country's own? Tonson's answer, in default of an actual dedication to
William, was to adjust the plates illustrating the *Aeneid,* so that the features
of Aeneas resemble those of William, rather than Charles II.[59] But Dryden's
answer to the same questions must be deduced from the entire volume:

[58] On the history of the Fronde, see Ernst H. Kossman, *La Fronde* (Leiden, 1954);
Pierre-George Lorris, *La Fronde* (Paris, 1961); A. Lloyd Moote, *The Revolt of the Judges: The
Parlement of Paris and the Fronde, 1643–1652* (Princeton, 1971). On French royalist iconogra-
phy at the time of the Fronde, see Erica Harth, *Ideology and Culture in Seventeenth-Century
France* (Ithaca, N.Y., 1983), and on the connections between the Fronde and the English civil
war see Philip Knachel, *England and the Fronde* (Ithaca, N.Y., 1967).

[59] The trials of being a conservative writer with a Whig publisher are recorded in Dryden's letter to his son. See *The Letters of John Dryden,* ed. Charles Ward (Durham, N.C.,
1942), p. 93: "[Tonson] has missed of his design in the Dedication: though He had prepared
the Book for it: for in every figure of Eneas, he has caus'd him to be drawn like K. William,
with a hookd Nose." That the visual emendation was generally understood as a Whig stratagem
is indicated in a contemporary satire, which remarked that "Old Jacob, by deep judgment
swayed, / To please the wise beholders, / Has placed old Nassau's hook-nosed head / On
poor Aeneas shoulders" and struck back with an unflattering "parallel" between William and
Aeneas. See Sir Walter Scott, *The Life of John Dryden* (1808), ed. Bernard Kressman (Lincoln,
Neb., 1963), p. 330.

from the dedications of the three parts of Virgil's canon, the last of which
became an extensive critical essay on the *Aeneid;* from the reassignment of
Ogilby's plates to the cultural aristocracy of the nineties; from Dryden's
strategies and nuances of translation; and, given the interpretive importance to such a project of all forms of introduction or theoretical preparation of the reader, both the *Life* of Virgil and the introductory essay on
pastoral poetry contributed anonymously by Dryden's friend Knightley
Chetwood. We can be sure (as from his dispute with Tonson) that Dryden
would not have allowed into his volume anything not concordant with his
own political opinions and purposes.

At first sight it might appear that the principle of blending the economics of subscription publishing with the politics of dedication (the
principle that Dryden learned from Ogilby) had been used to place this
volume firmly at the heart of the establishment. Unlike Ogilby's address to
a beleaguered and temporarily defeated upper class, Dryden's *Eclogues* are
entrusted individually to the protection (and self-interest) of men at the
very center of William's government: to John Sommers, the Lord Chancellor, to Thomas, Earl of Pembroke, the Lord Privy Seal, to Charles Sack-
ville, Earl of Dorset, the Lord Chamberlain, to Dorset's eldest son, Lionel
Cranfield, to James Bertie, Earl of Abingdon and Lord Chief Justice, and
so on. On the other hand, the *Eclogues* as a group are dedicated, with entirely different implications, to Hugh Lord Clifford, fourth son and heir of
the Thomas Clifford who had resigned from Charles II's Privy Council and
the Treasurership in 1673 when the Test Act against Catholics was passed
and who had died very shortly after, perhaps by suicide.[60] In the immediate aftermath of the resignation, Dryden had dedicated his tragedy *Am-
boyna* to Clifford, as a way of offering both his gratitude and his con-
dolences. And now, twenty years later, in Dryden's self-presentation to
Clifford's heir, two points are made that should have been critical for the
reception of the volume as a whole: first, that Clifford had been to Dryden
as the Roman patricians mentioned in the *Eclogues* had been to Virgil, true
patrons who made poetry possible; and second, that the warm cultural climate of the Restoration is now merely a memory:

> He was the Patron of my Manhood, when I Flourish'd in the opinion
> of the World; though with small advantage to my Fortune, 'till he
> awakened the remembrance of my Royal Master. He was that Pollio, or
> that Varus, who introduced me to Augustus: And tho' he soon dis-
> miss'd himself from State-Affairs, yet in the short time of his Admin-
> istration he shone so powerfully upon me, that like the heat of a Rus-

---

[60] Mysteriously, the *Dictionary of National Biography* states that Hugh Clifford died in
1690. However, Arthur Collins, *The Peerage of England* (London, 1710), p. 113, records him
as still flourishing twenty years later.

sian-Summer, he ripen'd the Fruits of Poetry in a cold Clymate; and gave me wherewithal to subsist at least, in the long Winter which succeeded.[61]

The *Eclogues,* then, are to be read primarily as an elegy for the Restoration before the rise of Shaftesbury, yet are addressed to someone who both embodies (by descent) the old values and represents a new and more hopeful generation:

> What I now offer to your Lordship, is the wretched remainder of a sickly Age, worn out with Study, and oppress'd by Fortune: without other support than the Constancy and Patience of a Christian. You, my Lord, are yet in the flower of your Youth, and may live to enjoy the benefits of the Peace which is promis'd Europe: I can only hear of that Blessing.

It is appropriate to Dryden's mood in this passage that the anticipated Treaty of Ryswick, which he implicitly compares to the Peace of Brundisium, both demonstrated the efficiency of William's government and left all the major issues of the war of the League of Augsburg undecided, ensuring a renewal of hostilities with France.[62] Nor need we suppose that his audience for this dedication, as represented by the Catholic Clifford, would have been deaf to the irony that a French victory in the war would have reversed the revolution of 1688 and almost certainly resulted in the restoration of the Stuarts.

According to this dedication, Dryden began work on the *Virgil* in his "great Clymacterique," that is to say, aged sixty-three, in 1694. There is a strong sense that he perceived it as both the climax of his career and a retrospective; and Chetwood's *Life* of Virgil enhances this inference by dwelling on the psychological aspects of Virgil's personal history, as well as on his legendary role as a cherished advisor to Augustus. Considering that Chetwood was translating from Donatus, it is remarkable how much he was able to personalize the old story, and how much of both pathos and contemporary nuance he was able to make the text of Donatus absorb. Here, for example, is the traditional account of the occasion of the *Eclogues,* re-

---

[61] *The Works of Virgil; containing his Pastorals, Georgics, and Aeneis; Translated into Verse by Mr. Dryden* (London, 1697), n.p.

[62] Compare the Whig application of Virgil to William's militarism in Nahum Tate's *A Pastoral Dialogue* (London, 1690), pp. 24–25, where, in response to one shepherd's request that his colleague repeat a heroic song about William's campaigns, the other replies that he must leave that task "To happy Swains . . . / Who sing beneath the Shade of their own Vine," and who therefore have the means to "rouze the noble Din of War. . . / And trace a Hero through the dusty Plain."

told in language appropriate to a readership that had experienced two revolutions, with all the shifts and reversals of party and personal fortune consequent upon them:

> Whilst Virgil thus enjoy'd the sweets of a Learn'd Privacy, the Troubles of Italy cut off his little Subsistance; but by a strange turn of Human Affairs, which ought to keep good Men from ever despairing; the loss of his Estate prov'd the effectual way of making his Fortune. The occasion of it was this; Octavius . . . by a Masterly stroke of Policy, had gain'd the Veteran Legions into his Service, (and by that step, outwitted all the Republican Senate:) They grew now very clamorous for their Pay: The Treasury being Exhausted, he was forc'd to make Assignments upon Land, and none but in Italy it self would content them. He pitch'd upon Cremona as the most distant from Rome; but that not suffising, he afterwards threw in part of the State of Mantua. Cremona was a Rich and noble Colony . . . [which] had done several important Services to the Common-Wealth. . . . But past Services are a fruitless Plea; Civil Wars are one continued Act of Ingratitude: In vain did the Miserable Mothers, with their famishing Infants in their Arms, fill the Streets with their Numbers, and the Air with Lamentations; the Craving Legions were to be satisf'd at any rate.
>
> (pp. 5–6)

This emotional tone extends into a causal explanation of the ninth eclogue, one that oddly anticipates the post-modernist emphasis on its fragmentary and memorial aspects. Recalling the episode of Arius the centurion and the forcible expulsion of Virgil from the lands he thought he had recovered, Chetwood explained that the poet was therefore "forc'd to drag a sick Body half the length of Italy, back again to Rome":

> and by the way, probably, compos'd his Ninth Pastoral, which may seem to have been made up in haste out of the Fragments of some other pieces; and he naturally enough represents the disorder of the Poets Mind, by its disjointed Fashion, tho' there be another Reason to be given elsewhere of its want of Connexion.
>
> (pp. 6–7)

The poem's thematization of the incompatibility between poetry and violence is thus presented as a biographical and psychological problem, the effect of stress on the mind's capacity for order; and if we turn to the translation itself we may deduce that Dryden also felt that inhibition, felt it as personally as had Ludovico Vives more than a century earlier, that in the 1690s the problem of Moeris was Dryden's own. In fact, his translation of

Moeris's complaints in the ninth eclogue seems infinitely more felt than those of Meliboeus in the first, who sounds less like an exile than a Restoration country gentleman having trouble with poachers:

> Did we for these Barbarians plant and sow,
> On these, on these, our happy Fields bestow?
> Good Heav'n what dire Effects from Civil Discord flow!
> Now let me graff my Pears, and prune the Vine;
> The Fruit is theirs, the Labour only mine.

By contrast, the distress of Moeris penetrates Dryden's couplets, and survives their smoothness:

> Under this influence, graft the tender Shoot;
> Thy Childrens Children shall enjoy the Fruit.
> The rest I have forgot, for Cares and Time
> Change all things, and untune my Soul to Rhime:
> I cou'd have once sung down a Summers Sun,
> But now the Chime of Poetry is done.
> My Voice grows hoarse; I feel the Notes decay,
> As if the Wolves had seen me first to Day.

And the application of the ninth eclogue to Dryden's own condition is confirmed, finally, by his translation of its closing lines. In place of Virgil's allusion to the mysterious "ipse" whose return will ensure "better songs" and whose anonymity contributes to his mythical potency, Dryden unequivocally locates the problem of Moeris in the contemporary world of preferment and factionalism:

> Cease to request me, let us mind our way;
> Another Song requires another Day.
> When good Menalcas comes, if he rejoyce,
> And find a Friend at Court, I'll find a Voice.

It would have been an unusually self-defeating enterprise, however, to have conceived and executed the *Virgil* solely or even primarily as a statement of personal and cultural decrepitude. As Steven Zwicker has shown in his analysis of the *Aeneid,* complete with its long interpretive dedication to the Earl of Mulgrave and its new series of individual dedications for each illustration, Dryden created out of that combination a last work of political propaganda: "maneuvering the *Aeneid* into an oppositional stance"; rewarding his friends, exposing his enemies to some highly oblique insults; and "asserting his literary and political identity under cover of epic enterprise."[63] But the contemporary allusions that Zwicker retrieved from the dedication to Mulgrave were already anticipated in the *Life*. The most striking example occurs in connection with a crucial story—crucial, we may be sure, for Dryden—when Virgil actually superseded the politicians in determining the emperor's policy. In retelling this anecdote, Chetwood put an unusual stress on motives, especially on those motives that both explain and discredit the political process. According to Chetwood, it was either because Octavian was bored ("cloy'd with Glory") or anxious "to gain the Credit of Moderation with the People, or possibly to feel the Pulse of his Friends" that he began to debate "whether he should retain the Sovereign Power, or restore the Commonwealth." These suggestions were all additions to the story as he found it in Donatus's *Life*. Because Agrippa and Maecenas gave him conflicting advice, Virgil, so the story went, was called in to mediate between them. "Thus a Poet had the Honour of determining the greatest Point that ever was in Debate, betwixt the Son-in-Law, and Favourite of Caesar." But before getting to that crucial "Point," Chetwood had inserted an analogy, which was yet *not* an analogy, between Octavian and Cromwell:

> That Emperour was too Politick to commit the over-sight of Cromwell, in a deliberation something resembling this. Cromwell had never been more desirous of the Power, than he was afterwards of the Title of King. . . . But by too vehement Allegation of Arguments against it, he, who had out-witted every body besides, at last out-witted himself, by too deep dissimulation: For his Council, thinking to make their Court by assenting to his judgment, voted unanimously *for him* against *his Inclination*.
>
> (p. 9)

When the advice is delivered, it too becomes subject to time-warp.

> The change of Popular into an Absolute Government, has generally been of very ill Consequence: For betwixt the Hatred of the People, and Injustice of the Prince, it of necessity comes to pass that they live in distrust, and mutual Apprehensions. But if the Commons knew a just Person, whom they entirely confided in, it would be for the advantage of all Parties, that such a one should be their Sovereign: Wherefore if you shall continue to administer Justice impartially, as hitherto you have done, your Power will prove safe to your self, and beneficial to Mankind.

[63] Steven Zwicker, *Politics and Language in Dryden's Poetry: The Arts of Disguise* (Princeton, 1984), p. 205.

Turning on those central "ifs," the verdict is certainly compatible with the conditional praise and support that Virgil and Dryden characteristically offered their monarchs. But Chetwood's added comment pushes what might otherwise have been perceived as loyalism, even to William, in another direction. Virgil, he wrote, spoke to the "true state of Affairs at that time: For the Commonwealth Maxims were now no longer practicable; the Romans had only the haughtiness of the Old Commonwealth left, without one of its Virtues." Given his earlier allusion to Cromwell, it takes little discernment to perceive that "that time" has at least two historical referents; the question remains open whether it has three, the third being the reign of the Whigs in the aftermath of the revolution of 1688, in which it was possible to argue (if one was a Whig) that there had been a return to the principles of the Commonwealth, in the absolute control of the monarch, the economy, and the army by parliament. The cynicism with which Chetwood presented Octavian's motives in initiating this consultation spreads through the entire passage, making it impossible to determine where this version of the *Life* stands in the ideological spectrum of the Glorious Revolution, and matching the paradoxical intentions of the *Virgil* as a whole: the life-work of a poet who had learned to accommodate republican principles to the service of empire, for the sake of stability, is translated into the last statement of a poet who had taken many turns in the service of constitutional government, but who in his last years was incapable of giving his loyalty to the ruler who embodied it.

Dryden's version of the *Eclogues*, then, cannot be understood without a grasp of what the *Life* of Virgil meant to him and his colleagues, as something which could explain the history of their country to them, and their own lives as part of this history. Dryden and Chetwood clearly saw the *Eclogues* as Servius and Donatus had presented them, as documents inextricably connected to Roman politics, and as texts deeply occasioned, in the sense of being part of a long chain of historical causes. From Dryden's perspective, of course, that chain had lengthened to include not one but two reenactments of Roman history as bounded by Virgil's life, the second of which was either incomplete as fact (pending a second restoration of the Stuarts), or incomplete as analogy, making it impossible to say whether William, or Cromwell, was to be recognized as Augustus. If Dryden's advice on this subject seems manifestly obscure (and markedly less courageous than Ogilby's in comparable circumstances) it must be remembered that he was not only old and depressed by 1697 but also working, in more senses than one, against time.

There is another paradox that attends his presentation of the *Eclogues* as a fin de siècle document. It arises from the presence in the volume, unmistakable but nonetheless ambiguous, of Neoclassical theories of pastoral imported from France and which run counter to everything stated above.

The subject of French Neoclassicism and the reading of Virgil's *Eclogues* that it produced will be taken up in detail in the next chapter; yet a reader of Dryden's *Virgil* who has also read Rapin and Fontenelle on the subject of pastoral will recognize a problem that cannot be entirely postponed for later discussion. On the one hand Dryden, in his dedication to Clifford, speaks of Fontenelle as "the living Glory of the French" and speaks of the pastoral in Fontenelle's terms, as essentially simple in nature and focused on love as its proper subject, from which it follows that Theocritus is superior to Virgil in his rusticity, and Virgil has erred in allowing into Eclogues 4, 6, and 8 "some Topicks which are above the Condition of his Persons." On the other, the *Eclogues* are preceded by Knightley Chetwood's preface on pastoral, which is almost entirely committed to an attack on Fontenelle. Chetwood's defense of the dignity of the life of shepherds in ancient cultures, which is not to be confused with the situation of seventeenth-century peasants, "leading a painful Life in Poverty and Contempt, without Wit, Courage, or Education," is primarily in refutation of the idealized, gentleman's version of pastoral promoted by Rapin and Fontenelle, from which not only rural labor but all consciousness of the "real" world, and especially political consciousness, were to be banished. As Chetwood wrote, in his comically explosive style:

> Mr. F. is a great deal too Uniform; begin where you please, the Subject is still the same. We find it true what he says of himself, "Toujours, toujours de l'Amour." He seems to take Pastorals and Love-Verses for the same thing. Has Human Nature no other Passion? Does not Fear, Ambition, Avarice, Pride, a Capricio of Honour, and Laziness it self often Triumph over Love?

It was precisely the workings of those other passions that were manifest in Dryden's re-presentation of the *Eclogues* to his countrymen at the turn of the century, and his hesitant expression to Clifford of the idealized and deodorized concept of pastoral that would later be endorsed by Pope is itself a cultural marker. Here, says the symptom of Dryden's self-contradiction, is a sign of mutation in process, of the disequilibrium induced by ideas new to ourselves but already fashionable elsewhere. And it is with those fashions, their French origins, and their sociopolitical substratum that the next chapter will now directly engage.

4

NEOCLASSICISM AND THE
FÊTE CHAMPÊTRE

When Love and Beauty heard the news,
 The gay green-woods amang, man,
Where gathering flowers and busking bowers
 They heard the blackbird's sang, man;
A vow they seal'd it with a kiss
 Sir Politicks to fetter,
As their's alone, the Patent-bliss,
 To hold a Fête Champêtre.

. . . .

When Politicks cam there, to mix
 And make his ether-stane, man,
He circl'd round the magic ground,
 But entrance found he nane, man:
He blush'd for shame, he quat his name,
 Forswore it every letter,
Wi' humble prayer to join and share
 This festive Fête Champêtre.

Robert Burns, "The Fête Champêtre" (1788)

Let the *fête champêtre* stand for the version of pastoral, sometimes denominated Neoclassical, that was promoted by French theorists in the second half of the seventeenth century and imported into England at the beginning of the eighteenth. What Robert Burns clearly saw, one year before the French Revolution, was the sociopolitical meaning of that version as it was represented in his own country, in the form of a pre-election garden-party held by a young Scottish aristocrat, supposedly to celebrate his majority but actually, it was suspected, to prepare for the coming election.[1] Burns's poem neatly allegorizes the double message of this Scottish gentleman's

---

[1] The gentleman was William Cunningham of Annbank. See W. E. Henley and T. F. Henderson, eds., *The Poetry of Robert Burns*, 4 vols. (New York, 1970), 2: 394.

193

pastoral, the magic circle of idyllic manners and aesthetic pleasure that were supposed to exclude political experience while implicitly supporting a conservative ideology. It would be putting it too strongly to call this version or theory of pastoral, and the reading of Virgil's *Eclogues* that it demanded, a cultural conspiracy. But the business of this chapter will be to tell a different story from the one currently enshrined in literary history about how Neoclassical pastoral was conceived, what it signified, and by what it was countered. In addition, the analysis should produce some reconsideration of what we mean by Neoclassicism, both as a cultural formation or movement, a complex of positions that replaced previous positions and would itself be replaced, and in its more technical sense (with a lowercase *n*) as the process by which classical texts are constantly rewritten.

Neoclassicism, as a term, is one of our self-imposed burdens, whether we struggle with it as literary or as art historians. Attended as it is by all the chronological difficulties of the comparable *Renaissance,* which can similarly designate cultural phenomena as much as a hundred and fifty years apart, *Neoclassicism* additionally embarrasses us by excluding from its temporal boundaries, however mobile or disputed, such imitators of classical antiquity as Petrarch or Marot or Marvell (to speak only of our literary self-contradictions). But it is also impossible to align Neoclassicism as a theory—of containment, of rationality, of a benevolent or idealizing view of the social order—whose cultural dominance defines a historical "period," with the actual practice of textual neoclassicism in that period. In practice, intellectuals continued to do through pastoral, and especially through their attitudes to Virgil's *Eclogues,* what they had done throughout the Renaissance and the earlier seventeenth century: to denote their ideological stance as writers in relation to their sociopolitical environment; and while some of them accepted and supported the premises of Neoclassicism, others, who were equally neoclassicist in their strategies, positioned themselves through irony, anxiety, or anger against the status quo. If Neoclassicism as a cultural formation was a stabilizing force, pastoral with its supporting and *competing* theories was potentially destabilizing.

This chapter will once again bring the cultural history of France and England back into a close and indeed causal relationship, by beginning with the disputes generated in France and imported into England as to what constituted correct or legitimate pastoral. What should gradually emerge is that this debate was never settled in favor of the aristocratic or gentleman's pastoral that certain French theoreticians desired, and that the closer France drew to the Revolution itself, the more likely were French intellectuals like Voltaire and Chénier to rediscover the anti-Neoclassical potential of Virgilian pastoral. In England, the debate initiated by Rapin and Fontenelle was taken up by Whig and Tory intellectuals in the first decade of the eighteenth century as a way of articulating their other divergences, initially over the question of a successor to Queen Anne (whose Stuart connections were based in France). The result was a quarrel between Pope and Philips and their various supporters that disrupted literary friendships for a generation and led, on Pope's side, to the renunciation of pastoral as a viable mode of expression, and its deliberate sabotage by the parodies of Gay and his followers.

England, of course, was meanwhile being rapidly transformed from an agricultural society into a modern commercial state. A massive reorganization of landownership dispossessed thousands of lease- and copyholders, not to mention cottagers and their time-honored though partial dependence upon commons grounds. The magic circle of exclusion recognized by Burns had therefore as its counter-image that of the enclosure, which was frequently performed in the service of the gentleman's park as well as for agricultural progress. So complete a transformation certainly encouraged a transfer of attention from pastoral as eclogue, with its comparatively simple model of agrarian policy, to the novel and to other more expansive genres such as the topographical poem or the philosophical travel-book, where the ideology of landownership could be aired in more detail. Fielding's *Tom Jones,* published in 1750, assumes that Squire Allworthy's "Inheritance of one of the largest Estates in the County" is compatible with his worthiness, and accordingly names it "Paradise Hall";[2] but as the sheer scale of enclosure mounted in the second half of the century such complacency became open to question, even in fiction.[3]

In Henry Mackenzie's *The Man of Feeling* (1771), both melancholy and irony invest the information that the squire has pulled down the schoolhouse "because it stood in the way of his prospects" and has ploughed up the green where the children used to play, "because, he said, they hurt his fence on the other side of it."[4] This point of view was rearticulated in the light of the French Revolution by John Thelwall, whose *Peripatetic,* a series of "Politico-Sentimental" journals, was published in 1793 under an epigraph from Virgil's second georgic. Thelwall inveighed against "improvements" that result in the tearing down of cottages in favor of finer views: "The imperious lord is not content with his own superiority; he envies the poor peasant (by the sweat of whose brow he eats) even the wretched offal of his own industry . . . or perhaps, his *tender feelings* can not endure the sight of such wretchedness; and he finds extermination less

---

[2] Henry Fielding, *Tom Jones,* ed. Sheridan Baker (New York, 1973), p. 27.

[3] After mid-century there was a steep increase in Enclosure Acts. As compared to the previous three decades, which showed, respectively, 33, 35, and 38 Acts, the next three produced, respectively, 156, 424, and 642. See April London, "Landscape in the Eighteenth-Century Novel," D.Phil. dissertation, Oxford, 1980, p. 108.

[4] Henry Mackenzie, *The Man of Feeling* (London, 1771; reprinted New York, 1974), p. 196. See also London, "Landscape, p. 108.

expensive than relief."[5] It was probably no accident that the Virgilian lines
with which Thelwall identified himself, "Me vero primum dulces ante
omnia Musae / quarum sacra fero ingenti percussus amore / [accipiunt]"
("first above all may the sweet Muses whose holy emblems, under the spell
of a mighty love, I bear, receive me," 2.475–76), expressed the poet's resolve to use his retreat in the country for philosophic purposes; nor that
they immediately followed Virgil's statement that Justice, as she quitted the
earth, left her last footprints in the country ("extrema per illos / Justitia
excedens terris vestigia fecit"). On the other hand, Thelwall's great antagonist Edmund Burke included in his *Reflections on the Revolution in
France* a satire on the architects of the new French constitution and their
"meddling . . . with rural economy." "At first, perhaps," Burke mocked,

> their tender and susceptible imaginations may be captivated with the
> innocent and unprofitable delights of a pastoral life, but in a little time
> they will find that agriculture is a trade much more laborious, and
> much less lucrative than that which they had left. After making its
> panegyrick, they will turn their backs on it like their great precursor
> and prototype. They may, like him, begin by singing "Beatus ille"—
> but what will be the end?[6]

And he quoted the cynical conclusion of Horace's second epode, where the
praise of the country life is revealed as the daydream merely of a usurer.

By the beginning of the nineteenth century the social (as well as the
sexual) premises of Jane Austen's *Mansfield Park* would have been clearly
recognizable as reactionary in the Burkean sense;[7] while the conservative
tradition in fiction continued to be challenged, as, for example, in Thomas
Love Peacock's satirical portrait of country landowners in his *Crotchet Castle*
of 1831. Their "game-bagging, poacher-shooting, trespasser-pounding,
footpath-stopping, common-enclosing, rack-renting, and all the other liberal pursuits and pastimes which make a country gentleman an ornament
to the world, and a blessing to the poor," are personified in Sir Simon
Steeltrap, whose name surely derives from William Cobbett's sarcastic
mention of a sign observed in his *Rural Rides* of the preceding year ("Para-

[5] John Thelwall, *The Peripatetic: or Sketches of the Heart, of Nature and Society, in a Series of
Politico-Sentimental Journals*, 3 vols. (London, 1793), 1: 134–35.
[6] Edmund Burke, *Works*, 16 vols. (London, 1826), 5: 344.
[7] The pastoral, Neoclassical, and aristocratic attributes of Mansfield Park—"elegance,
propriety, regularity, harmony—and perhaps, above all, . . . peace and tranquillity"—are defined by Fanny Price in contrast to the muddle of her lower-middle-class home. See Jane Austen, *Mansfield Park*, ed. Reuben A. Brower (Boston, 1965), vol. 3, Chap. 8, p. 298. The estate's social and moral enclosure of women is represented by the scene in vol. 1, chap. 10,
p. 76, where Maria Bertram escapes from the garden "without the key" and without her fi-
ancé's "authority and protection" in a figurative prolepsis of her later adultery.

dise Place: spring guns and steel traps are set here") that in turn reflects back on Fielding.[8] Cobbett himself began *Rural Rides* with an elegy for the misery of contemporary sheep-farmers unable to get a fair price for their animals, and proceeded, with or without conscious recall of Pope's eulogy to Windsor Forest, to decry that ultimate symbol of the policies of Pitt and Canning: the forest itself is "as bleak, as barren, and as villainous a heath as ever man set his eyes on. However, here are *new enclosures* without end." And Sunning Hill, on the western side of Windsor Park, "is a spot all made into 'grounds' and gardens by tax-eaters. The inhabitants of it have beggared twenty agricultural villages and hamlets."[9]

We can now begin to see, also, that the misappropriation of eclogue as a genre (as also of the georgic) to urban subjects, its weakening to the formal notion of dialogue, and its sabotage by parody may have causes beyond its own "decadence" or the perception of critics such as Samuel Johnson that certain aspects of classical pastoral, notably its *vocabulary,* had become vacuous. Theoretical uncertainties over the status of pastoral had, certainly, a social as well as an aesthetic content, and were connected to a reluctance among intellectuals to admit that the "golden age of power, privilege and increasing wealth" produced by industrialism was enjoyed only by the minority.[10] In the visual arts, John Barrell has brilliantly shown, this reluctance manifested itself in the development of English landscape painting, in the growing pressure for a native genre of landscape that would mediate between the neoclassical models of Claude and Poussin and the realism of Dutch painting; but the ideological restraints imposed, consciously or half-consciously, on Gainsborough and Constable, and even on the underdog sympathies of George Morland, produced in the second half of the century paintings in which pastoral was redefined by georgic elements, and georgic in turn redefined as the aesthetic containment of the working poor.[11] As the introduction of figures engaged in agricultural labor was necessary to the nation's view of itself and its class structure (a view that altered as the French Revolution approached and receded), formal strategies were developed to maintain an aesthetic distance from the "dark side of the landscape" and to support the fiction that the labor of

[8]Thomas Love Peacock, *Crotchet Castle* (London, 1831), in *Works,* ed. H. F. B. Brett-Smith and C. E. Jones, 10 vols. (New York, 1967), 4: 5–6, 65–66. William Cobbett, *Rural Rides . . . with Economical and Political Observations* (London, 1830), p. 209.

[9]Cobbett, *Rural Rides,* pp. 59, 61.

[10]J. H. Plumb, *England in the Eighteenth Century (1714–1815)* (Harmondsworth, 1950), p. 84. For an early and influential account of the agricultural revolution and its effect on writers, see Kenneth MacLean, *Agrarian Age: A Background for Wordsworth* (New Haven, 1950).

[11]John Barrell, *The Dark Side of the Landscape: the Rural Poor in English Painting 1730–1840* (Cambridge, 1980). Barrell, however, accepts as given the Neoclassical definition of *pastoral* as "idyll."

the poor was not oppressive to them, that it could even be conceived in the semi-pastoral language of Virgil's second georgic. So Constable exhibited *Dedham Vale with Ploughman* over a couplet taken from Robert Bloomfield's *The Farmer's Boy:*

> But, unassisted through each toilsome day,
> With smiling brow the Plowman cleaves his way.[12]

Virgil's own text had also to be reconceived in the light of progress as a less troublemaking document. As compared to Dryden's cynical and pointed emphasis on Roman history, for example, the translation by John Martyn, professor of *botany* at Cambridge, successively (as his translation changed its tone and format) directed attention away from its Roman historical context, reshaping the *Eclogues* into a treatise on Italian plants and their uses. As the century drew out, however, such massive cracks in the system as the American Revolution, the career of John Wilkes, and the Gordon riots of 1780 were accompanied by some striking experiments in political pastoral; the 1770s and 1780s produced a number of anti-slavery eclogues; and when the full significance of the French Revolution was grasped in England, it inevitably forced a reassessment of one of Virgil's most provocative pastoral concepts, liberty, in all its political, cultural, and psychological functions. Results varied from the marginally pastoral "eclogues" of Southey and Shelley to Wordsworth's sustained attempts to renovate the genre, rejecting, as we shall see in the next chapter, *both* the evasions of Neoclassical idealism *and* the excesses (in his view) of the new political realism.[13]

In France, as political history showed a more extreme fluctuation between stabilization—the chief objective of Neoclassicism as a cultural movement—and disruption, there was a more obvious (if inverted) relationship between pastoral as a cultural phenomenon and the real structures it has always described. The appropriation of pastoral by the court, and its sociopolitical decadence in the form of the *fête champêtre,* may not have caused but was certainly answered by the dismembering of the great aristocratic estates in the Revolution. Yet within that most sweeping of revisions there were all sorts of surprises and internal contradictions, and on the

---

[12] Barrell, *Dark Side of the Landscape,* p. 151.

[13] For Thomas Chatterton's *African Eclogues* (1770), Edward Rushton's *West-Indian Eclogues* (1787), and Henry Mulligan's *Poems Chiefly on Slavery and Oppression* (1788), see Stuart Curran, *Poetic Form in British Romanticism* (New York, 1986), pp. 95–99. Robert Southey's *Botany Bay Eclogues,* written in 1793 and published in 1797, extended the concept of the anti-slavery eclogue to social criminals extradited to Australia. Percy Bysshe Shelley's *Rosalind and Helen: A Modern Eclogue,* written in 1819, contains a digression on "Liberty" (lines 610–731), a paean to the early Romantic view of the French Revolution.

graph of French political history the impact of Virgil's *Eclogues* follows its own eccentric path.

Voltaire, whose career as a *philosophe* was one of the direct causes of the Revolution, recorded that career in hundreds of personal letters. Dozens of those letters are punctuated by deeply personalized allusions to the *Eclogues,* showing that he conceived of his role as a radical intellectual in terms of Virgil's analysis of both patronage and persecution. One would assume that Voltaire's disreputable enemy, the abbé Desfontaines, would have taken a different tack; yet he produced a translation of Virgil that combined a critique of Fontenelle's emasculated pastoral with implied attacks on the court and the Académie Française. André Chénier, in a mood of prerevolutionary reformism, wrote one of the century's starkest revisions of Virgil's first eclogue, transforming it into a cry for "La Liberté"; but Chénier was put to the guillotine. Jacques-Louis David, who above all is credited with supplying the Revolution with a Roman republican iconography, contributed, with his students Gérard and Girodet, to the most magnificent edition of Virgil that the French had produced since that of Marolles, the Didot edition of 1798; but while the edition may have been conceived in the spirit of the Revolution, it became in the course of production a reactionary monument. The languid and naked figures of the *Eclogues,* clearly in the spirit of David's post-revolutionary Hellenism, replace Virgil's historicized pastoral with a document more in the spirit of Winckelmann and his doctrine of *Heiterkeit,* or an idealizing serenity.

With these complexities in prospect, then, we can reapproach the question of what was, and who was responsible for, the Neoclassical reading of Virgil's *Eclogues.* The first point to be made, and it is a crucial one, is that Neoclassicism, with its emphasis on order and definition, shifted attention from the hermeneutics of pastoral to its theory—the theory of the genre conceived in abstraction. J. E. Congleton, whose account of this phenomenon I must on the whole disagree with, nevertheless remarked with some force that the amount of critical discourse expended on the theory of pastoral in this period was out of all proportion to either the quantity or the quality of pastoral writing.[14] What he did not consider is that the energy invested in writing *about* pastoral was symbolically displaced, that it signified the participation of intellectuals in bigger arguments otherwise beyond their intervention. The corollary, equally important, is that pastoral's representation of ideology now entered a new phase. As compared to the self-consciousness with which Renaissance pastoral functioned as a language, however encoded, of sociopolitical dialogue, the presence of ide-

---

[14] J. E. Congleton, *Theories of Pastoral Poetry in England 1684–1798* (Gainesville, 1952; reprinted New York, 1968), p. 295.

ology in eighteenth-century pastoral discourse is more inferred and inti-mated than spoken. This is especially true of the Neoclassical version, under the sign of the *fête champêtre*. In elucidating the texts of Rapin and Fontenelle and Pope we may also, as with the landscape of Gainsborough and Constable, have to think in terms of incomplete if not false conscious-ness, and to deal with repressions (and admissions) that were perhaps not fully understood by their authors.

When René Rapin published his essay *De carmine pastorali*, as a pref-ace to his religious eclogues in 1659, he wrote ostensibly as a good Aristo-telian. His stated object was to lay down rules for the writing of pastoral, as a genre that Aristotle had overlooked, by starting with a mimetic prem-ise—pastoral is "the imitation of the Action of a Sheapard, or of one taken under that Character"—and deducing principles of the appropriate subject-matter and style from the practice of Theocritus and Virgil, as Aristotle had done for epic from the example of Homer.[15] Yet he found himself caught (or at least we can find him so) in an ethical predicament. On the one hand his appeal to classical models required him to try to validate Virgil's practice at all costs; on the other, his personal preference was for an idealized pastoral from which not only the excessive rusticity of Theocritus but also the specifically Roman character of Virgil's eclogues should have been eliminated. What a Neoclassical pastoral should really imitate was nei-ther Theocritus nor Virgil so much as an idea, necessarily nonexistent, "of the simplicity and innocence of that Golden age" (p. 14) to which Virgil and Theocritus could only allude.

The nexus of this conflict between different types of mimesis was, of course, the Roman historical context or subtext of the *Eclogues*. Here Rapin sat unhappily on the fence:

> for tho as the Interpreters assure us; most of Virgils Eclogues are about the Civil war, planting Colonyes, the murder of the Emperor, and the like, which in themselves are too great and too lofty for humble Pastoral to reach, yet because they are accommodated to the Genius of Shepherds, may be the Subject of an Eclogue.
>
> (p. 26)

Yet he could not bring himself to accept the principle of "carmina maiora" in the fourth eclogue; expressed himself passionately on the subject of pas-toral's essential peacefulness, its ability to keep all thoughts of war in abeyance; and tried to bring Servius around to his own opinion: "And

---

[15] René Rapin, *Eglogae, cum dissertatione de carmine pastorali* (Paris, 1659); trans. Thomas Creech, in *The Idylliums of Theocritus, with Rapin's Discourse of Pastorals* (London, 1684). I cite from Creech in the edition by J. E. Congleton (Ann Arbor, 1947), p. 19.

upon this account I suppose 'tis that Servius in his Comments on Virgil's
Bucoliks reckons only seven of Virgil's ten Eclogues, and onely ten of
Theocritus's thirty, to be pure Pastorals" (pp. 26–27). That word *pure,* the
sign of a normative genre theory, was to have a long and dignified history
in European poetics, and many exclusionary actions would be committed
in its name.

We can see more clearly how revisionary was Rapin's response to Virgil
if we compare it with what had immediately preceded it. A mere two years
earlier Guillaume Colletet had published his *Discours du poëme bucolique,* in
which he restated the importance of the Servian/Renaissance hermeneutic.
Pastoral is the genre in which "Sous des termes de Pasteurs ils s'entretienent
des affaires du grand monde, des morts des Princes, & des autres hommes
illustres, des calamitez de leur temps, des changements des Estats & des
Empires, . . . & même lors qu'ils osent pousser leur voix jusques aux
oreilles des Consuls" ("Under pastoral language are discussed the affairs of
the great world, deaths of princes and other famous men, calamities of the
times, changes of states and empires, even to the extent that they dare address Consuls").[16] Virgil's own wish, in the sixth eclogue, that his "silvae"
might be "consule dignae," was still significant for Colletet in 1657; although, like Sebillet a full century earlier, the function of allegory is less of
a necessary protection for the French intellectual, and more of an opportunity for cleverness. The affairs of the great are presented "sous des termes
si agréables, & avecque des Allégories si ingénieuses & si justes, que les
intelligens en découvrent bien tost le secret, . . . ce qu'ils veulent cacher
sous un voile Pastoral" ("under such agreeable terms, and with such ingenious and apt allegories, that the intelligentsia quickly discover the secret
that they wished to conceal under a pastoral veil"). Nevertheless, the difference between his essay and Rapin's is both absolute and, given their chronological proximity, difficult to explain. Both wrote from a post-Fronde perspective, when the impulse to discuss "the alteration of states and empires"
was continually being satisfied, despite the controls exercised by Richelieu,
by all-too-historical fictions.[17] Both wrote within an institutional frame-
work that would seem to have promoted orthodoxy rather than dissent,
Colletet as one of the first members of the Académie Française, Rapin as a
Jesuit theologian.[18] Yet Colletet clearly respected the Renaissance/Servian
model and Rapin just as clearly wished it away. This difference can be ac-

---

[16] Guillaume Colletet, *Discours du poëme bucolique* (Paris, 1657), p. 18.

[17] See the account of the historical *romans à clef* by Erica Harth, *Ideology and Culture in
Seventeenth-Century France* (Ithaca, N.Y., 1983), pp. 99–103, 116–22, 129–79.

[18] Under Colbert, Rapin actually became a critic of the court hegemony and a defender
of an objective historiography, in his *Instructions pour l'histoire* (Paris, 1677). See Harth, *Ideology and Culture,* pp. 143–44.

counted for only partly by the fact that Colletet wrote descriptively of the past, and Rapin prescriptively for the future.

We can better understand Rapin, perhaps, by observing what he did with the theory of Ludovico Vives, an authority from the previous century he could afford neither to ignore nor openly to refute. As the first historicized account of the *Eclogues* and their subsequent reception, Vives's position could theoretically have allowed for further cultural adaptations. But what is astonishing about Rapin's response to Vives is that he quotes him as if he were an authority for the position argued in *De carmine pastorali*, calmly suppressing those parts of Vives's preface that dignified Virgil's *Eclogues* by reference to their Roman subtext, and changing Vives's vocabulary by misquotation so as to transform his preface into a Neoclassical document. Since the Golden Age is to be preferred to the heroic age, he argues, pastoral is superior to the epic, as it is also in the "unaffected neatness, elegant, graceful smartness of the expression, or the polite dress of a Poem." But the most telling passage is as follows:

> For tis not probable that Asinius Pollio, Cinna, Varius, Cornelius Gallus, men of the neatest Wit, and that lived in the most polite Age, or that Augustus Caesar the Prince of the Roman elegance, as well as of the common Wealth, should be so extreamly taken with Virgils Bucolicks, or that Virgil himself a man of such singular prudence, and so correct a judgement, should dedicate his Eclogues to those great Persons; unless he had known that there is somewhat more than ordinary elegance in those sort of Composures, which the wise perceive, tho far above the understanding of the Crowd: nay if Ludovicus Vives, a very learned man, and admired for politer studies may be believed, there is somewhat more sublime and excellent in those Pastorals, than the Common sort of Grammarians imagine.
>
> (p. 6)

A comparison with Vives's own statement (cited above, p. 89), or its Renaissance English translation by Latham (p. 165 above) will show the deliberate misprision. In place of Vives's defense of the hermeneutical dignity of the *Eclogues*, their ability to represent matters of national, international, and, ultimately, cosmic significance, we have here a defense of pastoral in formalist terms: "neatest Wit," "correct . . . judgement," "politer studies," Augustus Caesar "the Prince of the Roman elegance, as well as of the common Wealth"—this is the vocabulary of academic Augustanism.[19]

---

[19]This effect was not the product of Creech's translation. Rapin described Virgil's patrons as "Viros suavissimi ingenii, & aetatis omnium elegantissimae," and Virgil himself as "tam singularis prudentiae, judiciique tam politi virum." See *Hortorum libri, Eclogae, Liber de carmine pastorali* (Leiden, 1672), p. 76.

That Rapin was responsible for inaugurating a thoroughly idealized concept of pastoral is a familiar argument, although his aggressive relationship to Vives has not previously been explored. But according to Congleton, the critic most responsible for articulating English pastoral theory in this period, Rapin's opinions were of limited influence; Golden Age idealism was soon challenged in its basic premises and eventually replaced by a totally different theory of pastoral, originating in the *Discours sur la nature de l'eglogue* by Bernard le Bovier de Fontenelle, published in 1688, and translated into English in 1695 by Pierre Motteux.[20] Again according to Congleton, Fontenelle introduced into pastoral theory a rational critique of Neoclassicism, a rejection of neo-Aristotelian rules and definitions and their replacement by an account of how pastoral works, or ought to work, based on an empirical description of the human psyche. What the human mind desires, Fontenelle discovered by looking into his own, is a pastoral from which everything has been excluded except that vision of the countryside and its inhabitants which gives the most pleasure, a vision that permits us to grasp "l'idée de tranquillité," and of how little it costs to be happy ("le peu qu'il en coûte pour y être heureux").[21] Somehow, by focusing on the psychologism of Fontenelle's argument, Congleton managed to make him into the father of a rationalist "school" of thought which decried all imitation of classical pastoral and which led, therefore, to the celebration of "true" country poetry—in other words, to Romanticism.

Without for the moment attending to the logic whereby a theorist who rejects in Theocritus "la nature telle qu'elle est" ("Nature as it is," p. 59) could lay the foundations for Romanticism (whose founders claimed to prefer Theocritus to Virgil for precisely that quality), I wish to reexamine the question of Fontenelle's supposed antiphony to Rapin. For in fact Fontenelle makes perfectly clear what it is that he wishes to delete from pastoral tradition, and his motives for doing so—motives that differ from Rapin's only in being more explicitly sociopolitical. Fontenelle begins, not, as Congleton states, with the premise that all men wish to be happy but, rather, with a brief introduction of his own motives for embarking on this topic and of his own qualifications as critic, in which, interestingly, the "liberté" of the critic to strike out in new directions is twice mentioned; and he then contrasts the liberty of the shepherd in antiquity with the enslaved countryman of an advanced society like his own:

Il est assez vraisemblable que ces premiers pasteurs s'avisèrent, dans la tranquillité et l'oisiveté dont ils jouissaient, de chanter leurs plaisirs et

---

[20] Pierre Motteux, *Of Pastorals,* published with Bossu's *Treatise of the Epick Poem* (London, 1695).

[21] Bernard le Bovier de Fontenelle, *Oeuvres complètes,* ed. G.-B. Depping, 3 vols. (Geneva, 1968), 3: 56.

leurs amours. . . . Ils vivaient à leur manière dans une grande opulence, ils n'avaient personne au-dessus de leur tête, ils étaient pour ainsi dire les rois de leurs troupeaux; et je ne doute pas qu'une certaine joie qui suit l'abondance et la liberté, ne les portât encore au chant et à la poésie.

La société se perfectionna, ou peut-être se corrompit: mais enfin les hommes passèrent à des occupations qui leur parurent plus importantes; de plus grands interêts les agitèrent, on bâtit des villes de tous côtés, et avec le temps il se forma de grands états. Alors les habitans de la campagne furent les esclaves de ceux des villes; et la vie pastorale étant devenue le partage des plus malheureux d'entre les hommes, n'inspira plus rien d'agréable.

(3: 52)

It is quite probable that the first shepherds conceived, in the tranquility and leisure they enjoyed, of singing about their pleasures and their loves. They lived in their own way in great opulence, they had nobody in power over them, they were so to speak rulers of their flocks; and I have no doubt that a certain joy which results from well-being and liberty led them also into song and into poetry.

Society evolves, for better or perhaps for worse: but eventually men move on to occupations which appear to them more important; greater interests drive them, they build towns everywhere, and in time great states are formed. Then the inhabitants of the country become the slaves of those in the cities, and the pastoral life, having become the most unfortunate human lot, no longer inspires any pleasurable expression.

Given the premise that the lives of present-day peasants are "trop misérables" (p. 58) for them to sing about, Fontenelle could theoretically have argued either for a realistic poetry of country life (which implies the need for amelioration) or for a philosophical pastoral (the route taken by Wordsworth) that restated the hardships of rustic labor as a theme that can ennoble the spectator while leaving the social structure untouched. Instead, he proposed a Neoclassical solution, an idealized pastoral from which all signs of contemporary hardship were banished. "L'illusion et en même temps l'agrément des bergeries consiste donc à n'offrir aux yeux que la tranquillité de la vie pastorale, dont on dissimule la bassesse; on en laisse voir la simplicité, mais on en cache la misère" ("The illusion and at the same time the delightfulness of pastorals consists, then, in only offering to view the tranquility of the pastoral life, whose baseness is concealed; one shows the simplicity, but one hides the misery," 3: 59). The result was, inevitably, a depreciation of both Theocritus and Virgil as models: in

Theocritus it was the elements of rustic realism that Fontenelle despised; in Virgil the failure of *vraisemblance* and indecorous altiloquence of the "Pollio" and the "Silenus." But Fontenelle's exclusionary tactics were also strikingly personalized, in language revelatory of the political unconscious at work. Sannazaro's piscatory eclogues are antipastoral, because fishermen manifestly work: "j'y sens toujours que l'idée de leur travail dur me blesse" (3: 58). This admission leads to reflections on the role of sympathy, or psychological transference, in aesthetic pleasure:

> Quand on me représente le repos qui règne à la campagne, la simplicité et la tendresse avec laquelle l'amour s'y traite, mon imagination touchée et émue me transporte dans la condition de berger, je suis berger: mais que l'on me représente, quoiqu'avec toute l'exactitude et toute la justesse possible, les viles occupations des bergers, elles ne me font point d'envie, et mon imagination demeure fort froide. Le principal avantage de la poésie consiste à nous dépeindre vivement les choses qui nous intéressent.

> (3: 59)

> When someone represents to me the calm that reigns in the country, the simplicity and tenderness with which love is there experienced, my imagination, touched and affected, transforms me into the shepherd's condition, I *am* a shepherd: but when someone represents to me, although with all possible accuracy and justice, the wretched tasks that shepherds do, I cannot envy them, and my imagination remains stone cold. The chief advantage of poetry consists in painting for us vivid pictures of what interests us.

What we have here is a guilty conscience, and one that tells more than it meant to. "Leur travail dur me blesse." Their hard work pains him; therefore, for Fontenelle, being a shepherd is a negotiated condition, one that can only be maintained by a rigorous imaginative control over the idea of pastoral and an equally determined pretense that the experience so excluded was thereby socially and politically marginalized. That was, of course, the notorious "illusion" (Fontenelle's word) of Marie Antoinette, repeating the mimetic errors of Henrietta Maria, with equally violent consequences. But as an intellectual, Fontenelle's language is professionally, confessionally, precise. It is the intellectual's privilege to choose only those subjects for contemplation "qui nous intéressent," a phrase into which self-interest has textually insinuated itself. And, despite his rejection of Virgilian pastoral for not being ancient (primitive) enough,[22] Fontenelle's poetics have clearly

---

[22] Fontenelle was four times rejected as a candidate for the Académie Française because of his critique of the ancients; he was finally elected in 1691.

been infiltrated by the model he rejects. The aristocratic and academic privilege to exclude what one does not wish to contemplate is, again, "la liberté," and the "envie" he fails to feel for the pastoral life that fails to meet his standards of charm is clearly a distant echo of the envy that Virgil's Meliboeus *refuses* to feel for the idyll of Tityrus.

Instead, then, of being divisible into opposed theoretical camps, Golden Age Neoclassicists versus contemporary rationalists, both Rapin and Fontenelle were responsible for relocating pastoral under the sign of the *fête champêtre,* which excluded all the Virgilian dialectic, along with the "high" subjects of history, prophecy, and metaphysics, and the commentary tradition of hermeneutical difficulty and contingency. Sweet, docile, and untroubling, it was also, unmistakably, a gentleman's version of pastoral.

Pope and Philips: Pastorals at War

It was only natural, then (rather than being a sign of confusion or self-contradiction), that Alexander Pope should have appealed to both Rapin and Fontenelle in his *Discourse on Pastoral Poetry,* published in his collected *Works* of 1717. Pope suggested genially that "if we would copy Nature, it may be useful to take this Idea along with us, that Pastoral is an image of what they call the Golden age"; and two paragraphs later, that "we must therefore use some illusion to render a Pastoral delightful; and this consists in exposing the best side only of a shepherd's life, and in concealing its miseries."[23] We need, therefore, something more than the marginal differences between those French theorists to explain the extraordinary quarrel that occurred over the pastoral practice of Pope and Ambrose Philips, a quarrel that engaged on Pope's side Gay, Swift, Congreve, Walsh, and Arbuthnot, and on that of Philips, Addison, Steele, Tickell, and Dennis. The competition between Pope and Philips was formally initiated in 1709, when Tonson's *Miscellany* for that year included six pastorals by Philips as the first item in the anthology, and four by Pope as the last.[24] As Pope's modern editors have observed, "the opposing principles on which the two poets had fashioned their poems could not have been more dramatically suggested."[25] But those opposing principles were not, as was suggested by

[23] Alexander Pope, *Pastoral Poetry and an Essay on Criticism,* ed. E. Audra and Aubrey Williams (New Haven, 1961), pp. 25, 27.

[24] Jacob Tonson, ed., *Poetical Miscellanies: The Sixth Part* (London, 1709). Four of Philips's eclogues had previously appeared, in Fenton's *Oxford and Cambridge Miscellany Poems,* in January 1708.

[25] Pope, *Pastoral Poetry,* ed. Audra and Williams, p. 17.

Addison and Tickell, as patrons or promoters of Philips, a natural or native conception of pastoral (Philips) as against an artificial or neoclassical imitation (Pope). Philips was in fact as dependent on Virgil as was Pope, however differently they chose to interpret their model; and what each poet selected from Virgilian tradition was determined in large part by the role each wished to play in English affairs at the time.

Pope's editors cautiously admitted to there having been some element of political causation in the war over pastoral. I would say, rather, that it is absolutely unintelligible without the structural frame of Queen Anne's reign, her difficult relationship with Scotland, and the problem (once again) of the succession, created when her only surviving child, George, Duke of Gloucester, died in July 1700. The anxieties for a Protestant succession that had animated Sidney and Spenser in 1579–80 now activated the intellectuals of Anne's reign, not without direct allusion back to Elizabeth and, significantly, the pastorals of Spenser and Sidney. But loyalties now were divided between George, the Elector of Hanover, and James Stuart (the Old Pretender), a focus of Jacobite conspiracy and Roman Catholic hope who was, until the Peace of Utrecht in 1713 (when Louis XIV agreed to expel him from his dominions), domiciled in France.

We know that Ambrose Philips was prominent in pro-Hanoverian circles. He became Secretary of the Hanoverian Club, established in 1712, which, according to John Oldmixon, "met once a Week at Charing Cross, and took the Name from that Illustrious Family, for whose service they assembled."[26] In December 1712, Swift, who had two years earlier promised to solicit from Harley the post of queen's secretary in Geneva for Philips, reported to Stella that Philips had "run Party-mad" and forced him to withdraw his recommendation.[27] Pope, who continued to disclaim any active affiliation to the Tories, was, of course, a Roman Catholic. Although his first response to Philip's *Pastorals* was privately expressed as admiration, he was provoked into open rivalry by Addison and Tickell, who published their praise for Philips, declaring him the manifest successor to Theocritus and Virgil, in a way that was clearly intended to depreciate Pope.[28] Tickell

[26] John Oldmixon, *The History of England during the Reigns of King William and Queen Mary, Queen Anne, King George I* (London, 1735), p. 509. See also Robert Allen, *Clubs of Augustan London* (Hamden, Conn., 1967), p. 55.

[27] Jonathan Swift, *Journal to Stella*, ed. Harold Williams, 2 vols. (Oxford, 1963), 2: 589.

[28] Pope to Henry Cromwell, 30 October 1710, in Alexander Pope, *The Correspondence*, ed. George Sherburn, 5 vols. (Oxford, 1956), 1: 100–101. Addison announced in the *Spectator*, no. 523 (30 October 1712), that Philips had "given new Life, and a more natural Beauty to this way of Writing, by Substituting in the Place of these Antiquated Fables, the superstitious Mythology which prevails among the Shepherds of our own Country." See *The Spectator*, ed. Donald F. Bond, 5 vols. (Oxford, 1965), 4: 362–63. For Tickell, see John Calhoun Stephens, ed., *The Guardian*, nos. 22, 23, 28, 30, 32. Tickell's fourth essay suggests a political understanding of "Our own Country." Under the motto "Redeunt Saturnia Regna," Tickell set conditions for a new golden age, describing himself as "a good Patriot" whose

was himself a Hanoverian activist, described by Swift as one of the "Whiggissimi."[29] Addison had in 1707 accompanied Halifax on a diplomatic mission to the Elector, to invest him with the Order of the Garter; and when Addison became secretary of state in 1717 he chose Tickell as his undersecretary. Clearly more was at stake than whether one preferred the pastoral of the Ancients or of the Moderns.

If we reconsider the *casus belli*, the poems themselves, there are signs of ideological divergence from the start. Pope dedicated his first pastoral, "Spring," to Sir William Trumbull, who had been secretary of state under William but was now retired. Explicitly, the dedication praised the ethos of retirement, calling Trumbull "too Good for Pow'r" and inviting him to "Enjoy the Glory to be Great no more."[30] The poem itself is an elegant and seamless imitation of Virgil's third eclogue, underlining the formal principle of Theocritean song-contest ("Then sing by turns, by turns the Muses sing," line 41), and the connection of pastoral with the finely turned artifact, the carved wooden bowl that is simultaneously the singer's prize, an icon of the seasonal cycle, and an emblem of art's dependence on leisure.[31] Pope's emphasis on "Four Figures rising from the Work . . . / The various Seasons of the rowling Year" (lines 37–38) is a structural prolepsis of his four *Pastorals;* and in the 1717 edition of his *Works* the centrality of the bowl in his poetics is asserted visually, in the engraved headpiece by Simon Gribelin that we have every reason to suppose Pope himself carefully selected.[32] Compatible with this symbol, and with his emphasis in the *Discourse* on Neoclassical ideas of pastoral—it "consists in simplicity, brevity, and delicacy" (p. 25)—is Pope's system of Virgilian allusion. With one major exception, the *Pastorals* are constructed as an elegant tissue of echoes from Virgil, selected according to the principles of Rapin. There is no trace, in Pope's rewriting, of the Roman historical context, of war or dispossession. The only concerns are love or poetic competition; and as

definition of pastoral "will satisfie the courteous Reader that I am in the Landed Interest" (p. 128). Stephens (pp. 609–10) explains this in the context of the *Guardian*'s policy to mediate between the Whigs and the Tory landowners. The promotion of Philips, then, served not a rationalist view of pastoral but a nationalist one, a redefinition of "Country" interests in Hanoverian terms.

[29] Swift to Rev. Thomas Sheridan, 25 September 1725. See Jonathan Swift, *Correspondence,* ed. Harold Williams, 5 vols. (Oxford, 1963), 3: 101.

[30] Pope, *Pastoral Poetry,* p. 61.

[31] On the significance of the carved cups in Virgil, see Charles Segal, "Vergil's *caelatum opus:* An Interpretation of the Third Eclogue," *American Journal of Philology* 88 (1967): 280–83, reprinted in his *Poetry and Myth in Ancient Pastoral* (Princeton, 1981), pp. 234–70; and for a comparable account of Pope's imitation, see Martin Battestin, *The Providence of Wit* (Oxford, 1974), pp. 64–67.

[32] See Vincent Carretta, "'Images Reflect from Art to Art': Alexander Pope's Collected *Works* of 1717," in *Poems in Their Places,* ed. Neil Fraistat (Chapel Hill, N.C., 1986), pp. 195–233.

the *Discourse* also would make clear, one object of Pope's competitiveness was with Spenser, whose *Shepheardes Calender* he had also subjected to the ideal of simplification, reducing its twelve months to four tranquil seasons.

But (and this the exception) his adaptation of the riddles in Virgil's third eclogue served a rather different purpose: [33]

> Say, Daphnis, say, in what glad soil appears
> A wondrous Tree that Sacred Monarchs bears?
>
> . . . .
>
> Nay tell me first, in what more happy Fields
> The Thistle springs, to which the Lilly yields?
>
> (lines 85–86, 89–90)

The first riddle alludes, in the language of Stuart loyalty, to the escape of Charles II after the battle of Worcester by hiding in an oak tree; the second, to Anne's Scottish policy, beginning with her revival of the Order of the Thistle in 1703 and ending with the Act of Union between England and Scotland in March 1708. The "yielding" of the lily referred to the replacement of the fleur-du-lys by the thistle on the heraldic "fields" of the royal arms. The second riddle is therefore a statement of patriotism; the first keeps open at least the possibility of Jacobite sentiment.

These intimations would have been fully confirmed by the publication, in March 1713, of Pope's *Windsor-Forest,* a poem tightly connected to the *Pastorals* both in its closing lines, which echo the opening line of "Spring," and in its preliminary epigraph from Virgil's sixth eclogue, lines 9–10. Yet it marks a significant change in Pope's strategy, offering a generic compound that was at least *half* explicit about its engagement with contemporary events. The "Varus" invoked by the epigraph was at least as deeply involved with English politics as was the original with Roman: George Granville, Lord Lansdowne, a prominent Tory and known Jacobite, who in 1710 had replaced Walpole as secretary for war and was in 1712 one of twelve new peers created by Anne to give the Tories control over Parliament. This enabled the Peace of Utrecht, signed on 11 April 1713, an event to which Pope's poem looked forward and on which it presumably aimed to capitalize, as had Tickell's *Prospect of the Peace* six months earlier. In a series of contradictory and elliptical notes on his poem, Pope indicated his wish that it should be read as the product of two stages of his development as a poet, one prior to or at "the same time" with the *Pastorals,* in the year 1704, the other either (depending on which note one reads) 1710,

---

[33] For a discussion of the riddles, and Pope's revisions to them, between 1704 and 1707, to increase their topicality, see Pope, *Pastoral Poetry,* ed. Audra and Williams, pp. 39–41.

1712, or 1713.[34] Whatever the truth of Pope's compositional chronology, his seemingly obsessive concern to have the *Pastorals,* the *Discourse on Pastoral,* and part, at least, of *Windsor-Forest* back-dated to his adolescence should remind us of Marot's use of the trope of youthfulness as a way of claiming political innocence. It was Pope's stated strategy also to distinguish a "country" section of the poem from its political conclusion, with its survey of British history and its arguments both for peace and for peace's commercial benefits; but it is by no means clear where, if anywhere, such a line is to be drawn.

Ever since Earl Wasserman's brilliant reading of *Windsor-Forest,* however, it has been recognized that the entire poem is a subtle and encoded instrument of Tory policy and Jacobite sentiment, including an explicit identification of Anne as a Stuart monarch, an elegy for Charles I, a reference back to the riddle, in the first pastoral, about Charles II's concealment in the oak ("While by our Oaks the precious Loads are born," 1.31), and an attack on William III disguised as an attack on William the Conqueror. In addition, the hunting theme of the poem was revealed by Wasserman to be an allegory of the English constitution, in which Magna Charta and the Charter of the Forest, itself best represented by royal Windsor, are embodied in a modification of pastoral/georgic, the pacificism of the first blending with the activism of the second, yet excluding the militarism of the *Aeneid.*[35]

There were, however, two important Virgilian strategies that Wasserman overlooked. The first is the adaptation of the ancient pastoral theme of expropriation to William I's notorious creation of the forest for his hunt. "The Fields are ravish'd from th' industrious Swains" (line 65), wrote Pope, but "Succeeding Monarchs heard the subjects cries" (line 85), and reinstated "Fair Liberty, Britannia's Goddess" (line 91). The second is a quotation more clearly from the first eclogue than from *Georgics* 4.176 that functions as a key to the poem's entire metaphorical system. "Sic parvis componere magna solebam," wrote Virgil, speaking as Tityrus about his own attempts at metaphor, comparing the superiority of Rome over Mantua to that of dogs over puppies; and Pope, comparing the use of dogs in a hunt to the strategies of besiegers in a real war, used a similar disclaimer: "Thus (if small Things we may with great compare)" (line 105). The result is a neat and decorously Virgilian statement of *Windsor-Forest*'s relationship to larger political issues. And the conflicting and elliptical testimony of Pope's notes about its process of composition may not have been merely, as his editor's suggest, the result of faulty memory but, rather, an

[34] Ibid., pp. 125–28. See also the evidence assembled by Norman Ault, *New Light on Pope* (London, 1949), pp. 27–48, for an earlier planned edition of *Windsor-Forest* in the *Miscellaneous Poems and Translations* which appeared, with Pope as editor, in the spring of 1712.
[35] Earl Wasserman, *The Subtler Language* (Baltimore, 1959), pp. 101–68.

essential part of the camouflage. *Windsor-Forest*, in fact, goes far toward explaining the hostility of Philips to Pope, and his somewhat manic behavior
in April 1713, when he publicly charged Pope with disloyalty to the government and refused to turn over the subscriptions to Pope's *Homer* collected from members of the Hanoverian Club.

Philips had from the start been comparatively open about his Hanoverian sympathies.[36] His *Pastorals* were dedicated to Lionel Cranfield, seventh earl and first duke of Dorset, who in April 1706 had accompanied
Halifax on his mission to inform the Elector of the Regency Act, confirm-
ing his family as successors to the English throne provided they remained
Protestants. The second eclogue, under the figure of Menalcas, asserts its
author's gratitude to Addison. The third begins by tracing a genealogy of
pastoral as a form of address to a sovereign: Virgil to Augustus, Spenser to
Elizabeth, and (presumably) Philips to Anne; and it proceeds to lament,
under the figure of Albino, "Pledge of peaceful Times" (p. 19), the death of
the Duke of Gloucester. The sixth pastoral introduces a medley of Spenserian and Sidneyan speakers, including "Lanquet," or Hubert Languet,
Sidney's Huguenot mentor,[37] who explains the conditions under which
English pastoral may continue—that is, under the protection of Cranfield,
who has now replaced Sidney as "the Shepherds Friends":

> Thrice happy Shepherds now: for Dorset loves
> The Country Muse, and our delightful Groves;
> While Anna reigns. O ever may she reign!
> And bring on Earth a Golden Age again.

(p. 43)

For Philips, in other words, the Golden Age is, as it was for Virgil, a hypothesis, whose realization at this moment is as impossible as Anne's immortality. The absurdity of the appeal, "O ever," must have reminded the
audience of the problematic succession, as the analogy made between
Anne and "Eliza's Maiden Rule" would remind them of childlessness.
When the song contest ends, the series concludes, not with the Virgilian
evening shadows, but with the clouds of an unsettled political forecast:

> A mizling Mist descends
> Adown that steepy Rock: And this way tends

---

[36] I cite from *Tonson's Miscellany,* where Philips's *Pastorals* appeared on pp. 1–48, under
the date 1708, and under the Virgilian epigraph "Nostra nec erubuit Silvas habitare Thalia,
Virg. Ecl. 6."

[37] In a crucial eclogue in the *Arcadia,* Sidney's persona Philisides defers to "Languet, the
shepherd best swift Ister knew," for a fable about monarchy. See *The Countess of Pembroke's
Arcadia,* ed. Jean Robertson (Oxford, 1973), pp. 255–56.

Yon distant Rain. Shore-ward the Vessels strive;
And, see, the Boys their Flocks to shelter drive.

(p. 48)

To an alert reader of Tonson's *Miscellany,* then, as early as 1709 these different versions of pastoral could have been recognized as rivals in a more than literary sense. Two young men could be seen as making preliminary statements about the directions of English culture in the reign of Anne and beyond. Philips could plainly be identified as a Hanoverian poet, warning the queen and the nation about the dependence of literature upon a sure and stable Protestant succession. Pope could already be perceived as hedging his bets, as were most of the leading politicians of the day, while initiating a pattern that would be characteristic of his career and consistent with his pastoral *theory;* that is to say, espousing a poetics of retreat, defined in Virgilian terms,[38] while cautiously engaging in undercover warfare.[39]

What that public would *not* have been able to discern was any difference between Pope and Philips in the amount of obeisance paid to Virgil. As Robert Thornton was to remark a century later, Philips's second pastoral was an unmistakable rewriting of Virgil's first eclogue:

> Philips, an admirable poet, has ably imitated this first Pastoral of Virgil, and designates himself under the character of a shepherd, in order that he might publicly declare his gratitude to his patron; for he had come up a lad from Scotland to England with very scanty means, was attacked in his writings by ill-natured critics, and envious poets; but found at length a Maecenas . . . who stood forward as his friend, and brought him into public notice. . . . Thenot is the happy, and Colinet is the unhappy shepherd.[40]

While Thornton's chronology may have been somewhat erratic, reading the Pope/Philips quarrel back into the poetry that helped to cause it, we

---

[38] See Maynard Mack, "*Secretum Iter:* Some Uses of Retirement Literature in the Poetry of Pope," in *Aspects of the Eighteenth Century,* ed. Earl Wasserman (Baltimore, 1965), pp. 207–43.

[39] Despite Pope's protests against "party" writing (*Correspondence,* 1: 244–45, 246–47), and his suggestion to Gay that they shared Whig principles (1: 254), he had already been accused by John Dennis of Jacobitism by allusion. See Dennis, *Reflection Critical and Satyrical, Upon . . . An Essay Upon Criticism* (London, 1711; reprinted New York, 1975), p. 27. This was the first of many such accusations. See G. V. Guerinot, *Pamphlet Attacks on Alexander Pope, 1711–1744: A Descriptive Bibliography* (London, 1969). For Pope's later political involvements and his opposition to Walpole's Tory ministry, see Bertrand A. Goldgar, *Walpole and the Wits: The Relation of Politics to Literature, 1722–1742* (Lincoln, Neb., 1976), especially pp. 166–78, 208–16.

[40] Robert J. Thornton, ed., *The Pastorals of Virgil, with a Course of English Reading, Adapted for Schools,* 2 vols. (London, 1821), 1: 13.

can build on his basic insight. Philips's second pastoral was indeed the one in which he denoted his own stance as a poet, and claimed as his persona Meliboeus the exile (although the notion that he was a Scottish expatriate was Thornton's invention). As Colinet, who is *young* and unhappy, admits to the aged and would-be consoling Thenot, he succumbed to a "lewd Desire strange Lands and Swains to know" (p. 13); but the motive for departure is not, as it was in the original, an unwilled expropriation but, rather, a dimly perceived and unsatisfied subjectivity: "With wand'ring Feet unbless'd, and fond of Fame, / I sought I know not what, besides a Name" (lines 75–76).

This was a revision of Virgil that anticipated by a century one of the major premises of Romanticism, the conception of the intellectual as alienated from his culture, while leading more directly to Wordsworth's rethinking of the relationship between Recluse and Wanderer in *The Excursion.* Even more prophetic of Romanticism was Philips's transvaluation of the pastoral *umbra:*

> My piteous Plight, in yonder naked Tree,
> That bears the Thunder Scar, too well I see:
> Quite destitute it stands of shelter kind,
> The Mark of storms and Sport of ev'ry Wind:
>
> . . . .
>
> No more beneath thy Shade shall Shepherds throng
> With merry Tale, or Pipe, or pleasing Song.
> Unhappy Tree! and more unhappy I!
> From thee, from me, alike the Shepherds fly.

(pp. 10–11)

For Philips, the cultural shade that denotes protection of writers and the lightning-struck oaks that symbolized the revenge of Augustus have been folded together, as they had previously been collated by Petrarch, Sannazaro, and Marvell; but whereas those writers had seen the tree of patronage fall, leaving them destitute, the stricken tree here is the figure of the poet's *own* condition, a portent that remains untouched by the efficacy of Menalcas/Addison later in the poem. The symbol and the mood of desolation it extends are appropriate to the muted tone and warning function of the *Pastorals* as a group. Most significantly, it operates as the sign of a new direction in pastoral hermeneutics, a reading of the landscape that is performed *within* the poem, not imposed upon it by the learned commentator or annotator. The act of figuration is here decisively the poet's responsibility; he reads the landscape as tropical of his own feelings, which in the larger structure of his pastorals are culturally determined. Nor is his exile literally from anywhere; his melancholy is in being, or being afraid of being, athwart his social environment. Although in the most narrowly conceived view of his intentions Philips's forebodings were canceled by the accession of George I, in the larger sense his prognosis was sadly accurate. His career records the destabilizing effects of party politics on the older patronage system. And although there is no evidence that the mockery of Pope and Gay did Philips serious damage during his lifetime, he was subsequently the loser in the battle for canonicity and was driven into exile on the fringes of English literary history.

Philips's discovery—of pastoral as metaphor for imaginative work, for the ways in which the self registers its responsibility to, yet difference from, its environment—could conceivably have been widely acceptable to eighteenth-century men of letters of all persuasions. But because Philips also clearly believed that pastoral should engage major political issues, the local uproar so occasioned confused the issue and delayed until the following century the recognition of what he had accomplished. When that recognition came, it came in the highly eccentric form of Thornton's 1821 *Pastorals of Virgil,* a textbook for schoolboys in which analogues to and imitations of the *Eclogues* appeared as part of the interpretive apparatus. Along with the first eclogue, Thornton printed Pope's *Discourse on Pastoral Poetry* and Ambrose Philips's second pastoral; along with other conventional illustrations, there appeared the first and only woodcuts of William Blake, whom Thornton had commissioned to illustrate Philips's poem.

Pastoral and Social Protest

VOLTAIRE

Throughout his long and contentious career Voltaire, who renamed himself in the service of a secular free will,[41] did what he could to awaken the understanding of his contemporaries to the sociopolitical aspects of culture; and, at all stages of his development as a *philosophe* and champion of civil liberties, conceived of himself as an intellectual in Virgil's terms, most often in the terms of the first eclogue. The evidence for this is contained in the massive correspondence that has survived for our inspection, for Voltaire was an indefatigable letter-writer and reported extensively to friends on every phase of his battle for intellectual independence and survival, in a France that was both more tolerant of the witty *savant* than it was of Marot in the sixteenth century, and more arbitrary and cruel in its abuses of the *lettre de cachet.*

---

[41] See John E. N. Hearsey, *Voltaire* (London, 1976), pp. 33, 38.

In 1736, for instance, when Voltaire had retreated into the private world of study that he shared with Mme du Chatelet at Cirey, a copy of his unpublished poem *Le Mondain* got into the hands of the authorities. *Le Mondain* was not much more than a satire on the Golden Age, but its cheerful irreverence in favor of contemporary civilization looked sufficiently immoral to make prosecution inevitable, so Voltaire prudently took cover in Holland until the scandal died down. On 9 December 1736, he wrote to the count of Tressan complaining how his "repos" has been destroyed by this incident, and how, on account of "un badinage plein de naïveté et d'innocence," certain people have formed a design to chase him out of his own country:

> j'avais déjà quitté Paris pour être à l'abri de la fureur de mes ennemis. L'amitié la plus respectable a conduit dans la retraite des personnes qui connaissent le fond de mon coeur, et qui ont renoncé au monde pour vivre en paix avec un honnête homme dont les moeurs leur ont paru dignes peut-être de tout autre prix que d'une persécution. S'il faut que je m'arrache encore à cette solitude, et que j'aille dans les pays étrangers, il m'en coûtera, sans doute, mais il faudra bien s'y résoudre. . . . Vous m'écriviez: *"Formosam resonare doces Amaryllida silvas,"* faudra-t-il que je réponde, *"Nos patriam fugimus?"*[42]

> I have already left Paris to find a refuge from the fury of my enemies. The most respectable friendship has led into retreat those persons who know the depths of my heart, and who have renounced the world to live in peace with an honest man whose mores have perhaps seemed worthy of a reward very different from persecution. If it is necessary that I pluck myself out of this solitude again, and that I go into foreign lands, it will certainly cost me something, but I must resolve to do it. You have written to me, "You teach the woods to resound with the name of fair Amaryllis"; must I answer, "We are leaving our country behind?"

With remarkable precision and completeness Voltaire perceived, and articulated in his letter's lexicon *before* its Virgilian source is revealed, the match between his own circumstances and those of the protagonists—both of them—in the first eclogue; on the one hand, the possibility of a quiet idyll at Cirey ("repos," "solitude," "retraite," "innocence," "paix," even an "amitié" [however glossed as respectable] that fulfilled his need for

---

[42] Voltaire, *Correspondance,* ed. Theodore Besterman, 102 vols. (Geneva, 1953–65), D1222.

an Amaryllis of the flesh as well as of the mind); on the other, the exile from the "patrie," which for all it will cost him will confirm his status as a man of international significance. When, for example, news of his arrival in Amsterdam had reached London, a large group of his young admirers in England took the opportunity to visit this notorious celebrity. Voltaire was made increasingly aware that his relationship with his *patrie* was happy in inverse relationship to his fame abroad.

Two months later he had found a still more penetrating use for the dialectic of opposed fortunes. On 18 February 1737 he wrote to Pierre Robert Le Cormier that he could not imagine anything more pleasant than to sing with him "lentus in umbra," as compared to traveling in "le pays de démonstrations"; but that on the other hand it was important to be open to new experiences, to "ouvrir toutes les portes de son âme à toutes les sciences et à tous les sentiments" (D1285). Whether the "country of demonstrations" referred literally to France, to which he would return in March, or metaphorically to the condition of living with confrontation, on intellectual alert, the point Voltaire wished to make was the superiority of the Meliboeus role, the role of the wanderer, in contemporary culture. The importance of this statement from the future contributor to the *Encyclopédie* is that it implies the transfer of philosophy and rational inquiry from the recluse to the intellectual adventurer.

Back in Brussels briefly in 1739, though this time on his own business, Voltaire wrote in July to another friend, the marquis of Argenson, that he hoped to see him soon at the head of *belles lettres* in Paris, because the literary scene was in all other respects depressing in the extreme:

> La décadence du bon goust, le brigandage de la littérature me font sentir que je suis né citoyen. Je suis au désespoir de voir une nation si aimable, si prodigieusement gâtée.
>
> (D2054)

> The decadence of good taste, the pillaging of literature, make me feel that I was born a citizen. I despair to see so attractive a nation so extremely decadent.

The immediate cause of this chagrin was Richelieu's support for a court performance of Scarron's *L'Héritier ridicule,* of which the Comédie Française was so ashamed that they refused to play in it. But even that would be bearable if dedicated scholars were not to be persecuted by those without "esprit" or whose spirit is only for intrigue and *lettres de cachet*. "I say with you," wrote Voltaire, "*barbarus has segetes*" ("the seeds we sowed are now in the hands of barbarians"). And it is striking to hear his self-identification, in this anti-courtly context, as *citoyen,* a term which by mid-century had already, it seems, acquired a republican nuance.

There were, of course, occasions on which Voltaire exploited the text of the *Eclogues* for purely ritual or complimentary purposes, as in his letters to Frederick of Prussia, whom he honors as his Pollio or Augustus, with appropriate misquotation: "Deus nobis haec munera fecit," wrote Voltaire on more than one occasion ("It is a god who gave me these rewards," in place of Virgil's subtler "leisure").[43] But much more consistently, Virgilian pastoral functions for him, as it had for Marot two centuries earlier, as the model for an analysis of French culture and its apparent hostility to free thought. His own difficulties in gaining access to the Académie Française served as an emblem of the equivocal role played by that institution, the most prestigious academy in Europe, and yet one that had condemned itself, precisely because of the royal patronage under which it sheltered, to the dreariest of hegemonic routines.[44] It was not until the 1760s, when d'Alembert conceived the project of making the Académie a stronghold of the *philosophes,* that it would become an environment fruitful to Voltaire; yet from the early 1730s he passionately desired the acceptance that a *fauteuil* would symbolize.[45]

In April 1743 he wrote to Jean Dumas D'Aigueberre about the "petite persécution" that he had suffered at the hands of Boyer, the Bishop of Mirepoix, who had prevented his getting the seat vacated by Cardinal Fleury, and in the same letter he reported the imprisonment in the Bastille of the abbé Lenglet, for merely having published some notes supplementing the *Mémoires de Condé,* a historical work already well known and scarcely polemical. "Il a rendu un très grand service aux bons citoyens," wrote Voltaire bitterly (again using that term *citoyen*), "et aux amateurs des recherches sur l'histoire, il méritoit des récompenses, et on l'imprisonne à l'âge de soixante et huit ans. *Insere nunc Meliboee, pone ordine vites*" ("He has rendered a great service to good citizens, and to amateurs in historical research, he deserves some recompense, and they have put him in prison at the age of sixty-eight. 'Now, Meliboeus, go graft, set your vines in order'" [1.73], D2744). Here, obviously, was one reader of Virgil whom the ironic tone of Meliboeus's self-injunction did not escape.

In his old age Voltaire frequently referred to himself in the terms of Virgil's ninth eclogue, with respect to the failing voice of Moeris and the silencing vision of the wolf. The trope occurs in his writings four times

---

[43] Voltaire, *Correspondance,* D1255, D2020.

[44] For example, the competitions recorded in *Les Registres de l'Académie Françoise 1672–1793,* ed. Camille Doucet, 4 vols. (Paris, 1906), included a "prix de poésie" for 1743 on the subject "La Police perfectionnée sous le règne de Louis XIV," and one for 1780 on "La servitude abolie dans les domaines du Roi, sous le règne de Louis XIV" (4: 105, 108; Table Analytique).

[45] See Karlis Racevskis, *Voltaire and the French Academy* (Chapel Hill, N.C., 1975), pp. 71–75.

between 1756 and 1776, though more in the form of a modesty topos (apologizing to a friend for some inadequacy in his literary exchanges) than as an expression of the cultural frailty implied by Virgil (and transmitted by Dryden).[46] More significant for his self-image and its classical configurations was his decision in 1755 to go into voluntary exile in Switzerland, a move that ironically changed him, literally and in his imagination, back into the sheltered Tityrus whose security he had earlier rejected. Four times in these late letters Voltaire cites the statement of Tityrus that his liberty has been late in coming ("Libertas quae sera tamen respexit"), with the emphasis, presumably, on "late."[47]

What is even more striking is the way in which he remade his life in the image of the idyll described by Meliboeus, the happy life of the man who owns his own land and his own time. At Ferney, the philosopher became a farmer, and his estate became, as Hearsey puts it, something of an agricultural showplace. But it was also, clearly, a space for symbolic action: "Until 1772, when he reached the age of seventy-eight, there was one field which no one else was allowed to touch, and which Voltaire ploughed and sowed himself."[48] In 1773 he wrote to his lifelong friend, Charles Feriol, comte D'Argental, a letter that makes it clear how intensely the metaphors of Virgil were being reworked in actual experience:

> J'avoue que j'avais un peu de passion pour la scène française, mais les choses sont tellement changées, qu'il faut y renoncer. . . . Les affaires serieuses ne s'accommodent pas trop de la poésie. . . . Je n'ai plus de parti à prendre que celui de finir mes jours en philosophe obscur, et d'attendre la mort tout doucement, au milieu des souffrances du corps.
>
> (D18552)

> I admit that I have a small passion for the French scene, but things are so changed, that I must give it up. Serious matters can no longer be accommodated to poetry. I have no other role to play than that of finishing my days as an obscure philosopher, and of gently waiting for death, surrounded by bodily pains.

Insisting on maintaining his exile from the heart, or at the least the location, of French culture, while he continued to intervene from the sidelines

[46] Voltaire, *Correspondance,* D6999, D11117, D13491, D19848.
[47] In *Correspondance,* D8642, to Algarotti, 10 December 1759, on the subject of freedom of the press, Voltaire asked ironically whether the Jacobins had control over the library of a Roman senator, and added (in English), "Yes, good sir, I am free and far more free than all the citizens of Geneva." See also D8033, 8400, 8909.
[48] Hearsey, *Voltaire,* p. 314.

in its politics, Voltaire complained self-mockingly of business difficulties at Ferney, remarking that he had failed to find himself a "Mecène" and so did not know if in the end they would be able to speak of him as a "fortunate old man who retains his own lands" ("fortunate senex ergo tua rura mane-bunt," 1.46). In the last stage of this development, however, before his triumphal return to Paris as the grand old man and his ceremonial crowning at the Comédie Française, the querulousness induced by local frustrations made even that "if" seem overly optimistic, and on at least one occasion the threat of financial disaster brought back the other voice in the perpetual dialogue that was his life. "Tous mes travaux vont devenir inutiles; toutes mes peines perdues, et cent maisons que j'avais bâties vont être abandonnées. . . . *Insere nunc Melibeae piros pone ordine vites*" ("All my work is going to be useless, all my efforts lost, and a hundred houses that I have built are going to be abandoned. 'Graft your pear trees now, Meliboeus, set your vines in rows,'" D20325).

ANDRÉ CHÉNIER

Voltaire's Neoclassicism was, then, a mode of vocational self-analysis, resembling sixteenth-century humanism in constantly being excited by the experience or even the thought of persecution. For André Chénier, Neoclassicism was in a less egocentric way an aspect of his republicanism; and although one might suppose that the delicate Hellenism of most of his *Bucoliques* leaned as far as it could in the opposite direction from his political statements both in prose and poetry, the antithesis was neither unplanned nor absolute. In his poem on *L'Invention*, which actually consists of a powerful theory of imitation, Chénier began by invoking Virgil, "fils du Mincius . . . / Par qui le Dieu des arts fut roi du peuple roi" ("Son of Mincius / Through whom the god of art became ruler of a royal nation") who, together with Homer, bestowed on all subsequent poets "un ciel pur, les plaisirs, la beauté, / Des moeurs simples, des lois, la paix, la liberté" ("a clear sky, pleasure, beauty, / Simple customs, laws, peace, liberty").[49] In comparison with these monumental figures (whose contributions, however, are expressed in such anti-heroic terms as to suggest idyll), the contemporary poet, "L'esclave imitateur" passes away like a shadow in the night. In at least one important sense, then, "liberté" for Chénier meant the freedom of the originary imagination, slavery the condition of all who must remake and rewrite for their own culture what has already been done as well as it could be. Yet the poem moves, not entirely securely, to a definition of imitation that allows for a limited freedom:

---

[49] André Chénier, *Oeuvres complètes,* ed. Gerard Walter (Paris, 1958), p. 123.

Changeons en notre miel leurs plus antiques fleurs;
Pour peindre notre idée, empruntons leurs couleurs;
Allumons nos flambeaux à leurs feux poétiques;
Sur des pensers nouveaux faisons des vers antiques.

(p. 127)

We change their most ancient flowers into our honey; to paint our conception, we borrow their colors; we light our torches at their poetic fires; on the basis of new thoughts we erect antique verses.

The cultural restorations of Louis XIV and Colbert, especially in the drama, are compatible with such a program; but, more interestingly, the intellectual must now be able to reconcile classical poetry with the findings of modern science. And Virgil's is the name to conjure with here. As Democritus, Plato, Epicurus, Thales, have from afar whispered to Virgil the secrets of a nature for them "trop voilée," so Torricelli, Newton, Kepler, and Galileo, in their greater learning, have reopened Virgil's treasury of knowledge ("A tout nouveau Virgile ont ouvert des trésors," p. 125). This extraordinary statement, however implausible as a program for uniting all the arts and sciences (as Colbert himself had hoped to unite them in a single encyclopedic academy) nevertheless offers us a sharp view of the depth and originality of Chénier's thought, his grasp of where French and indeed European culture stood in the 1770s, and especially his insight into historical process.

These aspects of Chénier's thought are more fully articulated in the long but unfinished *Essai sur les Causes et les Effets de la Perfection et de la Décadence des Lettres et des Arts,* first published at the end of the nineteenth century by Abel Lefrance, who gave it that unwieldy title. The *Essai* was a sign of Chénier's astonishing ability to take the large and unprecedented view, all the more unusual given the fact that he was only twenty-three when he began work on it and only thirty-two when he left it, still in progress, to keep his appointment with the guillotine. Based on his reading both of classical authors and of Montaigne, Montesquieu, and Rousseau's *Contrat Social,* Chénier delivered an intelligently left-wing analysis of the relationship between literature and society. The golden moment for literature was, he hypothesized, after a young republic had stabilized, when the great actions that freed it from its enemies had been undertaken, and society had leisure to make monuments out of what has happened. Before this moment, the polis was "un peu rude et agreste"; afterward, it became decadent; but at that precise moment of equilibrium, "les arts de paix naquirent en foule." The arts of peace are born *en masse;* or, perhaps, for the masses. In this situation, letters become "augustes et sacrées, car elles étaient citoyennes" (pp. 622–23).

Given this language (which in *citoyennes* happens also to recall the Virgilianism of Voltaire) it takes little guesswork to imagine what historical model Chénier had in mind, for the only one to which his story could conceivably be accommodated is Augustan Rome. But his description of the era of decadence could be rather more widely applied, including to France under Louis XVI. Whereas in a healthy culture men of letters are integrated into the republic and can serve their country both physically and intellectually ("par la main et par le conseil"), in a decadent one there are two unacceptable alternatives: men of honor, excluded from fine action, console themselves with the fame of fine writing, usually in the role of satirist or sociopolitical critic; the majority, frightened by the danger involved in such alienation and attracted by financial incentives, "vendirent leur esprit et leur plume aux puissances injustes" ("sell their spirit and their pen to unjust powers"), teaching men to forget their rights, and only contesting as to who shall give the most illustrious examples of servitude. In such a culture, Chénier argued, men only read what was written yesterday, and neglect the study of "les lettres antiques." As for himself (and here the fact that France has been his subject is made explicit),

> ouvrant les yeux autour de moi au sortir de l'enfance, je vis que l'argent et l'intrigue étaient presque la seule voie pour aller à tout; je résolus donc . . . de vivre toujours loin de toutes affaires, avec mes amis, dans la retraite et dans la plus entière liberté.

> (p. 624)

> opening my eyes to what was about me as I emerged from childhood, I saw that money and intrigue were almost the only route to get anywhere; I resolved therefore always to live far away from all public affairs, with my friends, in retreat and in the most complete freedom.

Despite the fact that this resolution was broken by his membership in the Société de 1789 and his journalism (fatal to himself) on behalf of moderates and centrists during the Revolution, the opening analysis of the *Essai* nevertheless provides the best explanation we have for the *Bucoliques* and their extraordinary resistance (again with one exception) to Chénier's reformist passion.

The *Essai* also engaged directly with pastoral theory and practice. After a fragmentary statement on the origin of eclogues in comedic exchanges (*versibus alternis*), Chénier launched into an attack on Italian *favole boscherecce* and French *bergeries,* which, he argued, have rendered the idea of pastoral ridiculous. In particular he disliked authors who placed at the head of their *bergeries* a discourse on the theory of pastoral, since their theory and their practice are made for each other; and he contrasted the "nudité décente" of the ancient poetry with the "fades et énigmatiques subtilités appelées galanteries" (p. 661). And in a later section, he specifically attacked La Motte and Fontenelle for their attacks on the ancients (p. 664). Both of these men, he remarked astutely, were possessed "infiniment d'esprit et de connaissances," but neither of them had any talent for the fine arts. They were absolutely without taste, yet absolutely determined to be busy about such matters. In a crushing paragraph Chénier summed up the intellectual limitations that had had such pervasive influence on mid-century French culture:

> D'ailleurs, n'ayant aucune idée de la langue grecque, avec un caractère plus sage que grand, plus faits pour approuver que pour admirer, plus faciles à convaincre qu'à émouvoir, plus doués de raison que d'imagination, de finesse que de sensibilité, *moins amis de la liberté que du repos,* ils étaient absolument incapables de bien sentir et, par conséquent, de bien connaître jamais l'esprit, les moeurs, le génie des anciens peuples de l'Italie et de la Grèce, *quoiqu'ils ne fussent rien moins qu'ignorants dans leurs histoires.*
>
> (pp. 665)

> Besides, having no idea of the Greek language, having a character more knowing than great, more made for approving than for admiring, more ready to convince than to move, more gifted with reason than with imagination, with finesse rather than sensibility, *less friends of liberty than of repose,* they were absolutely incapable of ever really understanding and, in consequence, really knowing the spirit, the customs, the genius of the ancient peoples of Italy and Greece, *while they were nothing less than ignorant in their history.*

In the phrases that I have italicized lies the key to Chénier's personal brand of Neoclassicism: one that was deeply historicized, in the sense of insisting on knowledge of past cultures as a precondition of judging their products; and one that was passionately politicized, in the sense of recognizing the threats to the intellectual's "repose" that would inevitably be raised by a free, that is, democratized, society. What Chénier saw in La Motte and Fontenelle (for our purposes, most interestingly in Fontenelle) was both a failure of the historical imagination and a sociopolitical selfishness—the "repos" of a leisured class—that vitiated all their other accomplishments; *not* the invention of a new, rationalist approach to the arts that would, in banishing an outworn system of imitation, bring in modernity.

Knowing this, we can better appreciate Chénier's intentions in the one discordant unit of the *Bucoliques,* the poem entitled *La Liberté.* In his manuscript copy of this dialogue, Chénier had entered both its central premise and its date of composition, March 1787:

Un jeune berger libre et un esclave se rencontrent. L'homme libre fait à l'autre avec ravissement la peinture des beautés de la nature dont ils jouissent. . . . L'esclave répond qu'il ne les voit point . . . et oppose des malédictions contre lui-même à toutes les extases de l'autre. Le style de l'un est doux et fleuri, celui de l'autre dur et sauvage.

(p. 859)

A young shepherd, a freeman, meets a slave. The freeman rapturously paints for the other the beauties of nature which they enjoy. The slave replies that he does not see them, and opposes curses against himself to all the other's ecstasies. The style of the first is sweet and flowery, that of the other harsh and primitive.

In the poem itself the debate is between an unhappy shepherd and a cheerful goatherd, who addresses his companion as "berger infortuné," in unmistakable allusion to Meliboeus's "Fortunate senex." It takes little perceptiveness to recognize *La Liberté,* then, as Chénier's revision of Virgil's first eclogue, especially since the infertile landscape inhabited by the slave ("Un noir torrent pierreux y roule une onde impure") resembles the stony and marshy territory of Tityrus, whose long-delayed "Libertas," however, had finally rendered it a place of contentment and enough for him. In reversing the mental states of his personae and making the central issue not stability versus displacement but sociopolitical enslavement versus freedom, Chénier was able to accomplish two things: first, by suggesting the actual case of peasants in a still feudal agricultural system he flatly contradicted Fontenelle as to what pastoral should represent. Second, and more subtly, he suggested how central to a theory of pastoral is one's point of view, how absolutely penetrable is the genre by cultural presuppositions. When the goatherd speaks of the beauties of the maternal earth, the presence of the "agrestes déités" and the immanence of Peace and Hope, all ways of seeing one's relationship with the landscape that depend on certain idealizing preconceptions, the shepherd replies:

Sans doute qu'à tes yeux elles montrent leurs pas.
Moi, j'ai des yeux d'esclave et je ne les vois pas.
Je n'y vois qu'un sol dur, laborieux, servile,
Que j'ai non pas pour moi, contraint d'être fertile;
Où, sous un ciel brûlant, je moissonne le grain
Qui va nourrir un autre, et me laisse ma faim.
Voilà quelle est la terre. Elle n'est point ma mère.

(p. 51)

Without doubt they reveal their ways to your eyes. As for me, I have the eyes of a slave and I don't see them. I only see a harsh soil,

laborious, servile, which I am constrained, and not for myself, to
render fertile; where, under a burning sky, I harvest the grain that
will nourish another, and leave me hungry. *That* is what the earth
is like. She is not *my* mother.

It is beside the point, then, to call the poem a "false note" in the idyllic
context of the *Bucoliques,*[50] since by its presence Chénier was able to signify
that he recognized his own privileges for what they were: an enabling perspective that freed him and his imagination from the sourness of want and
the bitterness of meaningless labor.

CHARLES CHURCHILL

It is instructive to compare the social perspective of Chénier's dialogue, informed with sympathy for the underprivileged, with another pastoral dialogue that directly recalls Virgil's first eclogue. Written two decades earlier,
and for an English audience not yet alerted to the larger ideological tensions and class antagonisms perceived by Chénier, Charles Churchill's
Prophecy of Famine: A Scots Pastoral is nonetheless thoroughly unnerving to
read, even today, because it combines the most venomous satire against the
Scots with the misleading suggestion (carried by the title and the extremely devious use of pastoral conventions) that the poem was meant to
be read from their point of view. The point of the satire was Scots poverty,
both financial and cultural, a subject newly relevant with the accession of
George III in 1760 and the ascendancy of his Scottish tutor, Lord Bute,
who was promptly made Treasurer. Englishmen naturally feared once
more, as they had done in the early years under James I, an influx of Scots
hungry for place and privilege. The economic rivalry thus generated was
fed by the memories of the 1745 Jacobite rebellion, an event that revealed
Anne's Act of Union as a superficial compromise, utterly incapable of past-
ing over the ancient hostility between the kingdoms.

   This was not the first time that Virgil had been called in to authorize
some position on Anglo-Scottish relations. In 1669–70, when Lord
Tweeddale had proposed a union, Andrew Marvell had incorporated into
the text of his *Loyall Scot* a supporting argument that made use of Virgil's
cooperative bees in the fourth georgic, suggesting that Charles II, as the
"prudent Husbandman," could reconcile his island's quarrelsome swarms
by sprinkling them with dust.[51] His argument for union was motivated in

---

   [50] Here I disagree with Francis Scarfe, *André Chénier: His Life and Work 1762–1794* (Oxford: 1965), p. 66. Scarfe attributes *La Liberté* to the temporary influence on Chénier of V.
Alfieri's *Del principe et delle lettere* (1795), which Chénier had seen in manuscript.
   [51] Andrew Marvell, *Poems and Letters*, ed. H. M. Margoliouth, rev. Pierre Legouis,
2 vols. (Oxford, 1971), 1: 178. Compare *Georgics* 4.86–87.

part by hatred for the repressive Scottish bishops, especially John Maitland, second earl of Lauderdale. The fourth earl of Lauderdale, Richard
Maitland, an avowed Jacobite, was himself a translator of Virgil whose
work Dryden consulted in manuscript, and when Lauderdale's translation
was posthumously published in 1718 its editor remarked in his preface
that a comparison of Dryden's version with Lauderdale's would show "that
the Poetry of South and North Britain is no more Incompatible than the
Constitution."[52] Meanwhile Pope had alluded favorably, in his first pastoral, to the Act of Union by way of rewriting Virgil's riddles in the third
eclogue; and in 1742 James Hamilton had produced a prose translation of
both the *Eclogues* and the *Georgics,* with an explicit emphasis on contemporary agricultural theory and practice and "an Appendix, shewing Scotlands
chief and principal worldly interest."[53] Churchill's chauvinist Virgilianism
was not as eccentric, therefore, as it might otherwise seem, and it appears
that he was conscious of at least one of his predecessors in this continuous
polemic.

Churchill represents Scotland, with heavy irony, as the source of England's cultural enrichment:

> To that rare soil, where virtues clust'ring grow,
> What mighty blessings doth not England owe,
> What waggon-loads of courage, wealth and sense,
> Doth each revolving day import from thence?
> To us she gives, disinterested friend,
> Faith without fraud, and Stuarts without end.
> When we prosperity's rich trappings wear,
> Come not her generous sons, and take a share.[54]

Listing among these dubious Scottish imports Macpherson, author of
"That old, new, Epic Pastoral, *Fingal,*" and also Alan Ramsay, author of
the much-praised *Gentle Shepherd,* which was supposed to have set a new
standard of realism in pastoral, Churchill concluded:

> Thence simple bards, by simple prudence taught,
> To this wise town by simple patrons brought,
> In simple manner utter simple lays,
> And take, with simple pensions, simple praise.

(lines 135–38)

---

[52] *The Works of Virgil, Translated in English Verse, By the Right Honourable Richard Late Earl of Lauderdale* (London, 1718), folio A4v.

[53] James Hamilton, *Virgil's Pastorals Translated into English Prose; as Also his Georgiks, with Such Notes and Reflexions as Make Him Appear to Have Wrote like an Excellent Farmer* (Edinburgh, 1742).

[54] Charles Churchill, *The Poetical Works,* ed. Douglas Grant (Oxford, 1956), p. 198.

In other words, the political strategies of the poem are enfolded with contemporary pastoral theory, and a harsh connection is made between the new primitivism extolled by writers such as Hugh Blair and Joseph Warton and the naked greed and untrustworthiness that Churchill attributes to the Scottish national character.

What confuses this procedure and makes a reader's initial grasp of this poem uneasy is that it opens with a parody of the other alternative, the Golden Age pastoral, particularly as practiced by Pope. Churchill's ironic reference to "that rare soil, where virtues clustr'ing grow," looks suspiciously like an allusion to Pope's first pastoral, with its Stuart riddle, "Say, Daphnis, say, in what glad soil appears / A wondrous tree that sacred monarch bears." And his subsequent attack on a Neoclassicism that makes no effort at historical transvaluation seems therefore at first sight to be aimed at the type of pastoral that Pope first perfected and then disavowed:

> Trifles are dignified, and taught to wear
> The robes of Antients with a Modern air,
> Nonsense with Classic ornaments is grac'd,
> And passes current with the stamp of Taste.
> Then the rude Theocrite is ransack'd o'er,
> And courtly Maro call'd from Mincio's shore;
> Sicilian Muses on our mountains roam,
> Easy and free as if they were at home.

> (lines 43–50)

But this is a set-up. Accustomed to critiques of this kind, the reader expects it to be followed by an approving account of the new primitivism, already associated with Scottish poetry; but what he receives, after a heavy dose of political satire in the central section, is a parody of the new pastoral "realism."

Promising "a simple strain, / Which Bute may praise, and Ossian not disdain," Churchill in fact produced a debasing caricature of both Scottish pastoral and Anglo-Scottish relations. *Both* of his shepherds, as compared to Chénier's antithesis, inhabit a miserable and infertile region (the English view of Scottish agriculture) that is primarily characterized by thistles: "Thistles now held more precious than the rose" is perhaps another allusion to Pope's riddle. Jockey, the cheerful one, momentarily attempts to provoke Sawney into song; to which Sawney replies with a parody of the *adynata*, impossibilities, of Virgil's first eclogue:[55]

---

[55] The name Sawney, a diminutive of Alexander, was another uncomplimentary allusion to Pope. Compare *Sawney and Colley: A Poetical Dialogue*, a satire on Pope and Colley Cibber published in 1742. See *Popeiana XXV: Folio Verse Attacks, Defences and Imitations 1716–1743* (New York, 1975), GG.

Ah, Jockey, ill advisest thou, I wis,
To think of songs at such a time as this.
Sooner shall herbage crown these barren rocks,
Sooner shall fleeces cloath these ragged flocks,
Sooner shall Want seize shepherds of the south,
And we forget to live from hand to mouth,
Than Sawney, out of season, shall impart
The songs of gladness with an aching heart.

(lines 351–58)

Yet the point of the parody is to predict a change of fortune for the unhappy shepherds. For after a lament for the failed Jacobite rebellions of
1715 and 1745 has rendered them indistinguishable in point of view, the
goddess of Famine (a daughter of Pope's Dullness) raises her head and delivers a prophecy of a new golden age for the Scots:

For us, the earth shall bring forth her increase;
For us, the flocks shall wear a golden fleece;
Fat Beeves shall yield us dainties not our own,
And the grape bleed a nectar yet unknown;
For our advantage shall their harvests grow,
And Scotsmen reap, what they disdain'd to sow.

(lines 455–60)

The last couplet viciously translates Meliboeus's lament that he has tilled
his fields for another ("barbarus has segetes"), and as the prophecy continues, the twisted echoes of Virgil's first and fourth eclogues converge
with Churchill's deliberate misprision of the "happy man" passage from
the second georgic, where all the commercial and military activities of
which Virgil's rustics are innocent are triumphantly adopted by a new race
of Scottish peasant imperialists. Beyond the prophecy, however, is the
outer frame provided by the authorial voice, returning us from the dizzy-
ing experience of cultural inversion to candid polemic. The poem ends
with Churchill's plea to the English not to be deceived by false ideals of
peace into making friends with the Stuarts and forgetting what they owe
to William and to Protestantism.

In another way the *Prophecy of Famine* was actually prophetic, pointing
by its own linguistic and generic violence (however local may seem the
issue of anti-Scottish prejudice) toward the social agitation of the last
quarter of the century in England. The name of John Wilkes, whose career
was to be the focus of political radicalism from 1768 until the Gordon
riots of 1780, is already inscribed in Churchill's poem (line 159). But its
chief value, perhaps, is in showing, through its manipulation of realist/

idealist arguments, that pastoral theory and practice were now capable of being substituted for each other as metaphors for sociopolitical arguments.

OLIVER GOLDSMITH AND GEORGE CRABBE

Any discussion of pastoral as social protest in this period must take account of the controversial and contrasting figures of Oliver Goldsmith and George Crabbe, whose poems *The Deserted Village* (1770) and *The Village* (1783) were dialectically locked together from the moment that Crabbe published his poem, and whose relationship was clarified by Crabbe's attack on Goldsmith in *The Parish Register* (1807). There is nearly absolute critical disagreement about where these poems stood in the linked stories of pastoral and ideology. While some readers emphasize the radical socioeconomic posture of Goldsmith's poem, with its emotional indictment of the agricultural revolution and the increased pace of enclosures, others have criticized (or praised) his presenting in his "memories" of the now ruined village of Auburn an idealized and mythical vision of country life, which, if it had an empirical base, derived from Ireland, not England.[56] Crabbe, on the other hand, has been regarded by some as an important figure in the defeat of Golden Age pastoral by the new realism,[57] standing midway between Philips and Wordsworth, and his realism has sometimes been taken as coordinate with a radical critique of the social order, more soundly based on fact than Goldsmith's; whereas other readers, from Hazlitt to contemporary socialists, have seen him, rather, as a deeply conservative figure whose commitment to a factual account of the working poor was that of an "overseer."[58] To the extent that such divergences reflect the standing premises of their authors, they will probably have to remain unmediated; but some sharpening and even settling of the issues may result from a closer look at the Virgilian ingredients of both *The Village*, where the subject of Virgilian pastoral is addressed directly, and *The Deserted Village*, where its presence is only inferential.

Goldsmith's focus on the theme of dispossession might reasonably have been developed by some intelligent appropriation of Virgil's first eclogue.[59] But the Virgilian presence in *The Deserted Village* is manifestly

---

[56] Compare, for example, Barrell, *The Dark Side of the Landscape*, pp. 73–88, with Raymond Williams, *The Country and the City* (New York, 1973), pp. 75–79; and, for a sympathetic account of Goldsmith's "Politics of Nostalgia," Laurence Goldstein, *Ruins and Empire* (Pittsburgh, 1977), pp. 95–113.

[57] See Congleton, *Theories of Pastoral Poetry*, pp. 149–50; Oliver Sigworth, *Nature's Sternest Painter* (Tucson, 1965), p. 18–33.

[58] William Hazlitt, *Lectures on the English Poets* (London, 1818), pp. 190–92; Barrell, *The Dark Side of the Landscape*, pp. 73–88; Roger Sales, *English Literature in History, 1780–1830: Pastoral and Politics* (New York, 1983), pp. 36–51.

[59] As proposed by Ricardo Quintana, *Oliver Goldsmith: A Georgian Study* (New York, 1967), pp. 132–35.

the *Georgics,* as identified by its opening statement of subject: "Sweet Auburn! lovliest village of the plain, / Where health and plenty cheared the *laboring* swain." The part of the *Georgics* in question is the "happy man" passage in *Georgics* 2.458 ff., with its emphasis on the *secura quies,* rest without care, of the husbandmen; the poem's central argument is that enclosures, by depriving the village communities of England of their widespread agricultural base, deprived their inhabitants of the decent and not too arduous work on which their welfare (and, ultimately, their right to evening and holiday leisure) depended. Thelwall would later quote the same passage in his *Peripatetic,* in his own attack on enclosures. But Goldsmith's adaptation of Virgil was more precise and subtle. He carefully anticipated (though failed in the outcome to avert) the charge of unrealism by echoing Virgil's own admission that his country idyll belonged to the past. "Such a life the old Sabines once lived," wrote Virgil ("hanc olim veteres vitam coluere Sabini," 1.532); and Goldsmith:

> A time there was, ere England's griefs began,
> When every rood of ground maintained its man;
> For him light labour spread her wholesome store,
> Just gave what life required, but gave no more:
> His best companions, innocence and health;
> And his best riches, ignorance of wealth.
> But times are altered; trade's unfeeling train
> Usurp the land and dispossess the swain.[60]

He also absorbed from the *Georgics,* and perhaps also from Milton's *L'Allegro* and *Il Penseroso,* what was to be a profoundly influential formal device, of incalculable use to Wordsworth: the presence in this rustic idyll of the philosophic outsider, who distinguishes his own fully meditated happiness from the unself-conscious pleasures of the rustics. In Goldsmith's revision, however,the learned man returning from his travels in the hope of settling down as a country gentleman, his reward for intellectual labor, is deprived of his happiness by the ruin of the village:

> O blest retirement, friend to life's decline,
> Retreats from care that never must be mine,
> How happy he who crown in shades like these,
> A youth of labour with an age of ease;
>
> . . . .
>
> For him no wretches, born to work and weep,
> Explore the mine, or tempt the dangerous deep;

---

[60]Oliver Goldsmith, *Collected Works,* ed. Arthur Friedman, 5 vols. (Oxford, 1966), 4: 287.

No surly porter stands in guilty state
To spurn imploring famine from the gate,
But on he moves to meet his latter end,
Angels around befriending virtue's friend.

(lines 97–108)

It is impossible to miss the echoes of Virgil's "felix qui" and "sollicitant alii remis freta caeca" ("others disturb with oars the unknown sea"), though Goldsmith is also, with equal visibility, negating the premises of the earlier country-house poem, quintessentially expressed in Jonson's *To Penshurst,* and equally dependent on the second georgic.

There is a striking difference between Goldsmith's appropriation of georgic and that of Robert Dodsley, whose *Agriculture,* published in 1754 and dedicated to the Prince of Wales, was unabashedly hegemonic in intent. Fontenelle and his English followers had banished any sign of exertion from the pastoral; Dodsley attempted to do the same for the georgic, going so far as to describe the farmer in the reign of George II as "blest with ease": "he views / All products of the teeming earth arise / In plenteous crops, nor scarce the needful aid / Of culture deigns to ask."[61] Dodsley had Epicurus himself deliver an argument, typical of the second half of the century, that the agricultural laborer was especially happy in being denied unhealthy luxuries:

So small the wants of nature, well supplies
Our board with plenty, roots or wholesome pulse,
Or herbs, or flavour'd fruits, and from the stream
The hand of moderation fills a cup
To thirst delicious.

(p. 38)

But it was Goldsmith's bad luck, if discretion (by abstaining from name-calling) to have insufficiently specified his own position. *The Deserted Village* is not, therefore, as easily distinguished as it might have been from such invidious misrepresentations as Dodsley's; and if Goldsmith's critique of enclosure was as socially radical as that of those who had spoken against it a century earlier, his implied solution (a return to the supposedly good old days of a benevolent rural patriarchy) was conservative (in the sense of relying on nostalgia) and unrealistic (in the sense of being out of the question).

---

[61] Richard Dodsley, *Works* (London, 1797), p. 26.

No doubt the blurred intentionalist image of Goldsmith's poem also affected Crabbe, when he set out more than a decade later to "paint the Cot, / As Truth will paint it, and as Bards will not."[62] *The Village* has a still more undecided focus, since Crabbe's approach to the English landowning system, like Churchill's to Anglo-Scottish relations, at first represents itself as an essay merely on literary matters, an attack on the Neoclassical version of pastoral. It is further complicated by the fact that the most memorable lines in this opening polemic were contributed by Samuel Johnson:[63]

> On Mincio's banks, in Caesar's bounteous reign,
> If Tityrus found the Golden Age again,
> Must sleepy bards the flattering dream prolong,
> Mechanic echoes of the Mantuan song?
> From Truth and Nature shall we widely stray,
> Where Virgil, not where Fancy, leads the way.
>
> (1: 120)

The result is, as Terence Bareham noted, that we cannot be sure whether the real "motive-spring" of his most famous poem is "a political attack on the destruction of a way of life, a sociological attack on that way of life itself, or a poetic attack upon a superannuated genre."[64]

By its apparent focus on Golden Age pastoral, the approach via genre theory diverts attention from the other documents against which Crabbe's brand of realism set itself, namely, the versions of georgic which had also, in his view, distorted the reading public's view of rural life. It is here, of course, that *The Village* is inarguably radical in its analysis. Crabbe was determined to give an accurate account of the backbreaking work, poverty, ignorance, and brutality that from his perspective characterized rural life and rendered incredible any analogy between it and the classical happy husbandman. But it was clear that he made no political distinction between Goldsmith's emphasis on a well-earned country leisure and Dodsley's absurd denial that anybody worked at all. On the subject of the supposed healthiness of the country life, it was surely Dodsley's offensive remarks on nutrition that inspired one of Crabbe's most effective rebuttals:

---

[62] George Crabbe, *Poems,* ed. Adolphus Ward, 3 vols. (Cambridge, 1905–07), 1: 121.

[63] See James Boswell, *Life of Samuel Johnson,* ed. G. B. Hill, rev. L. F. Powell, 6 vols. (Oxford, 1950), 4: 175. For Johnson's own characteristically independent pastoral theory, see Leopold Damrosch, *The Uses of Johnson's Criticism* (Charlottesville, 1976), pp. 78–92. Johnson, who discussed the *Eclogues* in *Adventurer* 92, combined a distaste for Neoclassical artifice with respect for Virgil's first and tenth eclogues (but only those), on the grounds that they deal with real events.

[64] Terence Bareham, *George Crabbe* (New York, 1977), p. 135.

> Oh! trifle not with wants you cannot feel,
> Nor mock the misery of a stinted meal,
> Homely, not wholesome; plain, not plenteous; such
> As you who praise would never deign to touch.
>
> (1: 124)

Yet Crabbe was as hard on the poor as he was on the rich, undercutting such reproaches with a debasing account of peasant character, unrelieved by any argument that here were essentially decent people whom a better standard of living would improve. Even the country pleasures are not the rural games that Goldsmith remembered or imagined, but drinking, fighting, poaching, and smuggling. And if there are distinct limits to Crabbe's social sympathies, there are also inconsistencies in his approach to the classical pastoral as something that realism must leave far behind. For Crabbe's polemic was in fact constructed on a matrix of Virgilian postulates. We have already encountered, in Chapter 1, his version of the once protective but now stricken tree of patronage, the cultural *umbra*. This closing elegy to Sir Robert Manners, younger son of the family to which Crabbe owed his clerical living, reveals him as at the least conventional, at the worst complicit in a social structure that would remain unjust no matter how enlightened the aristocracy might be; and it is hard to argue with the critical and political outrage it has provoked. Yet it *is* possible to argue that in its very conventionality, Crabbe's allusion to the "ample shade" that was once the "guard and glory" of the "subject wood" was a self-conscious placement of himself in the long line of writer-intellectuals since Virgil who had recognized the impossibility, at least for themselves, of working outside the system. The very appeal (in Johnson's words) against the illusion of country prosperity ("Must sleepy bards the flattering dream prolong") is a conscious or unconscious echo of Eclogue 1.55–56, as mediated by Dryden's translation:

> The buisie Bees with a soft murm'ring Strain
> Invite to gentle sleep the lab'ring Swain.
> While from the Neighb'ring Rock, with rural Songs,
> The Pruner's Voice the pleasing Dream prolongs.[65]

We should also note that he chose to publish *The Borough,* his most extensive work of sociopolitical analysis, under the Virgilian sign "Paulo maiora canamus."

It is possible that Crabbe, for all the contradictions within *The Village,* and between *The Village* and his later poems on rural life, was less confused

---

[65] John Dryden, *The Works of Virgil* (London, 1697), p. 4.

than he seemed. In bringing his first and most radical poem formally under the shelter of patronage he confessed, symbolically, to the economic necessity that drove him originally to seek help from Burke and thereafter kept him in attendance on the Duke and Duchess of Rutland. And at the beginning of *The Parish Register* he admitted, along with his specific resistance to Goldsmith, his conviction that social change is incompatible with human nature since the Fall:

> Is there a place, save one the poet sees,
> A land of love, of liberty and ease;
> Where labour wearies not, nor cares suppress
> Th'eternal flow of rustic happiness;
> Where no proud mansion frowns in awful state,
> Or keeps the sunshine from the cottage-gate?
>
> . . . .
>
> Since vice the world subdued and waters drown'd,
> *Auburn* and *Eden* can no more be found.[66]

There is, however, one section of *The Village* that seems both relatively uncontaminated by this Calvinist view of the class structure and unmistakably pastoral in content and origin. To illustrate his argument that not even old age brings with it the leisure that Goldsmith has posited, that no one in the real countryside of Georgian England "crowns in shades . . . / A youth of labor with an age of ease," Crabbe introduced the figure of an old shepherd, clearly in the tradition of the Virgilian *infortunatus,* and especially as mediated by Ambrose Philips:

> For yonder see that hoary swain, whose age
> Can with no cares except his own engage;
> Who, propp'd on that rude staff, looks up to see
> The bare arms broken from the withering tree,
> On which, a boy, he climb'd the loftiest bough,
> Then his first joy, but his sad emblem now.

(p. 124)

And as the ruined shade-tree has, following Philips, been formally recognized here as an emblem of a later phase of pastoral, in which ease, whether financial, psychological, or both, is no longer available, so Crabbe develops at length the psychology of obsolescence, in language that admits also of socioeconomic criticism:

---

[66] Crabbe, *Poems*, 1: 158.

Oft may you see him, when he tends the sheep,
His winter-charge, beneath the hillock weep;
Oft hear him murmur to the winds that blow
O'er his white locks and bury them in snow.
When, roused by rage and muttering in the morn,
He mends the broken hedge with icy thorn:
"Why do I live, when I desire to be
At once from life and life's long labour free?
Like leaves in spring, the young are blown away,
Without the sorrows of a slow decay;
I, like yon wither'd leaf, remain behind,
Nipp'd by the frost, and shivering in the wind;

. . . .

These fruitful fields, these numerous flocks I see,
Are others' gain, but killing cares to me:
To me the children of my youth are lords,
Cool in their looks, but hasty in their words:
Wants of their own demand their care; and who
Feels his own want and succours others too?
A lonely, wretched man, in pain I go,
None need my help, and none relieve my wo."

(p. 125)

It would be Wordsworth's self-assumed responsibility to take this chilling emblem of cultural decay and convert it to a very different function. Wordsworth's similar denial that the shepherds of his world have any experience of the "smooth life" of classical pastoral is accompanied, in *The Prelude,* with a representation of the shepherd as an emblem of the nobility of spirit that only rural hardship is capable of producing but whose efficacy can be spread, through the mediation of poets like himself, to regenerate society from within; not, however, by any adjustment of the ratio between "killing cares" and "others' gain," that adjustment which was, even for Crabbe, easier to speak of before the collapse of the French Revolution.

Images of Belief: Illustrated Editions and Translations

A partial confrontation with the French *fête champêtre;* a botanist's close-up of Virgilian *flora;* naked and melancholy "Greek" shepherds; and Blake's visionary series of druidic figures: these were the major variants in the visual representation of Virgil's *Eclogues* in the last half of the eighteenth century and the first two decades of the nineteenth. All of the above refer to illustrated editions or translations of Virgil's text itself. I shall attempt here to account for this extraordinary divergence of interpretation, hoping to show not only the impact of local historical event and larger historical process but also the role of that unpredictable factor, individuality.

DESFONTAINES AND THE "DISCOURS DE RUELLE"

The earliest member of this series is a French translation of the *Oeuvres* by the abbé Desfontaines.[67] Published in 1743, the Desfontaines translation set out to establish itself as definitive by attacking previous French versions. The translation by Marolles is asserted to be "ridicule et barbare," the Jesuit Catrou's "toujours rampante & souvent burlesque," that by the abbé de la Landelle de S. Remy "froid & ennuyeux," and Fabre's "peu connue" (pp. i–iii). As part of his four-volume production, Desfontaines also included a preliminary "Discours sur la Traduction des Poètes," in which he outlined the principles of translation he supposed his own to exemplify.

Desfontaines was equally concerned with the status of pastoral in mid-century French society. Warning his readers, in a "Discours sur les Pastorales de Virgile," not to expect the inhabitants of a pastoral world to sound like their own, he unfavorably contrasted the "politesse" of modern French pastoral with the ancient "candeur," attributing the latter to the "liberté champêtre," and its disappearance to man's design for civilizing himself by imprisoning himself within walls. Rather than concluding, as had Fontenelle, that the modern pastoral should do all it could to conceal this original fall from freedom, Desfontaines argued instead that it should distinguish itself from contemporary mores and refuse to be appropriated by the court. Of Fontenelle's own pastorals, Desfontaines remarked that if one were to substitute for the (empty) signifiers "de hameaux, de brebis, de fleurs, de bois, de fontaines," Versailles, the Opera, the Tuilleries, nothing would have changed except that one would recognize without disguise "des entretiens de Cour & des discours de ruelle" ("the dealings of the court and the discourse of the bedchamber," p. lix), and he asked whether "la peinture d'une vie innocente & d'une société entièrement différente de la nôtre . . . n'est pas digne de notre attention" ("the representation of an innocent life and of a society entirely different from our own is not worthy of our attention," p. lxiii).

Accordingly, in 1643 Desfontaines issued his translation under an icon

⁶⁷Pierre François Guyot, *Oeuvres de Virgile traduites en françois, avec des remarques, par M. L'Abbé de Fontaines,* 4 vols. (Paris, 1743).

Figure 22. C. N. Cochin, "The Eclogues," from *Oeuvres de Virgile,* trans. Pierre François Guyot (Paris, 1743), vol. 1, frontispiece. By permission of Princeton University Library.

(Fig. 22) that set against each other, in visual contrast, these two conflicting styles of pastoral. Under a substantial shade-tree is seated a rustic group
of figures, dominated by the reclining figure of a young woman. Flanked
and supported by youths in peasant costumes, she dismisses with a gesture
of her left hand another boy on the right, dressed in the pretty outfit of a
Watteau *fête galante,* complete with beribboned staff and flute which he
holds out to her and which, by her gesture, she rejects. The meaning of the
group is explained in the two lines of verse at the foot of the engraving:

Je hais, jeune Berger, tous ces airs fredonnés.
Si vous voulez me plaire, imitez vos aînés.

Young shepherd, I hate these trilling airs. If you wish to please me,
imitate your elders.

In other words, the girl is no mere Amaryllis, but the spirit of an authen-
tically rustic pastoral, whose rejection of the courtly figure represents what
Desfontaines thought of both Fontenelle and Watteau, while the recommendation that the youth imitate his elders is clearly an appeal for a return
to antique pastoral models.

    There seems to be here, however, a conflict, over which Desfontaines
had no control, and that blurs the confrontation he intended, for the design by Cochin has a certain air of the rococo about it that sets form
against content, and a parallel incongruity certainly exists between Desfontaine's implied ethical argument—that contemporary French pastoral is as
morally decadent as the court where it flourishes—and his own character.
An ex-Jesuit who made his living partly by pirating other men's works, in
1725 he had been narrowly saved from being burned at the stake on a
charge of sodomy—saved by the intervention of Voltaire, whom he then
spent the rest of his life persecuting in the public press. In 1743, the same
year in which his translation of Virgil appeared with all its noble sentiments, Desfontaines was prevented by the authorities from continuing publication of his scandalous journal, *Observations.* Two years later, Hearsey
reported, "he was dead from dropsy, and Voltaire and the whole literary
scene in Paris were rid of a most dangerous enemy."[68] The story of pastoral
and ideology is continually throwing up such contradictions. But in terms
at least of Desfontaine's pastoral theory, somebody seems to have noticed
what was wrong. After the Revolution, and of course posthumously, his
translation was reissued in a larger and more expensive format, with the

----

[68] Hearsey, *Voltaire,* p. 135. Desfontaines also managed to outrage the Académie Française by his *Virgil,* which contained in its notes "des chose injurieuses à l'Académie en général
et à plusieurs de ses membres en particulier." See *Registres,* 2: 536.

icon of the rejected *fête champêtre* replaced by the figure of Virgil in Roman costume, receiving instruction from a distinctly intimidating female Muse.

JOHN MARTYN AND THE EYE OF SCIENCE

The decade in which Desfontaine's translation first appeared also produced a new English translation. John Martyn, professor of botany at Cambridge, had had a distinguished career as a scientist, was a member of the Royal Society, and corresponded with Linnaeus. At Cambridge, however, he discovered that no one would come to his lectures; we may speculate that this professional embarrassment had something to do with his rather strange decision to translate Virgil's *Eclogues*. Martyn began with the premise that a defense of Virgil needed to be conducted against both idealists and realists. His preface began by refuting Rapin, but proceeded to argue equally strongly against those whom nothing will please but "downright rusticity." To those who prefer the primitivism of Theocritus to Virgil's urbanity, he quipped: "If the Originals of things are always the most valuable, we ought to perform our Tragedies in a cart."[69] Yet he did in fact produce his own rather homely version of Fontenelle's theory of erasure:

> Surely, we ought to imitate that part of Nature, which is most agreeable and pleasing. . . . The lowing of the herds, the bleating of the flocks, the wildness of an extensive common, the solemn shade of a thick wood, and the simplicity of the buildings, furnish us with pleasing images: and whilst we are contemplating these beauties, we seldom have much inclination to admire the disagreeable, though natural, sight and smell of a dunghill, or a hogstye. We may therefore conclude, that though Nature is to be followed, yet we are not to represent everything that is natural, without distinction; but are to select such images only as are pleasing, *throwing a veil* at the same time over those which would give offence.
>
> (pp. vii–viii; italics added)

The hermeneutical veil so long associated with the *Eclogues* has traveled a long cultural distance to reach this point. Instead of being drawn aside by the learned interpreter so that the reader may penetrate the pastoral fiction and determine the higher meaning, it is now the protective covering drawn over our experience of the physical world, so that only those phenomena remain visible that are consistent with pleasure and decency.

---

[69] John Martyn, trans., *Pub. Virgilii Maronis Bucolicorum Eclogae Decem. The Bucolicks of Virgil, with an English Translation and Notes* (3rd ed., London, 1749), p. xviii. The two previous editions were in 1741 and 1746.

Apparently Martyn also wished to throw a veil over certain aspects of Virgilian reception, or, more accurately, to distinguish, in true Enlightenment fashion, between fact and legend. On the one hand, he included a Life of Virgil that consisted of solid Roman history, discrediting some of the Donatan anecdotes and locating the *Eclogues* in a rigorous, if hypothetical, chronology; on the other, he took issue with the Servian tradition of commentary, applying an intense logical scrutiny to all propositions that read Virgil's own life into (or out of) the text, and writing elaborate glosses, with references back to earlier commentators, to show that no allegory was intended. His comments range from the engagingly commonsensical to the downright distortive. On Catrou's fantasy that Tityrus represented not Virgil but his aged father and that Thestylis in the second eclogue configured his mother, Martyn remarked: "By this method of criticizing, we need not despair of finding out, not only the father and mother of Virgil, but even all his relations and friends" (p. 30). Vives, he thought, showed "more piety than judgment" in Christianizing the fourth and fifth eclogues (p. 148). The *libertas* awaited by Tityrus cannot possibly indicate that he was ever a slave, for he has a farm of his own; it must therefore refer to his "releasement from the bondage of his passion for Galatea" (p. 8). And "Servius has laid it down as a rule, in the life of Virgil, that we are not to understand anything in the Bucolicks figuratively, that is, allegorically" (p. 10). We can smile approvingly at the first and concur with the second, while noting the lack of a historicist hermeneutic. The third comment will seem more revealing now in the light of Chénier's dialogue between slave and freeman; but the bold-faced misprision of Martyn's last comment defies explanation, except in terms of a willed blindness to what one does not wish to see. For no one could accuse Martyn of not having had the necessary scholarship.

The overall effect of Martyn's volume is of different cultural imperatives wrestling in the same textual space. The classicist's attempt to deal with the history of Virgilian interpretation results in the display of rationalist preconceptions. The botanist's desire to make use of his special knowledge results in a large number of scientific footnotes identifying, in the most literal manner, the various flowers and herbs to which Virgil had alluded, however decorative, metaphoric, or even symbolic the allusion. Thus we are told the medicinal properties of the herbs pounded by Thestylis for the heat-exhausted reapers (while averting our eyes, of course, from the reapers themselves); and, on the fantasy of spontaneously colored fleece in the fourth eclogue, which Macrobius had related to Etruscan myths of state leadership, Martyn remarks that the *lutum* in question is the common dyer's weed. The tension between these two ways of reading the *Eclogues*—moderate Neoclassicism and scientific positivism—is amusingly registered by the two illustrations that Martyn chose for his volume; the first, in illustration of Eclogue 2.31, an engraving of Pan playing the pipes; the second, a folded insert of botanical drawings.

Ironically, some of this tension was resolved for Martyn after his death. In 1813 his translation was reissued in a new format. "The botanical disquisitions are put into an Appendix together with the figures of the plants referred to, and the literary annotations are separated; those which have a direct reference to the original Latin words are placed under the text, and those notes which serve to illustrate the story, are placed under the translation."[70] So the grammarian, the critic, and the botanist part company; Pan disappears; and the new volume is beautifully illustrated with full-page botanical drawings, in color. But what also disappear, silently, are Martyn's long arguments with his predecessors, and perhaps with himself, as to the presence of a Roman historical subtext to the *Eclogues*. Almost all that survives of that passionate dialectic is as follows:

> Amaryllis appears to be only a poetical name for a shepherdess. Those who understand this Eclogue in an allegorical sense, interpret Amaryllis to mean Rome; but this interpretation is liable to so many objections, that on the slightest consideration it must be entirely rejected. Servius in his life of Virgil, has laid it down as a rule, that we are not to interpret any thing in the Bucolicks figuratively: though this rule may not be always absolute, yet, bearing it in the mind, will often relieve the critic from many perplexities.
>
> (p. 17)

Modernism, which will manifest itself in the reception of the *Eclogues* as ahistoricism, has already arrived; hereafter it will be possible to read them increasingly *simpliciter;* and one of simplicity's forms will be that of the reader who, like Martyn, retires from the perplexities of national or international culture into horticulture. To mark the change, almost more neatly than one could hope for, the 1813 edition presented a visual interpretation (Fig. 23) of Virgil's "De coelo tactas memini praedicere quercus" (1.17), by now, as Martyn himself would certainly have known, heavily overdetermined. But nineteenth-century readers were not encouraged to be any less forgetful than Meliboeus himself. The 1813 text offers no reminder of the Servian gloss, with its reading of this line as a metaphor of Caesarian wrath, nor of the subsequent interpretive history of the British oak as a symbol for English kings and patrons. Instead, reversing the adage of the miraculous growth of the great from the small, the eye of science gives us a close view of the acorns of the "Common Oak."

---

[70] John Martyn, trans., *Virgilii Maronis Bucolica, The Eclogues of Virgil: With an English Translation and Notes, New Edition* (London, 1813), pp. iii–iv.

Common Oak
XXI

QUERCUS ROBUR

De coelo tactas memini praedicere quercus
Eclog.

Figure 23. "Quercus robur, Eclogue 1," from *The Eclogues of Virgil*, trans. John Martyn (London, 1813), plate 21. By permission of Princeton University Library.

THE DIDOT *VIRGIL:* REPRESENTATIONS OF
COUNTER-REVOLUTION

The Didot *Virgil* was, above all, an icon of a revolution that failed.[71] The
date on its title page is the first sign of its divided heart, Roman numerals
for 1798 balanced by the new (yet neoclassical) chronology, "Reip. VI." In
his preface, Pierre Didot the elder referred back to his earlier edition of
1791, articulating the principles of textual accuracy and typographical purity that informed it. The new edition matched the previous one in also
exhibiting the "elegantissimos . . . typos" cut for the family firm by his
brother Firmin Didot, and surpassed it in being not only printed on a
"pura and candidiora charta," in royal instead of regular folio, but also in
containing twenty-three engravings by (and I translate) the "eminent painters Gérard and Girodet (who occupy the places of honor in their art closest
to their master David)" (p. xi). This remark accretes significance when
compared to the preface to the 1791 edition, in which Didot had promised
that this second, greater volume would be ornamented with twenty-seven
engravings by "the chief of painters, David" himself, who "even now labors
assiduously to express [the spirit] of Homer, through his painting, to the
eyes and the mind."[72] Obviously, the commission to David had foundered
in the intervening seven years, resulting in its transfer to his students (as
well as a reduction in the number of engravings actually executed). What
complicates the story is the survival of proofs of the engravings, in a portfolio now in the Library of Congress, in which four that were attributed to
Gérard in the bound volume are instead identified as David's.

The cultural meaning of this extraordinary volume can be reconstructed from two directions, by looking first at the role of the Didot family in the development of the French press, and second at David's career
as chief iconographer for the Revolution. We can begin by translating
Maurice Audin's account of what he called "la révolution des Didot":

> The Didots, with the audacity of demigods born of academicism, at-
> tacked the sacrosanct round letter popularized by Garamond and
> against which no one, except Grandjean and his pupils, had dared to
> raise a hand. The "didot" looked austere, sober, constructed in severe
> pages, sometimes bounded by a rigid line. It was the same style as that
> of the compositions of the wild man David, transcribed into letters
> and textual masses, and it was also, in illustration, a theater in minia-
> ture where people were immobilized, transfixed before the grandeur of
> the spectacle. In art it was an infertile epoch, but it was necessary to

---

[71] Pierre Didot, ed., *Publius Virgilius Maro. Bucolica, Georgica, et Aeneis* (Paris, 1798).
[72] Pierre Didot, ed., *Publii Virgilii Maronis Bucolica, Georgica, et Aeneis* (Paris, 1791),
p. iv. Presumably Didot referred to David's "Funeral of Patroclus" (1778), "Andromache Bid-
ding Farewell to Hector's Corpse" (1783), and "Paris and Helen" (1788).

destroy what the eighteenth century had produced of the superficial, the facile, and the mannered and to rediscover the sincerity on which would be embroidered, brilliantly and inexhaustibly, the great romantic folly.[73]

In the development of their famous type, then, the Didot family, founded by François-Ambroise Didot, produced in aesthetic terms a revolutionary statement analogous to that of David's in painting; and they were also connected to the move in the French press to democratize the reading process by producing cheap and mass-produced editions bound in paper rather than leather.

Pierre Didot, who took over the press from his father in 1789, apparently brought with him to the task a sense of social responsibility that extended beyond the territory of typography and book distribution. In 1786 he had published a remarkable little volume entitled *Essai de fables nouvelles, dediées au Roi, Suivies de poésies diverses et d'une épître sur le progrès de l'imprimerie*. The epistle on the progress of the press, addressed to his father, supports the hypothesis that Louis XVI is the ideal patron and that the nation flourishes under his regime:

L'affreuse servitude en tous lieux abolie,
L'horreur de nos prisons par ses soins adoucie,
Le marine en vigueur, la liberté des mers,

. . . .

L'asyle des vertus est le coeur de Louis.

(p. 109)

Dreadful slavery is everywhere abolished, by his care the horror of our prisons has been mitigated, the navy flourishes, the sea is free; Louis's heart is the haven of virtue.

But the fables imply a rather different view of the ancien régime. The first, addressed directly to the king, advises him not to aspire to representation by the emblems of either lion or eagle, who both live by carnage ("Ce sont des tyrans, non des rois") but, rather, to emulate the cock, symbol of a more domestic and benevolent governance (p. 9). A later fable, "Les animaux devenus esclaves," begins with the nakedly republican statement that "l'homme est né pour la liberté" (p. 55). And in 1797, one year before the Virgil edition appeared, Pierre Didot addressed the National Institute on the necessity for the new republic of encouraging artists, so that they may share in the general enfranchisement.

Why, then, should Pierre Didot have thought it appropriate to bring

---

[73] Maurice Audin, *Histoire de l'imprimerie* (Paris, 1972), p. 186.

out the great *Virgil* in 1798, in a luxury format which, whatever the symbolism of its typography, would have been economically out of reach of all but a privileged few and which, in its choice of author, suggested the approach of imperialism? The paradox is only accentuated by the fact that he brought out simultaneously a small octavo version of the text alone, in the "éditions stéréotypes des citoyens" format. The illustrations raise still further problems, not least in the withdrawal of David from the project and in the character of what survives of his contribution.

Part of what happened is implicit in David's own history during these years. David's *Oath of the Horatii,* his first great Roman painting, appearing in 1785, was inevitably hailed for its "fierté républicaine" even before the revolution that it seemed, retrospectively, to have prophesied; and in stylistic terms it also, as Anita Brookner puts it, "reorganized the Neoclassical endeavour in France, and in bringing it to fruition made its life shorter."[74] In June 1789, when the Third Estate convened in the Jeu de Paume and swore to reconstitute the kingdom, David may well have been present in person as well as in imagination. His Salon picture of that year was *Brutus Receiving the Bodies of His Sons,* which again was read in the afterlight of history as a revolutionary document, a justification of violence in the cause of principle. In 1790 David embarked on his own form of revolutionary action, directed against the Académie Royale de Peinture, which had disappointed him by refusing a memorial exhibition for his pupil Drouais. Meetings of reformist academicians held at David's house sent petitions to the Constituent Assembly; in November 1792 he resigned from the Académie; and in August 1793 he successfully addressed the Convention on the need to abolish all "les trop funestes Académies, qui ne peuvent plus subsister sous un régime libre."[75]

His revolutionary fervor did not stop at the commonwealth of the arts. In September 1792 he was elected Deputy for Paris to the National Convention; in 1794 he took his turn as its president, and embarked vigorously on the signing of orders for arrest and execution; and on 2 August 1794 (15 Thermidor), in the immediate aftermath of Robespierre's fall, David himself was arrested, only narrowly escaping execution. In 1797 he had already received a generous offer from Napoleon to join him and become the official painter-historian of his battles; in December of the same year Napoleon made his triumphal entry into Paris, and David painted his first pre-Imperial portrait.

There follow from this chronology (more certainly than can usually be argued with respect to events in art and life) certain conclusions about the

[74] Anita Brookner, *Jacques-Louis David* (New York, 1980), pp. 68, 79. For David's Roman iconography, see also Ronald F. Paulson, *Representations of Revolution* (New Haven, 1983), pp. 10–12, 28–36.

[75] Brookner, *Jacques-Louis David,* p. 101.

Didot *Virgil*. In 1791, when Pierre Didot spoke of his intention to reissue a grander edition with David as its illustrator, the painter's political reputation was already established and its connection with his cult of antiquity assumed. The volume must, therefore, have been conceived in terms at least consistent with the idea of "un régime libre" and of a neoclassicism that stressed the republican phase of Roman history. It is hard to imagine quite how that would have been accomplished, but there is perhaps a record of the transitional phase in one of the designs attributed to David in the portfolio. David's choice of illustration for the second book of the *Aeneid* was, not surprisingly, the famous emblem of Aeneas escaping from Troy, with Anchises on his shoulders, and holding Ascanius by the hand (Fig. 24). But he shockingly reconceived the classical emblem of national *pietas*, patriarchy, and dynastic continuity in a newly darker language, showing the father as a sinister burden and Creusa not merely lost in the confusion but discarded at Aeneas's feet. We might be tempted to interpret this as a negative image of the ancien régime, and so perhaps it was for David when he started work on the project; but a counter-message seems unavoidable once we notice that the terrible weight of the father is surmounted by one of the Revolution's central symbols, the "liberty cap," whose shape echoes but is yet clearly distinguishable from Aeneas's heroic helmet.[76]

But few of the illustrations confess to experiences like these. The pervading tone is melancholy, sentimental, and, especially in the *Eclogues*, romantically Hellenistic. We know from Délécluze that David, when finally released under the amnesty of 1795, combined with his confessional rejection of the Revolution a commitment to a new aesthetic program, a different form of neoclassicism. Perhaps under the influence of Les Penseurs, a group of his pupils who deliberately espoused a new stylistic Hellenism, David transferred his allegiance from republican Rome to Greece, admitting for the first time the influence of Winckelmann and protecting himself, therefore, from an iconography all too capable of topical application. The Greek figure, especially in its nakedness, connoted simplicity, purity, the origin, formalism, first principles. "I have undertaken," David is reported to have said,

> to do something entirely new. I want to take art back to the principles laid down by the Greeks. When I painted the *Horatii* and *Brutus* I was still under the influence of Rome. But . . . without the Greeks, the Romans would have been little more than barbarians in artistic matters. One must therefore go back to the source. . . . I want to do pure Greek. . . . The Greeks . . . thought, and they were right, that in the

[76] On the liberty cap, see Lynn Hunt, *Politics, Culture, and Class in the French Revolution* (Berkeley and Los Angeles, 1984), especially p. 118.

Figure 24.   Jacques-Louis David, "Aeneid II," from *Publii Virgilii Maronis Bucolica, Georgica, et Aeneis*, ed. Pierre Didot (Paris, 1798). From the portfolio of proofs, Lessing J. Rosenwald Collection, Library of Congress, Washington, D.C.

arts the idea is much more fully contained in the manner in which one expounds it than in the idea itself.[77]

This program was, evidently, incorporated into the Didot *Virgil* of 1798, and fully adopted by Gérard and Girodet. It expresses both acceptance of Winckelmann's doctrine of *Heiterkeit,* serenity, and rejection of violence, however principled and however providentially arranged for. The illustrations to the *Georgics* are sentimental, eschewing any reference to the commonwealth of bees in Book 4 and instead choosing for emphasis the death of Euridice, and the *Aeneid* is provided with only one battle scene (in striking contrast to the Cleyn program for Ogilby's *Virgil*). But the tone of the volume is set most definitively by the six illustrations provided for the *Eclogues.* The fact that there are only six is itself significant, since it is here that the disparity between Didot's original plan and its execution can be located, at least in terms of numbers. Particularly distinguished by their absence are the plates for the fourth eclogue, with its freight of Christian allegoresis, and the ninth, with its reminders of an unsolved problem of landownership and its warnings that poetry cannot prevail in time of war. By the same token, the illustration of the first eclogue (Fig. 25) has been rendered politically neutral, its conversation between Tityrus and Meliboeus as untroubled as Cleyn's was dynamic, without a visual trace of the expulsions in the background; and that for the fifth eclogue (Fig. 26) is equally innocent of disturbing allusions to the death of a ruler.

The one discordant note in this program is the presence of the *Silenus,* a raunchy representation attributed to David (Fig. 27).[78] What it surely shows is David's familiarity with the royalist iconography of Franz Cleyn, as developed for the 1649 translation of Virgil's works by Marolles (compare Fig. 21). The presence of this visual echo in a volume otherwise dedicated to a contrary ideology is a symptom of the fundamental contradictions on which the Didot *Virgil* was based: an attempt to atone for an early republican commitment to all things Roman by Hellenizing the most Roman poet of all; a rejection, therefore, of previous traditions of interpretation, which nonetheless have left their traces; and the imposition of an aesthetic that privileged the *Eclogues,* while at the same time anticipating a new imperialism. It was a smaller step than perhaps Pierre Didot could have wished or realized, from the production of his Virgil edition to the

---

[77] Brookner, *Jacques-Louis David,* p. 134, translating Etienne Délécluze, *Louis David, son école et son temps* (Paris, 1855).

[78] The subject was more readily associated with French court painting. See G. de Tervarent, *Présence de Virgile dans l'art* (Brussels, 1967), pp. 14–15 and fig. 20, on the painting of the Silenus by Antoine Coypel (1700) for the Dauphin at the Château de Meudon.

Figure 25.   François Gérard, "Eclogue 1," from *Publii Virgilii Maronis Bucolica, Georgica, et Aeneis,* ed. Pierre Didot (Paris, 1798). From the portfolio of proofs, Lessing J. Rosenwald Collection, Library of Congress, Washington, D.C.

Figure 26. François Gérard, "Eclogue 5," from *Publii Virgilii Maronis Buco-lica, Georgica, et Aeneis,* ed. Pierre Didot (Paris, 1798). From the portfolio of proofs, Lessing J. Rosenwald Collection, Library of Congress, Washington, D.C.

Figure 27.   Jacques-Louis David, "Eclogue 6," from *Publii Virgilii Maronis Bucolica, Georgica, et Aeneis,* ed. Pierre Didot (Paris, 1798). From the portfolio of proofs, Lessing J. Rosenwald Collection, Library of Congress, Washington, D.C.

blatantly Napoleonic appropriations of the fourth eclogue for the birth of "le roi du Rome" in 1811.[79]

But the pacific quality of Didot's volume presumably did not displease him. Eight years later, Firmin Didot, the brother who had reformed the family firm's typeface, but who did not restrict himself to typographical projects, published and dedicated to his brother *Les Bucoliques de Virgile, précédées de plusieurs Idylles de Théocrite, de Bion et de Moschus, suivies de tous les passages de Théocrite que Virgile a imités; traduites en vers français;* in other words, a pastoral anthology, which also in its own way was determined to reverse literary history and return Virgil to his origins in Hellenistic culture. Most revealing of Firmin Didot's intention in this volume was his "Discours préliminaire sur les anciens poètes bucoliques," in which he set out the connection between the pastoral impulse, as he understood it, and the course of history.

> C'est sur-tout après de grandes révolutions politiques et quand les peuples sont fatigués du bruit de la trompette guerrière, que se fait entendre avec le plus de charmes le flageolet de la muse pastorale. Les conquêtes d'Alexandre venaient d'étonner la terre, . . . lorsque Théocrite parut: . . . César venait d'achever la conquête du monde alors connu, et Auguste recueillait avec peine un héritage sanglant, lorsque l'on vit paraître Virgile, Virgile admirateur passionné de Théocrite, et quelquefois son égal dans une langue moins riche. . . . Telles furent les époques remarquables du règne de la poésie pastorale chez les Grecs et chez les Romains: et il n'est pas impossible qu'elle ait un jour de la même sorte chez les Français.
>
> Dans ces temps de trouble, l'âme, tour-à-tour ebranlée, tantôt par l'espérance et par l'admiration, tantôt par l'inquiétude et la terreur, ramenée enfin à des idées générales de justice et d'ordre par ces images perpétuelles de ravages, d'incendies et de destructions, est disposée à contempler avec intérêt les tableaux d'une vie calme, silencieuse et pure; à aimer ces douces images, rendues plus douces encore par le contraste.
>
> (pp. 1–2)

It is especially after great political revolutions and when people are tired of the noise of the trumpets of war, that the charms of the flute and the pastoral muse make themselves heard to greater delight. Alexander's conquests had just astonished the world . . . when Theocritus appeared: Caesar had just achieved the conquest of the then known world, and Augustus gathered up with difficulty a bloody

---

[79] See, for example, M. de Loizerolles, *Le Roi de Rome, poème allégorique, imité de la quatrième Eglogue de Virgile* (Paris, 1811); and N. E. Lemaire, *Virgil expliqué par le siècle de Napoléon* (Paris, 1812).

inheritance, when men saw the appearance of Virgil, Virgil the passionate admirer of Theocritus, and sometimes his equal in a language less rich. These were the epochs remarkable for pastoral poetry among the Greeks and Romans; and it is not impossible that it will have a like day among the French.

In these times of trouble, the soul, continually diminished, as much by hope and admiration as by instability and terror, returned at last to general ideas of justice and order by these perpetual images of rapine, fire, and destruction, is disposed to contemplate with interest visions of a life that is calm, silent, and pure; to love these sweet images, rendered all the sweeter by the contrast.

This statement is, in effect, a description of the iconographical program of the Didot *Virgil*. But it speaks of far more than that. In one long historical curve, the ideology of Rapin is hereby linked to that of post–World War modernism, with its similar commitment to "poésie pure" and its similar belief that pastoral offers the mind relief from the experience of violence. Between them, and already being articulated by Wordsworth, is the complex aesthetic program of Romanticism, also directly a product of the French Revolution and equally committed to "general ideas of justice and order"—all the more general now that their enactment by political process had been seen to be so disastrous. But those "tableaux d'une vie calme, silencieuse et pure" that Firmin Didot had admired in his brother's beautiful volume, those "douces images, rendues plus douces encore" by erasures from earlier interpretive traditions, were quite explicitly connected to his own revolutionary experiences: "C'est peut-être aussi l'impression qu'a faite sur moi-même la lecture des pastorales, dans les temps d'une révolution orageuse, qui m'a déterminé à traduire les anciens poètes bucoliques" (p. 3). It was the effect that reading pastorals had on him during the Revolution that motivated his decision to translate the ancient bucolic poets. As we shall see in Chapter 5, the Romantic and modernist version of this relationship, of the connection between an idealized pastoral and violent political experience, would usually remain unspoken.

THORNTON AND BLAKE: REFORMIST TEXT
AND RADICAL IMAGE

In England, the Napoleonic wars made their own impact on Virgilian interpretation in the last of our four exhibits, Robert Thornton's *Pastorals of Virgil, with a Course of English Reading, Adapted for Schools,* published in 1821. We come back therefore, as promised, to William Blake's illustrations of Ambrose Philips's version of pastoral, an accident of cultural history that resulted in Thornton's *Virgil,* as it is familiarly referred to, acquiring a celebrity which some have thought was completely undeserved. In fact, as I shall argue, Thornton's *Virgil* was a far more complex document, as a whole, than is usually admitted, and not least in its mixture of sophistication and imperception, both of which are featured in Thornton's treatment of Blake. A botanist, like Martyn, Thornton approached this school edition of the *Eclogues* with very different motives and premises than his predecessor: rather than suppressing as far as possible the Roman historical context of the *Eclogues,* Thornton raised it to a prominence not seen in Virgilian interpretation since Ogilby and Dryden.[80] And like Ogilby and Dryden, Thornton subjected Roman history to contemporaneity, structuring his two-volume edition on the model of Renaissance *Virgils,* with their massive interpretive apparatus, but extending the commentary tradition explicitly into his own concerns.

One of his themes is, once again, the connection between pastoral and pacificism. In his commentary on the ninth eclogue, Thornton remarked, in clear defiance of Rapin, "The horrors of war, as afflicting the country, merit a place in Pastoral poetry. We are not, in such compositions, entirely to expect Arcadian scenes, or manners." But he then proceeded to personalize and topicalize the issue, in ways that clearly spoke to or, rather, against, the violence that from 1789 until Waterloo had structured European politics. "But when I contemplate civilized, nay Christian nations, butchering and murdering each other, and laying waste the fair peaceful scenes of Nature, my blood boils with honest indignation, and I attribute much of this to the fault of education" (2: 557). It was Thornton's program, only gradually revealed in the course of this, his third edition of the *Eclogues,* to exploit their complex dialectic on the subject of war and peace for political and educational ends simultaneously—that is to say, his own contribution to peace was to be an argument for the civic uses of a liberal education, and the provision of *the* text that for him could teach the humane values.

Thus his account of the ninth eclogue was as follows:

> Virgil, with great address, recommends himself to the favour of those in power, in order to preserve the lands about Mantua. . . . He therefore endeavours to shew, that if he can meet with encouragement, he shall be able to teach the Romans to surpass all other nations in the arts of peace, as they had already gained the superiority in the arts of war.
>
> (2: 540)

To drive home the point, Thornton inserted as analogues to the ninth eclogue his own poem *On the Horrors of War* and the second of Collins's

---

[80]The two previous editions were in 1812 (with some illustrations published separately in 1814) and in 1819.

Oriental Eclogues. And he was careful to point out that Virgil's chief ad-
dressee, Augustus, required some apology from the poet, "for he, as do all
tyrants, feared the soldiery, and only kept the people in subjection by
means of his armed force" (2: 547). The "moral" Thornton derived from
the poem, and focused on its final line, "quod nunc instat agamus," was
that his schoolboy readers must work as hard as they can. What Ogilby had
interpreted as a subdued campaign for royalist solidarity, and Dryden as an
appeal for patronage, Thornton read as an imperative to develop "a liberal
mind" (2: 548).

Thornton's skeptical portrait of Augustus was clearly intended to be
read in the light of his commentary on the fifth eclogue, from which he
extracted a critique of imperial ambition. "The following," wrote Thornton, under the pretext of discussing the later Roman emperors, "is a true
picture" of life "under a despotic government."

> There must be a state inquisition. The few, having a separate interest
> from the many, must be always on the watch, prepared to nip every
> conspiracy in the bud, and to quench every spark the moment it ap-
> pears, knowing that the least delay may cause a general conflagration.
> The despot must not enquire, if guilty or not guilty, but must at all
> events secure his own repose, by confining, by banishing, or by cutting
> off, all suspected persons. . . . In a country where the subjects are
> looked upon as enemies, we must expect to see state prisons inacces-
> sible to all, but the unhappy victims of the monarch's jealousy, or the
> favourite's revenge.
>
> (2: 263)

It was, in fact, the political context that best explains Thornton's motives in bringing out this third edition of his textbook, and in so massively
expanding its interpretive structure with annotations, illustrations, and
"imitations." By 1820, anti-Jacobin reaction and the economic tensions exacerbated by the Napoleonic wars had reached a climax in the Peterloo
Massacre and the Six Acts regulating all forms of assembly. By this time
Shelley, Southey, and Wordsworth had long abandoned their Godwinian
sentiments; but there can be no doubt that Thornton conceived of his
1821 edition of the *Eclogues* as an opportunity to take a stand, however
discreetly sheltered by the structures of academic discourse, against the
most disreputable aspects of Castlereagh's Tory government. And he was
probably aware that Blake, whom he accepted as one of the volume's illustrators, had moved in radical circles since the 1780s.[81]

[81] For Blake's associations, both social and conceptual, with the "remarkable coterie" of
Richard Price, Thomas Paine, Joseph Priestley, William Godwin, and Mary Wollstonecraft,
see Mark Schorer, *William Blake: The Politics of Vision* (New York, 1946), pp. 151–220; David
Erdman, *Blake: Prophet against Empire* (Princeton, 1954), pp. 138–47.

It is all the more ironic, therefore, that this celebrated commission should have resulted in an almost complete misunderstanding between Blake and Thornton, a misunderstanding that resulted from the clash between two different systems of encoding ideology. Whereas Thornton expressed himself primarily through significant juxtaposition, by aligning ancient against contemporary history and by setting the Virgilian text in a frequently contrastive frame of eighteenth-century "analogues," Blake proceeded to explore the emotional potential of Philips's second pastoral and to reinvest it with a deep social power.

While Blake's woodcuts have been almost universally admired (the strange exception being Thornton himself), the range of commentary on them has been oddly limited, perhaps because they fail to cohere with the general understanding of Blake's career, his philosophy of art and history, and his personal repertoire of symbols. This in itself is interesting, not least because in accepting the Thornton commission Blake apparently suppressed, or forgot, or rethought, his well-known antipathy to classical poetry, and especially to Virgil, an antipathy based on a view of Virgil as an emperor's apologist.[82] If, however, we reapproach Blake's Virgilian iconography in the light of its antecedents, images that are otherwise puzzling or disturbing fall into place, along with a plausible structure of motivation. The profound melancholy of Blake's interpretation can be recognized, not only as an expression of what has been called his "negative pastoral,"[83] his lifelong suspicion of natural phenomena when not read with visionary eyes, but also as an extension of a series that passed from Virgil's first eclogue through Clément Marot and Edmund Spenser to Ambrose Philips. In this series, the dialectic between the sad and happy shepherd had been continually revised, as we have seen, in the direction of cultural pessimism; and there was an increasingly close identification between the unfortunate shepherd and the poet himself.

It is all too easy to imagine how and why such a premise would have appealed to Blake at this late stage of his career, following his own unsuccessful experiment with "pastoral" life on Hayley's estate at Felpham, the total failure of his exhibition in 1809, his sense of neglect, and his decreased artistic activity. It has been suggested, for example, that the series of images represents "a dark allegory of the artist's subversion through patronage,"[84] the damage to his independence initiated by Hayley's demands and continued, out of necessity, in accepting this very commission. Blake

---

[82] See his remarks "On Virgil," *The Complete Poetry and Prose of William Blake,* ed. David V. Erdman (New York, 1982), p. 267.

[83] The phrase is Leopold Damrosch's, in *Symbol and Truth in Blake's Myth* (Princeton, 1980), pp. 229–30, n. 139. Compare Jean Hagstrum, *William Blake, Poet and Painter* (Chicago, 1964), pp. 52–53, and David Bindman, *Blake as an Artist* (Oxford, 1977), pp. 204–5. All read Blake's woodcuts (briefly) as visions of a "fallen world."

[84] See David Wagenknecht, *Blake's Night: William Blake and the Idea of Pastoral* (Cambridge, Mass., 1973), p. 8.

THENOT.

THENOT.

COLINET.

COLINET.

Figure 28. William Blake, "Imitation of Eclogue I," from *The Pastorals of Virgil . . . Adapted for Schools,* ed. Robert J. Thornton (London, 1821), vol. I, facing p. 15. Rare Books and Special Collections, Library of Congress, Washington, D.C.

himself has been seen in the figure of the traveler returning, in disillusion, to London (Fig. 28), by a milestone that marks his distance from the city as 63 miles, precisely the distance of Felpham.[85] The image is, then, a brilliant collage of autobiographical candor and illustrative sympathy, since Philips's "wandering feet unblest" were themselves set wandering by desire of "a Name." It is hard not to believe that Philips's poem articulated for Blake his own sense of cultural alienation:

> Hard is to bear of pinching cold the pain;
> And hard is want to the unpractis'd swain;
> But neither want, nor pinching cold, is hard,
> To blasting storms of calumny compar'd.

(p. 16)

And the fact that Blake's frontispiece (Fig. 29) specifically features the pastoral instruments hung up on a tree, the symbol of the shepherd who can sing no more ("Carmina nulla canam"), strongly suggests a personal and psychological motive for his acceptance of Thornton's commission, which in every other respect, given his expressed attitude to Virgil and the classical tradition, one might have expected him to refuse. If the frontispiece was also designed as an allusion to Blake's earliest and non-Virgilian pastoral, *The Songs of Innocence,* the visual echo serves to frame his career and to mark his own passage from innocence to experience.[86] It is also likely that Blake decided to work in wood, for the first and only time, as a late and apologetic tribute to Spenser's *Shepheardes Calender;*[87] and that the traveler's broad-brimmed hat and staff, recurrent in the Blake canon,[88] at last reveal their visual genealogy in recall of Spenser's "January" (compare Fig. 15).

---

[85] See G. E. Bentley, Jr., *Blake Records* (Oxford, 1969), plate XL; and Frederick Garber, "Intertext and Metatext in Blake's Illustrations to Thornton's *Virgil," Centennial Review,* forthcoming. For a telling statement by Blake about patronage, see *A Vision of the Last Judgment,* in *Complete Poetry and Prose,* p. 561: "works of Art can only be produced in Perfection where the Man is either in Affluence or is Above the Care of it . . . the Argument is better for Affluence than Poverty & tho he would not have been a greater Artist yet he would have produced Greater works of Art in proportion to his means."

[86] Garber, "Intertext and Metatext."

[87] Wagenknecht, *Blake's Night,* pp. 4–5, implies that the *Calender* contributed to Blake's idea of pastoral; but Robert Gleckner, in *Blake & Spenser* (Baltimore, 1985), p. 30, sees the *Calender* as to Blake the *least* interesting of Spenser's poems, at least in the 1780s. If, however, as Gleckner also argues, Blake was rethinking his relationship to Spenser in the decade immediately prior to the Virgil project, in preparation for his illustration of *The Faerie Queene,* 't seems unlikely that he would have ignored the *Calender.* In all, the visual similarities between the two series of woodcuts deserve reconsideration: the dimensions, the compressed urvilinear landscapes, the positioning and gestures of the figures, and even the echo, in Blake's Neoclassical mansion, of the Roman architecture of Spenser's "October."

[88] Garber, "Intertext and Metatext."

ILLUSTRATIONS

OF

IMITATION OF ECLOGUE I.

FRONTISPIECE.

THENOT AND COLINET.

The Illustrations of this English Pastoral are by the famous BLAKE, the illustrator of *Young's* Night Thoughts, and *Blair's* Grave; who designed and engraved them himself. This is mentioned, as they display less of art than genius, and are much admired by some eminent painters.

Figure 29. William Blake, "Imitation of Eclogue I, frontispiece," from *The Pastorals of Virgil . . . Adapted for Schools,* ed. Robert J. Thornton (London, 1821), vol. I, facing p. 13. Rare Books and Special Collections, Library of Congress, Washington, D.C.

Blake also seems to have intuited in Philips's poem (and in the tradition encapsulated by it) a social dynamic in which the distinction between the haves and the have-nots is underwritten by the power structures of society. While the first set of four woodcuts (Fig. 30) is devoted to exploring the emotional contrast between two versions of pastoral, most powerfully represented by Blake as that between the fruitful tree and the blasted one, the second set (Fig. 31) explores the economic relation between rusticity and success. The lines just quoted appeared in Thornton's *Virgil* facing (or against) two scenes that define the shepherd's misery only by contrast: the upper cut, with an elegant Georgian facade as background, shows a laborer dragging a heavy roller over someone else's lawn; the lower is a scene of festive and fashionable entertainment, a *fête champêtre* set in the garden of a Neoclassical mansion. That the first is in illustration of the poem's critique of wandering ("A rolling Stone is ever bare of Moss," line 79) only sharpens one's sense of Blake's overdetermination here; and that the second is Blake's response to the "yearly Wakes and Feasts" (line 114) presided over by the patron only adds another historical stratum to the social irony of "yearly."

What is most moving about these silent representations of social imbalance is what is also most definitively Romantic: their placement in a timeless world of natural phenomena, in which the tree of patronage is reabsorbed into a landscape of winding roads and winding rivers, is lit by sunsets and moonrises, and in which the melancholy imagination is denoted by the resemblances between milestones and gravestones, and among signposts, gibbets, and crosses. It is a landscape that might equally well have illustrated Wordsworth's revisions of pastoral, especially in *The Prelude*—except that, as we shall see in Chapter 5, by the time Wordsworth came to write the *Prelude* he had abandoned the social protest that underwrites Blake's visionary designs and contented himself with the vision.

These oblique protests against the class structure, along with the revolutionary affect of Blake's intentional primitivism, were apparently unintelligible to Thornton. The insulting introduction he provided to the series, describing it as displaying "less of art than genius," and his fortunately short-circuited attempt to have it recut by a professional engraver, were certainly understood by Blake in political terms. Six years later he wrote in the margin of Thornton's pamphlet on the Lord's Prayer that it was a "Tory Translation," celebrating a materialist religion. "Thus we see that the Real God is the Goddess Nature, & that [Thornton's] God Creates Nothing but what can be Touch'd & Weighed & Taxed & Measured; all else is Heresy and Rebellion against Caesar, Virgil's Only God. . . . see Eclogue i; for all this we thank Dr. Thornton."[89] Whatever Blake had intuited, through the

[89] See Geoffrey Keynes, *The Illustrations of William Blake for Thornton's Virgil* (London, 1937), p. 14.

Figure 30. William Blake, "Imitation of Eclogue I," from *The Pastorals of Virgil . . . Adapted for Schools,* ed. Robert J. Thornton (London, 1821), vol. I, facing p. 14. Rare Books and Special Collections, Library of Congress, Washington, D.C.

Figure 31. William Blake, "Imitation of Eclogue I," from *The Pastorals of Virgil . . . Adapted for Schools,* ed. Robert J. Thornton (London, 1821), vol. I, facing p. 16. Rare Books and Special Collections, Library of Congress, Washington, D.C.

mediation of Ambrose Philips, of another brand of Virgilianism had effectively been cancelled by another humiliation.

One has to conclude that Blake never read in Thornton's *Virgil*, when it appeared, beyond that ungenerous apology for his own contribution. Thornton's critique of everything that Blake meant by "Caesar" was as invisible to him as his revolutionary vision was aesthetically unavailable to Thornton. Once again, two versions of pastoral, two forms of neoclassicism, were in contest, but in this instance they were two who should have been natural allies. So Thornton's imperception alienated Blake, and Blake, who understood Virgil's first eclogue better than he either knew or cared to admit, allowed his own suspicions of the "Classical Learned," his own role as a cultural renegade, and especially his wounded pride, to turn him against the master-text whose other, destabilizing, voice he had so clearly heard.

5

POST-ROMANTICISM:
Wordsworth to Valéry

Oh, Meliboeus, I have half a mind
To take a writing hand in politics.
Before now poetry has taken notice
Of wars, and what are wars but politics
Transformed from chronic to acute and bloody?

I may be wrong, but, Tityrus, to me
The times seem revolutionary bad.

The question is whether they've reached a depth
Of desperation that would warrant poetry's
Leaving Love's alternations, joy and grief,
The weather's alternations, summer and winter,
Our age-long theme, for the uncertainty
Of judging who is a contemporary liar.

Robert Frost, "Build Soil: A Political Pastoral"

In 1932, in the context of Franklin Roosevelt's campaign for the presidency, America's most successful pastoral poet returned, uncharacteristically, to the classical origins of the pastoral mode. Driven by hostility to Roosevelt's social meliorism, which had already during his governorship of New York extended to agricultural reform, Frost delivered at Columbia University a long debate in verse on the policies that were shortly to become the New Deal.[1] The relationship to Virgil's first eclogue goes beyond

---

[1] Robert Frost, "Build Soil: A Political Pastoral," in *Poetry and Prose*, ed. E. C. Lathem and L. Thompson (New York, 1972), pp. 125–33. The poem versifies opinions expressed in an interview with Benson Landis, published in June 1931 in *Rural America*. See *Interviews with Robert Frost*, ed. E. C. Lathem (New York, 1966), pp. 75–78. For Roosevelt's agricultural policies in 1931 and 1932, see *The Public Papers and Addresses of Franklin D. Roosevelt,*

the names of the speakers; and like so much of Frost's spare and stoical New England country poetry, the dialogue thematizes the conceptual relationship between pastoral and georgic, and of both to the poet's trade. Articulate in "Build Soil" are certain key concepts of poetics that have been taken for granted since the opening of the nineteenth century, largely thanks to Wordsworth: the superiority of the poet-as-intellectual, here distinguished from his merely rustic interlocutor, who asks simple questions and receives long and abstract answers; the "natural" connection between thoughtful poetry and "country" phenomena; and the conclusion that pastoral is not, after all, to explore social and political issues, but to turn in upon itself and to replace reformist instincts with personal growth and regeneration. Explaining the metaphor of his title, Frost finally commits to Tityrus what we must surely recognize as his own poetic manifesto:

> Build soil. Turn the farm in upon itself
> Until it can contain itself no more,
> But sweating-full, drips wine and oil a little.
> I will go to my run-out social mind
> And be as unsocial with it as I can.
> The thought I have, and my first impulse is
> To take to market—I will turn it under.
> The thought from that thought—I will turn it under
> And so on to the limit of my nature.
> We are too much out, and if we won't draw in
> We shall be driven in.
>
> . . . .
>
> Keep off each other and keep each other off.
> You see the beauty of my proposal is
> It needn't wait on general revolution.
> I bid you to a one-man revolution—
> The only revolution that is coming.

(pp. 132–33)

But the poem remains a dialogue, however uneven; layered in the long shadow of Virgil's first eclogue were ironies that Frost must equally have chosen to recall. As the limitation of poetry's subjects (for which read pastoral's subjects) to love and the turning of the seasons recalls Neoclassicism, so can those earlier exclusions diagnose the modern ones as symptoms of ideological tension and a strain on the social conscience. The very fidelity

---

5 vols. (New York, 1938), 1: 140–55, 477–518, 693–711. For Frost's pastoralism, see John Lynen, *The Pastoral Art of Robert Frost* (New Haven, 1960), and Harold Toliver, *Pastoral Forms and Attitudes* (Berkeley, 1981), pp. 334–60.

with which Frost has reconstituted the older political issues that were thought to inhere in Virgil's text—the problems of patronage, personal liberty, and landownership—is a sign of the poem's confessional dynamic. One of the answers that Tityrus gives to Roosevelt's "socialism," expressed in the campaign as the rather naive plan to relocate the urban poor in the country, ironically reverses the Virgilian topos of dispossession by asserting the appropriateness of the status quo:

> Let those possess the land and only those,
> Who love it with a love so strong and stupid
> That they may be abused and taken advantage of
> And made fun of by business, law, and art;
> They still hang on.

(p. 130)

Yet the tenacity of the rural poor is presented with a condescension that itself descends from the ancient selfishness of the Tityrus position. On the still more controversial issue of the boundary between personal liberty and state intervention, Tityrus complains that "Everyone asks freedom for himself, / The man free love, the business man free trade, / The writer and talker free speech and free press"; and while greed has properly been taught "a little abnegation," the chief lesson he draws from all this jostling of freedoms is that of laissez-faire economics: "I'd let things take their course, / And then I'd claim the credit for the outcome." But the high-handedness of this conclusion was already established in the opening lines of the poem, where Meliboeus (who has lost his "interval farm" because potatoes are down to thirty cents a bushel) accosts Tityrus *on a university campus,* that green and pleasant modern replacement for Arcadia, and calls his bluff in advance:

> The Muse takes care of you. You live by writing
> Your poems on a farm and call that farming.

(p. 126)

Frost thereby admitted into his own poem the Virgilian unease at the doctrine of artistic selfishness and self-reliance he forged in defiance of the facts of his own life. As Elaine Barry remarked, since neither farming nor poetry could support him financially, from 1916 onward Frost depended on "the greatest of all modern patrons—the American University system."[2] The campus in question was not Columbia's but Amherst's, where

---

[2] Elaine Barry, *Robert Frost* (New York, 1973), p. 8. For an eloquent defense of Frost's aesthetic of selfishness, see Lawrence Thompson, *Fire and Ice: The Art and Thought of Robert Frost* (New York, 1942), pp. 208–13.

as poet-in-residence he was not required to teach. The predicament of the artist-intellectual takes a new twist in the institutional structures of modern academicism. Yet, as this chapter will argue, the *poetics* Frost here defended were more than a century older.

It is best to admit here to a double temerity, both in my governing premise that Wordsworth and Valéry might share the same cultural space, and in the assumption that more than two centuries can be fairly represented in a single chapter. Yet there is a certain poetic justice in such foreshortening, in that critical discourse from the beginning of the nineteenth century has been governed by the fiction that pastoral was either decadent, uninteresting, or dead.[3] This fiction, as we saw in Chapter 4, had its origins in a strain of Neoclassical thought which, for all that it could claim to be the dominant cultural position, was demonstrably challenged by writers and artists of considerable standing, while those who most wished to contain and aestheticize the pastoral idea often revealed their difficulties in doing so. At the turn of the nineteenth century, this impulse was redirected by the extraordinary cultural event we call Romanticism, although it might more accurately be named post-Romanticism, having been from the start a movement predicated, at least in its English manifestoes, on the abandonment of a romantic or utopian politics. Consider, as the premier example, Wordsworth's evocation in the 1805 *Prelude* of a dream of a new golden age, an international cultural revolution that would necessarily include and depend on political and social reform. "O pleasant exercise of hope and joy," wrote Wordsworth, *remembering* his youthful response to the French Revolution, as yet untested by the conflict of loyalties induced by the Anglo-French war of 1793, and unmarred by the Reign of Terror:

> For great were the auxiliars which then stood
> Upon our side, we who were strong in love!
> Bliss was it in that dawn to be alive,
> But to be young was very Heaven! O times,
> In which the meagre, stale, forbidding ways
> Of custom, law, and statute took at once
> The attraction of a country in romance!
> When Reason seemed the most to assert her rights
> When most intent on making of herself
> A prime enchanter to assist the work,

[3] See, for example, Raimund Borgmeier, *The Dying Shepherd: Die Tradition der englischen Ekloge von Pope bis Wordsworth* (Tübingen, 1976), whose premise is that Wordsworth marks the end of the genre. As Borgmeier observes (p. vi), the *Oxford English Dictionary* illustrates the meaning of the term *pastoral* by citing Thomas Hood's dictum that "The Golden Age is not to be regilt: Pastoral is gone out, and Pan extinct." Compare the defensive opening strategies of Richard Hardin, ed., *Survivals of Pastoral* (Lawrence, 1979), pp. vii–x, 1–3.

Which was then going forwards in her name!
Not favoured spots alone, but the whole Earth,
The beauty wore of promise—that which sets
(To take an image which was felt, no doubt,
Among the bowers of Paradise itself)
The budding rose above the rose full blown.[4]

This passage is located in Wordsworth's poetic autobiography at a point where the romance of radicalism has already been discarded as an illusion and where the deeply traumatized poet is already on the way to discovering its alternative: that is to say, an ideal of selfhood validated by introspection, and a noninterventionist view of society validated by an intense new relationship with physical nature.

Although there are obvious filiations between the program initiated by Rapin and Fontenelle—to isolate pastoral as an idea from major social and political issues—and the poetic revolution begun in England by Wordsworth and Coleridge, the motives, procedures, and consequences of the latter were unprecedented. Instead of the uneasy but unfocused perception of socioeconomic injustice that motivated eighteenth-century idyllicism, whether in literature or landscape painting, the new aesthetic movement was consciously postrevolutionary, partly conceived in response to the failure of the French Revolution. And as the other great formative influence was German transcendental philosophy, the result was a redefinition of the intellectual life and a mystification of ideas of art and the artist that have remained unchallenged long after transcendentalism ceased to be the dominant philosophical preterition. While metaphysics continues to grapple with the implications of Wittgensteinian language-games or Derridean deconstruction, aesthetics, at least as generally received, still takes for granted such concepts as artistic selfhood and imaginative genius, the alienation of the intellectual from the lesser minds that surround him, the capacity of art to embody general ideas of goodness, truth, and beauty, the privileging of the poet or *Dichter* as a special category of the writer-intellectual, and the superiority of the philosophical universal over the particular historical moment. It is not hard to see the connection between such an aesthetic and a post-revolutionary ideology that substitutes introspection for social analysis, and imaginative and spiritual advances for institutional change. These were the principles that informed and motivated Wordsworth's version of pastoral, and very little distance separates it from the characteristically modern definition of pastoral as interior landscape, the pastoral of the

---

[4]Wordsworth, *The Prelude: A Parallel Text,* ed. J. C. Maxwell (New Haven, 1971), p. 440.

mind. In the twentieth century, the impetus given to such thinking by the cataclysmic spectacle of two world wars and, in America, of the Vietnam war has also been only what one would expect.[5]

For despite the premise of pastoral's obsolescence, nineteenth- and twentieth-century writers and artists continued to interrogate its history, its theory, and its founding texts, and Virgil's *Eclogues* have experienced a remarkable series of reincarnations. Some of those reincarnations depend, like Frost's New England dialogue, on the original Virgilian dialectic for their very form and claims to legitimacy. Others, like the dozens of academic books *about* pastoral that have appeared in this century, are the distant descendants of Virgilian commentary, whether in its Servian form as extended annotation of specific texts, or as an essay in genre theory, on the model (unrecognized) of Vives or Rapin. Still others are editions or translations of Virgil's *Eclogues* that continue the business of rewriting the classical text in the language of the day, including the visual language of illustration. In all of these forms of reception there appear, as in Frost's poem, signs of ideological activity, evidence that pastoral continues to evolve in response to historical circumstances, even when the objective is most resolutely to deny its historical connections or conditions.

As with the massive subject of Renaissance humanism, the story of post-Romantic pastoral will have to be told selectively. It must begin with Wordsworth, who more than any other Romantic was responsible for articulating the new aesthetic, and whose responses to pastoral anticipate, almost concept for concept, those of Frost. Samuel Palmer's illustrated translation of the *Eclogues* in the mid-nineteenth century is a complex example of the intricate Victorian conscience at work, one that connects both backward to Blake's Virgilian woodcuts and forward to William Butler Yeats. Fin de siècle decadence might seem to be worlds apart from even the least idealized account of classical pastoral; yet André Gide found in Virgil's first eclogue a metaphor for his turn-of-the-century anomie. Another telling transitional exhibit is the polyglot translation of the *Eclogues* produced by Count Harry Kessler at the Cranach Press, with woodcuts by Aristide Maillol; a document that is contextually rich in the culture of the Weimar Republic, but which also looks back, in the field of fine bookmaking, to the aesthetics of William Morris and the Kelmscott Press. And, for the period of the Second World War, a group of French illustrated translations culminates in the remarkable joint production of Paul Valéry and the Cubist painter Jacques Villon. I shall let this volume, published in 1953,

---

[5] The point has been made before. Charles Segal, in his finely balanced introduction to *Poetry and Myth in Ancient Pastoral* (Princeton, 1981), p. 7, asks whether it is "coincidental that the remarkable efflorescence of studies of the *Eclogues* and the strongest new directions in approaches to ancient pastoral in the United States came when we were involved in a costly, unpopular, and divisive war."

stand as the last word in the development I have been tracing. Although there are signs in Virgilian scholarship that another phase of interpretation is just over the critical horizon, I prefer not to conclude with an analysis of late-twentieth-century pastoral theory, but rather to let my readers compare what they find in the modern "commentary tradition" with the story of pastoral and ideology as retold up to this point. And because Valéry himself played a crucial role in the formulation of modernist poetics in France, the powerfully revealing preface that he wrote at the very end of his career, his personal *Variations* on the *Eclogues,* can serve as a better peroration than anything I could provide.

Wordsworth's Hard Pastoral

It is the emphasis on the efficacy of the countryside, first nurturing, then healing, and finally enlightening in a way that renders the Enlightenment obsolete, that distinguishes Wordsworth's version of the Romantic ideology from that of any other English Romantic except Keats;[6] the same emphasis places him firmly, though controversially, in the long history of pastoral as one of the languages through which ideology speaks, with or without the knowledge of the speaker.

Wordsworth's relationship to pastoral is controversial in at least two ways. The first concerns classical poetry. Either as a consequence of seeing Wordsworth as a successor to Crabbe and the so-called realists or, more persuasively, as an innovative genius who almost single-handedly transformed the character of English (and American) poetry for a hundred years, it is often assumed that Wordsworth deliberately discarded the classical pastoral for himself and effectively buried a tradition that was already discredited. If he had a residual affection for classical pastoral, it is argued, it was only for Theocritus, whom he was reading enthusiastically in 1799 and writing about to Coleridge.[7] It is generally assumed that an enthusiasm for Theocritus implied a distaste for Virgil and that Wordsworth's poetic revolution, especially as formulated in the 1800 Preface to *Lyrical Ballads,* implied not a continuation of pastoral tradition but a total break with the past, and reconstitution from first principles. "Humble and rustic life

[6] For a response to A. O. Lovejoy's call for a "discrimination of Romanticisms," see Jerome McGann, *The Romantic Ideology: A Critical Investigation* (Chicago, 1983); also David Aers, Jonathan Cook, and David Punter, *Romanticism and Ideology: Studies in English Writing 1765–1830* (London, 1981).

[7] See Stephen Parrish, *The Art of the Lyrical Ballads* (Cambridge, Mass., 1973), pp. 166–67; and, more generally, Leslie Broughton, *The Theocritean Element in the Works of William Wordsworth* (Halle, 1920).

was generally chosen," Wordsworth wrote of his subject matter in the *Lyrical Ballads,*

> because, in that condition, the essential passions of the heart find a
> better soil in which they can attain their maturity, are less under re-
> straint, and speak a plainer and more emphatic language; because in
> that condition of life our elementary feelings coexist in a state of
> greater simplicity, and consequently, may be more accurately contem-
> plated, and more forcibly communicated; because the manners of rural
> life germinate from those elementary feelings, and, from the necessary
> character of rural occupations, are more easily comprehended, and are
> more durable; and, lastly, because in that condition the passions of men
> are incorporated with the beautiful and permanent forms of nature.[8]

This all-too-familiar passage, by laying claim to the "natural," has obscured
from many of its readers the fact that its central terms, *essential, elementary,
durable, permanent,* and above all *simplicity,* belong to an idealized poetics
and a Neoclassical theory of pastoral rather than to the empirical mimesis
of rural life that Wordsworth seemed to promise, and in some of the *Lyrical
Ballads* actually offered. This language nevertheless persuaded the public
that the call for a totally new, anti-classical pastoral had been answered:[9]
and by the middle of the nineteenth century the great Virgilian editor John
Conington, who regarded the "corruption" of pastoral as "chargeable" to
Virgil, announced the death of the earlier tradition:

> It was not to be expected that a thing so purely artificial could outlive
> that general questioning of the grounds of poetical excellence, which
> accompanied the far wider convulsions at the end of the last century.
> Whether it is now to be registered as an extinct species, at least in En-
> gland, is perhaps a question of language, rather than of fact. The po-
> etry of external nature has been wakened into new and intenser life,
> and the habits of the country are represented to us in poems, remind-
> ing us of the earliest and best days of the Idyl: but the names of
> Eclogue and Pastoral are heard no longer.[10]

[8] Wordsworth, *The Poetical Works,* ed. E. de Sélincourt and Helen Darbishire, 5 vols.
(Oxford, 1940–49), 2: 386–87. Unless otherwise stated, citations from Wordsworth's
poems will be from this edition.
[9] So argues Stuart Curran, *Poetic Form and British Romanticism* (New York, 1986),
pp. 99–100. As Curran points out, "the well-known terms by which Wordsworth propa-
gated his new poetic are all not only appropriate to commentary on the pastoral, but the actual rubrics used for it during the eighteenth century."
[10] John Conington, ed., *The Works of Virgil,* 3 vols. (London, 1858–71), pp. 2–3. One
of Conington's chief complaints about Virgilian pastoral was that "the shepherd is mixed up
with the poet": "The danger was one to have been apprehended from the first. So soon as
pastoral poetry came to be recognized as a distinct species, the men of letters who cultivated

To equate *pastoral* with "the poetry of external nature" implies, then, that the term stands for the entire Wordsworthian aesthetic. Yet Wordsworth *also* chose to preserve the term *pastoral* as a separate category of thought and experience, adding it to the title of the *Lyrical Ballads* of 1802 and building it as a subtitle into a few significant poems. And, as we shall see, the influence of Virgilian pastoral is much stronger in Wordsworth's canon than critics such as Conington have imagined. His schoolboy translations from the *Georgics* were followed in the 1820s by a massive attempt to translate the *Aeneid*. Between them comes the marvelous ode "Intimations of Immortality," published in 1807 under the Virgilian sign of a higher pastoral, "Paulo maiora canamus." [11] And Wordsworth's program was not only to regenerate pastoral for his own generation but specifically to answer the conceptual challenges of all of Virgil's *Eclogues*, not merely the messianic fourth, while responding also to the classical chain-reaction between pastoral and georgic.

Politics is the other arena in which Wordsworth's response to pastoral has been, and will surely continue to be, contested. While few would deny that he became as reactionary in old age as he had once been revolutionary—opposing the Reform Bill of 1832, for example, because it undid the traditional restriction of the franchise to landowners—the timing of his reaction is still in question. Wordsworth's "development," notoriously confused by revisionist habits of composition and the deceptively recursive autobiography offered in *The Prelude,* has been minutely scrutinized for evidence of political commitments or waverings. Carl Woodring's scrupulous *Politics in English Romantic Poetry* found the *Lyrical Ballads* still empowered by "democratic individualism" and social protest, although he admitted that Wordsworth sometimes "had difficulty in avoiding the appearance of honoring the poor for their utility to him." [12] E. P. Thompson, speaking himself out of strong left-wing sympathies, wrote a passionate "lay sermon" to defend Wordsworth against the charge of apostasy; yet by showing the degree to which he was actually intimidated by the British government's anti-Jacobin measures, beginning with the treason trials of 1794, Thompson himself contributed to the tendency "to press the moment of political disenchantment further and further back." [13] James Chandler persuasively argued that the "Genius of Burke," whom Words-

---

it, perhaps themselves grammarians or professional critics, were likely to yield to the temptation of painting themselves in bucolic colours, instead of copying the actual bucolic life which they saw or might have seen in the country" (pp. 10–11).

[11] See Peter J. Manning, "Wordsworth's Intimations Ode and Its Epigraphs," *Journal of English and Germanic Philology* 82 (1983): 526–40.

[12] Carl Woodring, *Politics in English Romantic Poetry* (Cambridge, Mass., 1970), pp. 97, 135.

[13] E. P. Thompson, "Disenchantment or Default? A Lay Sermon," in *Power and Consciousness,* ed. Conor Cruise O'Brien and William Dean Vanech (London, 1969), p. 149.

worth, in a passage written in the 1820s, incorporated as one of the Muses of the 1850 *Prelude,* had already penetrated the text of the 1805 *Prelude,* even in the very passage where Wordsworth describes the Romantic dream of international social change.[14] And Marjorie Levinson's subtle probing of "Tintern Abbey" establishes that poem as a half-deliberate, half-unconscious farewell to political activism, modifying the ballad (populist) dimension of the *Lyrical Ballads* in the direction of the lyric (personalist) and hence socially neutral mode. "Tintern Abbey" accomplishes this by strenuous imaginative erasures. So Wordsworth excluded from his field of vision both the signs of the industrial revolution visible in the Wye's traffic and its pollution, and the indigents and vagrants who scratched out a living by begging or charcoal burning in the vicinity of the Abbey—sights to which Wordsworth's own guidebook must have drawn his attention. It was Levinson's brilliant insight that the term *pastoral* in this poem was also not innocent. The "pastoral farms, / Green to the very door" that Wordsworth perceived as idyllic in this landscape were so because "the common lands had been enclosed some time back and the only arable land remaining to the cottager was his front garden."[15]

Here and elsewhere, Wordsworth actually pinpointed for his readers the ideological issues that he and they certainly knew had historically accrued to the category *pastoral* from Virgil's *Eclogues* onward. He invited, in fact, the following questions: What *is* the ideological content of "Michael: A Pastoral Poem," which explores the ancient pastoral theme of a shepherd who loses his patrimonial lands? What are the intimations of "The Idle Shepherd Boys: A Pastoral," whose title patently alludes to the classical ideal of *otium?* What is to be thought of "The Ruined Cottage," nearly published in 1798 as a separate poem in the new genre established by Goldsmith and Crabbe, of social meditation on the contemporary rural economy, yet based even more clearly than *The Deserted Village* on a matrix of Virgilian eclogue? And why did Wordsworth build into *The Prelude* a mini-history of pastoral that contrasts the past with the present, central Europe with northern England, and concludes with an accolade to the hard but noble life of the *working* shepherd? Are these the contributions of a man whose social and political instincts were outraged by the hardships

[14] James K. Chandler, *Wordsworth's Second Nature: A Study of the Poetry and Politics* (Chicago, 1984). F. M. Todd, in *Politics and the Poet: A Study of Wordsworth* (London, 1957), pp. 81–82, argues that the turning point occurred in late 1794, partly as a reaction to the treason trials, and was marked by his abandoning plans for a new monthly journal, *The Philanthropist.*

[15] Marjorie Levinson, *Wordsworth's Great Period Poems: Four Essays* (Cambridge, 1986), pp. 14–57; quotation from p. 30. Her argument was in part anticipated by Kenneth Johnston in "The Politics of 'Tintern Abbey,'" *The Wordsworth Circle* 14 (1983): 6–14. Johnston, more so than Thompson and Levinson, is prepared to accept Wordsworth's "retrenchment" as "part of the cost of his becoming a poet," a cost that Johnston charges "to his conscious artistic control of his unconscious sublimation, or a little of both" (p. 12).

attributable to the industrial and agrarian revolutions? Or are they, rather, subtle contributions to the counter-revolutionary programs of the British government, promoting a conservative ideology based on the "georgic" values of hard work (by others), landownership (Wordsworth became a freeholder in 1803), and, above all, the premise that hardship is to be countered by personal "Resolution and Independence" rather than social meliorism?

To pose these sets of questions is not to invite easy answers in either direction, or to forget the degree to which, in Wordsworth, the workings of the conscience and the unconscious, political or otherwise, resist formulation.[16] Few writers have left as much evidence of confused intentions, changes of plan, and the signs of personal "Guilt and Sorrow." It would be extraordinary if, in his transit from one end of the political spectrum to the other, Wordsworth had always known exactly where he stood or what his feelings meant. What we can ascertain, despite and because of the complex chronology and textual history of his work between 1797 and 1805, is that Wordsworth unquestionably made the same associations between pastoral and the socioeconomic structure of his own society as did the writer-intellectuals who preceded him, and that he felt the same urgency to define his own position as an intellectual by renegotiating the terms that pastoral-as-ideology provided.

"The Idle Shepherd Boys: A Pastoral," which appeared in the 1800 *Lyrical Ballads,* may seem to carry no significance until it is placed in the context of contemporary socioeconomic discussion. In turn-of-the-century England, economic hardship in the countryside was extreme, as the damage done to small freeholders by accelerating enclosures and to cottage industry by factory competition was exacerbated by bad harvests. Yet Frederick Eden's three-volume study of *The State of the Poor* (1797) declared that the chief cause of rural misery was the "improvidence and unthriftiness" of the lower classes.[17] Those who see in the *Lyrical Ballads* a "turn towards a more theoretical, disinterested, and spiritually focused philanthropic mode" would probably dispute the statement that Wordsworth had already decided that some of the poor were indeed lazy.[18] Yet the conclusion of this small tale of childish irresponsibility, resulting in a lamb

---

[16] For an extreme version of the benevolent view, see Kenneth MacLean, *Agrarian Age* (New Haven, 1950), especially pp. 87–99. MacLean, however, had difficulty documenting his thesis, admitting that Wordsworth had misrepresented the situation of the Cumberland farmers as freeholders, when they were in fact copyholders, and that he was "silently satisfied . . . that a touch of feudalism should remain in society" (p. 101). For an extreme version of the negative view, see Roger Sales, "William Wordsworth and the Real Estate," *English Literature in History 1780–1830: Pastoral and Politics* (New York, 1983), pp. 52–69.

[17] See MacLean, *Agrarian Age*, pp. 21–26.

[18] Cf. Levinson, *Wordsworth's Great Period Poems*, pp. 19–20, agreeing with Marilyn Butler, *Romantics, Rebels and Reactionaries: English Literature and Its Background 1760–1830* (Oxford, 1982), p. 31.

strayed and almost drowned, is that the lamb is rescued by the poet: "And gently did the Bard / Those idle Shepherd-boys upbraid, / And bade them better mind their trade" (1: 241). However "gently" he imagined himself as speaking, the word is inevitably double-edged with class-consciousness.

"The Last of the Flock" deals with a larger problem. Readers have been moved by its Old Testament quality, its evocation of ritual but painful sacrifice,[19] and it has been cited as evidence that Wordsworth considered the social causes of rural poverty—in this instance, the fact that the parish requires the farmer to sell his sheep before qualifying for relief. But if we ourselves are to be serious about the relationship between poetry and ideology, it must be admitted that this is neither the point on which the poem turns nor even a stated reason for indignation. The official position, "How can we give to you . . . what to the poor is due?" is scarcely presented as inhumane, nor does the poem encourage analysis of the shortsighted policy that will only produce more poverty. Instead, Wordsworth relocates the inhumanity of the system in the obsession of the sheep-farmer, who loves his dwindling flock more than the children whose appetites he has come to feel are the real cause of his sacrifice.

As is now well known, one of the complimentary copies of the 1800 *Lyrical Ballads* that Wordsworth and Coleridge distributed to influential people was sent to the Whig statesman Charles Edward Fox. Wordsworth's covering letter to Fox contained an emotional appeal on behalf of "small independent *proprietors* of land here called statesmen, men of respectable education who daily labour on their own little properties . . . which have descended to them from their ancestors."[20] But the letter does not speak, as Goldsmith would have spoken, against enclosures, the chief cause of the virtual disappearance of the small freeholders for whom Wordsworth claimed to speak. It speaks, rather, against the reorganization of society, and *especially* against such welfare measures as then existed, "workhouses, Houses of Industry, and the invention of Soupshops." The effect of such measures, Wordsworth argued, was to produce "a rapid decay of the domestic affections among the lower orders of society," by reducing "the spirit of independence." Apparently Wordsworth believed that reading the *Lyrical Ballads* would bring Fox round to his own opinion: that state assistance to the rural poor would ultimately destroy the nation's moral fiber.

One of the two poems that Wordsworth drew to Fox's attention was "Michael," and attempts have therefore been made to correlate its "message" with the letter's argument—namely, that "the little tract of land" that

---

[19] See Geoffrey Hartman, *Wordsworth's Poetry, 1787–1814* (New Haven, 1964), pp. 143–44.

[20] *The Letters of William and Dorothy Wordsworth*, ed. E. de Sélincourt, rev. C. L. Shaver (Oxford, 1967), p. 314.

distinguished the small freeholder from the rest of the "lower orders" was a "rallying point for their domestic feelings." But again, once one has set aside the emotional impact of Wordsworth's biblical language, the patriarchal dignity of Michael's character and the deep psychic constraints that words such as *covenant* impose,[21] the argument of the poem will not support even the dubious social message that Wordsworth, in commending it to Fox, must have thought it did. Rather, it narrates how Michael, in effect, sacrificed his son for his land, by exposing him to the temptations of city life; but even that sacrifice, it appears, was unnecessary. The financial threat to the estate vanishes, although no evidence is given that Luke ever sends the money that will prevent his father from having to sell "a portion of his patrimonial fields" (line 224). The land is only sold "into a stranger's hand" after Michael and his wife are dead; the idea of pastoral dispossession is, therefore, deprived of its ancient political underpinnings. The only forces that control the poem are personal weakness, parental grief, and natural decay, that which has transformed the ruined sheepfold into an object of aesthetic and imaginative interest. It is difficult, then, to read "Michael" as testimony of Wordsworth's residual social reformism or even as a deeply bifurcated poem. But it is equally impossible to derive from "Michael," as one can from the letter to Fox, a literal argument for Burkean traditionalism, unless by positing that that message has been translated into *literary* conservatism, the ideal of continuity being represented not by the passage of land from father to son but by the lasting symbol of the ruined sheepfold and its permanent inscription in the legend that is the poem.

"Michael," therefore, remains politically indistinct and historically nonspecific; that, many readers would affirm, is just as it should be. It was not until 1820 that Wordsworth published a "pastoral" that made his ideology as plain as the poem is trivial. "Repentance: A Pastoral Ballad" fully explains the connection between rustic improvidence and the decay of the old way of life, not without its own parodic echoes of Virgil's first eclogue:

> The fields which with covetous spirit we sold,
> Those beautiful fields, the delight of the day,
> Would have brought us more good than a burthen of gold,
> Could we but have been as contented as they.
>
> . . . .
>
> With our pastures about us, we could not be sad;

---

[21] Compare Hartman, *Wordsworth's Poetry*, pp. 265–66, where an analogy is suggested between Michael's story and Abraham's near-sacrifice of Isaac. See also Lore Metzger's chapter on "Michael," "Wordsworth's Pastoral Covenant," in *One Foot in Eden: Modes of Pastoral in Romantic Poetry* (Chapel Hill, N.C., 1986), pp. 137–58, an attractive but overly generous reading, which accepts at face-value all of Wordsworth's evaluative claims.

Our comfort was near if we ever were crost;
But the comfort, the blessings, and wealth that we had,
We slighted them all,—and our birthright was lost.

Oh, ill-judging sire of an innocent son
Who must now be a wanderer.

(2: 46–47)

In this poem the responsibility of the dispossessed for the loss of their patrimonial fields is laid squarely at their own door, and the ambiguities that
"Michael" had generated, not least by its emotional primitivism, are here
resolved in unmediated social condescension.

"The Ruined Cottage," later to be incorporated into *The Excursion,*
was complete enough as a separate poem for Wordsworth to offer it to
Joseph Cottle for publication in March 1798, although the volume actually published in that year was, of course, the first edition of *Lyrical Ballads*.[22] It too needs to be read in the context of contemporary economics,
but also of contemporary aesthetics. The rural cottage, the poem's nominal
subject, was commonly featured in discussions of the picturesque. Compared with that kind of aestheticizing, Wordsworth's story of the destruction of Margaret's family and the gradual disintegration of her cottage still
delivers an emotional jolt, powered by Wordsworth's deep insights into
family psychology, that is easy to mistake for humanitarianism. But the
poem's message is not the injustice of the social system that drives "shoals"
of the unemployed to "hang for bread on parish charity," or the factories
that are putting the cottage weavers out of business. Margaret's personal
disaster is caused by her weaver-husband's desertion of the family for the
army. True, he originally enlisted to rescue them from indigence, but the
poem makes it clear that it is the endless waiting, not knowing whether he
is alive or dead, that destroys Margaret emotionally, so that she in turn becomes a deserter, no longer adequately nurturing her children or maintaining her cottage and its garden. After her death, the poet-narrator and the
pedlar meet at the ruin, where among the symbols of nature's reclamation
of its own is "the useless fragment of a wooden bowl" (line 91) that in
another culture would have signified a rural idyll.

Wordsworth makes explicit, through the pedlar, the proper purpose of
retelling this tale. It is to move the reader, together with the poet-narrator,
from the simple emotion of pity to the complex one of *meditation,* a word
central to the poem's conclusion, where it is named as the process that
transforms human tragedy into peace of mind—for its interpreter. The

---

[22] See James Butler, ed., *"The Ruined Cottage" and "The Pedlar"* (Ithaca, N.Y., 1979),
p. 21. All my citations are from ms. D in this edition.

subject of meditation is the *naturalness* of the forces that have brought the cottage to ruin, from the bad harvests that initiated the cycle of poverty to the beautiful weeds that encroached on Margaret's garden. This, then, is Wordsworth's rewriting of the pastoral elegy, its generic origins declared in a passage added in 1799:

> The Poets in their elegies and songs
> Lamenting the departed call the groves,
> They call upon the hills and streams to mourn,
> And senseless rocks, nor idly; for they speak
> In these their invocations with a voice
> Obedient to the strong creative power
> Of human passion. Sympathies there are
> More tranquil, yet perhaps of kindred birth,
> That steal upon the meditative mind
> And grow with thought.
>
> (lines 73–82)

If it is reasonable to hear in this passage a deliberate allusion to Virgil's elegy for Daphnis ("vos coryli testes et flumina Nymphis," 5.21), it is more important to recognize in *meditate,* both here and in the final statement of catharsis, an echo of Virgil's definitive *meditaris.* As Wordsworth certainly knew, the word had already been appropriated for the English pastoral elegy in *Lycidas,* and, like Milton, Wordsworth had clearly determined by this time that pastoral meditation—that which defines the intellectual—had to be redeemed from its negative associations with Tityrus, that is to say, from associations with empty leisure or unfeeling happiness. It was surely for this reason that in 1798 he attached to "The Ruined Cottage" the opening distinction between the narrator and another gratuitous figure who has no role at all to play in the narrative action. The poem opens with an experience of extreme summertime heat or, rather, of variant experience of that heat, described as being:

> Pleasant to him who on the soft cool moss
> Extends his careless limbs beside the root
> Of some huge oak whose aged branches make
> A twilight of their own, a dewy shade
> Where the wren warbles while the dreaming man,
> Half-conscious of that soothing melody,
> With side-long eye looks out upon the scene,
> By those impending branches made more soft,
> More soft and distant.
>
> (lines 10–18)

It would have been impossible for Wordsworth to write these lines *without* conceiving of his "dreaming man" as Tityrus, whose late-eighteenth-century version of *otium* renders everything as "soft and distant," a merely picturesque landscape. In contrast, the narrator's "other lot" is the hard pastoral: "Across a bare wide Common I had toiled. . . . And when I stretched myself / On the brown earth my limbs from very heat / Could find no rest." His physical restlessness will be shortly transformed, under the pedlar's guidance, into imaginative work, which in turn transforms "a common tale" of suffering into philosophy. Without that thoughtful and active engagement with the "scene," each would be merely, as the pedlar put it, "an idle dreamer" (line 231). The soft pastoral, then, both of antiquity and as emasculated by Wordsworth's immediate predecessors, is replaced by the hard pastoral of the mind at serious work. The claim has obvious attractions. Wordsworth has been praised for developing, here and elsewhere, a "labor theory of poetic value";[23] yet such appropriations of Marxist terminology have been trenchantly discarded by Fredric Jameson, on the grounds that "writing and thinking are not alienated labor" in Marx's sense, and that it is "fatuous for intellectuals to seek to glamorize their tasks . . . by assimilating them to . . . genuine manual labor."[24]

The Prelude, in both its 1805 and 1850 versions, confirms that the idea of work was problematic for Wordsworth and that he conceived of that problematic in terms of the category *pastoral.* In the opening lines of "Michael" Wordsworth had allowed himself an admission that perhaps he had not fully penetrated. He calls it the first of the tales that spoke to him of "Shepherds . . . men / Whom I already loved;—not verily / For their own sakes, but for the fields and hills / Where was their occupation and abode" (2: 81). "Shepherds," wrote Wordsworth in the eighth book of the *Prelude,* "were the men that pleased me first"[25]—a statement that will introduce a definition of pastoral worthy of his project, the epic to answer Coleridge's demands for a great philosophical work. And as the passage recalling the romance of political reformism is located in the poem only after its spell has been broken and its rationalist basis rejected, so the account of pastoral appears in the poet's autobiography as a meditation on his experience of the city, London, in all its sublime and demonic aspects. But while the poem's structural strategy continues to display one of its central theses—that memories make us what we are—the chronological reversion here permits a conceptual examination of that special form of memory that pastoral represents. Through this generic exercise, Wordsworth appar-

---

[23] See Kurt Heinzelman, *The Economics of the Imagination* (Amherst, 1980), p. 221.

[24] Fredric Jameson, *The Political Unconscious: Narrative as a Socially Symbolic Act* (Ithaca, N.Y.: 1981), p. 45.

[25] *The Prelude: A Parallel Text,* p. 306.

ently came to terms, at the level of conscious theory, with the implications of that potentially shocking admission in "Michael": that what shepherds had come to mean to him had less to do with *their* experience as representatives of the agricultural working class than with their symbolic function for himself.

This section of *The Prelude* is sometimes read as if it were a statement like Crabbe's in *The Village,* distinguishing a conventional or literary pastoral from a "real" rusticity. In fact, Wordsworth's major distinction here is again between a soft or leisured, and a hard or working pastoral, both of which could exist in the real world, and each of which is articulated through a carefully marshalled series of literary echoes. The soft pastoral is introduced as confined to the past:

> Smooth life had flock and shepherd in old time,
> Long springs and tepid winters, on the banks
> Of delicate Galesus; and no less
> Those scattered along Adria's myrtle shores:
> Smooth life the herdsman, and his snow-white herd
> To triumphs and to sacrificial rites
> Devoted, on the inviolable stream
> Of rich Clitumnus; and the goat-herd lived
> As calmly, underneath the pleasant brows
> Of cool Lucretilis, where the pipe was heard
> Of Pan, the invisible God, thrilling the rocks
> With tutelary music, from all harm
> The fold protecting.

(lines 312–24)

This loving evocation of Arcadianism is rich in data about Wordsworth's pastoral theory, not least because of its subtle Virgilianism. The allusion to Pan, "from all harm / The fold protecting," is clearly in recall of Virgil's second eclogue, "Pan curat ovis oviumque magistros" (line 33), with the emphasis on *curat* rather than its origin in Theocritus *Idyll* 8.48—an echo that permits Wordsworth to focus on the *security* of the soft pastoral. More revealing in their origins are the allusions to the two rivers, Clitumnus and Galaesus. The first occurs in *Georgics* 2.146, at the point where Virgil turns to describe the Italian landscape, superior to the rest of the ancient world, as a home of olives and joyous herds, without wild beasts, a place of eternal spring. The second, equally significantly, marks the homeland of the old Corycian in *Georgics* 4.125–46, another idyllic region where the land provides the farmer with all he needs, along with contentment equal to the wealth of kings. It is no coincidence that in both instances Wordsworth turns for his pastoral sources to the *Georgics,* for this predicts both his solution to contemporary debates on pastoral theory, and, more importantly, his response to the socioeconomic conflicts that underwrite the literary ones.

Despite having defined the soft pastoral in terms of classical allusion, Wordsworth now proceeds to argue that the "smooth life" is not entirely out of reach, even in his own day. "I myself, mature / In manhood then, have seen a pastoral tract / Like one of these," he asserts, locating it in Goslar, Germany. But its description is no less dependent on memories of Theocritus as rewritten by Virgil. That ideal German landscape, Wordsworth asserts, resounds with the "flute or flageolet" of shepherd songs, because the hours are marked only by "unlaborious pleasure, with no task / More toilsome than to carve a beechen bowl / For spring or fountain, which the traveller finds, / When through the region he pursues at will / His devious course." In "The Ruined Cottage," the beechen bowl had already been found, in fragments, by precisely such a visitor; this passage makes it whole again and reminds us of its origins in Virgil's third eclogue, where its figurative expression of art's relation to leisure was perfectly understood.

Without, therefore, denying that "unlaborious pleasure" can still, in certain circumstances, be part of "real" pastoral experience, Wordsworth proceeds to his second definition of the hard pastoral, vicariously experienced by himself as a child, in observing the shepherds of his "native region."

> There, 'tis the shepherd's task the winter long
> To wait upon the storms: of their approach
> Sagacious, from the height he drives his flock
> Down into sheltering coves, and feeds them there
> Through the hard time, long as the storm is locked,
> (So do they phrase it) bearing from the stalls
> A toilsome burden up the craggy ways,
> To strew it on the snow . . . .
>
> . . . .
>
> And when the flock, with warmer weather, climbs
> Higher and higher, him his office leads
> To range among them, through the hills dispersed,
> And watch their goings, whatsoever track
> Each wanderer chooses for itself; a work
> That lasts the summer through.
>
> (lines 359–66, 370–75)

For the guardianship of Pan, "Invisible God," the hard pastoral substitutes the selfless and paternal human care, the "office" (the word is surely chosen for its classical connotations of ethical responsibility) of the shepherd himself. And, according to Wordsworth, unlike the miserable old shepherd in the "realistic" pastoral of Crabbe's *The Village,* the Lake District shepherd has his own interior rewards:

> He feels himself,
> In those vast regions where his service is,
> A freeman, wedded to his life of hope
> And hazard, and hard labour interchanged
> With that majestic indolence so dear
> To native man.

(lines 385–90)

It is impossible not to see in these lines, given the Virgilian entry codes that Wordsworth had so carefully provided, a position being taken in a long debate whose starting point was Virgil's ambiguous *libertas* in the first eclogue, the condition of pastoral happiness. But we have come a long way from the republican glosses of Servius or Landino, or even from Chénier's appropriation of the debate to the plight of peasants in the ancien régime. Wordsworth's solution was, in effect, to collapse the Virgilian dialectic between Tityrus and Meliboeus into a single, composite figure whose experience is a mixture of pain and pleasure; to stress the protector rather than the protégé; to note that the shepherd, for all his hard work, yet has time to "lie down upon some shining place, / And breakfast with his dog," and that, moreover, he often stays at rest "beyond his time" (lines 238–39); and, most significantly, to transform what others might see as agricultural slavery into a "service" to higher powers. It is this perception that makes him a spiritual "freeman."

We can now grasp why Wordsworth turned to the *Georgics* for his classical definition of the soft pastoral; it leads to a hard pastoral whose entire rationale is georgic. The solution to the ethical dilemma posed by rural labor, as Wordsworth now saw it, was both to endorse its necessity and to insist on its dignity, and in the occupation of the shepherd as it actually survived in the Lake District he was able to reconcile his own poetic program with a philosophical view of work that transcended and obscured the social issues. He thereby avoided both Goldsmith's sentimental nostalgia and Crabbe's unhidden contempt for the poor, as well as the contradictions generated by his own thoughts on landownership. The solution, however, depends on his "imaginative alchemy," on the subtle persuasions of "sagacious," "office," and that brilliantly oxymoronic "majestic," which controls even an earned and momentary "indolence." And it is equally clear that no socioeconomic cause is to be posited, let alone blamed, for the harshness of the northern English pastoral; on the contrary, the only antagonist is the weather. And Wordsworth's essential point is that this kind of hardship, independent, isolated, and, above all, *natural,* ennobles. That is to say, it ennobles the spectator; for the poem finally obscures the question of what the shepherd really feels, by literally objectifying him, turning him into an aesthetic object, which can only be perceived externally: [26]

> His *form* hath flashed upon me, glorified
> By the deep radiance of the setting sun:
> Or him have I descried in distant sky,
> *A solitary object and sublime,*
> Above all height! like an aerial cross
> As it is stationed on some spiry rock
> Of the Chartreuse, for worship. Thus was man
> Ennobled *outwardly* before mine eyes,
> And thus my heart at first was introduced
> To an unconscious love and reverence
> Of human nature.

> (lines 404–14; italics added)

In the 1850 *Prelude* Wordsworth carefully emended the two sections where social issues were embedded. At the point where he mentions the shepherd's brief moments of leisure, he excised the suggestion that the worker usually "stayed . . . beyond his time," replacing it by a much more constrained and improbable assertion:

> When they have stolen,
> As is their wont, a pittance from strict time,
> For rest not needed or exchange of love,
> Then from his couch he starts; and now his feet
> Crush out a livelier fragrance from the flowers
> Of lowly thyme, by Nature's skill enwrought
> In the wild turf.

> (lines 238–44)

The *conventional* pastoral diction here acts like an antimacassar, protecting the reader's mental furniture, especially in the ingenious relationship between "strict time" (the employer's time scheme) and the "lowly thyme" of a natural overseer whose fragrance rewards the unslothful. Finally, just before the crucial lines in which Wordsworth declared that the reward of

---

[26] Compare John Barrell's suggestion, in *The Dark Side of the Landscape: The Rural Poor in English Painting 1730–1840* (Cambridge, 1980), p. 139, that this passage is the textual equivalent of Constable's landscape paintings, in which "only by being kept at a distance are men . . . able to be seen as at one with the landscape." We need, however, to remember Wordsworth's own critique of this approach to landscape as the point of view of the "dreaming man" at the opening of "The Ruined Cottage."

hard service is the consciousness of freedom, he inserted a telling admission of where such a consciousness is really to be found:

> Philosophy, methinks, at Fancy's call,
> Might deign to follow him through what he does
> Or sees in his day's march; himself he feels
> In those vast regions where his service lies,
> A freeman.

(lines 249–53)

Between the two major versions of the *Prelude* stands another monument to Wordsworth's meditation on Virgilian pastoral and georgic, another attempt to adapt them to the needs of his own generation. As I have argued at length elsewhere, the *Excursion*, published in 1815, was an extended dialectic on the "choice of life" theme, as represented by the two types of the Wanderer and the Solitary.[27] Although these figures are developments of the Virgilian options of *otium* and exile, with the ethical preference going to the Wanderer, while the Solitary is presented initially as a disillusioned cynic, the poem is more continuously fueled by the "happy man" passage in Virgil's second georgic, with its crucial distinction between the country philosopher, who knows the causes of things, and the mere rustic, whose ability to conceptualize his happiness Virgil was the first to interrogate. And by 1815, Wordsworth seems to have admitted to himself not only that the admirable domestic emotions of the rural poor *were* under siege but that he himself had sentimentalized the idea of rural labor. In book 8 of the *Excursion*, in a debate on industrialization and its effect on English culture, the Wanderer delivers a formal lament for the disappearance of the georgic values, as the country children are sucked into the urban vortices and, as prisoners of towns and factories, lose their birthright:

> Oh! where is now the character of peace,
> Sobriety, and order, and chaste love,
> And honest dealing, and untainted speech,
> And pure good-will, and hospitable cheer;
> That made the very thought of country-life
> A thought of refuge.[28]

But it is the Solitary, now gradually emerging from his cynicism, who delivers an attack on rural ignorance and on the sentiment that assumes that

---

[27] In "Wordsworth's Georgic: Genre and Structure in *The Excursion*," *The Wordsworth Circle* 9 (1978): 145–54.

[28] *Poetical Works*, vol. 5: *The Excursion*, book 8, lines 239–44.

all is well on the farm. The ploughboy one actually meets, he points out, as distinct from the one usually represented "in soft verse" as "whistling . . . gladness to the morning air," is probably stiff-jointed, thick-legged, and low-browed, with eyes "wide, sluggish, blank, and ignorant," revealing the mental torpor within. "In brief," the Solitary concludes, "what liberty of mind is here?"

The Wanderer's solution to this challenge is to propose a program of national education for urban and rural children alike, which will produce something like "true equality" (9: 248); and in the light of a symbolic sunset, a "local transitory type" of the great Christian consummation, the Pastor (the third alternative) looks forward to a georgic not merely brought up to date but absolutely redeemed, a "blest day" when happiness will be equally distributed to all, whatever their "choice or lot" (9: 663–72). Whatever one may think of this last solution or of the quality of the *Excursion* as a whole, it is to Wordsworth's credit that he became temporarily dissatisfied with the pastoral ideology of the *Prelude*. At least as an (aberrant) phase between the two versions of his greatest poem, he had more than "half a mind / To take a writing hand in politics," and a politics of social meliorism, the choice that Frost's Tityrus, Wordsworth's direct descendant, considers but discards.

Samuel Palmer's Virgil con Amore

> Landscape of any kind is poor work without its persons,
> politics and human associations—expressed or
> understood.
>
> *(Letter to Frederic George Stephens, September 1875)*

Samuel Palmer has been called "a major influence in contemporary British painting and a key figure in Romantic art";[29] and it is a commonplace of art history that he was himself deeply influenced, as a painter, by William Blake's Virgilian woodcuts, the series commissioned by Robert Thornton for his 1821 edition of Virgil. John Linnell, who had introduced Blake to Thornton, now introduced Palmer to Blake. The meeting, momentous for Palmer, occurred in 1824, and either then or later Palmer was given one of the rare proof sheets of the Virgil series.[30] In a statement that

---

[29] Carlos Peacock, *Samuel Palmer: Shoreham and After* (London, 1968), p. 22.

[30] See Samuel Palmer, *The Letters of Samuel Palmer,* ed. Raymond Lister, 2 vols. (Oxford, 1974), 2: 707–8. Unless otherwise indicated, Palmer's correspondence is cited from this modern edition.

was forcefully to influence Yeats, he recorded in his notebook his first response to that early-nineteenth-century version of Virgil: "I happened first to think of their sentiment," wrote Palmer, in a highly self-revelatory statement. He proceeded to interpret Blake's woodcuts with a religious and sentimental fervor that would probably have deeply offended their author:

> They are visions of little dells, and nooks, and corners of Paradise; models of the exquisitest pitch of intense poetry. . . . There is in all such a mystic and dreamy glimmer as penetrates and kindles the inmost soul, and gives complete and unreserved delight, unlike the gaudy daylight of this world. They are like all that wonderful artist's works the drawing aside of the fleshly curtain, and the glimpse which all the most holy, studious saints and sages have enjoyed, of that rest which remaineth to the people of God.[31]

In 1826 Palmer settled in the country, at Shoreham in Kent, and produced a series of visionary landscapes inspired, it has been suggested, especially by the sixth woodcut in Blake's Virgil series—a moonscape, with the stricken tree that Philips had converted into a symbol of imaginative failure, in a field of windblown corn.

But the influence of Blake alone will not explain the project to which Palmer committed the last years of his life and which apparently became an obsession with him. That project was a new verse translation of Virgil's *Eclogues*, with a prose commentary, an introductory essay "On the Country and on Rural Poetry," and a series of etchings which he never completed.[32] In January 1872 Palmer wrote to the artist Philip Hamerton to ask about "the best way of disposing of a completed verse translation of Virgil's *Eclogues*" which he was, "right or wrong, . . . resolved to print." He added, "Whatever my version may be, it is a work done *con amore* in the superlative degree; but so is murder by a zealous 'Thug.' It has been 'bread eaten in secret,' as no one but my son knows of it" (2: 835). It was Hamerton who persuaded him that the volume would never find a market unless it were illustrated, and so launched Palmer on the second half of his passionate project, to produce a series of etchings, one for each eclogue, in which the influence of Blake as an artist was merged with the seemingly incompatible models of Claude and Poussin. This part of his dream proved impossible of fulfillment. When the volume was finally published in 1883, two years after his death, a long preface by his son explained how the task of finishing the volume had been bequeathed to him by his father on his deathbed. Both there and in his biography of his father, Alfred Herbert

---

[31] Recorded in A. H. Palmer, *The Life and Letters of Samuel Palmer* (London, 1892), pp. 15–16.

[32] Samuel Palmer, *The Eclogues of Virgil: An English Version* (London, 1883).

Palmer told from his perspective the story of the volume's genesis and motivation. Among his father's comments on the Virgil project was this astonishing statement: "When an artist sees at last what he ought to do, and
gathers himself up for the effort, I believe it is a sign that his days are
numbered." [33]

We face, therefore, the most intensely personal response to Virgilian
pastoral of all that this study has so far considered. It was, to begin with,
recorded by the second son of a father who, if we can judge from his correspondence, focused all his parental attention on his eldest son, Thomas
More (named for the great humanist), who was treated by his father as a
genius. In the summer of 1861 More died of brain fever, believed to have
been brought on by excessive study. Herbert states that the Virgil project
was conceived about 1856; [34] but there is no reference in Samuel Palmer's
correspondence to such a project until after More's death, when, it appears, he turned to the translation out of therapeutic motives. A fragment
of a letter to Edward Calvert, written in December 1863, admits that he
had "for many months" been working on the classical text "as a resource in
the deepest distress of mind."

It is hard to believe that Herbert did not himself experience powerfully
ambivalent feelings as the executor of a psychic trust whose origins were so
tied to the loss of the firstborn and whose fulfillment, as a test of his own
claims to his father's affection, could not possibly receive its reward. [35]
Freudian psychology seems particularly relevant to Herbert's language in
the *Life*, where he describes the *Virgil* as "an ill-fated project" conceived by
a man "blinded" by the ambition "of having his name associated, within
the covers of a real, published book, with the work of an immortal poet,"
an ambition which, when extended to the idea of an illustrated edition,
"betrayed him into trying to use pen and ink in a manner which was un-
natural to him." [36] Both in the *Life* and in his preface to the *Virgil*, Herbert
speaks in derogatory terms of his father's translation and apologizes for the
illustrations, but no passage is more responsible for conveying the sense of
a guilty aberration than this:

> If the friends who from time to time paid us an evening visit at Furze
> Hill had closely examined the piles of books which lay on my father's
> table, they would have found among them one in manuscript—a
> manuscript so interlined, erased, and cut about for the insertion of

[33] A. H. Palmer, *Life and Letters*, p. 159.
[34] Both Palmer's sons were apparently always called by their second names.
[35] Palmer's treatment of his younger son, who was ten when his brother died, seems to
have been worse than neglectful. Alfred describes himself at this time as "shut up in the house
of mourning, unable to read or write; without toys; without any resources and actually
dresed in petticoats with a frill for a collar and a coat so outlandish that all who saw me
smiled." See S. Palmer, *Letters*, 2: 675 n. 2.
[36] A. H. Palmer, *Life and Letters*, pp. 155–56.

slips of new matter, that but little of the original remained. He was never to be found by strangers with the volume in his hand, for a knock at the door was the signal for its being put out of sight.

(p. 155)

We need, therefore, to approach the question of Palmer's Virgilianism with a certain caution, for it is possible that its obsessive character is partly the creation of the son. The letter just mentioned, for example, survives only in the biography as a fragment, but even as a fragment its message is extremely complex, indicative both of the emotional relationship that Palmer established with Virgil's *Eclogues* and of the long cultural history of the text that enabled that relationship and gave it conceptual as well as pathetic force. "In the most successful of the few photographic portraits of my father," wrote Herbert, "he is holding in his hand a small volume which he took to London for that express purpose."[37] By one of the many coincidences of Virgilian reception, this volume was a copy of Martyn's translation of the *Eclogues,* in the 1813 edition, for Herbert describes it as containing "a series of figures of Virgilian plants."

It had been given to Palmer by Edward Calvert, and the larger text of the letter already quoted accompanied a copy of the photograph, as an expression of gratitude for the gift. The photograph itself (Fig. 32) speaks, as they say, volumes—about self-deprecation, economic hardship (the ancient and torn overcoat), and the meaning (physical, psychic, cultural) of the book. And what Palmer wrote to Calvert was not the simple exchange of courtesies that most of us are familiar with:

> The photograph of that Virgil you so kindly gave, it is but fair that you should have it, so I enclose it. You can cut it out and throw the old man who holds it into the fire. The old man was obliged to sit, as it was for a set of the Water-Colour members which Mr. Cundall in Bond Street had published; so he took your Virgil in his hand; which, indeed, is seldom long out of it. . . . I have been as a resource in the deepest distress of mind, employed for many months in endeavouring to sift the *Eclogues* thoroughly, to the last exactness of meaning and expression. With the exception of a few verses, I have now gone through the whole ten, and long after the Latin is thoroughly construed there are certain difficulties, here and there, which puzzle all the commentators.
>
> (2: 684–85)

Few letters can be more revelatory of the way the mind works: beginning with a gesture of self-abasement, which transforms the conventional hu-

---

[37] Ibid., p. 155.

Figure 32.   Portrait of Samuel Palmer, reproduced from Carlos Peacock,
Samuel Palmer: Shoreham and After (London, 1968), Plate 21. By permission of
John Baker (Publishers) Ltd.

mility topos of letter-writing into an expression of self-erasure ("cut it out
and throw the old man who holds it into the fire"), the text gradually suc-
cumbs to the *interest* of the work of translation and interpretation. And for
all his emphasis on his own age, the inference that he is used up and ready
for the (eternal) incinerator, Palmer has obviously been engaged in a serious

work of scholarship, tracking the Virgilian commentary tradition and prepared to commit himself to the *solution* of ancient interpretive problems.

A still more remarkable letter, dense with information about Palmer's state of mind just a few months after More's death, was written to William Linnell at the end of January 1862:

> To look up from this den of horrors to our felicity one would hardly think 'twere the same planet. My earthly hopes are in the grave and I have said unto the worm "thou art my sister." Earthed up thus to the very neck so far as this life is concerned I trust it shows some little virtue to look with envy upon your bright lot. "O happy if their happiness they knew," says Virgil—but when men are very happy they seldom know it—but stooping to snap at a shadow lose the substance or entangle themselves in anxieties, in the endeavour to unite several pleasant things each good in itself but incompatible with each other. Simply great was N. Poussin peopling his solitude with the mighty past and taking his evening walk on the Pincian. "How I pity you," said the Lord Bishop, "that you have no servant." He answered, "How I pity your Lordship who has so many. . . ."
>
> Mr. Severn says this is a Claude country where you may see his very trees. Ah where is the Virgilian muse? At the railway whistle she fled for ever. Yet her very oxen wander about the Eternal City disconsolate—but can it be? Have Corydon and Thyrsis met in Corduroys and Manchester cottons? "Yes," say the men of matter, "and it is out of the present that the true Poet weaves his Fable" . . . Mr. Blake would have said, "That is a lie." I say nothing but feel sick of the stomach. . . . Virgil was great but a godly crossing-sweeper is greater. . . . One of our greatest writers says that the doings of St. Giles's are the true materials for new epics. The Epic is far above me—but having formerly taken a daily walk in that neighbourhood before breakfast I doubt its eligibility for the pastoral and decidedly prefer the sentiment of Southern peasants making [ricotta] on the mountains. But those dear old Roman oxen, have they not lovely eyes? Well! "Trade's proud empire hastes to swift decay" and far ahead with the race to dust and ashes I remain, Yours most truly.

(2: 636–37)

As in the letter to Calvert, the text is, as it were, edged with black, beginning with Job 17:14 on the sisterhood of the worm—probably as mediated by Blake's aphorisms "for Children" in *The Book of Paradise*—and ending with dust and ashes. But the body of the letter is alive with allusions to Palmer's literary and painterly experience, all feeding into each other and including in the general ferment a level of social consciousness.

The literary allusions all have pastoral connections (though Palmer himself does not make the connection): the quotation of Virgil's "sua si bona no-rint" (*Georgic* 2.458); less obviously, the statement of Meliboeus in Eclogue 1.11 that he does not envy his neighbor's superior fortune, probably as Keats had restated that proposition in the *Ode to a Nightingale,* "'Tis not for envy of thy happy lot, but being too happy in thy happiness"; [38] and the final quotation from Goldsmith's *Deserted Village.* But thinking about happiness leads Palmer to the "simple" greatness of Poussin and Claude, whose Neoclassical landscapes he deeply admired and preferred to English landscape painting. This, in turn, leads to an ironic series of remarks on the possibility of a modern, Victorian pastoral, or a contemporarized aesthetic, as asserted by the "men of matter," a possibility that Palmer denies with the sardonic force he imagined Blake would have used. The letter, therefore, as an impromptu record of mental process, changes before our eyes from an act of mourning to one of cultural criticism. It is closely connected to a letter written to Laura Richmond in December of the same year, in which Palmer stated as one of the rules of art that "Classical subjects are peculiarly fit to be painted just now, as a protest against the degraded materialism which is destroying art," and adding, in a more Blakean manner, "Hogs live in the Present; Poets in the Past" (2: 672).

Virgilian pastoral, then, encapsulated a set of values that gave Palmer emotional support as he struggled to come to terms with his bereavement, but which quickly expanded beyond the scope of personal therapy. The full statement of what was at stake appears in the "Observations," which precede his translation and constitute a defense of poetry (for which read *pastoral*) against Victorian materialism. As Palmer had sentimentalized Blake's woodcuts, so in the "Observations" he reconceived the *Eclogues* in ideal terms, both as a landscape of the mind and as an actual countryside to which the men of his own generation ought to retreat whenever they could. But—and this is the central paradox of his work—*because* Palmer approached the *Eclogues* as a traditionalist, he was brought face to face with issues that were incompatible with either idyllicism or reclusiveness, issues that render his account of pastoral socially problematic where he most asserts its simplicity, and a product of historical change while he claims it as a refuge from history.

The "Observations" begin with a dramatic re-creation of the opening of Virgil's first eclogue:

---

[38] Keats's representation of himself as Meliboeus, and of the nightingale as Tityrus, singing "In some melodious plot / Of beechen green, and shadows numberless," is one of the Romantic allusions to Virgilian pastoral that has gone unnoticed. Palmer cited the *Ode to a Nightingale,* along with the ending of *Lycidas,* in a letter of 1851 (S. Palmer, *Letters,* 1: 485).

It was in the pleasant vale of Bickley that an accomplished friend, to whose conversation I am indebted for some of the happiest hours of life, sat down under a tree and solaced himself by repeating aloud in the sonorous original, passages from one of Virgil's Eclogues. "O you poor lost creature!" cried an acquaintance who had accidentally wandered to the spot, and thus detected his weakness. To a sharp man of the world, both verse and philosophy are superfluous; routine and the market have shaped and set him to a mediocrity for which epic is too high and the bucolic too lowly; and if he believe all poetry to be useless, by which diminutive of contempt will he designate its pastoral mood, with its wax-jointed pipes and poetic sheep which never come to mutton.

(p. 1)

In this literary idyll, the role of Tityrus is claimed by Palmer and his friend (identified by Herbert as Edward Calvert), while that of Meliboeus, "accidentally wandered to the spot," has been rewritten as the Victorian realist or materialist, who perceives idyllicism as failure. Palmer's project in the "Observations" was to disarm such prejudice, by moving to and fro on the interface between the literal and the metaphorical countryside, between culture and agriculture, mental and physical ecology: "Have we a patrimony?" he asked, suggesting that *reading* pastoral might then "persuade us to reside upon it":

Our capital is over-peopled, and human lungs are breathing an atmosphere which decomposes stone; the Western end of the New Palace had begun to peel or crumble, before the East was finished: then the whole was permeated by alarming smells from the river; which no future Denham is likely to select either for his theme or his "example."[39] It is said that out of town we merely vegetate; better so than wither.

(p. 3)

One of Palmer's central arguments was a very old one indeed, that pastoral serves as "a wholesome moral counterpoise and complement" to the art of politics. So it should alternate, in any statesman's experience, with the reading of history:

Yet history must be read, because the past is the exploration of the present, and the horoscope of the future, but ever and anon it will be

---

[39]The reference is to John Denham's *Coopers Hill*, a topographical poem published in 1642 and commenting, with occasional allusions to Virgil's *Georgics*, on the early stages of the English civil war.

well for us to make holiday among the quiet people by whose healthy labour we subsist and eat the fatness of the earth: then the happiness of Virgil's husbandmen in the second *Georgic* will be the better understood.

(p. 6)

His model for that happiness is, preeminently, the gentleman owner of a manor with its well-kept farms, or, better still, a retired politician with the "leisure to peruse himself . . . and revise the imaginations and desires of the interior polity" (p. 7). But however much this position seems to ally him with the country-house poets who supported and were supported by a Stuart aristocracy, there are nuances in Palmer's argument that make such a simple alignment impossible. One of his exemplary statesmen, for instance, is the surprising figure of Charles Edward Fox, whose liking for the *Eclogues* redeems him, in Palmer's eyes, from the bad company he has (like Blake) been keeping.[40]

Nor does Palmer avert his eyes from the agricultural laborer on the gentleman's estate, or pretend, like Robert Dodsley, that peasant life was delightful, or suggest, like the Wordsworth of the *Prelude,* that toil ennobles. In fact he reproaches Virgil for naïveté on that point:

> It is nothing to the purpose [to argue] that he and the farmer might have changed manners had they changed places; that was in Virgil's mind when he praised a country life, for he was simple enough to suppose that it had a moral influence upon our common nature; nor was he aware that the cultivation of the earth was a stupefying employment, and the peasant skilled in the varieties of labour, a log: No! "Non omnia possumus omnes"—that discovery was reserved for us. How could Virgil anticipate our progress, with whom the "bucolic mind" has become the synonym of fatuity? But those who are "behind the age," and not very anxious to overtake it, will discern in their ancient friends—in the Ploughman who lives in Chaucer's verse, and his kindred, something better than a barbaric foil to the intelligence of the modern artizan—especially to the hapless one dwarfed within some one of the minute divisions of labour, ever putting heads upon pins.

(p. 6)

So irony at the expense of the Victorian ideal of progress finds that quotation from Virgil's eighth eclogue, "We cannot all do everything," the motto

---

[40] See also S. Palmer, *Letters,* 2: 993: "'There is nothing like poetry!' said Charles Fox, who might often be found engrossed by Virgil's Eclogues in the intervals of a very different career."

that humanist culture had made proverbial for humility, and transforms it into something *approaching* Marxist thought on the division of labor; and in his acknowledgment of the "stupefying" effect of farmwork Palmer speaks like the atypical Wordsworth of *The Excursion*.

The same pattern emerges from the "literary" level of Palmer's pastoral theory; for his reading leads him to consider the question of pastoral's supposed decadence as a genre. Here a statement that people of "good taste" were revolted by the pseudo-pastoral of the Augustan "coffee-house poets," with its "spurious and tawdry" poetic diction, leads to a different sort of criticism. Much more offense must have been given, Palmer assumes, "by a glance at the Arcadia of Louis the fifteenth, at crooks tipped with silver and tittering shepherdesses who left their 'chers moutons' for a day's holiday to enjoy the tortures of Damiens" (p. 1). And when he turned to the question of whether pastoral is entitled to deal with the high subject, Palmer stated his religious belief that in the fourth and sixth eclogues Virgil had established the supremacy of pastoral even over epic, by telling of events—"the creation of the universe and the final restitution, compared with which, the fall of Troy, nay, even the founding of Rome, are but an interlude" (p. 9); but he also launched into an astonishing attack on Fontenelle:

> In the age of Louis the Fourteenth, when war was supposed to be the proper employment of gentlemen, rural culture a servile drudgery, it was not unlikely that a French critic, Fontenelle, would censure loftiness of thought as a breach of pastoral decorum, and that the Eclogue which delighted Cicero would seem grotesquely absurd to the eulogist of the Academy. The condition too of the French peasantry was deplorable, and pastoral poetry is read at a disadvantage when nothing that we have ever seen resembles it; . . . whenever misgovernment or encroaching wealth, garden-filching, enclosure, and violation of common-right, are making the country life a term convertible with stinted food, squalid habitations and sordid manners, bucolic poetry departs: the rural Thalia may blush, may weep, but cannot sing.
>
> (p. 9)

What began as a comment on generic hierarchies becomes, irresistibly, an argument for the causal equivalence of literary and social repressions, and the demise of pastoral in Victorian England now appears a product of the exterior as well as the interior polity.

It has been strenuously argued by Geoffrey Grigson, moved by anxiety lest Palmer's admiration for Blake tar him with the same radical brush, that Palmer was as conservative in his politics as he was in his cultural instincts. According to Grigson, the social unrest of the 1820s and 1830s caused

Palmer to retreat "to the primitivism of a Christian age of gold," a program institutionally compatible with "the Anglican Church of his fathers" and "the High Tories." Again according to Grigson, Palmer shared with Constable and Coleridge a dread of the Reform Bill: "Rick-burning, riots, machine-breaking, the wild speculation and greed and collapse of 1824–26 —all such things could be put down to the agitation of Whigs and dissenters and the influence of the new money-makers it was proposed to enfranchise."[41] This argument is based primarily on an anonymous *Address to the Electors of West Kent,* dated 4 June 1832 and attributed to Palmer by his son, which fulminates against the Reform Bill as the "Annihilation" of "good old England." But neither Grigson nor Palmer's later biographer Lister made any attempt to analyze his long-term opinions or to weigh that early and anonymous pamphlet against the evidence of Palmer's later statements.

There is certainly evidence in Palmer's letters of attempts to soften Blake's political profile. He claimed to one correspondent that Blake never praised the American republic (!) (2: 663) and suggested to another that his radicalism was the effect of keeping the wrong company: "Thrown early among the authors who resorted to Johnson, the bookseller, he rebuked the profanity of Paine, and was no disciple of Priestley; but, too undisciplined and cast upon times and circumstances which yielded him neither guidance nor sympathy, he wanted the balance of the faculties which might have assisted him in matters extraneous to his profession. He saw everything through art" (1: 509). And in 1828 he wrote of his political disagreements with Linnell, now his father-in-law, in terms that could be taken to support Grigson's hypothesis:

> Politics we dabble in:[42] Mr. L. though of no party magnifies the peasants; I also, as you know, of no party, as I love our fine British peasantry, think best of the old high tories, because I find they gave most liberty to the poor, and were not morose, sullen and bloodthirsty like the whigs, liberty jacks and dissenters; whose cruelty when they reign'd, was as bad as that of the worst times of the worst papists; only more sly and smoothlier varnish'd over with a thin shew of reason.
>
> (1: 37)

But it would be equally plausible to credit Palmer's statement that he was politically nonpartisan, a statement repeated in a letter of 1839 in which he

[41] Geoffrey Grigson, "Samuel Palmer: The Politics of an Artist," *Horizon* 4 (1941): 314–28. See also his *Samuel Palmer: The Visionary Years* (London, 1947), pp. 104–5, 150n.

[42] Raymond Lister explains this phrase, written in 1828, as alluding to the *Address,* written four years later. Yet it clearly refers solely to Palmer's disputes with Linnell on his unfortunately structured "family" honeymoon.

claimed that his principles were merely the general ones of Christian decency.

And there is ample evidence that Palmer was, or became, disillusioned with the social policies of the Victorian state. In 1876, for example, he praised Oliver Cromwell for having a more objective theory of history than that permitted by the stultifying "Divine Right politics of advanced ritualists" (2: 925). The same letter opens with a sardonic reference to contemporary "Political Science," which is only withheld "because of some lingering prejudices against homicide" from offering worn-out agricultural laborers prussic acid, so as to remove them from the list of welfare recipients. Another letter deplores Victorian moral cant about the morals of the poor. Palmer "really can not see how any of us can be quite sure that we are better than they, so much depends on surrounding influences and early habits." What he is certain of is that "Sin lies heavily at the door of those who have suffered the poor to live in pig-sties and have filched from them their gardens" (2: 938). The last phrase echoes the "garden-filching" of the "Observations." Another letter explicitly refers to Thomas Paine's *Rights of Man,* asserting "the right of the less voracious to restrain those who are more so," and again connecting political philosophy to the question of land use and ownership. "The rights of the poor majority are pure air, and pure water, and sufficient space to walk about in,—when the rich minority are befouling the air with manufactories, poisoning the rivers, and . . . adding 'field to field till there is no place left,' and the villagers can not step out of the dusty high road without a trespass" (2: 975–76). Significantly, this letter also refers to "our dear cheerful peace-loving Virgil" and quotes the *Georgics.*

We should, therefore, reconsider the strange texture of that turbulent letter to William Linnell, written at the inception of the Virgil project, and especially the point of Palmer's retelling of the anecdote about Poussin from Bellori's *Lives of the Painters.*[43] That vision of Poussin "peopling his solitude with the mighty past" is not merely a statement about Neoclassical landscape and the visual allure of nostalgia and repose, for the cardinal (whom Palmer calls a bishop) is presented as a typical materialist, whose own gentlemanly leisure is supported by large numbers of servants, whereas Poussin represents an ideal of self-sufficiency, a refusal to be complicit in the social structure of the ancien régime. And while Palmer's contempt for the contemporary culture that elevates a "godly crossing-sweeper" above Virgil may seem to conflict with so democratic a reading of Poussin, later and less volcanic letters clarify Palmer's growing realization of what Victorian pieties managed to conceal. The older he became (and the connec-

[43] G. P. Bellori, *Le vite de' pittori, scultori et architetti moderni* (Rome, 1672), p. 441.

tion with his work on the Virgil project cannot be fortuitous), the sharper became his sense of the socioeconomic causes of poverty.

This did not, however, induce in Palmer a belief in political solutions. In the summer of 1880, a year before his death, and just after the return of Gladstone's Liberals to power, Palmer opened a letter with the "fact" that "the French peasantry are in much better circumstances than before the Revolution," the result of "a more equitable distribution of property, and deliverance from unbearable oppression." In England, however, he believed that no such major change was likely. "Political reform has done so little to make us better that the old maxim which the liberals used to laugh at so much, 'Let each reform himself,' seems respectable advice after all." And he cited John Stuart Mill on liberty as "depending upon the character of the free" (2: 1013).[44] It was this interior liberation that Palmer read into Virgilian pastoral, as into the landscapes of Claude and Poussin, and which he passionately wished to make available to as many as his Virgil could reach.

We need this other view of Palmer to counteract Grigson's profile of the high Tory, as well as to comprehend the internal contradictions of his *Eclogues*. Given the tendentious structure of the tradition he had inherited, the scholarly way he went about mastering it, and the holistic nature of the "version" he desired, it would have been surprising if Palmer's *Eclogues* had managed absolute coherence of tone and statement. Nobody before him, with similar ambitions, had managed it, though some—Landino, Spenser, Ogilby—had turned ambiguity and dialectic to their own ends. But in Palmer's composite act of interpretation—a mixture of extremely free translation with scrupulous annotation, with a theoretical preface that extends the meaning of *pastoral* into the sociopolitical arena, and a series of etchings that limit it almost exclusively to natural images of a peaceful if inhabited landscape—self-contradiction becomes itself holistic. Palmer's version of the *Eclogues* is a Victorian statement of anti-Victorianism, a counter-cultural document that offers pastoral as a cure for society's ills but in which the diagnosis of the ills and the vision of the cure are formally and conceptually incompatible.

We can follow some of Palmer's contrary impulses in the notes that locate his version in the commentary tradition, most authoritatively represented for him by Martyn and Conington, but to which he brings his own instincts and preoccupations. So he bowdlerized the second eclogue, converting it (as had Marvell) into a decorously heterosexual poem; in the fourth eclogue he accepts, as a "conjecture," the medieval reading of the poem as "an antepast of the Final Restitution" (p. 45). But the fifth eclogue, which he reads metaphorically as an elegy for Julius Caesar, is

---

[44] John Stuart Mill's essay *On Liberty,* the classic expression of nineteenth-century liberalism, was published in 1859.

therefore a "kind of tacit satire upon war . . . in which no pastoral combat with bear or wolf, or other imagery, indicates the soldiership of the world's greatest captain; while the better parts of his nature, clemency and benevolence, are deified; virtues which, undisplaced by more violent impulses, would render war impossible" (p. 51). It is hard not to believe that Palmer intended this commentary as his own "tacit satire" on Disraeli's imperialism. He certainly made the most of the Roman historical context of the first eclogue, which he read as "a thank-offering to Augustus; a persuasive to extend to others the justice he had rendered to Virgil in the restitution of his inheritance, and incidentally, as a protest against military outrage and the national corruption which engenders civil war" (p. 17). And no passage more fully explains the connections among his commitment to Virgil, his own past experience at Shoreham, and his mature meditations on the social system than his evocation of Meliboeus and the language of dispossession:

> Have we a distant hope; shall I at last
> Return, when travel has confused the past,
> From bleak exile, and wondering at the change
> Come, at a turn, upon the byres, the grange,
> Lowly and thatched with turf, where I was born;
> A realm to me, a loss I vainly mourn,
> Thrust headlong by a soldier from the soil
> Rich with my kindred's immemorial toil?

> (p. 22)

Despite his reluctance to assume that the *libertas* of Tityrus carries any of the old republican implications, and his acceptance of the alternatives proposed by Martyn and Conington, Palmer had clearly intuited the ideological density of the first eclogue. "Apart from allegory, there is, perhaps, a by-play glancing at public affairs and at the poet himself, which it is now impossible to trace: his words are two-edged, a single one is often an abridgement of many, and its meaning expands like the widening circle when a stone is thrown into the water" (p. 99).

Palmer's notes, then, take for granted that the text of the *Eclogues* is problematic and that it bespeaks a range of ideological activity. His illustrations, on the other hand, seem mostly to assert the absence of any concepts other than those subsumed by idyllicism, and because they are usually discussed only as etchings, by art historians, little consideration has been given to the way in which they must interact with the larger structure of text, preface, and commentary. In addition, art historians have been wary of the Virgil etchings because of their incompletion, and the necessary interventions of Herbert Palmer, which involved not only completing some of the plates but selecting those designs that had not been begun on copper and which were subsequently reproduced by photogravure. Only that for the eighth eclogue was finished (and published separately, under the title of "Opening the Fold"). Herbert suggests that "the laden apple tree in the twilight pastoral [of the first eclogue], . . . and the huge cedars overshadowing Daphnis's mourners, may be cited as thoroughly realizing the views of the veteran etcher" (p. xiii). But for the tenth eclogue he added an "older" and presumably discarded design on the grounds that it was "strikingly original and characteristic" (p. xiv). To further complicate matters, he also included in the volume an alternative design for the first eclogue, never intended for the volume; it was, rather, a large watercolor exhibited in 1877.

Yet if we do approach the illustrations as part of the larger structure, they change their appearance, becoming less a vision of undifferentiated pastoral calm and more a record of the conceptual paradoxes that underlie Palmer's Victorian Virgilianism—an effect only accentuated by the choices made by Herbert Palmer. "Opening the Fold" (Fig. 33), the plate with which Palmer began, has an ambiguous Claudian repose that could be read simply as generic pastoral landscape. As Herbert remarked, no one, when it was published, "suspected that it was the 'hapless Damon' who leaned against the olive tree."[45] Likewise, the illustrations for the second, sixth, and ninth eclogues reduce them all to the same vespertinal moment when shepherds may rest: Corydon disappears, along with the critique of erotic pastoral; there is no trace of Silenus or the creation-song; and both the painful journey and the cultural anxieties of Moeris and Lycidas are displaced by the lyric fragment from Theocritus, which now, in Palmer's unauthorized expansion, invites Galatea to "recline" in a "shaded" cave, to "watch the West, / And timely, with the sun, together rest" (p. 87). For the fifth eclogue (Fig. 34) on the other hand, he chose a scene of intense emotion, expressed in Blakean gesture and texture, and the "great *pathetic* lines" that Palmer believed the engraver should first reach for.

And although the illustrations show not a trace of the Roman historical context examined in the notes, the alternative design for the first eclogue (Fig. 35), unlike the nonspecific and soothing scene of a ploughman returning home or the vision of evening hospitality under the apple tree, cannot be understood solely as landscape, or even solely as idyll. In its handling of the figures in the landscape, it faithfully translates the ancient iconography of Tityrus, the man at rest, and Meliboeus the traveler, complete with the conical straw hat that has itself traveled a long journey from the illustrated *Virgils* of the early Renaissance; while the evocation of Claudian landscape and perspective, with the fortified building in the

---

[45] A. H. Palmer, *Life and Letters*, p. 159.

Figure 33. Samuel Palmer, "Eclogue 8: Opening the Fold," from *The Eclogues of Virgil: An English Version* (London, 1883), facing p. 76. Rare Books and Special Collections, Library of Congress, Washington, D.C.

Figure 34. Samuel Palmer, "Eclogue 5," from *The Eclogues of Virgil: An English Version* (London, 1883), facing p. 54. Rare Books and Special Collections, Library of Congress, Washington, D.C.

Figure 35. Samuel Palmer, "Eclogue 1," from *The Eclogues of Virgil: An English Version* (London, 1883), facing p. 20. Rare Books and Special Collections, Library of Congress, Washington, D.C.

distance, serves in this instance as a subtle allusion to the Roman background, established as part of the visual tradition of the *Eclogues* by the
woodcuts of Sebastian Brant.

Which brings us back to Palmer's letter to Stephens cited as an epigraph for this section, a letter that moves in the same paradoxical way as
Palmer's thought in general, from the politics of landscape to the idealism
of Claudian landscape, and from there to an idea of the Golden Age. In
that letter Palmer had been speaking of the many traditions, warlike, romantic, and sacred, that inhere in Yorkshire landscape and that could supply a landscape painter with his figures:

> and landscape is poor work without its persons politics and human
> associations—expressed or understood. In Yorkshire scenes, you get
> your landscape from the past; and though it is just now the fashion to
> say that great geniuses have been distinguished by their sympathy with
> the then present, I think their works have always synchronized with
> the past, though as men and moral agents it is to be hoped they sym-
> pathized with people about them and did what good was in their
> power. A preference for the present as a matter of taste is a pretty sure
> sign of mediocrity. . . . And the best poets and painters appeal to this
> faculty and instinct within us:—and I do not think that it is either the
> truth of his colour or the charm of his trees, (unrivalled though they
> be,) or the gold of his sunshine, that makes CLAUDE the greatest of
> landscape painters, but that Golden *Age* into which poetic minds are
> thrown back—on first sight of one of his genuine *Uncleaned* pictures.
>
> (2: 923–24)

So Palmer's own idiosyncratic classicism defines itself against the dominant
culture of Victorian England, as a nostalgia for the past which is yet intended to improve the present, and a politics of landscape which can only
be "expressed or understood" in images of a world innocent of politics.

It is not surprising that this inverted ideology should have failed to
make itself understood. And as Palmer's reputation as an artist has been
based (rightly) on the products of his Shoreham period, so his early response to Blake's Virgil has loomed much larger in his profile than his own
syncretic and problematic *English Version* of Virgilian pastoral. William
Butler Yeats read that early statement in the *Life and Letters,* misquoted the
phrase "mystic and dreamy glimmer" as "*misty* and dreamy glimmer," and
proceeded to build what *that* phrase evoked for him into much of his es-
capist poetry of the 1890s.[46] Even when Yeats himself moved on to cultural

---

[46] See Elizabeth Loizeaux, *Yeats and the Visual Arts* (New Brunswick, N.J., 1986), pp. 80,
208.

criticism on the grand scale in his late poems, Palmer still represented a more innocent idealism than his own "cold eye" could now contemplate. He wrote in *Under Ben Bulben* that when the "greater dream" of Quattrocento painting was past,

> Calvert and Wilson, Blake and Claude,
> Prepared a rest for the people of God,
> Palmer's phrase, but after that,
> Confusion fell upon our thought.[47]

Under Ben Bulben is dated 4 September 1938, the month of the Munich conference, six months after Hitler's invasion of Austria. At that moment Yeats's nostalgia for an earlier aesthetic is understandable, however unforgivable the direction of his own political sympathies. But it would be fairer to Palmer, now that we have more of the record before us, to say that he articulated his own cultural confusion and stored it for our benefit in a time capsule we are now capable of opening.

André Gide and Fin de Siècle Pastoral

Yeats had initially assimilated his own conception of Palmer to the cultural pessimism that seems, at the end of the nineteenth century, to have become among European intellectuals virtually a new dominant ideology, although its forms varied from Yeats's escapes into Irish mythology to the programmatic decadence of Rimbaud or Wilde and should probably include the amoralism of Nietzsche and his redefinition of freedom as the will to power. Among the French purveyors of anomie, well before Durkheim resurrected the term, was André Gide; and among Gide's preoccupations, as he struggled to liberate himself from his rigid Protestant upbringing, were Virgil's *Eclogues*. An eccentric case, Gide's *Corydon*, a manifesto for homosexuality, was published, privately and anonymously, in 1911. Aside from its title it bears no formal or hermeneutical relationship to Virgil's second eclogue. But already in 1889 Gide had published a parody of Virgil's first eclogue as part of *Le Prométhée mal enchaîné* and in 1895, more significantly, a brief autobiographical novel with the alternative titles of *Paludes (Swamps)* and *Journal de Tityre*.[48] The connection between the two titles derives from Virgil's description of Tityrus's farm as infertile, characterized

---

[47] W. B. Yeats, *Collected Poems* (London, 1950), p. 400.
[48] I cite from André Gide, *Paludes* (Paris, 1973). See also *Marshlands and Prometheus Misbound*, trans. George D. Painter (New York, 1953), whose translation I partially adopt.

by "bare rocks and slimy marsh reeds" ("quamvis lapis omnia nudus / limosoque palus," lines 47–48), but what was accidental in the original becomes structural here. "Paysage" equals "l'état de l'âme." The marshes from which Tityre will not depart are a psychic terrain, a cultural stagnation.

Structured as a journal, *Paludes* records the thought processes, conversations, and minimalist social experiences over a six-day period of a writer-intellectual (Gide's persona) who is currently working on an autobiographical novel entitled *Paludes* whose protagonist is Tityre. Yet author, persona, and protagonist merge under the sign *Tityre,* as the subject of *Paludes* 1 is the writing of *Paludes* 2, and so on in a presumably infinite series.

The strategy is that of the *mise en abîme* or mannerist gesture of self-referentiality so important to post-modernist aesthetics,[49] but that Gide had, significantly, defined in his personal journal long before post-modernism, or for that matter modernism, took programmatic shape. "What I like in a work of art," wrote Gide,

> is when one finds the very subject of the work transposed, with specific reference to the characters in it. . . . Thus, in certain paintings by Memling or by Quentin Metzys a small convex dark mirror reflects on its own the interior of the room where the painted scene occurs.[50]

This perception arose as a comment on *Hamlet;* and Gide's persona shares with Shakespeare's most self-conscious intellectual a propensity to self-recording. At a moment of what is supposed to be intense mental suffering, he cries, "Tiens! une phrase! Notons cela," and reaches under his pillow for paper (p. 94), in unmistakable allusion to Hamlet's famous recourse to his writing-tables at the moment of the Ghost's revelation.

The subject, then, of *Paludes* is the creative process itself—except that it is not creative. The writer-figure offers a series of increasingly morose definitions of what his novel purports. First, it is the history of one who cannot travel, whose life, like the marsh around him, is static, stagnant. In an earlier conception of the work that had focused on sexuality, or fear of it, as the central problematic, Gide had projected the title as "Angèle ou le pauvre petit voyage."[51] This survives, without the "poor," as the subtitle of the novel's last section, in which the writer and Angèle do indeed take the smallest of journeys, a picnic in the country. The narrator's incapacity to travel, except in imagination to destinations he refuses to specify, is the subject of several central dialogues. Within the novel he writes, the symbol of his condition is Tityre, whose *contentment* with his swampy environ-

---

[49] I refer to its appropriation, and its conceptual darkening, by Jacques Derrida, in *Of Grammatology,* trans. Gayatri Chakravorty Spivak (Baltimore, 1974), p. 163.

[50] Cited in Tadeusz Kowzan, "Art 'en abîme,'" *Diogenes* 96 (1976): 67.

[51] See Vinio Rossi, *André Gide: The Evolution of an Aesthetic* (New Brunswick, N.J., 1967), p. 117.

ment is extracted from Virgil's text and made the figure of cultural impotence. The "story" is restated as that of a bachelor in a tower surrounded by marshes, who spends his time fishing, of course unsuccessfully, from the windows of his tower. He has insufficient bait but "multiplication des lignes (symbole)" (p. 21), the parenthesis a deliberate parody of Gide's own earlier Symbolist phase. And when Angèle fears that this story will be slightly boring, the narrator cries out in exasperation that that is precisely its point: "L'émotion que me donne ma vie, c'est celle-là que je veux dire: ennui, vanité, monotonie" ("What I want to express is the emotion my life has given me: the boredom, the emptiness, the monotony," p. 23). It is never entirely clear whether the purpose of writing *Paludes* both 1 and 2 is, as the narrator sometimes claims, to cure himself and his friends from the narrowness and mediocrity of their lives, or whether he indulges in anomie for its own sake, an "inutile contemplation . . . devant les délicates choses grises" (p. 44), an unprofitable contemplation in the face of delicate grey phenomena.

At a party for Paris intellectuals in Angèle's salon the narrator finds himself on the defensive, forced to define his project in ever more shifting allegorical terms. It is the story of the neutral ground we all share, of the ordinary man, as whom we all begin, of the third person (the French *on*) who survives us all, and, because Virgil defined Tityrus as *recubans,* it is the story of the "homme couché." This phrase, made newly enigmatic by its urbane translation and by the narrator's tendency to spend longer and longer in bed, is also revealed as an allegory, even a critique, of existentialism, long before that stance had been rendered formally philosophical by Heidegger and Sartre. For action, the narrator explains as best he can, contains its own principle of inertia, our desire for continuity ensuring that action, instead of being a "repoussoir," jumping-off point, becomes instead the bed on which we fall back *recubans,* supine as before (p. 85). The narrator's position is not that action is freedom, but that only the free act is truly responsible; he wishes not to engender action, but to disengage liberty; but the moral philosopher in the group accuses him of the paradox, by his writing *Paludes,* of wishing to compel others to be free (pp. 80–81).

In a letter to a friend, Gide made explicit the therapeutic intentions of *Paludes,* as well as its lightness of tone, its deliberate absurdity. "I hope to make people laugh and think. You'll see that I have put myself in it. Besides, it is a satire of ourselves."[52] That it also freed him to write *Les Nourritures terrestres,* a more extreme manifesto for personal liberation (and also peopled with names from Virgil's *Eclogues*) is taken for granted by Gide's biographers. But more to our purpose here are the insight and the discipline with which, in attempting to comprehend Paris at the turn of the

---

[52] Ibid., p. 88.

century, Gide turned backwards for his vocabulary of cultural criticism. Like Frost in "Build Soil," his engagement with the *Eclogues* was one of remarkable fidelity to the Virgilian pastoral dialectic, reproducing the ancient points of ideological pressure—happiness versus its opposite, stasis and recumbency versus travel and action, liberty versus slavery—and reinscribing them in an avant-garde analysis that was years ahead of its own time.

"A Book for Kings, Students or Whores": The Cranach Press Eclogues

Count Harry Kessler knew André Gide, whom he met at a large social occasion in 1928.[53] He knew everyone. He went to school in Paris; in Ascot near London, along with Winston Churchill and Roger Fry; and in Hamburg; and to university in Bonn and Leipzig. He fought in the First World War in Belgium, Russia, Poland, Hungary, and France. In 1916 he held a position in the Foreign Office with responsibility for German cultural propaganda and for secretly investigating the terms of peace with France. In Switzerland, he participated in the negotiations for the return of Lenin to Petrograd, in the famous sealed train; and at the end of the war he escorted General Pilsudski, the new Polish dictator, back to Poland. In Poland, Kessler served as the first German minister to Warsaw, his mission being to organize the peaceful withdrawal of German troops. Back in Berlin, he led a cosmopolitan and complicated life as diplomat, patron of the arts, political journalist, and publisher of fine books. He was a close friend of Walther Rathenau, who became foreign minister of the Weimar Republic, and after Rathenau's assassination in 1922 Kessler wrote his biography. His friends included Albert Einstein, Bernard Shaw, Auguste Rodin, Henry van de Velde, Diaghilev, Josephine Baker, Jean Cocteau, Max Reinhard, Hugo von Hofmannsthal, Richard Strauss, Paul Valéry (whom he failed to persuade to translate the *Georgics*)—and Aristide Maillol, out of whom he coaxed the illustrations for the *Eclogues*. Kessler was in almost every respect the living symbol of the political and cultural ideals of the Weimar Republic before it succumbed to the Depression and Nazism.[54]

---

[53] Kessler, *In the Twenties: The Diaries of Harry Kessler*, introduction by Otto Friedrich, trans. Charles Kessler (London, 1971), p. 343. Kessler's diaries were first published in Germany under the title *Harry Graf Kessler, Tagebücher 1918–1937* (Frankfurt, 1961).

[54] See Peter Gay, *Weimar Culture: The Outsider as Insider* (New York, 1968). Gay frequently cites Kessler's *Tagebücher* for both historical data and insight into various Weimar personalities. For Kessler's biography, see Renate Müller-Krumbach, *Harry Graf Kessler und die Cranach-Presse in Weimar* (Hamburg, 1969).

His cosmopolitanism was not untheorized, the lucky product merely of birth and affluence. Kessler had been influenced as a student by the more constructive strains in Nietzsche's thought, the call in *Beyond Good and Evil* for a new internationalism that would rise above German Romanticism and patriotism, those "atavistic attacks of fatherlandishness and soil addiction," and produce a new generation of "good Europeans."[55] Overlooking Nietzsche's far more dangerous argument that national boundaries were being eradicated by an international democratic movement that was preparing the majority for slavery and the exceptional few to become the new ruling caste, Kessler saw only a pandemic ideal of polity and culture, compatible with his own instinctive pacifism. In February 1919, Kessler was meditating what response the Weimar Republic should make to Woodrow Wilson's League of Nations, an entente he regarded as "animated by the old spirit and barely disguising the imperialist intention of a number of states to enslave and pauperize their defeated enemies." "A mistake that leaps to the eye," Kessler wrote in his invaluable *Tagebücher,* is that the plan "has originated with states, political entities which are by nature rivals, rather than with those major economic and humanitarian interests and associations which inherently incline to internationalism" (p. 69). He thought in terms of labor organizations, international trading and banking consortia, and major religious communities.

In international policy, then, Kessler was both more visionary and more radical than Rathenau and the Social Democrats, seeing his own League as a way of allying Germany with Russia. His "concise definition" of the plan stated that "supreme power . . . respecting war, peace, and international law shall not lie with a league of sovereign states but with *an organization of those organizations which in any case support peace and are international*" (p. 74). But there were also, in Kessler's thinking, the strong and conflicting impulses of an intellectual aristocrat. His scheme required "the surrender of democracy for the sake of human personality . . . the individual plays a vital part instead of functioning as a mere digit" (p. 97). In April, Kessler had actually persuaded the Cabinet to introduce his proposal as the official German alternative to Wilson's plan. "I am really surprised how vigorously this idea . . . is making progress," Kessler noted, "the notion of the state restrained by the universal forces of humanity. Born of despair, it can perhaps shape humanity's future and guide it to a fresh flowering" (p. 96).

He later discovered that official support was nothing but a rhetorical gesture of despair, not expected to go anywhere; and by the spring of 1925, on one of his many lecture tours in aid of the League as Wilson had

[55] Friedrich Nietzsche, *Beyond Good and Evil,* trans. Walter Kaufmann (New York, 1966), pp. 174–77.

defined it, Kessler perceived himself as one of the "preachers in the wilderness" (p. 253) on the subject of peace and international accord. When Germany formally entered the League of Nations in 1926, Kessler asked for a place on the delegation, but nothing came of it; and in October 1933 he recorded the "coup de tonnerre" of Nazi Germany's official withdrawal from the League. It is impossible to tell in what mental tone of voice he wrote the following entry, but irony is strongly to be suspected:

> Thursday, 19 October 1933. Paris. In the morning visited Hermann Keyserling. He has been taking part here in a congress of the *Coopération Européenne* and was in a state of the most exuberant excitement. He and Paul Valéry conducted the entire congress, he had to make speeches the whole time, and everything went off splendidly. He has hopes of the alliance between a few hundred European intellectuals proving the salvation of European civilization. Lack of intellectuality is the most terrible thing about the Hitler regime. For the time being, though, there is nothing to be done about it other than creating a haven where the intellectuals can take refuge.
>
> (p. 463)

Without this insight into Kessler's convictions, the Cranach Press *Eclogues* would be intelligible only as an aesthetic object, an experiment in fine bookmaking that engaged him primarily as a patron of the arts. Certainly this is the message of the *Prospectus* issued to advertise the English edition.[56] This document takes a strongly intentionalist position on the meaning of the volume and hence of Virgil's *Eclogues* themselves:

> In September 1927 the Cranach Press, set up by Count Harry Kessler at Weimar, will publish the Eclogues of Virgil, with an English translation, and woodcuts by Aristide Maillol. . . . The aim of the Press in this book, has been to print an edition of the Eclogues in which the type used for the text, the illustrations and the paper should be in perfect keeping with one another, and so to emulate the unity of text and illustrations which we see in Carolingian manuscripts and in the illustrated incunabula.

Kessler then described the special paper, which was handmade, largely of Chinese silk, by Maillol's brother Gaspard, and stated that, owing to the revolution in China, a shortage of silk had meant that the English edition

---

[56] The *Prospectus* was published in 1927, and reproduced in Roderick Cave, *The Private Press* (New York, 1983), p. 146. There were separate editions of the *Eclogues,* each with a different translation: in French by Marc Lafargue, in German by Thomas Achelis and Alfred Koerte, in English by J. H. Mason.

would be printed instead on a special Japanese paper. Finally, he explained how the dominant aesthetic of the volume was established by Maillol's woodcuts:

> The text, the illustrations, and initials were conceived architecturally from beginning to end. . . . The woodcuts of Aristide Maillol were designed for the text as set in this edition. From the beginning, he has based his work on the tone of the type in mass and on the proportions of the page, with a vew to securing a harmony of line and tone between text and illustrations. Within these limitations he has given his imagination and sense of form the freest play. The Hellenic grace and fertile invention of this great plastic artist is admirably seen in these forty-three woodcuts. The designs may be compared to a series of delicate Hellenistic reliefs decorating the severe typographical architecture.

There are certain congruities here with the typographical revolution accomplished by the Didot family in France at the end of the eighteenth century: the same emphases on simplicity and harmony, the conception of the typeface as carrying its own ideology. But there the ideology was Roman austerity, a reproach to the social and aesthetic frivolities of a decadent aristocratic culture. Here it is Hellenism that speaks through the *Prospectus,* and in Germany Hellenism also carried an ideological freight. Originating with Winckelmann, it became in Goethe a defense against the emotional excesses of Romanticism, and in Hölderlin, as rediscovered by the circle of Stefan George, a new version of nationalism, Griechendeutschland.[57]

What Hellenism meant to Kessler is problematic. Certainly he associated it with Maillol, both as an artist for whom Greek art was the ideal and as a personality. In the spring of 1908, Kessler had visited Greece with Maillol and Hugo von Hofmannsthal, and later that year he had collaborated with Anton Kippenburg on a fine edition of the first two books of the *Iliad* and of the *Odyssey,* with woodcuts by Maillol and initials by Eric Gill. In 1925, at a time when Maillol was consistently at work on the *Eclogues,* Kessler described him as having the face of "a Greek shepherd poet" (p. 243); and in 1930, when the Virgil project was success in the past, he recorded a visit with Maillol and his mistress-model to the School for Physical Culture in Grünewald in language indistinguishable from the manifestos of Griechendeutschland:

> In the magnificent grounds and glorious sunshine the sight of almost naked young people performing athletic exercises was reminiscent of

---

[57] See Gay, *Weimar Culture,* p. 59. And for German Hellenism, see Eliza Butler, *The Tyranny of Greece over Germany* (Cambridge, 1935), and Henry Hatfield, *Aesthetic Paganism in German Literature from Winckelmann to the Death of Goethe* (Cambridge, Mass., 1964).

ancient Greece. In many ways, especially in Germany, we are returning, unconsciously and naturally, to the habits of the Greeks. Nudity,
light, fresh air, sunshine, worship of living, bodily perfection, sen-
suousness without either false shame or prudishness. . . . Maillol
asked me to photograph two youngsters who were "beaux comme des
dieux antiques."

(p. 395)

Yet Kessler would have been appalled at the inference such a comment
would later carry, in the light of the Nazi emphasis on the perfection of
the species, and he was alert enough to the political implications of Goethe's "classical epoch" to remark that it was "caused to a considerable degree by inevitable deference to the feelings and outlook of the Weimar
court" (p. 318). The result, Kessler suggested, was that Germany had been
"cheated" of the realistic and political writings that Lessing and the younger
Goethe had led it to expect. How, then, could he himself reconcile the sinu-
ous forms and perfect nudity of Maillol's designs for the *Eclogues* with his
own political activism and tireless campaigning for the League of Nations?
How could he write a *Prospectus* for the volume that said not a word about
Virgil or Rome, let alone the Augustan peace and the shadows of civil war,
and which would have been far more appropriate an advertisement for a
collectors' edition of the *Idylls* of Theocritus?

There is no simple answer to this question. We need to begin by noting that the Virgil project was not solely a product of the late 1920s, but
had been conceived simultaneously with the Cranach Press itself. Kessler
had become interested in the art of fine printing through his editorial work
for *Pan,* the quarterly journal of the arts, which in 1896 printed facsimiles
of work by the Kelmscott Press. In 1902, when Kessler became director of
the Art Museum in Weimar, he came into contact with Henry van de
Velde, the Belgian architect who founded the State School of Arts and
Crafts, later to become the Bauhaus. Under van de Velde's influence Kessler
began to see Weimar as the confluence of an artistic renaissance which
would transcend national boundaries. His early experiments with fine
printing, including the *Homer,* with its German, French, and English participants, were part of that larger concept. Kessler's plan to found his own
press was conceived in 1904; and by 1910, when Kessler turned to Emery
Walker, founder of the Doves Press, for advice, work on the *Eclogues* had
already begun. Through Walker, Kessler negotiated with A. H. Mason,
formerly a compositor for the Doves Press, who then taught at the Central
School of Arts and Crafts in London, where he passed on both the typographical idealism and the social doctrines of William Morris. When
Kessler first visited Mason in London in 1913, he already had with him, as
a visual prospectus, several of Maillol's completed woodcuts, and it was

these that apparently persuaded Mason to commit himself to the project and to visit Weimar to supervise the setting up of the press.[58]

From its inception, then, the Virgil project was defined both by Maillol's illustrations and by Kessler's *Kulturpolitik,* a program in which art proclaimed its own internationalism and in which Weimar, as a historical center of German culture, should be the site of this ideal collaboration. Yet the most cosmopolitan aspect of the edition, its presentation in three European languages, seems to have been the least significant aspect of the project as Kessler defined it. The contributions of Marc Lafargue, Thomas Achelis, and Alfred Koerte went unnoted in the *Tagebücher,* where Kessler recorded with loving precision the evolution of the woodcuts; and the English translation by A. H. Mason was an afterthought, conceived only when Mason, on one of his postwar visits to Weimar, showed Kessler his own translation of one of Erasmus's dialogues as an example of the quality of printing done at the Central School.

Moreover, the *Eclogues* were conceived in a prewar period of optimism, rather than out of the climate of constant crisis and uncertainty, however exhilarating, that marked the Weimar Republic. The project was completely halted during the war, but it was not the war's offspring; nor is there any evidence that Kessler made a conceptual equation between pastoral as a genre and his own political pacifism. Insofar as the project was dictated by *Kulturpolitik* it was the collaboration of artists that made the statement, not the content of the work itself. Early in 1919, Kessler recorded a conversation with the painter George Grosz in which Grosz declared his new commitment to realism and didactic art, whereas Kessler "made the reservation that . . . it is uneconomic to use art for purposes which may be achieved just as well, if not better, without artistic propaganda." On the other hand, he agreed with Grosz that there may be "events of an ethical character which perhaps art alone is capable of conveying" (p. 64). The Cranach Press *Eclogues* do indeed convey to the bibliophile certain assumptions about the interface between ethics and aesthetics, but they do so precisely because Kessler accepted the formalist position articulated in the *Prospectus* as the work's entire and self-justifying intention.

What, then, do Maillol's woodcuts say? They speak, first of all, of the primacy of line and form in the art of book illustration, and of the comparative insignificance of narrativity, the visual elucidation of the text, or other conceptualized modes of representation. The overwhelming effect of the volume is that of *design,* of the reduction of the human figure and landscape to a few eloquently curved lines. When Kessler was coaxing the de-

---

[58] See Müller-Krumbach, *Harry Graf Kessler,* pp. 25–29; Leslie Owens, *J. H. Mason, 1875–1951: Scholar-Printer* (London, 1976), pp. 71–92.

signs for the Virgil initials out of Maillol, he remarked with fascination on
the ease and speed with which he worked: he "shakes them so to speak out
of his sleeve, the profusion of forms alive in him appears miraculous"
(p. 263). But it would be a mistake to assume that Maillol's woodcuts have
no interpretive force. Not only do they resolve Virgilian pastoral back into
its Greek origins, eliminating all traces of its Roman historical context and
every phase of its subsequent cultural history, they also represent Greek
pastoral in a mode of which Nietzsche would have approved, an utterly un-
German mode of lighthearted and elegant sexuality. As Müller-Krumbach
puts it, "Nymphs and Naiads move contentedly in the sheer pleasure of
existence."[59]

The indolent, nakedly erotic tone is set definitively by the opening image of Pan (Fig. 36), whose dominance over the first eclogue, rather than
the second, accords with Maillol's emphasis on the idea of the satyr, fully
exploited in the woodcuts to the sixth eclogue (Fig. 37). The representation of Silenus himself echoes the Pan in seeming compressed into the
frame, and hence more powerful than if unconstrained, while the witty relationship between the bag on which Silenus leans and his emphatic geni-
talia is both a denial of the philosophic content of the poem and a typically
Maillolian gesture toward the creation-song. Several of the designs have no
discernible connection with the text—for instance, in Eclogue 9, the boy
mounting a goat (Fig. 38) in a highly ambiguous image of play. It is true
that these images are partly countered by the appealingly simple family
group suggestive of Christian iconography that Maillol designed for
the fourth eclogue, and by the austere representation of Daphnis's tomb
(Fig. 39). In fact, although Maillol supposedly modeled this design on a
monument in his own French countryside,[60] it strongly resembles the
matching woodcut in the Grüninger *Virgil* by Sebastian Brant (Fig. 40).
But the total effect of the volume remains best expressed in a phrase that
Kessler produced as a description of Maillol himself: it is Virgil presented
"with an artful, benevolent smirk, half that of a guilty schoolboy and half
that of an old sage" (p. 261).

When Maillol was criticized for having produced a naïve Virgil, since
Virgil himself was not naïve, but elegant and urbane, he replied that he had
not tried to reproduce Virgil accurately. Who can replicate Virgil? he
asked. He asserted that what he had tried to create instead was something

---

[59] Müller-Krumbach, *Harry Graf Kessler,* p. 47. On Maillol's sexual energy, resulting in
his affair at sixty-seven with his model, Lucile Passavant, see Kessler, *In the Twenties,* pp. 383–
84, 386–89.

[60] *In the Twenties,* p. 241: "Maillol showed me what he regards as the most beautiful
grave in [Banyuls], a low tomb surrounded by a small grove of olive trees and cypresses, right
in the middle of a meadow. He modelled his Virgilian woodcut on this tomb, he told me, just
as the spring with its nymph in Eclogue IX had its origin in a small spring where we pic-
nicked years ago."

P. VERGILI MARONIS ECLOGA PRIMA
MELIBOEUS ET TITYRUS

INCIPIT MELIBOEUS
TITYRE TU PATULAE RECUBANS SUB
TEGMINE FAGI, SILVESTREM TENUI MU
SAM MEDITARIS AVENA; NOS PATRIAE
FINIS ET DULCIA LINQUIMUS ARVA.
NOS PATRIAM FUGIMUS: TU TITYRE
LENTUS IN UMBRA, FORMOSAM RE
SONARE DOCES AMARYLLIDA SILVAS.

Figure 36. Aristide Maillol, "Eclogue 1," from *Eclogae,* trans. Thomas Achelis and Alfred Koerte (Weimar: Cranach Press, 1926), p. 4. Lessing J. Rosenwald Collection, Library of Congress, Washington, D.C.

P. VERGILI MARONIS ECLOGA SEXTA
SILENUS

Figure 37. Aristide Maillol, "Eclogue 6," from *Eclogae,* trans. Thomas Achelis and Alfred Koerte (Weimar: Cranach Press, 1926), p. 54. Lessing J. Rosenwald Collection, Library of Congress, Washington, D.C.

lovely, something that blended with the typography. He did not illustrate Virgil, he illustrated the paper, and they had brought him a beautiful paper. Whether it was now a book for kings, for students, or for whores, it all began with beautiful paper.[61] No further comment seems necessary on the ideology of the Cranach Press *Eclogues,* except to suggest that the final product was perhaps no more intelligible to Kessler than his own remark on German athletics and the "unconscious" return of the nation to the habits of the Greeks. What he did produce, unquestionably, was a monument to an aristocratic cultural ideal: in the supremely beautiful book (no

[61] Henry Frère, *Gespräche mit Maillol* (Frankfurt, 1961), p. 162.

MÉRIS
Et ces vers qu'il n'a pas achevés et qu'il chantait à Varus:
VARUS SI SEULEMENT MANTOUE NOUS RESTE
MANTOUE TROP VOISINE DE LA MALHEUREUSE

CRÉMONE Ô VARUS C'EST JUSQU'AUX ASTRES
QUE LES CHANTS DES CYGNES PORTERONT
TON NOM
LYCIDAS
Puissent tes essaims fuir les ifs de l'île de Corse; puis-
sent tes vaches, nourries de cytise, avoir leurs mamelles
gonflées de lait! Mais commence, si tu sais un chant.
Et moi aussi, les Muses m'ont fait poète. Moi aussi je

Figure 38. Aristide Maillol, "Eclogue 9," from *Eclogae,* trans. Thomas Achelis and Alfred Koerte (Weimar: Cranach Press, 1926), p. 89. Lessing J. Rosenwald Collection, Library of Congress, Washington, D.C.

DAPHNIS EGO IN SILVIS
HINC USQUE AD SIDERA NOTUS
FORMOSI PECORIS CUSTOS
FORMOSIOR IPSE

Figure 39.   Aristide Maillol, "Eclogue 5," from *Eclogae,* trans. Thomas Achelis and Alfred Koerte (Weimar: Cranach Press, 1926), p. 48. Lessing J. Rosenwald Collection, Library of Congress, Washington, D.C.

longer supported, as it had been with Morris and the Kelmscott Press, by a program to reintegrate art and labor), Kessler himself created the equivalent of what Keyserling and Valéry had attempted with their 1933 congress on "Coopération Européenne," a visual and tactile "haven" from reality, which only "a few hundred European intellectuals" could hope to share.

Paul Valéry and the French Fine Book

One year before Paul Valéry signed and dated the introduction to his translation of the *Eclogues,* on 20 August 1944, there appeared another translation by Xavier de Magallon, illustrated with the lithographs of Ker-Xavier

Figure 40. Sebastian Brant, "Eclogue 5," from Virgil, *Opera* (Strasbourg, 1502), fol. XVIr. Lessing J. Rosenwald Collection, Library of Congress, Washington, D.C.

Roussel and with "pages liminaires" by Fernand Mazade.[62] Although Valéry's translation did not appear from the Société Scripta et Picta until 1953, along with its own lithographs by Jacques Villon, the proximity of the two enterprises points to a phenomenon in French culture of the period of the Second World War and beyond, that is to say, a remarkable interest in Virgil's *Eclogues* and an equally remarkable assumption that there was a market for new translations of the work, especially when presented in an expensive, illustrated format. Between 1942 and 1962 there were half a dozen such productions, including the Valéry/Villon *Eclogues*. The origins of this movement go back to the previous decade, but it recedes in a way that only clarifies its causal connections to the Second World War and especially to the position of artist-intellectuals in Vichy France.

Mazade's preface was actually written for a 1930 edition of Magallon's text that appeared without benefit of illustration and with an unusual ge-

---

[62] Xavier de Magallon, trans., *Les Bucoliques* (Paris, 1943). Only 120 copies were printed.

netic history. "Un jour du mois d'avril dernier," Mazade explained, "quelques hommes de lettres se trouvaient réunis chez Henry Charpentier" ("One day last April several men of letters found themselves at a reunion at the home of Henry Charpentier," p. 4). He proceeded to describe how they formed a plan to celebrate the Virgil bimillennial by collaborating in a new translation of the *Eclogues,* which were to be divided among the ten friends. They had three months to realize this project, but during that time, instead of translating merely his own assignment, which happened to be the fourth eclogue, Magallon became inspired. In a mere ten days he produced a verse translation of the *Eclogues* in entirety. "La belle fièvre ne le quitta pas," wrote Mazade in a fever of his own. "Traduction? Non: communion, fusion." It is not explained how his colleagues took the news of this inspired appropriation of what was to have been a joint effort, but Magallon's translation was promptly published.

Beyond these defensive moves, Mazade's preface is full of information about the state of French culture between the wars. In the first instance, as even his account of "the fine fever" of composition indicates, this is a document in which Romantic notions of art and genius are still deeply embedded. Mazade's view of the history of French literature was that a huge hiatus occurred between the death of Racine and the appearance of Chénier, but that all was set right during the "grand siècle lyrique" of the nineteenth century. Verse, for him, was "l'expression naturelle d'une crise enthousiaste et mystique de l'âme" ("the natural expression of a crisis, enthusiastic and mysterious, of the spirit," p. 2). But a few pages later, he described Magallon's achievement in more sober, even sombre terms:

> Et c'est la vue nette de l'objet sous une lumière attentive et pure qui m'autorise à écrire que, par sa fidelité dans la liberté, cette transposition des Eglogues constitue une oeuvre unique parmi notre littérature. Elle arrive à son heure en ces fêtes virgiliennes et mistraliennes de fraternité latine au-dessus d'un ciel orageux.
>
> Marmontel pensait qu'il n'est pas de galerie si vaste qu'un peintre ne pût décorer avec une seule des Eglogues. La ville y brille à l'horizon. Le sentiment civique y traverse les caresses. En même temps que l'aménité, le calme, la mélancolie, une volupté nuancée comme un ciel d'automne, on y respire la grandeur romaine, l'amour des lois. Elles seraient à notre temps une lecture salubre. Souhaitons que beaucoup de nos contemporains les considèrent et dans leur splendeur latine et dans le miroir français.
>
> (p. 13)

And it is the clean view of the object under a pure and perspicuous light that authorizes me to write that, on the grounds of its fidelity that is also freedom, this translation of the *Eclogues* makes a unique contribution to our literature. It arrives punctually at these Virgilian celebrations of the Latin fraternity, in a mistral and under a stormy sky.

Marmontel thought that there was no gallery so vast that it could not be decorated with a single Eclogue. The city shimmers on the horizon. The civic spirit comes through the caresses. Simultaneously with charm, calm, melancholy, a subtle voluptuousness like an autumn sky, one breathes the grandeur of Rome, the commitment to law. The *Eclogues* will be a salubrious lesson to our own times. Let us hope that many of our contemporaries meditate upon them, both in their Latin splendor and in the French mirror.

The Virgil bimillennial of 1930 coincided with the National Socialists' first electoral success, three years before they were to assume power. The political forecast was threatening to a degree that Mazade's rhetoric barely indicates, and the notion that reading the *Eclogues* would serve as a warning to France seems ludicrous in the light of Europe's failure to grasp the dimensions of the threat. When Mazade's preface was reprinted in 1944 under the Vichy regime its haplessness must have been fully apparent. And the lithographs of Roussel, himself residual from another era (having been a member of the Nabis or artistic mystics who gathered around Sérusier at the turn of the century), were visually unequal to even the oblique monitions of the text—a series of misty figures, standing or dancing, without distinct form in themselves or any discernible connection to the text, and certainly without a trace of "sentiment civique" or "grandeur romaine."

Henry Charpentier, the poet in whose house the collaborative Virgil project was formed, was not apparently as feverish a Virgilian as Magallon; his own translation appeared in 1946, with lithographs by René Demeurisse.[63] Demeurisse offered the postwar reader not the disintegrating figures of Roussel, but a comforting image of shepherds in antique costume, naturalistic and sentimental in style. The eclogues were visually differentiated, with a clearly recognizable nativity scene for the fourth, a peaceable kingdom for the fifth, Silenus in person in the sixth, and in the first eclogue, two shepherds standing in conversation under a tree. But the volume is more distinguished by Charpentier's own afterword, which offers, like Mazade's, both a modernist poetics and a historicist hermeneutics, with a naked conflict between them.

Charpentier explained to his audience (we might have guessed) that his tenth eclogue was originally written for the Virgil bimillennial of

---

[63] Henry Charpentier, trans., *Les Bucoliques* (Paris, 1946). The edition is dated "18 January." Only 220 copies were printed.

1930. It is almost a word-for-word translation of the original. But for the other nine a different theory of translation was developed:

> Nous avons tenté dans notre transcription de faire éprouver que Virgile est d'abord un poëte. Pour y réussir nous avons cru devoir préférer le sens littéral aux périphrases qu'employa souvent l'érudition dans le louable dessein de traduire et de commenter tout ensemble. . . . S'il nous fût parfois demandé de choisir entre ces développements savants, qui, sans doute, éclaircissent, et le son, nous avons toujours opté pour le son, premier élément du poëme . . . Nous laissons au lecteur désireux d'approfondir la résonance secrète et les subtiles intentions, qui ondoient au fil des Bucoliques, le soin de les découvrir, élucidées dans les travaux des grammairiens et de scoliastes que ne manquent point et qui sont mieux instruits que nous en ces matières. Il ne s'est agi pour nous ici que du poëme pur.
>
> (p. 84)

We have tried in out translation to prove that Virgil was above all a poet. In order to succeed, we believed we ought to choose the literal sense over those periphrases that often use erudition in the admirable project of translating and commenting at the same time. If we were sometimes asked to choose between such learned developments, which, no doubt, do clarify, and the sound of the word, we have always opted for the sound, poetry's primary element. We leave to the reader who desires to plumb the secret resonance and the subtle intentions that wind their way through the *Eclogues* the task of discovering them, fully explained, in the works of grammarians and scholiasts, of whom there are plenty and who are better instructed than we in such matters. Our only concern here is the pure poem.

This passage is resonant with all of the aesthetic premises of modernist poetry, significantly attached to the term *pure* as Valéry had given it currency;[64] but at the same time, from the vantage point of this study, we can recognize in it the voice of older prejudices, the attack on learned exegesis and on subtexts that disturb. What they disturb, in the 1940s, is the poem's musicality, not, as in Fontenelle and Rapin, an idea of pastoral that is soothing to the social conscience. But the ideology of a "pure" poetics requires interrogation nonetheless, not least because Charpentier's own

---

[64] Valéry's famous essay on "poésie pure," or a system of linguistic relations "unconnected with the practical order," was first published in an English translation by Malcolm Cowley in the *New York Herald Tribune,* 15 April 1928.

postscript brings it into question and suggests the direction that questioning should take.

Just before his defense of "poésie pure," Charpentier explained precisely what anxieties such an aesthetic transcended, and at the same time developed the historical analogy invoked by Mazade:

> Toujours le cours des siècles recommence. Virgile vécut en des temps qui ressemblèrent au nôtre. Les guerres, longues et cruelles, étaient suivies de confiscations et d'exils. Les vainqueurs étaient durs; les poëtes doux et craintifs. Ils aimaient la louange et les honneurs et changeaient facilement de camp pour obtenir quelques réparations ou quelques avantages des nouvelles puissances. Mais, en dépit de ses soucis temporels, trois préoccupations essentielles emplirent la vie et l'âme de Virgile: La contemplation de la nature périodique, mystérieuse et belle; l'étrange Eros qui joint et divise tous les êtres; et le secret métaphysique enfin, la solution du problème de la destinée qui ne se laisse, et si faiblement, entrevoir que par l'homme capable d'appeler à l'aide la science, la mythologie et la magie ou, si l'on préfère, l'observation, les analogies et l'intuition.
>
> (p. 83)

> The course of centuries always repeats itself. Virgil lived in times that resemble ours. Wars, long and cruel, were followed by confiscations and exiles. The victors were harsh; the poets mild and fearful. They loved praise and honors and readily changed sides in order to obtain certain reparations or certain advantages from the new holders of power. But, despite temporal troubles, three essential preoccupations filled the life and soul of Virgil: the contemplation of nature—cyclical, mysterious, and beautiful; the strange power of Love which unites and divides all beings; and finally the metaphysical secret, the solution of the problem of destiny which only lets itself be glimpsed, and ever so faintly, by the man capable of calling to his aid science, mythology, and magic; or, if you prefer, observation, analogy, and intuition.

In the French mirror Charpentier observed an analogy to Virgil's own situation that could act as a powerful interpretive tool—too powerful, perhaps, in its reflection back again onto postwar culture of the Virgilian analysis of hegemony, the necessity, as Servius saw it, of adapting one's voice to the "nouvelles puissances." Charpentier's solution to this painful insight was first to admit it and then immediately to repress it, by asserting that Virgil's "essential preoccupations" were not those of historical self-definition and vocational anxiety but, rather, the great themes of post-

Romantic transcendentalism. His final move, which would lead into the defense of "poésie pure," was to make the transaction of modernism: "En outre, Virgile savait que le lien de toutes connaissances est le style" ("Moreover, Virgil knew that what links all knowledge is style," p. 84).

Similar persuasions, in variant combinations, show up in the work of Charpentier's contemporaries. In 1951 the early-nineteenth-century translation by Jacques Delille was recuperated in a fine edition with woodcuts by Lucile Passavant—a highly erotic development of the Maillol interpretation of the *Eclogues,* with a more explicit theme of rampant sexuality, even across the species.[65] In 1952 a new translation by "un auteur incertain" preceded each eclogue with an "argument" taken from Servian commentary and even went so far as to draw attention to the "termes d'ESCLAVE, de SERVITUDE," which are to be taken allegorically, because "Virgile et son père étaient nés de condition libre."[66] But the accompanying etchings by Marcel Roche turn the reader's attention from this historical version of the *Eclogues* to the idea of landscape as a subject in its own right. No distinction is made among the eclogues; the melancholy figures in antique costume are easily transferable, and more often the subject is landscape empty of figures, a single tree. This development is carried to its logical extreme in the *Bucoliques* translated in prose by André Berry and produced in 1962 with etchings by Jean Commère.[67] Here a deliberate attempt has been made to merge the figures into the landscape: the primary subject of contemplation is a tree, or a field of sheaves, or, for the ninth eclogue, two full pages showing agricultural laborers naked to the waist, not for pleasure but for work; and for the first eclogue, a row of leafless trees receding into the distance. Pastoral has returned to what Raymond Williams, in 1973, defined as its "original substance," the depiction of life in the country.[68]

When Count Harry Kessler approached Paul Valéry in 1927 with a request for a translation of the *Georgics,* Valéry refused, on the grounds that he knew nothing about agriculture. A similar statement appeared in the 1944 preface to his translation of the *Eclogues,* produced at the request of Valéry's personal physician, A. Roudinesco: "La vie pastorale m'est étrangère et me semble ennuyeuse. . . . La vue des sillons m'attriste—jusqu'à ceux que trace ma plume. Le retour des saisons et de leurs effets donne

[65]This is a strange partnership—between the abbé Delille, whose translation of the *Eclogues* first appeared in 1811, and Lucile Passavant, Maillol's mistress, whom Kessler (*In the Twenties,* pp. 387, 390, 394) described as having considerable artistic talent, and who clearly learned from Maillol her stylistic eroticism.

[66]*Les Bucoliques,* trans. "par un auteur incertain," "gravures sur cuivre de Marcel Roche" (Paris, 1952), p. 8. There were 190 copies printed.

[67]*Les Bucoliques,* ed. Pierre de Tartas, trans. André Berry, "gravures sur cuivre de Jean Commère" (Paris, 1962). There was also a translation by P. F. Tissot, with watercolors by Gaston Barret, published in Paris in 1959, which I have not seen.

[68]Raymond Williams, *The Country and the City* (New York, 1973), p. 21.

l'idée de la sottise de nature et de la vie, laquelle ne sait que se répéter pour subsister" ("Pastoral life is quite foreign to me and strikes me as tedious. I am depressed by the sight of furrows, including those made by the pen. The recurrence of the seasons and of their effects illustrates the stupidity of nature and of life, which can persist only by repeating itself").[69] This statement, with its affectation of Gide's *ennui*, is potentially interpretable as a lack of commitment to the project, and it has been argued that Valéry's preface "not only betrays but emphasizes a distaste for, even a dislike of . . . the pastoral Virgil."[70] Although the author of this statement subsequently produced some counter-evidence from Valéry's correspondence, especially with Gide, the inferences remained that here was a great modern poet unsuitably matched and that the resulting translation showed unfortunate signs of being a chore rather than a labor of love.

This misconception needs to be laid to rest. But before approaching that extraordinary preface, which, as Roudinesco observed, might well be considered "le testament poétique de Valéry,"[71] we should note that simultaneously with his "Variations" Valéry was at work on another "variation" on "the pastoral Virgil," the *Dialogue de l'arbre*. This prose meditation on the first eclogue was read at the annual joint session of the Cinq Académies in October 1943, where Valéry mentioned "a certain circumstance—a chance, since chance is the fashion," that had recently brought him back to Virgil's *Eclogues*.[72] The subject of the dialogue is the tree itself, the pastoral *umbra* under which the poet, identified as Tityrus, is still to be found, even or especially in Vichy France, and speaking to the Académies. But the other speaker is not now Meliboeus, but Lucretius, and the new dialectic is now between the poet as intuitive lyricist and the intellectual as metaphysician.

Lucretius both envies and condescends to Tityrus for his intense response to the natural object:

> This great Tree is for you only your fantasy. You think you love it, Tityrus, but only see your charming fancy there, which you bedeck with leaves. You love only your hymn—and so please me the more. From the majestic Beech you take wherewith to sing the eddies of its form and its sonorous birds, its shade which welcomes you from the

[69] Paul Valéry, trans., *Les Bucoliques de Virgile*, ed. A. Roudinesco, with lithographs by Jacques Villon (Paris, 1953), p. xi; English translation from Valéry, *Art of Poetry*, trans. Denise Folliot (Princeton, 1958), in Paul Valéry, *Collected Works*, ed. Jackson Matthews (Princeton, 1956–75), 7: 296.

[70] L. A. Bisson, "Valéry and Virgil," *Modern Language Review* 53 (1958): 501–11.

[71] See Roudinesco's introduction to the unillustrated edition of Valéry's translation (Paris, 1956), p. 14.

[72] Paul Valéry, *Dialogues*, trans. W. M. Stewart (New York, 1956) in Valéry, *Collected Works* 4: 152.

burning heart of day, and, by the Muses blest, you duly celebrate upon
your fragile reed the mighty giant's charms.

(4: 156)

Tityrus, more generously, replies:

Well, sing yourself in turn; to nature give decrees, to the vast earth, to
bulls, to rocks, and to the sea; give to the waves its law, give to the
flowers their form! Think for the universe, a monster without head,
which, for itself, in man searches for reason's dream; but O do not disdain your simple listener.

(4: 157)

So the stage is set, misleadingly, for an updated version of the contrast between simple and complex, low and high pastoral. As the dialogue continues and becomes a discussion of the relationship between form and idea,
between creation and the notion (for Lucretius, a fallacy) of a creator or
author, Tityrus more than holds his own in abstraction, while Lucretius
becomes less the philosopher and more the vatic poet. "O, Tityrus," he
cries, "It seems to me that I am sharing with my whole being in that meditation—powerful, active, and rigorously followed up in its design—which
the Plant bids me make" (4: 172). And when Tityrus questions how the
tree can meditate, Lucretius provides his own final gloss on the opening
lines of Virgil's poem: "I say that if someone on earth does meditate, it is
the Plant" (4: 173). Abandoning all pretense of rational control, the philosopher gives himself up to communion with nature: "Radiant meditation fills me with rapture. . . . And in my soul I feel all words atremble."
The audience is left to decide how much, if any irony, inheres in this
conclusion, as Tityrus bids him farewell: "I leave you in that admirable
state. . . . Mind the cool of the evening—it comes so quickly" (4: 174).[73]

The *Dialogue de l'arbre* was published under the general title *Arbres,*
accompanied by eighteen photographs of trees. It therefore presented itself
as a post-Romantic meditation on "real" nature, while at the same time
implying a certain skepticism about the products of such meditation.
Nothing could more sharply define, by contrast, the tone and preoccupations of Valéry's preface to the *Eclogues,* significantly entitled "Variations."
As Roudinesco pointed out in his own preface to the volume, the chief
justification for this new version of the *Eclogues* was that previous illustrated editions had only represented the text "sous son aspect exclusive-
ment pastoral." In fact, he asserted, Virgil had borrowed nothing from

---

[73] The *Dialogue* is sufficiently *clair-obscur* to have attracted structuralist and post-
structuralist attention. See Alexandre Lazaridès, *Valéry: Pour une poétique du dialogue* (Mon-
treal, 1978).

Theocritus except a genre, and his eclogues were something very different from a story of herdsman and goats. Virgil was a difficult author, and especially "citadin." He wrote in the context of Caesar's assassination, of the new triumvirate, of proscriptions and exactions; and the first eclogue was, above all, "politique." It expressed in two voices a personal predicament:

> Virgile fut brutalement expulsé de son domaine paternel de Mantoue. . . . Sa plainte amère s'exprime ici par la voix de Mélibée. *En quo discordia cives produxit miseros!* Tityre le console. . . . Mais ce Tityre n'est-ce point encore Virgile? On sait qu'il est allé à Rome voir Octave qui lui promit la restitution de sa terre et le prit à son service. Il n'y a pas de gloire sans plume. Virgile fut-il sincère, ou était-il divisé lui-même?
>
> (n.p.)

> Virgil was brutally expelled from his patrimonial estate in Mantua. His bitter lament is expressed in the voice of Meliboeus. "See how strife renders our citizens unhappy!" Tityrus consoles him. But isn't Tityrus also Virgil? We know that he went to Rome to see Octavian, who promised to restore his land and engaged him in his service. There is no glory without literary record. Was Virgil sincere, or was he self-divided?

But for all his revisionist emphasis on the Roman historical context of the *Eclogues* as a group and on the ambiguous ideological stance of the first eclogue in particular, Roudinesco's preface reminded the French reader of the mid-twentieth century that the *Eclogues* were a study in contrasts, a dialectics of form and stance in which the "aspect pastoral" was only one possibility.

Valéry rose to the challenge with all the daedalian and gordian faculties he had developed in and for survival and success. In 1927 Kessler had described him as already "an old *grand seigneur,* a fairly harmonious mixture of philosopher and businessman laced with intellect and malice, a gleaming surface of manners and intelligence over an abyss of obscurity which is difficult to define and perhaps deliberately veiled."[74] In 1944, one year before his death at seventy-four, Valéry wrote as the grand old man of French letters, who in 1931 had delivered the address welcoming Marshal Pétain into the Académie Française, who had been able to continue his wartime career without major interruption, but who had already, in his articles and lectures of the late thirties, shown a few signs of vocational anxiety.[75] In

---

[74] Kessler, *In the Twenties,* p. 327.

[75] See Valéry's lecture on "La Liberté de l'esprit," delivered at the Université des Annales, 24 March 1939, in *History and Politics,* trans. Denise Folliot and Jackson Mathews (New York, 1963) in *Collected Works,* 10: 204–8; and the essay "L'Esprit est-il un luxe?" discussed shortly.

his *Variations* the task of theorizing his own endeavor produced a manifesto that can indeed, as Roudinesco suggested, stand as his testament, both in poetics and in politics. And it is fascinating to follow the logic of this testament, as it moves not, as with Charpentier, from political self-consciousness to "poésie pure," but in the opposite direction.

Thinking about the art of translation, Valéry began with a post-Romantic defense of poetic process: the passivity of the poet, "poised between his ideal of beauty and his nothingness," in "a state of active and questioning expectation"; the "indefinable singing force" that "exacts" from him a whole series of possible verbal correlatives to his "desire"; and the choice of the one word that does not correspond to his "thought" exactly, for "that is the business of prose," but is, rather, a "precious and unique solution to a problem that is formulated only when it is solved." This meditation on linguistic choice leads him to Latin, and a different system of values: the slender knowledge of the "langage de Rome" that he still retains is "infiniment précieuse," a humanist emotion that allows him to discern the grain of truth in all the self-defensive posturing of the so-called humanities; that is to say, Latin is the language to which the French owe all that is most solid and dignified in the monuments of their own tongue,[76] which connects them with their country's ancient history.

On Virgil himself Valéry pronounces himself an amateur (the by now familiar disclaimer of specialized knowledge); but an amateur, it seems, who has developed an intimacy with Virgil as a personality, and especially a split personality:

> Virgil, who felt himself divided between the different ways of looking at the country around him, Virgil, whose view was double, sometimes invested the countryside with the contentment, fears and hopes of a man who possesses and is often obsessed by the cares of the property that provides him with a living. At other times, a different consideration assailed him. His ambitions ceased to be rural; he was no longer a simple man; there emerged in him a polished spirit, learned in Greek refinements and attracted by subtler compositions than these songs of the artless herdsmen. *He could have written an eleventh eclogue between him and himself.* But then he was, or had just become, a victim of the disorders that civil war and its brutal consequences had brought into the orbit of his life.
>
> (7: 309–10; italics added)

This divided Virgil, part simple husbandman, part literary aesthete, part participant in history, was to produce the finest development of the Latin

---

[76] Valéry, *Art of Poetry,* pp. 300–301.

language, with all its "musical and plastic means in a field of political forces."

How much of his patrician self Valéry read into this sketch is difficult to estimate. He had already written that eleventh eclogue, the "dialogue between him and himself" in the *Dialogue de l'Arbre,* but I see no trace here of a "distaste" for the Virgil of the *Eclogues.* On the contrary, his consideration of Virgil's career becomes "a good place" for Valéry to insert a general essay "On the Relations of Poetry with Various Regimes or Governments." The problem of intellectual independence, Valéry writes (though he does not use that phrase), has as many solutions as there are individual temperaments and circumstances:

> There are economic solutions—for one must live. Others are of a moral order. And some are purely affective. A regime attracts either by its material perfections or by its glory and triumphs; one leader by his genius; another by his liberality, sometimes a mere smile. In other cases . . . the man of intellect rebels more or less openly or shuts himself up in a work that secretes a kind of intellectual insulation about his sensibility. In fact, every type can be observed. Racine adores his King. Chénier curses his tyrants. . . . Goethe prefers injustice to disorder. Majesty dazzles. Authority impresses. Freedom intoxicates. Anarchy terrifies. Personal interest speaks with a powerful voice. One must not forget, either, that every individual distinguished by his talents places himself in his heart among a certain aristocracy. . . . he notices that democracy, egalitarian in its essence, is incapable of pensioning a poet. Or else, judging the men in power and the men dominated by these, he despises both, but feels the temptation to appear in politics himself and to take part in the conduct of affairs. This temptation is not infrequent among lyric poets. It is remarkable that the purest of human occupations, that of taming and elevating beings by song, as Orpheus did, should so often lead to coveting the impurest of occupations.
>
> (7: 310–11)

And, as he considered the temptation to self-interest that beset Virgil "in professing to praise Caesar, even to deifying him," Valéry forgave him or, rather, he submerged the negative judgment that, as a "modern," he thought he ought to render—submerging it not merely in historical relativism ("in those days there was as yet no question of the Rights of Man") but in completely unanswerable questions: "If the submission to a despot, the acceptance of his favors, which degenerates into, or reveals itself in, expressions of gratitude and praise, is a condition of the production of works of the first order, what is one to decide, to do, to think?" (7: 311–12). Can we doubt that here, through engagement with the *Eclogues,* Valéry's own situation as the leading man of letters in Vichy France had become perspicuous to himself? Modern history had led Valéry to a position not very different, after all, from that of Servian commentary; and at the end of his career he rediscovered for himself the ancient ideological tension that Virgil had built into pastoral, the intellectual's mirror.

We should note the synonymity of Valéry's analysis, as well as the synchronicity, with Hermann Broch's *Death of Virgil,* written in Broch's American exile and published in 1945. Indeed Broch's pressure on the analogy between Rome under Augustus and Europe in Hitler's grip can reciprocally illuminate Valéry's remarks about despots. But because Broch turns finally to otherworldly solutions and makes the *Aeneid* bend to the fourth eclogue and messianic prophecy, Valéry, with his urbane sense of all the ethical alternatives, is the more typical link in the long chain I have been building, the artist-intellectual *par excellence,* "who places himself in his heart among a certain aristocracy" and to whom self-knowledge comes not out of the psychic depths explored in Broch's novel but out of the European cultural tradition.

Valéry's "Variations" represent, in this inquiry, the last major modern interpretation of the *Eclogues.* But its message was not completed until 1953, when it appeared with the lithographs of Jacques Villon, born Gaston Duchamp, whose arrival at the *Eclogues* had perhaps a different interior logic than Valéry's. Born in 1875, Villon was, like Roussel, originally associated with the semi-mystical theories of Sérusier. In 1910–11, the three Duchamp brothers were at the center of the Orphist movement, a group of artists discussing ideas of pure number and proportion which, it was thought, might lead to an absolute painting, independent of natural observation and yet grounded in the rules of things. Apollinaire entitled this ideal painting "peinture pure," a term explicitly applied to Cubism by Maurice Raynal.[77] The product of these discussions was a journal, the *Section d'Or,* but no significant transfer of theory to practice, since none of the participants was talented enough to conceive a major formal breakthrough. The dominant style of the moment was analytical Cubism, developed by Picasso and Braque out of the geometric insights of Cézanne. From 1914 to 1919, Villon fought in the First World War. When he returned to painting, he returned to Cubism, which he developed into a softer, more lyrical system than Picasso's and with a characteristically brighter palette; but he began with an observed object, which was then

---

[77] On Apollinaire and Raynal, see Edward F. Fry, *Cubism* (London, 1966; reprinted 1978), pp. 100–101. See also Werner Haftmann, *Painting in the Twentieth Century,* trans. Ralph Manheim, 2 vols. (London, 1965), pp. 110–14. For an eloquent description of Villon's late style, see Haftmann, *Painting,* p. 332, and see Dora Vallier, *Jacques Villon: Oeuvres de 1897 à 1956* (Paris, 1957), pp. 16, 18, 81, 84, for Villon's comments on his theories of color, the chromatic circle, and the pyramid as the essential form.

analytically broken down into semi-abstract proportions and crystalline planes. Instead of Picasso's disconcerting wit, which requires the viewer to revise all his formal and phenomenological expectations, Villon's Cubism offers us a world refracted from the surface of a prism, controlled by a rigorous geometric pattern but still recognizable.

After the First World War, some of Villon's strongest compositions reflected his combat experience; in 1940 he fled before the German army and spent several months near Toulouse. And when he agreed to illustrate Valéry's translation, he undoubtedly understood the nature of the assignment and where the volume was to be located in French ideology and culture. Instead of the shadowy figures of Roussel, the eroticism of Maillol and Passavant, the sentimental naturalism of Demeurisse, or the subdued landscapes and lone trees of Marcel Roche, Villon's lithographs accost the viewer with a dazzle of color, at first sight inappropriate. But one gradually discovers that color is here Villon's first means of discrimination among the eclogues. So a vision of the Golden Age as one huge open-air picnic with crowds of happily naked figures is expressed in a medley of bright pinks, yellows, and apple-green, whereas the equally naked mourners over Daphnis's dead body are recorded in grey, black, and a deep lavender blue.

The second means of discrimination is recorded in the table of contents, where the subjects of the lithographs are explained by their titles. Here Roudinesco's conception of the volume is further clarified: whereas the first illustration to Eclogue 5 is "La Mort de Daphnis," the second is merely "Pastorale." Eclogue 7 is illustrated solely by two "pastorales," and Eclogue 8 begins with a "pastorale" but adds two abstract symbols of "Incantations." And for Villon, *pastoral* in this sense means an image only of sheep or goats, with a shepherd piping against a tree. In striking contrast to these are the massively detailed scene of "La Rome impériale" that is part of the visual interpretation of the first eclogue, and the dynamic "Création du monde," with the chariot of the sun bursting out of an aureole as Pyrrha casts her stones into the air. Here the high subject is fully recognized.

The challenge to post-Romantic versions of pastoral goes deeper still. As the Latin text is set in Didot type, so, it appears, Villon went back to older iconographical traditions. In his Silenus, with two over-attentive nymphs, the burly and splayed legs hint at the precedents of Cleyn and David. The eloquent scene of Moeris and Lycidas on their anxious journey, walking in a blue mist with a background of lake and mountain, is strongly reminiscent of Cleyn's two designs for the ninth eclogue, one for Ogilby and one for Marolles. And for the first eclogue, the premise of the entire volume is rendered up in terms of ethical, aesthetic, and historical choice. There in his Cubist modernity is Tityrus (Plate 6) under his tree, in a pose unquestionably derived from Simone Martini's Virgil (compare

Plate 1), with a roll of parchment that marks his origin as older than the codex; and facing him (Plate 5) is a figure with the same iconographical history but a still more complex resolution. We recognize the pointing finger as that of the interpreter, but he stands now in a posture of outright accusation. Holding in his right hand neither the shepherd's crook nor the traveler's staff, but the soldier's sword, we see also that he has absorbed the epic dignity of Simone Martini's Aeneas. The table of contents tells us that the subject of these paired images is "Virgile expulsé de sa terre par un Centurion," but the disposition of image and text tells us that the figure of strength and accusation is Meliboeus, whose new gesture manifests an unprecedented yet intelligible challenge to the intellectual's repose. The meaning of this coalescence of eras, of figures and their ideological functions, is clarified by Villon's selection of the volume's closing image. Entitled "Lycoris à l'Armée du Rhin," a phrase unauthorized by the text of the tenth eclogue, it shows a band of unidentifiable soldiers building trenches on the banks of the Rhine. A disembodied girl's face floating in the foreground imparts the theme of sexual infidelity, now brought up to date by female collaborators, and standing inferentially for the theme of a general collaboration.

This, then, is Virgil visualized by an artist who had experienced two world wars and had fought in one himself. In its representational vigor, Villon's style of illustration breaks through even his modified Cubism and challenges the viewer to rethink the modernist commitment to abstraction in the visual arts, while demanding self-consciousness about the status of the arts in wartime. Yet it must also be said that the volume's primary message—the confrontation of the secure artist-intellectual by his other self—remains finally inhibited by the very form in which it has been articulated: the precious volume designed for the discriminating few. The Bibliothèque Nationale possesses Villon's personal copy, specially bound for him by friends in an inlaid geometric pattern of pastel leathers (reflecting his own style) and gilt-tooled with the title: "Virgile/Valéry/Villon." The object speaks for itself—and for all beautiful books that aspire to cultural statement.

Luxury editions or accounts of the *Eclogues* are, nevertheless, only extreme examples of the dilemma that besets the twentieth-century intellectual, whatever his or her field, in negotiating ideology, financial support, and institutional status. As I have chosen not to belabor the connections between academic pastoral theory of the late twentieth century and the often extraordinarily protected situation of those who have articulated it (including, of course, myself), so Valéry can speak for me on the modern phase of the intellectual's historical evolution. In July 1937, Valéry published in *Le Figaro* an essay on the question, "L'Esprit est-il un luxe?" ("Is the Mind a Luxury?") Although in the title of his essay he answered the question by asserting "la nécessité de l'inutile," its text was not so certain:

> But that labor of the mind which develops the mind itself, which tends to increase this strange power of transformation which is in man, showing itself in the noblest branches of science, or embodied in works of art and giving order to the compositions of poets, although it is often and nearly everywhere honored, celebrated, and even "encouraged," rewarded, indeed subsidized, is nonetheless held to be a *luxury* and is kept in that condition with a care and strictness manifested precisely in the very honors and advantages accorded to it. This is the way *ladies* used to be treated. They were showered with attention, they governed manners, but their gallant privileges stopped there, and their authority vanished at the smallest piece of serious business.[78]

What Valéry here recognized were the negative consequences of the rich legacy of Romanticism—its shifting of the concept of the intellectual from someone admittedly in service, however equivocally, to a community or its leaders, to someone who, on the basis of self-scrutiny, "places himself in his heart among a certain aristocracy." This self-appointed meritocracy, whether of writers or artists or teachers (of the humanities), has willingly, by insisting on the unique and mysterious character of what they do and on sanctions for it that transcend the general comprehension, contributed to their own marginalization.[79]

In so doing they have had to lean on a massive fiction, since in the late twentieth century the interior life of the mind proceeds most successfully with institutional support and approval. Where would pastoral theory be today without the *otium* of a paid sabbatical? How, then, can its practitioners continue to speak of "pure pastoral" and to reproach "contemporary history" for shattering "the fragile integrity of the genre"?[80] This book would not have been written without the pastoral supports of tenure, a leave of absence, and more than one grant. I hope that in writing it I have contributed to ideological candor in that part of the intelligentsia to which, by profession at least, I belong. Valéry's mid-century view of his

---

[78] Valéry, "Is the Mind a Luxury?" in *History and Politics*, pp. 366–67.

[79] Compare the description of modernist aesthetics in Malcolm Bradbury, *The Social Context of Modern English Literature* (New York, 1971), especially pp. 116–17.

[80] This is the position of Robert Coleman, in the introduction to his widely used edition of the *Eclogues* (Cambridge, 1977), especially pp. 33–34. Although he attributes these distortions to Renaissance pastoralists rather than to Virgil himself, who managed a "fine balance of myth and reality," Coleman's normative impulse remains clear, along with his sense that true pastoral needs to be anchored in the "real countryside"; his notes therefore show the preoccupation with actual Italian flora that entered the interpretive tradition with Martyn.

own cultural situation seems, if anything, too sanguine as a description of where we stand today; but if his own analogy with feminism holds, nothing but complacency requires that this situation should continue. Virgil himself both regretted and denied the inefficacy of song (for which read humanist writing) in the hard times, *tela inter Martia,* doves among eagles; yet the ninth eclogue taught us the necessary conclusion:

Desine plura . . . et quod nunc instat agamus.

Index

Designer: Janet Wood
Compositor: G&S Typesetters, Inc.
Text: 10/12 Galliard
Display: Galliard
Printer: Braun-Brumfield, Inc.
Binder: Braun-Brumfield, Inc.